How to Do *Everything* with

Microsoft® Office 2003

Laurie Ann Ulrich

McGraw-Hill/Osborne

New York Chicago San Francisco Lisbon
London Madrid Mexico City Milan New Delhi
San Juan Seoul Singapore Sydney Toronto

The McGraw·Hill Companies

McGraw-Hill/Osborne
2100 Powell Street, 10th Floor
Emeryville, California 94608
U.S.A.

To arrange bulk purchase discounts for sales promotions, premiums, or fund-raisers, please
contact **McGraw-Hill**/Osborne at the above address. For information on translations or book
distributors outside the U.S.A., please see the International Contact Information page
immediately following the index of this book.

How to Do Everything with Microsoft® Office 2003

234567890 CUS CUS 019876543

ISBN 0-07-222937-3

Publisher:	Brandon A. Nordin
Vice President &	
Associate Publisher:	Scott Rogers
Acquisitions Editor:	Marjorie McAneny
Project Editor:	Janet Walden
Acquisitions Coordinator:	Tana Allen
Technical Editor:	Will Kelly
Copy Editor:	Bart Reed
Proofreader:	Claire Splan
Indexer:	Claire Splan
Composition:	Carie Abrew, Tara A. Davis
Illustrators:	Kathleen Fay Edwards, Melinda Moore Lytle, Lyssa Wald
Series Design:	Mickey Galicia
Cover Series Design:	Dodie Shoemaker
Cover Illustration:	Eliot Bergman

This book was composed with Corel VENTURA™ Publisher.

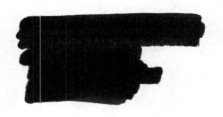

Contents at a Glance

Part I   **Office 2003 Common Elements**

1	What's New in Office 2003	3
2	Common Office Features	17
3	Using Images in Documents, Worksheets, and Presentations	45

Part II   **Creating Documents with Word**

4	Building a Basic Document	65
5	Proofing, Printing, and Saving Documents	81
6	Effective Document Formatting	101
7	Working with Long Documents	129
8	Structuring Documents with Tables	143
9	Creating Form Letters, Envelopes, and Labels with Mail Merge	163

Part III   **Crunching Numbers and Keeping Lists with Excel**

10	Building and Formatting Worksheets	175
11	Working with Formulas and Functions	197
12	Building and Maintaining List Databases	209
13	Charting Excel Data	223
14	Printing and Publishing Worksheets	235

Part IV   **Creating Presentations with PowerPoint**

15	Planning and Building a Presentation	249
16	Enhancing a Presentation with Graphics and Charts	267
17	Building an Effective Multimedia Slide Show	281

Part V   Managing Data with Access

    18   Getting Started with Access Databases   299
    19   Simplifying Data Entry with Forms   317
    20   Extracting Data with Queries   331
    21   Documenting Your Data with Access Reports   343

Part VI   Keeping in Touch and on Schedule with Outlook

    22   Communicating with Email   357
    23   Scheduling Tasks and Appointments   381
    24   Building a Contacts List   395

Part VII   Designing Web Pages with FrontPage

    25   Planning a Website   407
    26   Building a Website   419
    27   Posting Pages to the Web   439

          Index   447

Contents

	Acknowledgments	xix
	Introduction	xxi
PART I	**Office 2003 Common Elements**	
CHAPTER 1	**What's New in Office 2003**	**3**
	The New Office "Look"	4
	The New Task Pane	7
	Expanded Use of Smart Tags	8
	Customizing the Display of Toolbars and Menus	8
	Faxing via the Internet	8
	Office Watson to the Rescue	8
	The Picture Library	9
	The XML Factor in Office 2003	10
	What's New in Word	10
	New and Improved in Excel	12
	PowerPoint's Enhancements	12
	Access Improvements	13
	Outlook's New Features	13
	Upgrade Considerations	14
CHAPTER 2	**Common Office Features**	**17**
	Common Workspace Elements	18
	Working with Office 2003 Toolbars	21
	Using Toolbar Buttons	21
	Displaying Different Toolbars	22
	Moving Toolbars	22
	Working with Office 2003 Menus	23
	Making Menu Selections	23
	Common Menu Elements	23
	Using the Task Pane	24
	Displaying the Various Task Panes	26
	Turning Off the Task Pane	26

Working with Smart Tags Across the Office Suite 27
Using the Office 2003 Clipboard 28
    Moving Content with the Cut Command 29
    Sharing Content with the Copy Command 29
    Pasting Clipboard Selections 30
    Storing Multiple Clipboard Selections 32
    Deleting Clipboard Content 32
    Customizing the Clipboard Task Pane 33
Using the Paste Special Command to Insert Clipboard Content 34
    Creating a Paste Link 35
    Embedding Selections and Editing Tools 37
Working with Speech Recognition 39
    Turning Speech On 39
    Training the Speech Tools for Your Voice 40
    Dictating Documents, Spreadsheets, and Presentations 41
    Giving Commands Verbally 41
Getting the Office 2003 Help You Need 42

CHAPTER 3   **Using Images in Documents, Worksheets, and Presentations** **45**
Inserting and Manipulating Graphics 46
    Adding Images to Word Documents 46
    Using the Picture Toolbar 51
    Using Images in Excel Worksheets 53
    Enhancing Presentations with Clip Art and Photos 53
Capturing Images Digitally 54
Taking a Tour of Office 2003's Picture Library 55
    Creating Shortcuts to Your Images 56
    Opening an Image 56
    Renaming Images 56
    Sharing Images via Email 57
Editing Your Digitally Captured Images 60

PART II   **Creating Documents with Word**

CHAPTER 4   **Building a Basic Document** **65**
Getting Started in Word 66
    The Not-So-Blank Document 66
    Starting with a Template 68
Typing Your Document Content 70
    Working with Word Wrap 71
    Working with Paragraph and Line Breaks 71
Navigating a Word Document 73
    Moving Around with the Mouse 74
    Keyboard Navigation Techniques 74

Selecting and Working with Text 76
    Selecting Text via the Keyboard 76
    Using Your Mouse to Select Text 76
    Editing Your Text 78
    Rearranging Words, Sentences, and Paragraphs 78

CHAPTER 5   **Proofing, Printing, and Saving Documents** **81**
Proofing Word Documents 82
    Handling Errors as You Type 83
    Running the Spelling and Grammar Check 84
Making Automatic Corrections 85
    Creating AutoCorrect Entries 87
    Editing and Removing AutoCorrect Entries 88
Customizing the Proofing Tools 89
    Customizing the Spell-Checking Process 89
    Adjusting the Standards for Grammar Checking 90
    Turning As-You-Type Proofing On and Off 91
Viewing Your Document's Readability Statistics 91
Printing Your Document 92
Saving Word Documents 94
    Performing a First-Time Save 94
    Updating a Saved File 96
    Saving a Document with a New Name 96
Creating Document Templates 97
    Building Template Content 97
    Creating New Documents from Your Templates 99
    Template Tips and Techniques 99

CHAPTER 6   **Effective Document Formatting** **101**
Changing the Appearance of Text 102
    Choosing the Right Font and Size 103
    Applying Text Color 104
    Applying Special Text Effects 105
Altering Text Position and Flow 106
    Changing Paragraph Alignment 106
    Indenting Text 107
    Adjusting Line Spacing 109
    Understanding Text-Flow Controls 110
    Creating Lists 112
Working with Styles 114
    Creating Styles 116
    Locking Styles and Formatting to
        Prevent Changes to Your Templates 118

Customizing Page Layout 119
    Setting New Page Margins 119
    Adjusting Page Orientation 120
    Changing Paper Size 121
Working with Tabs 122
    Creating a Tabbed List 122
    Using Word's Default Tabs 122
    Setting Tabs from the Ruler 123
    Using the Tabs Dialog Box 125
    Setting Up Multiple Tabbed Lists in a Single Document 126
    Editing Tab Settings 126
    Adjusting Tab Positions 126
    Changing Tab Stop Alignment 127

CHAPTER 7   **Working with Long Documents** **129**
Inserting and Formatting Page Numbers 130
Working with Headers and Footers 131
    Inserting Header and Footer Content 132
Creating a Table of Contents 134
Searching for and Replacing Document Content 135
    Using Find to Move Through a Document 135
    Replacing Text 136
    Replacing Special Codes 136
Working with Columns 137
    Building a Newsletter Document 138
    Applying Columns to Existing Text 139
    Setting Up Columns Before Typing 140
    Customizing Columns 141
    Setting Up Multiple Column Configurations in One Document ... 142

CHAPTER 8   **Structuring Documents with Tables** **143**
Structuring Documents and Text with Tables 144
    Building a Uniform Grid 144
    Entering Table Content 147
    Navigating a Table 148
    Selecting Table Columns, Rows, and Cells 148
Formatting Tables 149
    Resizing Columns and Rows 149
    Adding and Deleting Columns and Rows 151
    Splitting and Merging Cells 152
    Applying Borders and Shading 153
Drawing a Freeform Table 155
    Drawing Table Cells 155

	Erasing Table Cell Walls	156
	Working with the Tables and Borders Toolbar	157
	Nesting Tables	160
CHAPTER 9	**Creating Form Letters, Envelopes, and Labels with Mail Merge**	**163**
	Starting the Mail Merge Process	164
	Creating a Form Letter	164
	Creating Mailing Labels	167
	Choosing the Right Label	168
	Selecting Your Data Source	169
	Merging Data with Your Labels	169
	Printing Labels	172
	Mail Merge Troubleshooting	172
PART III	**Crunching Numbers and Keeping Lists with Excel**	
CHAPTER 10	**Building and Formatting Worksheets**	**175**
	Touring the Excel Interface	176
	Starting a New Workbook	176
	Understanding Worksheets	177
	Navigating Worksheets	180
	Entering Worksheet Content	181
	Editing Cell Content	183
	Selecting Cells, Blocks, Columns, and Rows	184
	Inserting Rows and Columns	185
	Saving Workbook Files	185
	Saving a New Workbook	186
	Saving a Workbook as a Template	186
	Formatting Worksheet Content	188
	Applying Numeric Formats	189
	Changing Fonts and Sizes	190
	Aligning Worksheet Content	191
	Shading Worksheet Cells	193
	Applying Borders	194
	Copying Cell Formats	195
CHAPTER 11	**Working with Formulas and Functions**	**197**
	Understanding Spreadsheet Calculations	198
	Performing Quick Addition with AutoSum	199
	Using the AutoSum Function	200
	Pasting the AutoSum Function	200
	Creating Simple Formulas from Scratch	202
	Editing Formulas	203
	Understanding Relative vs. Absolute Addressing	203

Controlling the Order of Operations 204
Using 3-D Formula References 205
Using Excel's Built-in Functions 206

CHAPTER 12 **Building and Maintaining List Databases** **209**
Understanding Database Concepts 210
Database Terminology 210
Excel List Database Requirements 212
Building a List 212
Sorting by a Single Field 213
Sorting by Multiple Fields 213
Creating a Subtotal Report 214
Searching for Specific Records 217
Using AutoFilter to Locate and Display Records in a List 217
Setting Up Advanced Filters 218
PivotTable Basics 219
Building a PivotTable 219

CHAPTER 13 **Charting Excel Data** **223**
Using Charts to Enhance Worksheets 224
Understanding Chart Types 224
Understanding Chart Elements 226
Building a Chart 228
Selecting Data for Charting 228
Setting Up a New Chart 228
Updating and Changing Charts 230
Changing Chart Types 232
Formatting a Chart 232
Editing Chart Text 233
Resizing and Moving Charts 233
Deleting Charts 233

CHAPTER 14 **Printing and Publishing Worksheets** **235**
Printing Workbooks and Worksheets 236
Printing an Entire Workbook 237
Printing Individual Worksheets 238
Printing a Range of Cells 238
Controlling Page Breaks and Page Count 238
Working with Print Options 241
Setting Up Headers and Footers 242
Publishing Excel Content to the Web 243
Saving Your Worksheet as a Web Page 243

PART IV	**Creating Presentations with PowerPoint**	
CHAPTER 15	**Planning and Building a Presentation**	**249**
	Planning Your Presentation	250
	Organizing Your Presentation Content	251
	The PowerPoint Environment	251
	Deciding on a Presentation Template	252
	Choosing Slide Layouts	254
	Inserting New Slides	254
	Deleting Slides	255
	Inserting Slide Text	256
	Working with Bulleted Text	256
	Typing Paragraphs	258
	Inserting Extra Text Boxes	259
	Formatting Slide Text	259
	Repositioning Text Objects	260
	Aligning Text Objects	261
	Resizing Text Objects	261
	Saving a Presentation	263
	Printing Your Slides	263
	Printing Color Options	264
	Creating Notes and Audience Handouts	265
CHAPTER 16	**Enhancing a Presentation with Graphics and Charts**	**267**
	Using Graphics Effectively in a Presentation	268
	Adding Clip Art and Photographs	268
	Drawing and Manipulating Shapes and Lines	269
	Drawing Shapes	270
	Drawing Lines and Arrows	270
	Formatting Graphic Elements	271
	Applying Fills and Outlines	271
	Typing in Shapes	272
	Rotating Shapes and Lines	272
	Aligning Graphic Objects	273
	Changing the Stacking Order of Graphics and Drawn Objects	273
	Grouping and Ungrouping Objects	273
	Creating a PowerPoint Chart	273
	Selecting a Chart Type	275
	Customizing the Chart	275
	Building an Organization Chart	276
	Filling in the Chart Boxes	277
	Adding New Boxes to the Chart	278
	Formatting the Organization Chart	278
	Creating a Diagram	279

CHAPTER 17	**Building an Effective Multimedia Slide Show**	**281**
	Previewing Your Slide Show	282
	Rearranging, Duplicating, and Deleting Slides	282
	Applying Slide Transitions	284
	Animating Individual Slide Elements	286
	Animating Text	286
	Animating a Bulleted List	288
	Applying Animation to Charts and Diagrams	289
	Making Pictures and AutoShapes Move	289
	Setting Up a Slide Show	289
	Inserting Links to Files, Presentations, and Web Content	290
	Using Slide Elements as Hyperlinks	291
	Working with Action Buttons	292
	Publishing a Presentation for Use on the Web	294
PART V	**Managing Data with Access**	
CHAPTER 18	**Getting Started with Access Databases**	**299**
	What Is a Database?	300
	Understanding Database Concepts	300
	Understanding Database Objects	301
	Viewing Objects in Your Database with the Database Window ..	301
	Designing Tables to Store Your Data	301
	What You Need to Know about Tables Before You Begin	303
	Viewing a Table and Its Data	304
	Creating a Table	305
	How to Connect Tables with Relationships	313
	Understanding Relationship Types	314
	Creating Relationships	314
CHAPTER 19	**Simplifying Data Entry with Forms**	**317**
	Creating a Form with the Form Wizard	319
	How to See the Form Design and Data	319
	Understanding Some Basic Form Concepts	320
	Using the Form Wizard to Create a Form	320
	Modifying Your Form	321
	Managing the Controls on Your Form	321
	Making a Pick List with the Combo Box Control	323
	Adding a Title to Your Form	325
	Changing the Appearance of Controls by Formatting	325
	Entering Data in Your Form	327
	Data-Entry Tips	327
	Navigating Through Records	328

CHAPTER 20   **Extracting Data with Queries** **331**
Understanding Query Types 332
Viewing Query Designs and Data 333
Using the Simple Query Wizard to Make a Select Query 333
Designing a Query in the QBE Grid 334
Ordering Your Records with the Sort Row 336
Writing Criteria to Select Specific Records 338
Selecting Data from Multiple Tables 340

CHAPTER 21   **Documenting Your Data with Access Reports** **343**
Exploring Report-Development Options 344
Simplifying Report Design with the Report Wizard 344
Creating a Report with the Report Wizard 347
Changing the Margins to Fit More Data per Page 352
Printing Your Reports 353

PART VI   **Keeping in Touch and on Schedule with Outlook**

CHAPTER 22   **Communicating with Email** **357**
About Email Accounts 358
Touring the Outlook Interface 360
Working with Messages 361
Attaching Files to Messages 363
Working with Message Flags, Levels, and Receipts 364
Sending Your Message 366
Replying to Messages 369
Forwarding Messages 370
Formatting Email Messages 370
Setting a New Default Font 371
Choosing Stationery 371
Formatting Message Text 373
Working with Signatures 373
Creating a Signature 374
Establishing Signatures for Different Email Accounts 375
Creating Folders to Organize Email 376
Setting Up Inbox and Sent Items Folders 376
Moving Messages Between Folders 377
Deleting Messages 378
Filtering Junk Email 379

CHAPTER 23   **Scheduling Tasks and Appointments** **381**
A Tour of the Outlook Calendar 382
Understanding Calendar Entries 384
Creating Appointments, Events, and Meetings 385
Scheduling a Meeting 388

Customizing the Calendar 389
Working with Tasks 390
    Creating a New Task 390
    Assigning Tasks 391
Printing Your Schedule 392

CHAPTER 24   Building a Contacts List **395**
Working with Contacts 396
    Entering a New Contact 397
    Editing Contact Information 399
    Contact Tracking 401
Printing Your Contacts List 402

PART VII   Designing Web Pages with FrontPage

CHAPTER 25   Planning a Website **407**
What Are Your Online Goals? 408
    Personal and Family Websites 409
    Sites that Advertise 409
    Sites that Sell 409
Planning Your Site's Content 410
    Understanding Graphic Requirements 410
    Working Within Color Limitations on the Web 412
    Gathering Your Graphic Images 412
    Collecting Text Content 413
Building Your Website Blueprint 414
    Creating a Site Map 415
    Storyboarding Your Individual Page Content 416

CHAPTER 26   Building a Website **419**
Getting Started with FrontPage 420
Starting a New Website 420
    Adding Pages to Your Site 422
    Rearranging the Site Structure 423
Applying a Theme to Your Website 424
Adding Page Banners 426
Inserting Navigation Bars 427
    Adding Navigation Buttons to the Home Page 427
    Adding Navigation Buttons to Subpages 429
Building Web Page Content 429
    Inserting Text Content 430
    Making Text Links to External Web Pages and Sites 430
    Adding Images to Your Web Pages 432
    Editing Images 432

Structuring Pages with Tables 434
    Inserting a Table 435
    Resizing Tables 436
    Merging and Splitting Cells 436
    Modifying Table Properties 436

CHAPTER 27   **Posting Pages to the Web** **439**
Previewing Pages Through a Browser 440
    Selecting a Preview Browser 440
    Checking Your Site for Errors 441
    Publishing Your Website 443

Index 447

Acknowledgments

Updating my previous edition of this book has been a lot of fun—I've been able to work with some of the same people I worked with on the XP edition of the book, and I've had the pleasure of meeting and working with new people, as well. Although I'm sure I'll end up leaving someone out, I want to individually acknowledge the following people at McGraw-Hill/Osborne, without whom this book would just be a lot of text taking up space on my hard drive:

- Margie McAneny, for orchestrating this new edition and coordinating the project
- Laura Stone, Elisabeth Manini, and Tana Allen, for being so well-organized and easy to work with
- Janet Walden, for her great work in dealing with the chapter layouts and handling all the loose ends that turn text and images into a book
- Will Kelly, for insightful and accurate technical edits
- Bart Reed, for great copy edits
- Claire Splan, who worked hard to index the book
- McGraw-Hill/Osborne's production and illustration departments for the page layouts and for expert art handling

I must also thank my contributing authors:

- Ken Cook, who wrote the chapters on Access, is an expert on virtually everything Office-related, and the readers should thank me for not writing the Access chapters myself—you're much better off in Ken's hands. I encourage you to visit Ken's website at www.kcookpcbiz.com to find out about all of Ken's services and areas of expertise.
- Robert Fuller, who wrote the Outlook and FrontPage chapters, is a talented and experienced web designer, a gifted computer trainer, and the author of *HTML Virtual Classroom*, also from McGraw-Hill/Osborne. I hope you'll check it out once his chapters on FrontPage whet your appetite for real web design.

Thanks must also go to my agent, Margot Maley, who takes very good care of me, and to my students and readers who teach me new things all the time.

Introduction

Office 2003 is the latest version of Microsoft Office, the most popular suite of desktop applications on the planet. The suite's popularity is due not only to the incredible power Microsoft has acquired through its distribution of the Windows operating system, but due to the fact that the applications—Word, Excel, PowerPoint, Access, Outlook, and FrontPage—are truly great tools for both business and home users.

The Office applications are relatively easy to use, and as someone who has been using and teaching them for more than a decade, I can say they offer just about everything you'd want from a word processing, spreadsheet, presentation, database, email/scheduling, and web design application. I've taught more than 10,000 people to use Office, and my hope is that your experience with this book will be similar to sitting in on one of my classes. My goal was to create both an effective jump start for new users and an effective reference for both experienced and novice users alike as they upgrade to the new release.

Although everything you might already know about Office 97, 2000, or XP (2003's predecessors) will still apply to your use of Office 2003, this version of the software contains some exciting additions and improvements that you'll enjoy using. If you're new to the Office suite or to any of the individual applications within it, you'll find this book to be a significant tool in shortening your learning curve. If you already know one or more of the applications, you'll find this book useful in terms of learning how all the applications work together, and will want to pay particular attention to the first chapters and sections of other chapters throughout the book which cover the elements that are common to all the applications and the suite's cross-application features.

The book is divided into seven parts, six of them devoted to individual applications, and one of them to the features you'll find throughout the suite:

- Part I: Office 2003 Common Elements
- Part II: Creating Documents with Word
- Part III: Crunching Numbers and Keeping Lists with Excel
- Part IV: Creating Presentations with PowerPoint
- Part V: Managing Data with Access
- Part VI: Keeping in Touch and on Schedule with Outlook
- Part VII: Designing Web Pages with FrontPage

The names of these parts are rather self-explanatory—each one contains three or more chapters that break an application down into the main tasks that the application enables you to perform, such as typing a letter or report, setting up a list database, creating presentation slides, merging letters and labels with a database, setting up data entry forms, sending email, maintaining personal and business calendars, scheduling and inviting coworkers to meetings, building websites, and designing web pages. Although this book never intends to present soup-to-nuts coverage of the Office 2003 suite, it does cover a comprehensive set of tasks, and shows you how the applications work so you can do whatever you want to do with greater confidence and creativity. My approach in choosing and executing the book's topics was similar to the old "teach a man to fish" analogy—if I show you how to perform key tasks correctly and give you a solid foundation in the applications, there's nothing you can't do on your own.

Throughout the book, you'll find a few special elements that were added to increase the amount of information shared through the book without adding significantly to the book's length. You'll find special Note, Tip, Caution, and Shortcut paragraphs:

NOTE *Notes delve into related topics and provide information that will support you in whatever the main topic of the chapter might be. I enjoy going through a book and reading just the notes (and other special paragraphs) to pick up some quick information before I begin reading the book cover to cover, or before I put the book on my shelf for future reference.*

TIP *Tips are short asides that offer information related to the subject at hand or that relate to something you might want to do now that you've mastered whatever is covered in the chapter. It's like having me there next to you, saying, "Oh! By the way, did you know that you can...?"*

CAUTION *Cautions are my way of helping you avoid common pitfalls and errors that will cause you frustration.*

SHORTCUT *These paragraphs cut to the chase and show you the quickest, most direct way to complete a task.*

In addition to the special paragraphs, you'll also find text boxes with the titles, "How to..." and "Did You Know?" The text in these boxes explains how to perform a key task, or provides helpful information related to the topic at hand.

Here are some other things to look for: new terms or lingo are in *italics*, and followed by a definition or example as explanation. Keyboard shortcuts, such as CTRL-P, are also formatted to stand out amongst the rest of the text so that you can easily refer to the book as you work through a procedure.

As I mentioned, I welcome your comments and questions. I can be reached via email at laurie@planetlaurie.com, and hope you'll check out my website, www.planetlaurie.com. I try to respond to all email queries within 24 hours of receiving them, but please be patient if an answer takes a little longer. I look forward to hearing from you, and I hope you enjoy this book and find it useful in your learning and using Microsoft Office 2003!

Part I

Office 2003 Common Elements

Chapter 1

What's New in Office 2003

How to...

- Identify new features in the interface
- Make use of the new features
- Customize basic settings to create a comfortable transition

Office 2003 has an entirely new look—and that's what you'll notice right away. Understandably, the first thing you'll spot is the new design of the buttons, menus, and the more web-like, colorful task pane on the right. There's a lot more to the new version of Office than such window dressing, however—there are significant changes to Office's "underpinnings" in the form of XML support and how Outlook works. You'll also find that helpful tools such as smart tags have been integrated into all the applications in the suite, making the applications not only smarter but also more consistent.

The New Office "Look"

That new Office look I said you'd spot right away involves a much more web-like appearance. The changes in the look are consistent across the suite, in terms of the menus, toolbars, and the task pane, as you can see in each application shown in Figures 1-1, 1-2, 1-3, 1-4, and 1-5. Whether you're learning Office for the first time, or if you're a veteran Office user who needs to support other users at work, you'll find that the new interface is easy to navigate, and therefore a short learning curve can be expected.

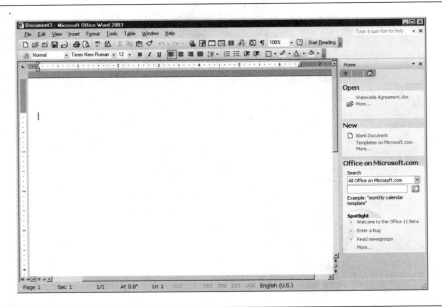

FIGURE 1-1   The gradient fill that makes the menu bar and toolbars look three-dimensional helps you keep visual track of onscreen features.

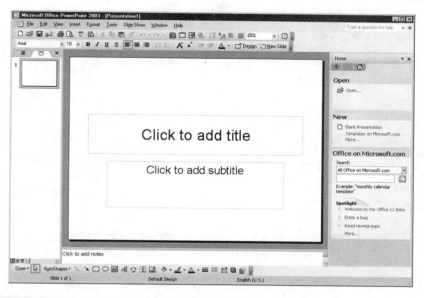

FIGURE 1-2   PowerPoint's workspace contains the required elements for building, editing, formatting, and animating slides—all in Office 2003's clean new look.

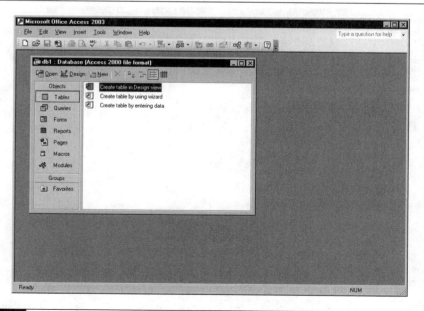

FIGURE 1-3   The simple Access worksheet remains in Office 2003.

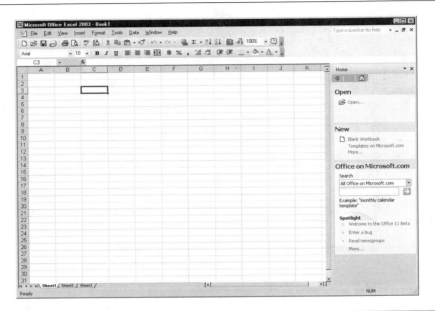

FIGURE 1-4   Excel's worksheet is unchanged, but the workspace has Office 2003's new look and an enhanced task pane.

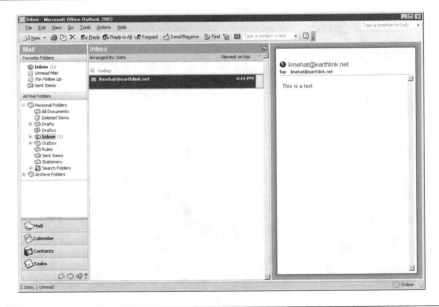

FIGURE 1-5   The workspace layout is different in Outlook, and you'll like the logical configuration, even if you're quite accustomed to the Windows 2000 or XP environment.

Outlook has undergone the most changes, as the location and appearance of its onscreen elements—folder lists, tools, and the message preview pane—look vastly different (see Figure 1-5). The environment is much friendlier to use and much more logically laid out. Also, you have more options for customizing the view, such as changing the location of the preview pane and the look of the message being previewed, which now appears more graphically realistic.

The New Task Pane

You'll find that the increased use of color in the task pane (the Word version of which is shown in Figure 1-6) makes it more inviting and easier to use, and if you're like me, you'll find that you stop turning the task pane off so readily—now that it's more visually friendly, it doesn't seem to simply be taking up workspace!

The use of the task pane hasn't changed much—you can just click the text and graphic links to explore different areas of the application. Note the word "Home" at the top of the pane, however. This is a definite visual reference to the web, and it makes it easier for you to return the pane to its default setting.

FIGURE 1-6   The task pane employs colors, varied fonts, and graphics—all designed to make the pane less of a pain to use.

 *The Research button, found on all Office 2003 applications' toolbars, opens the Research task pane and accesses the web to facilitate researching just about any topic. You must be connected to the Internet to use Research, but assuming that's not a problem, you'll find this new feature quite useful.*

Expanded Use of Smart Tags

All the applications—Word, Excel, PowerPoint, Access, and Outlook—now employ smart tags. Of course, the tags themselves vary by application, but the methods for adding, using, and deleting these tags remain constant throughout the suite (Tools | AutoCorrect Options). Of particular interest is the ability to associate smart tags with cells in an Excel worksheet. You can assign names, dates, financial symbols, phone numbers, and times with any cells in the worksheet, making it possible to bring more data into the worksheet than is directly contained within its cells.

Customizing the Display of Toolbars and Menus

By default, the menus in Office 2003 display a shorter set of commands—typically the most often used commands. You can turn this option off, thus displaying the entire menu the first time, every time, by choosing Tools | Customize. In the Customize dialog box, check the Always Show Full Menus box. You'll have to enable this option in each application if you want to see all the menu commands throughout the suite.

 The growing popularity of tablet devices has led Microsoft to make tablet support a standard feature within the Office 2003 suite. If you have a tablet installed on your computer, Office 2003 will detect it upon installation of the suite, and you'll be all set to write your letters, insert data via pen to Excel, scribble email messages, and so on.

Faxing via the Internet

You can now use the Internet to fax any Office document–based file. By choosing File | Send To | Fax Service, you'll access a fax website that processes your file and sends it to the computer or fax machine you indicate.

Office Watson to the Rescue

Has Word crashed again? Is Excel acting flaky? Office Watson will gather information on the glitch and report any problems back to Microsoft via the web. In addition to bona fide crashes, Office Watson will report on alerts, error messages (of the nonfatal variety), and any other unexpected "events" that make you want to throw your computer out the window.

The Picture Library

To help you name, organize, and share your images, Office 2003 offers the Picture Library. Unlike the Clip Gallery, which functioned *within* the Office applications, the Picture Library is an application unto itself. You can edit images—cropping them, resizing them, and removing common problems such as red eye and bad contrast or color problems—and you can create small-sized files that are perfect for sharing via email. When you run Picture Library for the first time, you'll be able to choose which graphic file formats will be opened by default (see Figure 1-7). If you usually edit your images in another application, such as Adobe Photoshop or Macromedia Fireworks, don't check any of the formats—you'll still be able to open them in Picture Library, but you won't turn Picture Library into your default editing program. It's a convenient tool, but not a robust one.

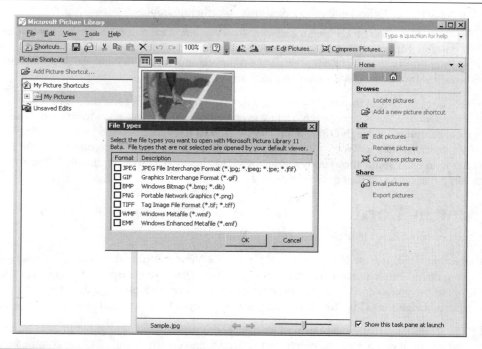

FIGURE 1-7   Want to do a quick edit or rename a file for easier retrieval next time you need it? Try Office 2003's Picture Library.

The XML Factor in Office 2003

You may be asking, "What *is* XML, anyway?" If you are, you certainly won't be alone among most Office users. All users will experience the benefits of Office 2003's use of XML, but many of the beneficiaries have no need to understand the nuts and bolts. Assuming you just want the basic facts, here goes:

■ *XML stands for Extensible Markup Language.* This means that XML is a language designed for structuring data in clear, simple ways.

■ *XML is a meta-markup language.* This means that XML structures data in a way that makes it much more universally compatible with a variety of diverse data-sharing tools and environments.

■ *XML is considered a public standard.* Created by the W3C (World Wide Web Consortium, the organization that decides on standards for the structure and functionality of the web), XML isn't owned by anyone and is therefore much more reliable—nobody's going to upgrade it (like Office) and render data created earlier unusable.

■ *XML protects data by keeping it separate from the interface that displays it.* This makes it possible for the same data to be used in many different ways, by many different people, thus increasing and hastening the return on investment in database development because stored data can do more in more ways for more people.

So what does this mean to you? If you're not designing databases for use on the web or throughout a network, maybe not much. If, however, you'll be designing ways to store and use data that's accumulated through Office applications such as Excel and Access and displaying it through applications such as Word, you'll want to make use of the Save As command (found in the File menu in each application) and choose XML Document (*.xml) from the list in the Save As Type drop list, at the bottom of the dialog box.

What's New in Word

Here's a list of some new features you'll enjoy in Word:

■ Reading Layout view (found, in of all places, the View menu) makes it easier to read long documents onscreen, as shown in Figure 1-8. The page is displayed along with tools that allow you to quickly search the document and view multiple page thumbnails to speed navigation. This view is much easier on the eyes for extended reading sessions.

■ The Comments feature is improved, with the commented text highlighted in light blue and a callout containing the comment text neatly and clearly pointing to the commented text in the document (see Figure 1-9). The Reviewing Pane (more of a toolbar) offers more tools for managing comments throughout a group editorial process.

■ Track Changes is also improved, making it much easier to track who has done what to your documents. You can now mark up a document in "ink" using a tablet device, which is great for people who are accustomed to traditional editing symbols and techniques. In addition, you can now decide which parts of your document can be edited, and by whom, making it easier to control the editorial process.

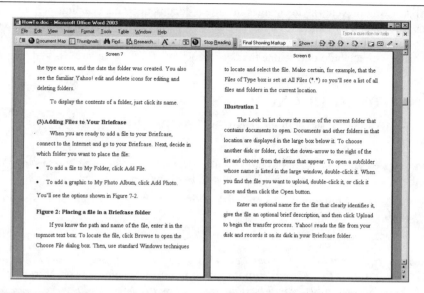

FIGURE 1-8   Take it easy on your eyes by switching to Reading Layout view when you have a long document to review.

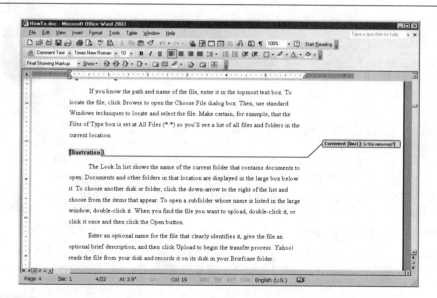

FIGURE 1-9   Never again will you wonder which text is associated with a comment—it's perfectly clear in Office 2003.

■ Style Locking prevents style changes in certain documents. This is a huge benefit to those of us who design templates for others to use—we desire the consistency that a template affords, but prior to Style Locking, couldn't prevent individual users from tweaking the template, which would undermine the consistency of custom template-based documents.

New and Improved in Excel

Whether you're new to using Excel or an experienced user, you'll find the following enhancements to be quite useful:

■ Smart tags can now be linked to individual cells, bringing date, time, names, phone numbers, and lists to the tags associated with worksheet data.

■ Excel's statistical functions are improved, giving you more statistical-analysis tools to work with.

■ You can use a pen device to mark up your Excel worksheet.

Through its compatibility with pen devices, Office 2003 will also be compatible with Microsoft's Tablet PC. Though initial reviews of this new computer are mixed, it's nice to know your new software will be able to make use of the technology.

PowerPoint's Enhancements

The tools for creating presentations aren't vastly different, but some of the tools for making presentations, sharing them with others, and navigating during a presentation are greatly improved:

■ The Viewer has been improved to make it possible for more people to run PowerPoint presentations on their computers, even those PCs that don't have PowerPoint installed. Also, users of earlier versions of PowerPoint will find it easier to run a presentation that was created with PowerPoint 2003.

■ The Package to CD feature makes it possible to place an entire presentation (or group of presentations) on CD. This makes it much more cost-effective and less labor-intensive to distribute educational and sales presentations to a wider audience. The aforementioned Viewer can also be placed on the CD, thus expanding the audience further.

■ The Windows Media Player is now part of PowerPoint, thus improving the playback of video and streaming audio.

■ The Thesaurus, previously a Word-only feature, is now available in PowerPoint.

■ You can mark up your slides in "ink" with a pen/tablet device, writing comments onscreen during a presentation. This is a vast improvement over attempts to annotate slides onscreen with the mouse.

Access Improvements

XML makes its biggest impact in Access. Through enhanced XML import and export tools for Access data, more people in more places, using more environments for accessing and using data, can now work with the data you've stored in Access. In addition to this overarching change, you'll enjoy the following enhancements to Access:

- AutoCorrect, which used to be available in Word, Excel, and PowerPoint only, is now available in Access. This will be a big help to people who want to make sure that data is entered consistently and that common spelling and abbreviation errors don't stand in the way of easily filtered and sorted data.

- Forms and reports benefit from enhanced error-checking tools. Access points out errors and makes suggestions for resolving them.

- Your Access databases can now be backed up from within the Access application. You don't have to manually copy your .mdb files to disk or CD anymore; you can now issue a backup command through the application itself and know that you're backing up your tables, forms, reports, and all other related content.

Outlook's New Features

Outlook is the most changed of the Office applications. As communication has become the heart of just about every organization's life and success, the ability to use Outlook to communicate more effectively is clearly a priority for Microsoft Office's design team. Here are some enhancements you can look forward to:

- New panes for navigating folders and messages and reading email are now available. Like Word's Reading Layout view, the Reading pane (the right-hand pane of Figure 1-2 shown earlier in the chapter) mimics a paper reading environment and is much easier on the eyes, especially in a long email-handling session.

- Search folders make it easier to use simple criteria for finding and grouping e-mail messages by category.

- Quick Flagging simplifies the process of marking messages for follow-up action, be it to respond to important messages, delete unwanted messages, or move certain messages to particular folders.

- You can block junk email with a "web beacon" that includes inline references to external content—pictures, sounds, web pages, and so on. This will get rid of a large percentage of the spam that may currently plague you, especially if your ISP doesn't offer any spam-blocking features of its own.

- Unique email signatures can be set up for multiple accounts. If you have several email personas, each one can now have its own signature—one for your personal email, one for your business email, and one for any email identities you have for other organizations, such as your church, clubs, mailing lists, and so on.

■ Better thread management tools make it easier to manage long conversation threads and to find the most recent messages in a given thread.

Perhaps the most exciting improvement in Outlook is the new connections between your calendar and your contacts. You can now view multiple calendars simultaneously (see Figure 1-10), making it possible for you to keep track of personal and business events in separate calendars *and* see both calendars side by side to make time management easier. You can also see your calendar and contacts at the same time, so you can make visual associations between your appointments and the people related to them.

Love Instant Messenger? Now Office 2003 offers instant messaging, making it possible to start a conversation with people in your Contact list or people whose names are found in a smart tag list. You can check to see who's online, and you can do it from within any of the Office applications.

Upgrade Considerations

If you're an individual user working in a small or home office, you probably don't have anything other than cost to dictate whether you upgrade from Office 97, 2000, or XP to Office 2003—assuming, of course, you're running the right version of Windows, because Office 2003 runs only in

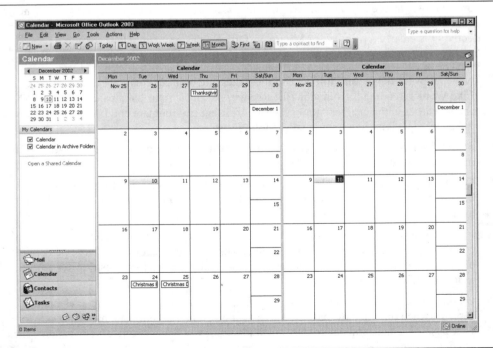

FIGURE 1-10 Got a life? How about two lives? Now you can schedule and view your activities in separate calendars, viewable side by side.

an XP or Windows 2000 environment. If you're reading this book, you probably already made the decision, and it came down in favor of the upgrade. For larger offices, however, the decision can be more complex—the cost, certainly, is a factor, plus the learning curve for users who need to master the new version, the compatibility with other companies or divisions within the same company that may not be upgrading, and whether the upgrade offers features that are really worth the challenges entailed in an organization-wide upgrade.

> NOTE   *If you have Windows 2000 running on your computer now and have not yet installed Office 2003, you'll need to install the latest service pack (SP 3 as of this writing) in order for Office 2003 to install and run properly.*

With regard to the learning curve, it should be very short. There are very few major differences between the last two versions of Office and this one, except with respect to Outlook—and there, the changes are positive ones that make the application work more the way people want their email, scheduling, and contact-management tools to work. The result? The new features are quickly mastered because they make sense.

With regard to compatibility, users of Office 2000 and XP will have no problems opening files created in Office 2003. Further, if very old versions of Office still survive in some parts of your organization or within your pool of customers and suppliers, Office 2003 users can save to a variety of older and non-Microsoft versions of the applications (see Figure 1-11). This makes it very easy to keep things running smoothly and simply once the upgrade is performed.

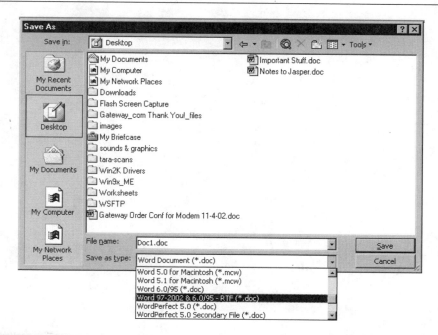

FIGURE 1-11   You can turn back the hands of time when you save files for use by people using very old versions of the Office applications.

Chapter 2

Common Office Features

How to...

- Display and use toolbars
- Work with menus
- Use the enhanced task pane
- Access and train Office 2003's Speech Recognition feature
- Use smart tags to extend Office's capabilities
- Work with the Clipboard to move and share content between Office applications
- Use Office 2003 Help

The main applications within Office 2003—Word, Excel, PowerPoint, Access, and Outlook—have a lot of common features, and understanding them will enable you to master all the applications much more quickly. What you learn about the toolbars and menus in the application you use most will be applicable to the other applications, making it easier to use them and to share files between applications within the suite.

Common Workspace Elements

This book covers the five applications that are part of the Office 2003 suite: Word, Excel, PowerPoint, Access, and Outlook. The workspaces you see in Word, Excel, and PowerPoint are very much the same, and you'll have little or no trouble transferring what you've learned about one to another. If, for example, Word is your primary application, you'll find it very easy to learn Excel and PowerPoint as well as to find tools for common activities such as opening, saving, and printing files. You'll find that among these three applications, the only differences in their workspaces are the features specific to these applications, as shown in Figures 2-1, 2-2, and 2-3.

When it comes to Access and Outlook, the menus and toolbars are quite different from the ones in the other applications, mainly because Access and Outlook are so vastly different in terms of how they work and what they do. The Access and Outlook toolbars are entirely specific to what these applications do—that is, they maintain a database of information and keep track of contacts and appointments, respectively.

When it comes to Access (shown in Figure 2-4), once you have an understanding of database management and how a relational database-management application works, what it does, and so on, you'll find the Access workspace more intuitive as well.

In the case of Outlook (see Figure 2-5), you'll find that although the workspace and tools are very different from those in Word, Excel, and PowerPoint, the features are so familiar that you'll have no trouble learning the application, even if you're someone who has been keeping track of people and places manually.

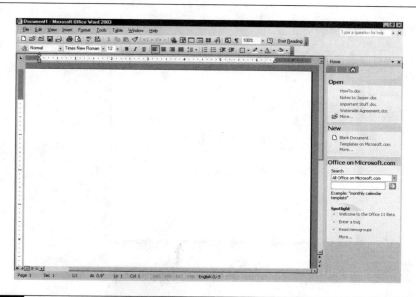

FIGURE 2-1   The Word workspace offers tools for formatting and laying out a document.

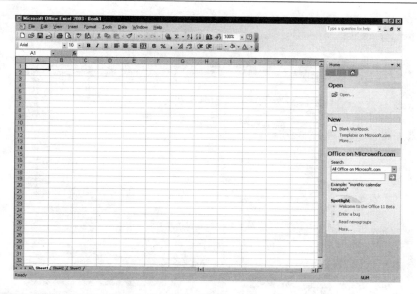

FIGURE 2-2   All the tools you need to edit and format your worksheet content are found in the Excel workspace.

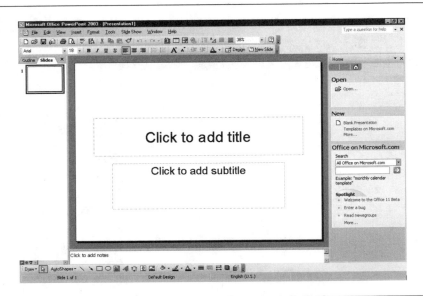

FIGURE 2-3   PowerPoint provides everything you need to insert text and graphical content onto your slides.

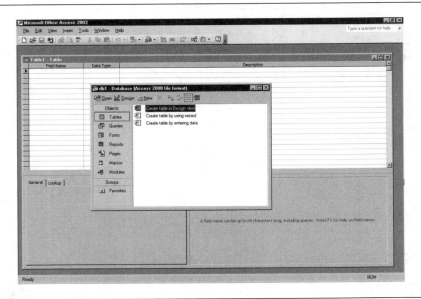

FIGURE 2-4   The Access workspace provides some common features, but many of its tools pertain solely to database management.

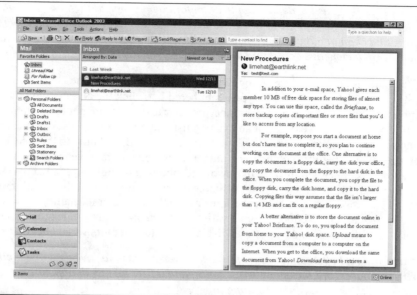

FIGURE 2-5   Although not common to the other applications, the tools in Outlook are fairly self-explanatory.

Working with Office 2003 Toolbars

The three primary applications—Word, Excel, and PowerPoint—offer two main toolbars, and you see them as soon as you open the applications for the first time. The Standard toolbar is on top, and it contains tools that generally pertain to the entire document, workbook, or presentation. Commands allow you to open, save, print, and add important elements such as tables (in Word), formulas (in Excel), and a grid to assist in object placement (in PowerPoint). Other than the application-specific tools, most of them are common to all three applications and are found in the same place on the Standard toolbar, no matter which application you're in. The second toolbar is the Formatting toolbar. Its set of buttons pertains to how the content of a file looks, including fonts, text sizes, colors (in all three applications), and numerical formats (in Excel).

Using Toolbar Buttons

Toolbar buttons are easy to use—just click them. Of course what you do before or after the click is where it can get a little tricky. For example, most of the Formatting toolbar buttons work best if you select some text—either in your document, on your slide, or in the cells of your worksheet—before you click them. This helps the application know which content the activated formatting should apply to. For example, if you click the Bold button with nothing selected in the document, worksheet, or slide, the application will assume that the format should apply to the next thing you type rather than to text that has already been typed.

Outlook uses Word as the default application for composing, editing, and formatting email messages. Therefore, you'll use the same tools and techniques for entering, editing, and changing the appearance and placement of text in messages as you do in actual Word documents. You'll find these familiar features in the message window.

Many of the buttons are toggles, meaning that you turn them on with one click and off with a second click. For example, if you want to type a numbered list, click the Numbering button and then type your list. When you want to stop numbering your text, click the button again to turn this feature off. Conversely, you can select an existing list and number it by clicking the button once. If the list was not numbered previously, numbers are applied, and only to the selected list. If the list was already numbered, clicking the Numbering button will remove those numbers.

Toolbar buttons accompanied by a small downward-pointing triangle offer a list of options when clicked. For example, the Font button (available on the Formatting toolbar in all three main applications) can be clicked to see a list of the fonts available for use in formatting your text. You can also click the Size button to choose from a variety of point sizes for your text, and the color buttons (Text Color, Fill Color, and so on) will display a palette of colors when clicked.

Not sure what a button does? Point to it and hover your cursor over it without clicking. Keep your mouse still for about two seconds, and a ScreenTip will appear containing the name of the button you're pointing to.

Displaying Different Toolbars

If you want to see and use toolbars in addition to the default Standard and Formatting toolbars—or if one (or both) of them is not showing and you want it back—pick one of the following methods to view a list of available menus and display them in the workspace:

- Choose View | Toolbars. A submenu appears, listing the toolbars available in the application you're using. The items in the list with check marks next to them are already displayed.
- Right-click any currently displayed toolbar or the menu bar and then choose a toolbar from the shortcut menu. Again, those with check marks are already displayed.

Moving Toolbars

If, for some reason, you want to change the stacking order of your toolbars (such as moving the Formatting toolbar on top of the Standard toolbar or adding the Drawing toolbar to the top of the workspace, taking it away from its default location at the bottom of the workspace), follow these steps:

1. Point to the left end of the toolbar you want to move. Your cursor will turn into a four-headed arrow.

2. Drag the toolbar to a new spot within the area where the toolbar is currently displayed (changing its stacking order with the neighboring toolbars), or to the top or bottom of the workspace.

3. If desired, you can drag a toolbar out onto the workspace to turn it into a floating toolbar, as shown here. Once set to float, a toolbar can be closed (by clicking the X), moved (by dragging it by the bar containing the toolbar's name, also called its *title bar*), or reattached to the top or bottom of the screen (by dragging it back to the top or bottom of the workspace and releasing the mouse when the toolbar's title bar disappears).

Working with Office 2003 Menus

As is the case with the toolbars, you'll find many of the same menus and menu commands in the same places in Word, Excel, and PowerPoint. When it comes to the File and Edit menus, you'll even find common ground when you venture into Access or Outlook, too. No matter which Office 2003 application you're in, you'll always have the File, Edit, Window, and Help menus. The others vary by application.

Making Menu Selections

To make a selection from a menu, use your mouse to pull down the menu and then click the command you want to use. If the command requires another level of interaction from you, either a submenu (for a refinement of the command choice) is offered or a dialog box appears so you can give the application specific instructions.

TIP   *You can also use the menu hot keys—the underlined letters on menu names and in menu commands—to open a menu and issue a command. Press ALT plus the underlined letter to open the menu and then just press the underlined letter for the command you want from within that menu.*

Common Menu Elements

Within the menus shared by all the Office applications, you'll find several common elements. You'll also find that having these items in the same menu, in roughly the same order within the menu (give or take a few application-specific commands), will help you learn and master the Office 2003 applications more quickly. Here are some common elements to look for in the menus:

- A list of the most recently used files is available at the foot of the File menu. This provides a quick way to reopen a file you were working with in your last session. You can increase (to 9) or reduce (to 0) the number of listed files, using the Options dialog box. The default setting for the Recently Used File List option is 4.

NOTE   *To access the Options dialog box (for changing many aspects of Word's functionality, including the number of Most Recently Used files listed in the File menu), choose Tools | Options. The Most Recently Used files option is found on the General tab.*

- Keyboard shortcuts (the keyboard equivalents of using the menus or clicking toolbar buttons to issue commands) are listed on the right side of the menus.

- Toolbar button equivalents are shown down the left side of the menu. These appear in the menus so that people who prefer the toolbars can learn which buttons perform the same tasks as certain menu commands.

- Submenu triangles appear to the right of any command that will spawn a submenu.

- An ellipsis after a menu item tells you that choosing this command will open a dialog box. Dialog boxes allow you to fine-tune how the command will be applied or to tell the application exactly what to do. For example, if you use the File | Print command, the application will open the Print dialog box from which you can choose how many copies to print, which pages to include, whether any other options exist (such as printing in black and white rather than color, or sending the print job to a different printer), and which ones you'd like to employ.

Using the Task Pane

New to Office XP and now greatly enhanced and expanded in Office 2003 is the panel of commands that appears on the right side of the workspace. This panel is called the *task pane*, and for good reason (see Figure 2-6). It offers a list of commonly performed tasks, making them more accessible than they were in versions of Office prior to Office XP. For example, you can open files, start new files based on a particular template, or access the Office web pages at Microsoft's website, www.microsoft.com.

FIGURE 2-6   With a distinctly web page–like look and a much more effective interface, the task pane puts specialized tools, commands, and features in easy reach.

TIP   *You'll find that Office 2003 is very much web oriented. Many features, such as the Research button (found on the Standard toolbar) and the Office on Microsoft.com feature in the task pane, assume that you're online and ready to access the web when you click them. You don't have to be online to use Office 2003, certainly, but if you want to access information to use in your Office documents, worksheets, presentations, and email, you'll want to have Internet access available for the times you need it.*

Displaying the Various Task Panes

In addition to the default Home task pane, you can choose task panes for a variety of other sets of activities, as shown here:

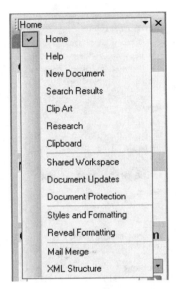

For example, in Word, you can access a Clipboard pane, a Research pane, and panes for applying styles and formatting, performing a mail merge, and getting help.

In PowerPoint, you can view task panes for Clipboard and Search (the same as Word) as well as panes for adjusting slide layout, slide design templates, color schemes, and animation schemes. You can also access custom animation and slide-transition tasks through specialized panes. Overall, the task pane options for all applications are roughly the same, with the exception of tasks that are specific to each application.

Turning Off the Task Pane

To temporarily turn off a task pane (it'll reopen when you ask for it from the View menu) click the X button in the upper-right corner of the pane.

NOTE *If you don't want to use up any of the workspace displaying the task pane, you can turn the task pane off by selecting it in the View menu. If the task pane is displayed at the time, selecting it will toggle it off.*

Working with Smart Tags Across the Office Suite

Smart tags give you the ability to perform content-specific tasks, based on the content in your documents, worksheets, and presentations. For example, if Word spots someone's name in a document, it will offer up a series of smart tags, asking whether you want to make this person into a new contact (in your Outlook Contacts database), for example, or perhaps schedule a meeting with them. If you're in Excel, and a stock symbol (a company's symbol on the NYSE or NASDAQ) is spotted, a smart tag for inserting a stock quote can be applied to the cell containing that symbol.

If the smart tags feature is turned on, you'll see a small button appear next to content that the Office application feels may need tagging. If you want to apply a smart tag, click the drop-down arrow next to that button and choose the type of tag you want to use, as shown in Figure 2-7.

To turn smart tags on (or to customize how they work), choose Tools | AutoCorrect Options, and in the resulting AutoCorrect dialog box (see Figure 2-8), click the Smart Tags tab.

Using the tab, you can click the Label Text with Smart Tags box (it appears as Label Data with Smart Tags in Excel) to place a check mark in it. Once this option is turned on, the Recognizers list becomes available, and you can choose which types of text or data will be seen as potentially smart tag-able.

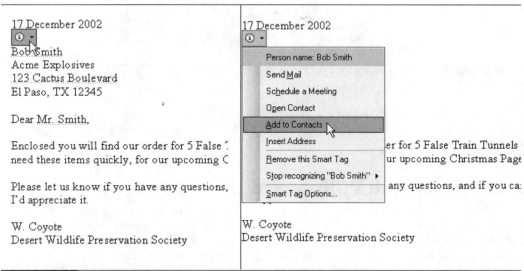

FIGURE 2-7   Any text or data that could be tagged will get a smart tag button next to it (left), which you can use or ignore. If you want to apply a particular smart tag, pick it from the list (right).

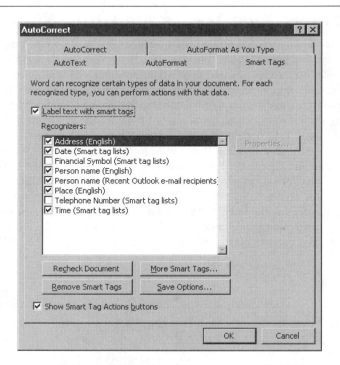

FIGURE 2-8   Considered an automatic "correction," smart tag settings can be found in the AutoCorrect dialog box.

Click the More Smart Tags button to go to the web and download more smart tags from the Office website.

Using the Office 2003 Clipboard

The original version of the Clipboard was actually part of Windows, not specific to the Office suite or any of its applications. It worked between any Windows-based applications, enabling people to take artwork from Paint (one of the Windows accessories) and paste it into a document, for example, or to take a section of text from one manufacturer's word processor and use it in another manufacturer's spreadsheet files. The interoperability this provided to users became an integral selling point for Windows users, and one of the most popular features of what was then a new thing for PC users: a graphical interface that made a lot of previously labor-intensive tasks much easier to perform.

In its original (and current) form, the Office Clipboard allowed you to cut or copy content from any file and use it elsewhere in that same file or in another file. Imagine needing to rearrange paragraphs or pages of text in a document—this belongs on page 5, not 7; that belongs at the end, not the beginning. Without the Clipboard, such rearrangements would require a great deal of typing and, with that, a large margin for error and lost consistency.

The Office Clipboard makes it possible to take content from a *source* file and move (cut) or share (copy) it and then to paste it within a *target* file. It has done this, with nearly perfect results, from the beginning. Office 2003 gives you the ability to cut and copy up to 24 selections, and through this enhancement, the Office Clipboard remains a staple in the day-to-day creation and maintenance of documents, spreadsheets, presentations, databases, and web content.

Moving Content with the Cut Command

Moving takes something from point A and repositions it at point B, requiring the use of the Cut command rather than the Copy command. The Cut command can be invoked in any one of the following three ways, each beginning with your selection of the content to be moved:

■ Press CTRL-X. This keyboard shortcut will remove the selected content and place it on the Clipboard, awaiting your use of the Paste command to place it somewhere else.

■ Choose Edit | Cut. Again, the content is removed and can be pasted to another spot in the same file or in another file.

■ Right-click the selected content and choose Cut from the shortcut menu that appears. If you're a fan of the right-click as a tool for displaying context-sensitive tools and commands, you'll be able to use it for the Paste half of this process, too.

TIP   *If you want to move content from one place to another within a small area of your document, presentation, or worksheet, you can drag it with your mouse—no need to use the Clipboard. Simply select the content to be moved and point to it with your mouse. The mouse pointer will turn into a left-pointing arrow. Drag the content from where it is to where you want it to be and then release the mouse.*

Sharing Content with the Copy Command

When you copy content, it is assumed that you want to share it—that is, to use it again somewhere else but leave the selected content right where it is. The ability to do this can be very handy if you want to make two documents identical or make sure that sections of a worksheet contain the exact same numbers and formulas.

To copy content, select it and then choose one of the following methods to place it on the Clipboard:

■ Press CTRL-C. You won't see anything exciting happen because, unlike Cut, this command won't remove the selected content. If you have the Clipboard task pane displayed (more about this later), you'll see your selection appear there, but nothing else happens when the command is issued.

■ Choose Edit | Copy. Again, no fanfare, just a duplicate of the selected content placed on the Clipboard.

■ Right-click the selected content and choose Copy from the shortcut menu.

TIP *If you want to copy content from point A to point B and both points are visible onscreen at the same time, you don't need to use the Clipboard—just use Drag and Drop. Here's how: select the content and release the mouse. Take your mouse back to the selection and point to it. The mouse pointer turns into a left-pointing arrow. While pressing CTRL on your keyboard, drag the selected content to its new location. A plus (+) sign will accompany your mouse pointer to indicate that a copy is being dragged. When your mouse is pointing to the desired "point B" location, release the mouse and then CTRL. Even though you never issue a Cut or Copy command, the content you drag and drop is pasted.*

Pasting Clipboard Selections

The obvious culmination of cutting or copying content to the Clipboard is pasting it into the spot where it belonged (if you're moving content) or where it is needed in addition to where it already is (if you're sharing content). To execute the Paste command, choose from these four techniques:

- Press CTRL-V. Why V? Because it's right next to X (Cut) and C (Copy), and if you look at it, it sort of looks like a down-pointing arrow, saying "insert this here." That's one way to remember it, anyway.

- Choose Edit | Paste.

- Right-click the spot where you want to place the cut or copied content and then choose Paste from the shortcut menu. If the Paste command is dimmed in the menu, you didn't successfully cut or copy, and you should go back to the original content and redo that portion of the process.

- If you have multiple cut or copied selections on the Clipboard and the Clipboard task pane is displayed, click once to position your cursor where the content should appear and then right-click the selection in the task pane. Choose Paste, and the content appears in the document, worksheet, presentation, email message, or data table. It is accompanied by a Clipboard symbol.

If you want to change the formatting of the pasted content, point to the Clipboard symbol and click the drop-down arrow that appears (see Figure 2-9).

From the resulting menu, choose how to apply formatting:

- **Keep Source Formatting**   This is how the content looked when you originally cut or copied it.

- **Match Destination Formatting**   This option formats the content to match its new surroundings.

- **Keep Text Only**   This option removes any formatting from the source and doesn't follow the formatting in the target location.

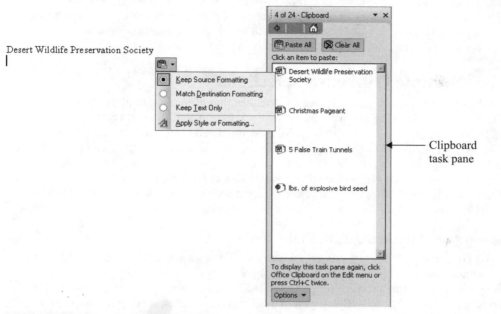

Desert Wildlife Preservation Society

FIGURE 2-9 You can ignore the Clipboard symbol or
click it to display a list of formatting options.

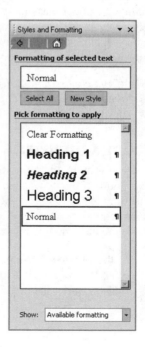

■ **Apply Style or Formatting**   Use this option if
you want to format the content differently from
how it was or is. When you select Apply Style
or Formatting, a series of formatting options
appears in the task pane, shown here, allowing
you to apply formatting and styles as desired.

 *Although it's rarely appropriate, if your situation calls for it, just click the Paste All button at the top of the Clipboard task pane, and every item in the Clipboard will be deposited at your cursor (in your document or presentation) or into your worksheet, starting with the active cell.*

Storing Multiple Clipboard Selections

Most of the time, you only need to copy or cut one selection from place to place, and that's it. You don't need to do anything else with that particular selection, and you don't care what happens to the Clipboard's content after you've pasted the cut or copied content where you want it. Ever since the release of Office 2000, however, the Clipboard could hold multiple selections (12), and Office 2003's Clipboard can hold 24. The selections can be pasted as many times as you want to, to as many locations within Office files as you want. This expanded functionality does not apply outside of the Office suite, however. You cannot copy more than one thing to the Windows Clipboard at a time.

Displaying the Clipboard Task Pane

When you could cut or copy only one selection to the Clipboard at a time, there was little or no need to actually *see* the Clipboard. You knew what you'd cut or copied, and you knew it was there until you cut or copied something else or exited Windows. Easy enough. With the ability to cut or copy up to 24 different selections to the Clipboard, however, it becomes essential to be able to see the selections so you can choose which one to paste.

Office 2003 makes dealing with the expanded functionality of the Clipboard much easier by providing a Clipboard task pane in each of the suite's applications. You can display this task pane whenever you know you're going to select and cut or copy more than one thing to the Clipboard. To display it, click the drop-down arrow at the top of the task pane and choose Clipboard. It will also appear automatically as soon as you cut or copy more than one selection to the Clipboard.

 If you choose not to display or use the Clipboard task pane to paste content, you'll get the last thing cut or copied to the Clipboard when you issue the Paste command, no questions asked.

Deleting Clipboard Content

What if you want to add more items to the Clipboard and you already have 24 items in it? What if one or more of the items shouldn't be there and you don't want to risk accidentally clicking and inserting them? You can get rid of individual items in the Clipboard, or you can empty the Clipboard entirely.

To delete individual Clipboard items, follow these steps:

1. In the Clipboard task pane, point to the selection you want to delete. A box forms around it, and a drop-down arrow appears. Be careful not to click the item when you point to it; that will paste the item rather than give you the chance to delete it.

2. Click the drop-down arrow and choose Delete from the resulting menu, as shown here.

> **TIP** *You can also right-click any item in the Clipboard task pane and choose to delete or paste it from a resulting shortcut menu.*

3. Repeat steps 1 and 2 for as many individual selections as you want to delete.

To remove all the items from the Clipboard in one fell swoop, simply click the Clear All button at the top of the Clipboard task pane. Do this with care, however, because there is no confirming prompt as you might be accustomed to whenever you delete something. Every item on the Clipboard will be deleted, and if some of them were items that you cut, they're really gone now.

> **CAUTION** *There's no going back after emptying the Clipboard or deleting one of the items on it. Undo won't help you. Exercise care and restraint when using any of the Clipboard's features, including pasting and deleting content and emptying the Clipboard.*

Customizing the Clipboard Task Pane

Office 2003 gives you options for when, how, and where the Clipboard task pane appears. By default, as soon as you cut or copy two items to the Clipboard, the task pane changes to display the Clipboard version. If the task pane is not displayed when you make your second selection, the task pane, in Clipboard mode, will appear. This is the most efficient way to work because it saves you having to ask to see the task pane. The task pane is essential for dealing with multiple selections, so it comes up automatically as soon as you have more than one selection to deal with.

If, however, you don't want the task pane to appear unless you specifically ask for it, you can tell Office 2003 how you want it to behave with respect to the task pane in general and the Clipboard version of it specifically. To adjust its settings, click the Options button at the foot of the task pane, as shown here.

The options are fairly self-explanatory. You can choose that the Clipboard task pane stays hidden, even if you make multiple selections, or you can leave it set to come up automatically. With respect to the content of the Clipboard task pane, you can choose whether the Clipboard icon will appear in the taskbar (giving you another way to open the task pane once multiple items are on it) and whether to display a little status comment when items are added to the Clipboard.

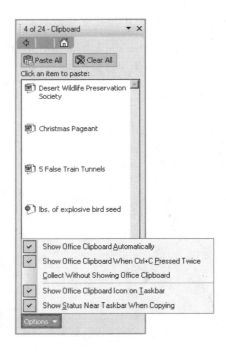

Using the Paste Special Command to Insert Clipboard Content

When opening the Edit menu to execute the Paste command, you've probably noticed the Paste Special command directly beneath Paste. You might have even been tempted to click it, even if you had no idea what would happen as a result. When you click the Paste Special command, a dialog box appears, its content dependent on what has happened prior to the command being issued. The dialog box gives you options for just how special your paste will be—and "Special" refers to the additional functionality that can be added by choosing Paste Special. You can create a link between the source content (what you cut or copied) and the target location (where you paste it). By creating this link, you make it possible to continuously update the target to reflect changes made in the source. The source and target can be the same document, two different files generated by the same application, or files created in two very different applications, such as Word and Excel.

What do I mean by that? Imagine an Excel worksheet that contains expense data for your department, and suppose you have to turn in a report to your manager every month, summarizing your expenses and showing year-to-date expense information as well. Your report is done in Word, and it uses the data from the Excel worksheet, where the actual expenses are entered and stored. Wouldn't it be great if you could copy the content from the worksheet and paste it into the Word document, and then each month update the document to include your latest entries into the worksheet as well as the ever-accruing year-to-date expense data?

If you use Paste Special to insert the Excel content into your Word document, this sort of automation can eliminate you needing to repeatedly paste each month's entries and updated totals, and it eliminates typos if you normally type the numeric data into your document rather than do a simple paste.

Creating a Paste Link

So you're sold. You like the idea of being able to have a linked portion of an Excel worksheet in your document or presentation, or a chart from a PowerPoint presentation in your document, or a chart from Excel in your PowerPoint presentation and have the target versions keep in sync with the source information. It saves time, saves effort, and keeps all your records in tune with each other. To create this sort of connection between your source content and its target version, follow these steps:

1. Select your source content—a section of a worksheet, text from a document, or a chart or text from a presentation.

2. Choose Edit | Copy, right-click and choose Cut from the shortcut menu, or press CTRL-C. You can use any method to copy the content; just don't cut it. If you cut it, there won't be any source to link with!

3. Go to your target location and choose Edit | Paste Special. There is no keyboard shortcut or shortcut menu alternative for this command.

4. Click the Paste Link radio button on the left side of the resulting dialog box.

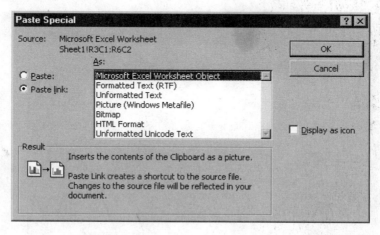

5. From the As text box, select the type of object you're inserting. For example, if the content comes from Excel, choose Microsoft Excel Worksheet Object.

6. Click OK.

The source content now appears in the target location, and it doesn't look any different from something you simply pasted. The difference between a simple Paste and Paste Special won't become evident until you change something in the source version of the content or reopen the target file. While the connection to the source and target is maintained, any time you open the target file, you can "update" it (that is, you can edit the target to reflect any changes made at the source since the paste or the last update).

Updating Linked Content

The nice part about linking a source and a target is the fact that the updates from the source to the target don't have to be automatic. If you want to control the updates, use the Links dialog box (see Figure 2-10) that appears when you choose Edit | Links in the target file. You can use this dialog box to update your target file only when you want updates to occur. You can update at any time, even if you initially don't update the target file, but later want to. Why not update? You might need the file to remain in an out-of-sync state, perhaps to print out last week's version before this week's changes are inserted. You can protect the target until you're ready.

Severing Links Between the Source and Target

A link between source and target files remains intact until you perform one of the following actions:

- Delete one or both of the files
- Rename one or both of the files

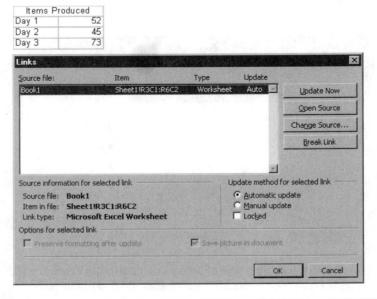

FIGURE 2-10   You can manage your links—and update them when it suits you—through the Links dialog box.

■ Move one or both of the files to another drive or folder

■ Use the Links dialog box to sever the link intentionally

The fact that deleting one or both of the linked files can sever the link requires no explanation, of course, but why does renaming or moving break the link? Because the link is based on a path from the source to the target. If you rename or move the file, the path becomes invalid. It would be like changing the numbers on the front of your house or mailbox and then expecting someone with your old address to be able to find your house. If you actually moved to a new house, finding you would be even more difficult.

If you do accidentally delete or rename a file, you can reestablish the link by repeating the process of building the link through the Paste Special command. Just go back to the source file, select the content, copy it to the Clipboard, and then use Paste Special to insert it into the target file. Remember to use the Paste Link option and select the object type from the As list, as described previously in this chapter.

To sever the link between source and target on purpose, you can go to the target file and choose Edit | Links. In the resulting dialog box, click the Break Link button. A prompt will ask you to confirm your intention to break the link.

Embedding Selections and Editing Tools

Another way to use content from one application in another is to create a new object from another application in your open file. This will place content from another application in your file and give you access to that application's tools for use in editing the object. Why would you do this? Imagine that Excel data in your Word document again. Wouldn't it be great to be able to double-click the Excel data in the document and have Excel tools appear in the Word window so you could edit the data and perform Excel tasks, such as creating formulas and formatting numbers? If you've placed an Excel chart in a PowerPoint presentation, the ability to use Excel's charting tools to edit it is of obvious value, and such power is only possible through the embedding of one application's object into another application's file. To do this, follow these steps:

1. In the target file (the file that will contain the other application's object), click to place your cursor where the object should appear once inserted.

2. Choose Insert | Object. The Object dialog box appears.

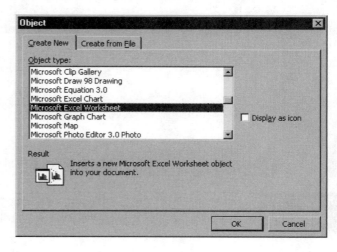

3. Click the Create New tab to insert a blank object. You'll be able to fill the object (say, an Excel worksheet or a Word document) later.

4. Select the object type you want to insert. You'll have a list that includes objects from every Windows application on your computer, not just Office 2003 applications.

5. Click OK to insert the object. As shown in Figure 2-11, an object appears in your file.

The object can be edited right away, or you can click away from it to deselect it and then return to the open file's application tools to continue working on the target file. When you're ready to edit the object, just double-click it to display its native application tools.

> **TIP** *You can choose to display the embedded object as an icon, which takes up less space than the actual content you're embedding. It also leaves it up to the person viewing the file that contains the embedded content whether to explore that content. If they choose to view it, all they have to do is double-click the icon, and the embedded content is fully displayed.*

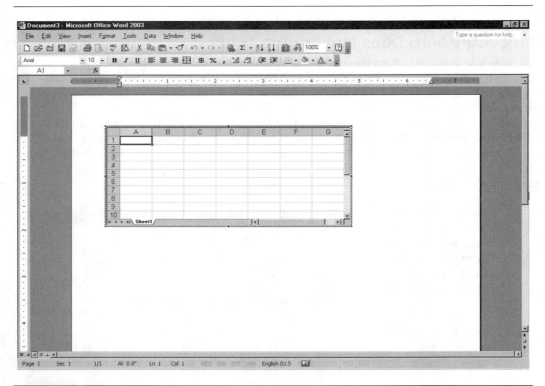

FIGURE 2-11 The blank object awaits your entry (you can even paste into it from another source file) and formatting, using the native application's tools.

2

If you want to insert an object from an existing file, you can click the Create from File tab in the Insert Object dialog box and then select the file to insert. You'll be inserting a copy of the file, not the original file. If you want to establish a link between the original file and this object, click the Link to File option.

Virtually all the features discussed in this chapter are available in any of the Office 2003 applications. You can cut, copy, paste, and use Paste Special in just about all the applications, and the ability to insert objects—both blank and based on existing files—is supported in Word, Excel, and PowerPoint. Access supports only the Cut, Copy, and Paste commands, and it makes use of the Paste Append command, which you'll find out about in the section of this book that covers Access. Outlook allows you to cut, copy, and paste text, worksheet content, and graphical content to and from the body of a message, but it doesn't support Paste Special or the insertion of objects, simply due to the nature of the application. There's really no need to do so.

Working with Speech Recognition

Like its predecessor, Office XP, Office 2003 gives you the ability to speak to your computer. You can dictate letters, fill in worksheets, tell PowerPoint what text to type onto a slide, and you can also give commands, telling an application to perform such tasks as printing a document or saving a file. Obviously, to take advantage of this feature, your computer must be equipped with the ability to play and record sound. Any computer with a sound card and speakers probably has a microphone built in, or you can buy one.

It's suggested that you invest in a headset microphone (you'll look like an air traffic controller or a telephone operator) that picks up your voice right at your lips. Why? To improve the chances of the speech-recognition software properly interpreting your words. People who speak quickly, have thick accents, or might not be completely fluent in the language they work in will want to give the software every advantage in understanding them as they speak.

The benefits of having speech-recognition capabilities are obvious. You can avoid typing your letters, read from typed or written copy to fill in a document or worksheet, and speak to your computer to design presentations. Further, to keep your hands free to perform other tasks—filing, writing, leafing through papers, or drawing—you can give your computer commands. You can tell it to save a file, print a file, apply a font—do anything that can also be done from the toolbars or menus.

Turning Speech On

If you installed the speech-recognition feature when you installed Office 2003, all you need to do is choose Tools | Speech to turn on this feature and invoke its tools. If you didn't install it, when you choose Tools | Speech, a series of prompts will take you through the process of installing the feature from your Office 2003 CD-ROM.

Once you've got speech recognition running (a series of buttons will appear above your workspace, as shown in Figure 2-12), you can click the Microphone button to have the software start "listening" to you speak. Your two modes of operation are Dictation and Voice Command. Dictation mode will type whatever you say into the open document (Word), cell (Excel), or slide (PowerPoint). If you want to give your computer commands instead, click the Voice Command button.

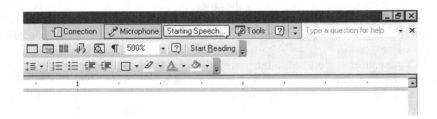

FIGURE 2-12   When you choose Tools | Speech, a set of voice-recognition tools appears at
the top of your screen.

Training the Speech Tools for Your Voice

The first time you use the Office speech-recognition feature, you're taken through a series of
steps that help train the software to respond accurately to your particular voice. The speed at
which you speak, your accent, your pronunciation, and anything unique about the way you speak
needs to be learned by the software so that when you say "Dear Bob" the computer doesn't type
"Ear Blob" or something that just *sounds* like what you said.

The training process involves you reading a series of sentences, and it takes about five to ten
minutes to complete the process. As you speak, reading the prompts onscreen, the text that you're
reading is highlighted (see Figure 2-13). You don't have to wait for the computer's highlighting

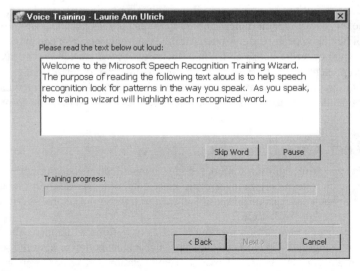

FIGURE 2-13   Read the sentences as they appear, allowing the software to get used to the way
you speak.

to catch up to your speaking. Just keep talking until, and unless, you see that the computer has stopped following you. If this happens, just go back to the first word after the highlighting ends and repeat the sentences.

It's suggested that you run through the training process twice, and it's alleged that the accuracy will improve to approximately 95 percent, meaning for every 100 words you say, the software will correctly recognize 95 of them. Not too shabby, especially for people who hate to type or who type so slowly as to reduce their own productivity. People who like to type or for whom typing is not an insufferable chore might never even bother with the speech-recognition software. It's nice to know it's there, however, in case you ever sprain your wrist or break your arm. Losing the use of even a few of your typing fingers can make it nearly impossible to get work done on the computer.

> **NOTE** *If your work involves esoteric terms, uncommon names, or anything that you find the speech-recognition software is just not interpreting properly, you can add these words and names to a personal list. Assuming you say them the same way every time, the list will help the software understand you when you use specialized medical or legal terms, foreign terms, or names of people and places that aren't found in a typical dictionary.*

Dictating Documents, Spreadsheets, and Presentations

To have the speech-recognition software insert the words you're saying, follow these steps:

1. Choose Tools | Speech to turn speech recognition on. The Microphone and Tools buttons appear at the top of your screen.

2. Click the Microphone button to tell the software that it should begin listening to you.

3. Position your cursor in the document, worksheet, or slide by clicking with your mouse where the new content should be inserted.

4. Click the Dictation button to tell the software that it should type what you say rather than perform tasks or commands.

5. Begin speaking. Speak clearly and at an even pace. Don't speak like Frankenstein, as though every word is a challenge, but speak more slowly and evenly than you would in an animated conversation.

6. When you're finished dictating, click the Microphone button to tell the software to stop listening, or click the Voice Command button if you want to give the computer instructions.

Giving Commands Verbally

When you need to give instructions to your computer without your mouse or keyboard, what's left? That's right, your voice. Although we've all been speaking to (or maybe even yelling at) our computers for years, they haven't been able to respond until recently. Speech-recognition applications have been available for the last five or six years, and in the last year or so they've become quite accurate and useful. In response to the improved technology and user demand for it, Microsoft has added speech recognition to Office 2003. You can use it to write letters, fill in a worksheet or database, or flesh out the text in a presentation, as described in the previous section. You can also give your computer commands by following these steps:

1. Turn on the speech-recognition feature by choosing Tools | Speech. The Microphone and Tools buttons appear at the top of your screen.

2. Click the Microphone button to tell the computer that it should begin listening to you speak.

3. Click the Voice Command button to tell the software that rather than dictating content, you'll be giving instructions.

4. Say the name of any menu or toolbar button, and the computer will respond as though you clicked that item with your mouse. In the case of menus, say the menu command that follows it as well as any submenu commands, such as "Insert, Picture, From File."

5. If a dialog box opens, say the words you see in it. For example, if you've said "File, Print" to open the Print dialog box, say "Number of Copies" and then the number you want. To wrap up this sample procedure, you'd say "OK" when you were ready to print.

6. When you no longer want to give voice commands, click the Microphone button so that the software will cease listening to you, or click Dictation if you want to start entering content verbally.

Getting the Office 2003 Help You Need

The Help features in Office 2003 haven't changed dramatically from the previous version of Office, and they continue to be consistent throughout the applications. For example, whatever application you have open, you'll see a text box in the upper-right corner of the window with the instructions "Type a question for help" in it.

This allows you to type any question—"How do I print the odd pages?" or "How do I create a toolbar button?"—and see a list of the Help articles that the active application (the one that's on top on your screen) thinks match your question. Sometimes the listed articles won't be appropriate, but at least one of the responses is usually relevant and will, if pursued, give you the help you need.

TIP *If you like working with task panes, you can choose to view the Help task pane and use it to interface with the Help files—posing questions or key words to search for and navigating the Help articles presented in response to your queries.*

Now, you may be wondering what I mean by "if pursued." I mean that the listed article titles must be clicked, as in Figure 2-14 (they're hyperlinks to the actual articles). Within these articles are usually terms and topics that are underlined (indicating that they're hypertext, too). If you click them, you get additional and more focused help, which appears in a window alongside (sort of overlapping the right side of) your application window. You can resize this window as needed by dragging its sides (your mouse cursor will turn to a two-headed arrow), and you can use the sizing icons to minimize, maximize, or close the Help window as needed.

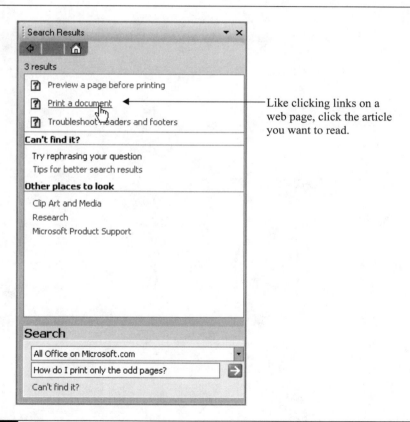

Like clicking links on a web page, click the article you want to read.

FIGURE 2-14   Click the listed article that seems the closest match to the question you asked.

Chapter 3

Using Images in Documents, Worksheets, and Presentations

How to...

- Add graphics to your documents, worksheets, and presentations
- Use the Picture toolbar to resize, crop, and rotate images
- Capture images with a scanner or digital camera
- Open and utilize the Picture Library
- Adjust brightness and contrast, and remove red eye and other image problems

Inserting and Manipulating Graphics

It's easy to add images to your Word documents, Excel worksheets, and PowerPoint presentations. The directions for inserting images into these three types of Office files follow in this section of the chapter, and you'll find a great deal of similarity among the procedures, resulting in a much shorter learning curve for you, and giving you the ability to quickly use the same images in related files—reports, financial data, and slide shows—that pertain to the same topics. This sort of consistency is at the heart of any comprehensive use of Office 2003, and hopefully this chapter will give you some ideas for ways to use images that you may not have considered before.

NOTE   *You can also add images to Outlook email messages and, of course, to FrontPage web pages. The procedures for performing these tasks are found in Chapters 22 and 26, respectively.*

Adding Images to Word Documents

Word is the most used of the applications in the Office suite, yet the inclusion of images in documents is probably the most underused when it comes to Word. Many users don't even think of Word when they want to create a document with pictures. They'll readily use Publisher or go outside the suite to an application such as QuarkXPress or PageMaker to build a newsletter or lay out a publication, leaving Word as a sadly untapped resource, right on their desk. But not you! Not after reading this, anyway.

To add an image to a Word document, you have a few choices. Before implementing any of these techniques, however, it's important that you position your cursor where the image should appear on the page. You can always move it later, but it's a good idea to click and place your cursor in the general vicinity of the final location. After placing your cursor where the image should appear, pick one of these methods for inserting the image:

- Choose Insert | Picture | Clip Art.
- Choose Insert | Picture | From File.
- With the Drawing toolbar displayed, click the Insert Clip Art button.

In the case of inserting clip art, after you make this selection, the Insert Clip Art pane will appear on your page (or the task pane, if already displayed, will change to offer tools to search for clip art images, as shown in Figure 3-1). You can then search for and select an image, and it will appear at your cursor position, right on the document page.

After inserting an image, you might want to resize it and perhaps move it. You can also change how the text and the image on the page react to one another. By default, the image breaks the text, and appears on a line between two sections of the existing text. If this isn't the result you want, you can force the text to wrap around the image, run behind the image, or flow right over the image. Word also makes it easy to change the appearance of the image, using either the Picture toolbar or a new application called Picture Library. Both will be discussed later in this chapter.

Resizing Images

Resizing images is very simple and can be done two ways: by eye, using your mouse to drag the object's *handles* until the object is the desired size, or by precise measurement, using the Format Picture dialog box and entering a specific width and height for the image. The easiest way to

FIGURE 3-1   Search for clip art using keywords and refine the results by choosing the type of media you're looking for—photos, clip art, even movies and sounds.

FIGURE 3-2   Point to a handle and drag it to resize the image.

resize an image is to use the handles, as shown in Figure 3-2 (above). The handles appear on the corners and on each side as soon as you click the image to select it.

When you point to a handle with your mouse, the mouse pointer turns to a two-headed arrow. Dragging on the handles resizes the image. Drag outward to make it bigger, inward to make it smaller. If you want to keep the picture's current proportions (width-height ratio, also known as the *aspect ratio*), use a corner handle and drag diagonally. As you drag, a dashed border follows you. As soon as you release the mouse, the image takes on the dimensions of the dash-bordered box.

TIP   *To resize the image on both the left and right (using a side handle) or top and bottom (using either the top or bottom handle), press and hold CTRL as you drag the image handle. If you drag from a corner handle with CTRL depressed, the image will resize from all four corners at the same time.*

If you need to resize your image to very specific measurements, you can use the Format Picture dialog box, which opens if you right-click the image in question and choose Format Picture from the resulting shortcut menu. In the dialog box, click the Size tab (see Figure 3-3) and enter the desired width and height for the image. You can also use the scaling options to increase the image size by a specific percentage—for example, you can double its size by typing **200** as the percentage in the width and height scaling options.

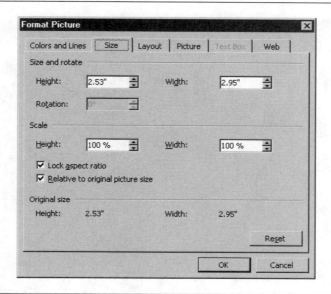

FIGURE 3-3   Need an image to be exactly 2 inches square? Adjust the current measurements through the Format Picture dialog box.

Changing Text Flow

In a Word document, you might want text to flow around the image instead of breaking before and continuing after it. Flowing text around an image saves space on the page because less space is taken up by the image. You can set the flow so that the text runs right next to the image, or you can set it so it keeps a polite distance, forming a tidy square around the image. Once the flow is set, you can move the image anywhere on the page and the text will follow your settings for the relationship between it and the image. To set text flow for your image, follow these steps:

1. Right-click the image and choose Format Picture from the shortcut menu. You can also click the image once with your left mouse button to select it and choose Format | Picture.

2. In the resulting Format Picture dialog box, click the Layout tab, as shown in Figure 3-4.

3. Choose the wrapping style that suits your document. In Line with Text is the default, which allows for no wrapping. The Square and Tight options allow text to flow around the image, and Behind Text and In Front of Text will do just as their names imply, and no wrapping occurs.

4. If you want the text to always fall on the left or right side of the image, choose Left or Right from the Horizontal Alignment options, which become available as soon as Square or Tight is chosen from the Wrapping Style options.

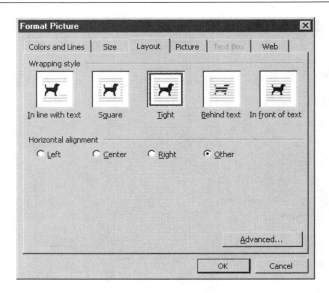

FIGURE 3-4 View your text wrapping options in the Format Picture dialog box.

5. Click OK to apply your changes to the image and close the dialog box. The following shows an image with Tight wrapping:

This lovely home on a private lake can be yours for just $3,250,000.00. The home includes 6 bedrooms, 4 baths, and a lovely guest cottage (not pictured) at the rear of the property. The kitchen was recently remodeled, but maintains the look and feel of the century in which the house was built.

Other amenities include a library, a game room, and a modern gym, including a lap pool and sauna. The master suite includes a sitting room, small office area, bedroom, and large bathroom with whirlpool bath and steam room.

Showings are by appointment only, and are generally scheduled for after 1 pm on weekdays and before 2 pm on Saturdays. Please call at your earliest convenience:

3

Moving Images

You can't move an inserted image until some text-flow setting is created. Until then, the image is locked on the line with the cursor. Once you've applied a text-flow setting, however, you can move the image anywhere on the page—just point to the image, click it, and drag your mouse. Wherever the image is when you release the mouse will be its new home. By default, the image appears on the document at the cursor, but you can move it anywhere after that. Here is an example of an image in transit:

This lovely home on a private lake can be yours for just $3,250,000.00. The home includes 6 bedrooms, 4 baths, and a lovely guest cottage (not pictured) at the rear of the property. The kitchen was recently remodeled, but maintains the look and feel of the century in which the house was built.

Other amenities include a library, a game room, and a modern gym, including a lap pool and sauna. The master suite includes a sitting room, small office area, bedroom, and large bathroom with whirlpool bath and steam room.

Showings are by appointment only, and are generally scheduled for after 1 pm on weekdays and before 2 pm on Saturdays. Please call at your earliest convenience.

Using the Picture Toolbar

As soon as an image is selected for the first time, the Picture toolbar appears onscreen. The toolbar offers a series of buttons, each designed to make some change to your image or to offer up tools that will enable you to resize, crop, or otherwise edit the image. A much more extensive set of tools is available through the Picture Library, an application new to Office 2003 (which we'll discuss later in this chapter), but for quick manipulation, especially resizing and cropping, the Picture toolbar's tools are quite effective.

The toolbar's tools are pretty simple to use, and their names are fairly illustrative of their purpose. Table 3-1 lists each button on the Picture toolbar and describes how you'd use it to alter the appearance of an image.

TIP   *If the Picture toolbar isn't showing when you select an image, choose View | Toolbar | Picture to display it. You can also right-click the menu or any displayed toolbar and choose Picture from the resulting shortcut menu.*

Button	Name and Description
	Insert Picture This button has the same effect as choosing Insert | Picture | Clip Art. It opens the Insert Clip Art pane, from which you can select an image to insert.
	Color Click this button to choose from Auto (the default for the selected image), Grayscale, Black & White, and Washout. The names are pretty self-explanatory!
	More Contrast Click this button to make the colors more intense in the image.
	Less Contrast This button washes out the image colors, making them less intense. In black-and-white images, it reduces the stark contrast between lights and darks.
	More Brightness This button makes the image brighter, adding more white to all the colors in the image.
	Less Brightness Click this button to reduce the amount of white in the colors and to add more black. This has the net effect of graying out the image, even if it's currently in color.
	Crop This tool allows you to remove portions of the image from along its edges. Click once on the button and then drag on the image handles to crop away content. Note that the content is hidden, not really taken away. If you reverse your dragging with this tool on, you can bring back what you cropped away.
	Rotate Left You can turn an image on its side with this button. Successive clicks of the button continue to rotate it 45 degrees at a time, clockwise.
	Line Style This button displays a palette of line thicknesses and styles (double, dashed, dotted, and so on). The palette's options are only available if the selected image is a line. It doesn't work if your image is clip art or a photograph.
	Compress Picture This tool reduces the pixel depth, or dots per inch, of a picture—handy if the document and image are bound for the web, where small images load faster. Click the button to display a dialog box that gives you all your compression options for images that will be printed versus displayed online.
	Text Wrapping Similar to the Layout tab on the Format Picture dialog box, this button displays the options for the way text will relate to the selected image.
	Format Picture Click this button to open the Format Picture dialog box.
	Set Transparent Color You can pick one of the image's colors and make it transparent, so if text is set to flow behind the image, the text will be visible behind the portions of the image that are the selected color.
	Reset Picture If you've just tweaked the image using the tools on the Picture toolbar and hate your results, click this button to return the image to the way it looked before you started tinkering.

TABLE 3-1   The Picture Toolbar

Using Images in Excel Worksheets

Although you'll find more clip art and photographs in a Word document than you will on a typical worksheet, graphics can enhance your Excel worksheets considerably. How? By adding to the story told by the numbers and text in the worksheet. Imagine a worksheet that includes sales figures for a particular product. Including an image of that product on the worksheet makes the data more interesting to look at, and it clears up any confusion as to which product is reflected in the sales numbers. This can also make the worksheet more effective as a marketing tool, if you're sharing it with a customer, in which case you'd probably want to also insert your company logo on the worksheet.

Inserting any type of image into an Excel worksheet is the same as inserting an image into a Word document. Click the Insert Clip Art button on the drawing toolbar or choose Insert | Picture | Clip Art or From File. You'll know which command to use, depending on the type and location of the image you want to insert—use Insert | Picture | Clip Art if you're inserting a piece of the clip art that came with Office, and use Insert | Picture | From File to insert a graphic you've downloaded, designed yourself, or purchased on CD.

Whichever method you choose, after you select an image, that image appears on the worksheet, floating over the surface of the sheet. The image is not inserted into a cell on the worksheet, nor is it attached to anything on the sheet. You can resize and move the image just as you would an image in a Word document. There are no wrapping options for images on a worksheet, so placing the image without obscuring worksheet data is your responsibility.

TIP *Charts provide interesting graphic content and also directly reflect the content of the worksheet because they're based directly on the worksheet data. Find out more about creating charts from Excel worksheets in Chapter 13.*

Enhancing Presentations with Clip Art and Photos

PowerPoint presentations should consist largely of images—graphics and charts—rather than text. A presentation should keep the attention of its audience, and nothing loses attention faster than a slide filled with text. The technique for adding graphics to a PowerPoint presentation is the same as it is in Word and Excel:

1. Display the Drawing toolbar and click the Insert Clip Art button.

2. Choose Insert | Picture | Clip Art (if you're adding an image from the clip art collection that came with Office) or Insert | Picture | From File (if you're inserting a graphic you designed or downloaded).

PowerPoint's presentation templates include graphics that appear on the background of each slide in the presentation. This does two things: It adds a graphical component without you having to select and insert individual graphics, and it makes the careful selection of your additional graphics important. Keep the tone and style of the background graphics in mind and don't pick images that clash or that create a visually overwhelming design when combined with the background.

If you have multiple images on your document, worksheet, or presentation and they overlap, you can right-click any of them and choose Order, Send to Back or Bring to Front to change the order of the overlapped images. You can also choose Send Backward or Bring Forward to move one image in a stack of three or more up or down in the stack rather than moving it all the way to the top or bottom of the stack. By default, images appear in order, with the most recently added images on top.

Capturing Images Digitally

If the image you want to use isn't online or within the clip art and photograph collections you find through the Clip Art task pane, but exists on paper instead, you can scan it to get it into your computer and then place it in your document, worksheet, or presentation. Scanning, of course, requires a scanner. If you have one attached to your computer, Office will "see" it, and you can use the Insert | Picture | From Scanner or Camera command. When you issue this command, the scanning software that came with your scanner is invoked, and you can capture the images—photographs, drawings, handwritten letters, old documents, anything that's on paper—and turn them into image files (see Figure 3-5). Once scanned and saved as an image file, the image can be used repeatedly in any document, worksheet, or presentation you wish, and you can use the Picture Library's editing tools to improve the quality of the image as needed.

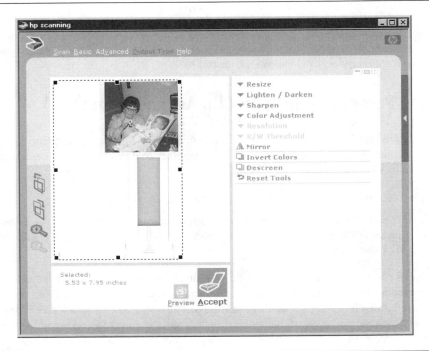

FIGURE 3-5   The software that came with your scanner may be different, but the basic tools and scanning procedures are the same.

Taking a Tour of Office 2003's Picture Library

When you open the Picture Library application (choose it from the Programs list in your Start menu), you're presented with a window consisting of three main parts—a series of picture shortcuts on the left, an area that shows images in particular folders in the center, and a pane listing tools for displaying, editing, renaming, and sharing images on the right. Figure 3-6 shows the Picture Library workspace, with an image selected and ready for editing.

Click Home to go back to the default set of Picture Library links.

Add Picture Shortcut creates a link to a folder with images you may want to edit now or in the future.

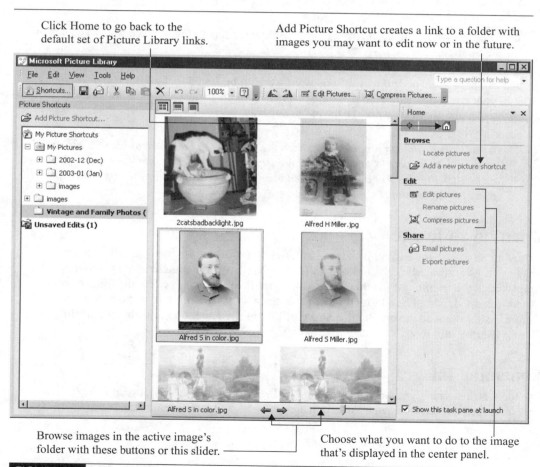

Browse images in the active image's folder with these buttons or this slider.

Choose what you want to do to the image that's displayed in the center panel.

FIGURE 3-6   The Picture Library window puts all the library's tools within easy reach.

Creating Shortcuts to Your Images

Unlike Office XP's Clip Gallery, which looked to preset folders of images that came with Office, the Picture Library assumes you have your own images, stored in folders of your choosing. By default, it already has one shortcut set up—it points to the My Pictures folder. You can set up other shortcuts, each pointing to folders where you store images for use in your Office files and other applications' files. To set up a new shortcut, follow these steps:

1. Click the Add Picture Shortcut link at the top of the Picture Shortcuts panel.

2. Using the Add to Picture Shortcuts dialog box, navigate to the folder you want the shortcut to point to.

3. Click the Add button. The dialog box closes, and a link to the selected folder appears in the Shortcuts list.

You can have as many shortcuts as you want—they'll be stored in the My Picture Shortcuts folder in your computer. However, these are just the shortcuts themselves—the folders you're designating for the shortcuts won't be moved in any way.

> **TIP** *If you'd like, you can rename your shortcuts. By default, the shortcut name is the same as the folder name, but that's not always useful. To rename the shortcut (not the folder), right-click the shortcut and choose Rename. Then type a new name for the shortcut and press ENTER to confirm.*

Opening an Image

Choosing an image for editing is easy—just click the shortcut for the folder that contains the image you want to work with, and when the thumbnails for the images in that folder appear, simply click the thumbnail for the image you want to edit. Once opened, the image can be edited, renamed, compressed, or emailed. You can also add a shortcut to the individual picture, using the Add a New Picture Shortcut link in the panel on the right side of the Picture Library window.

Renaming Images

The tools for renaming your images are found on the right side of the window, and the link is very intuitively named—Rename Pictures. Click the link, and the current name is displayed

Choose how the new name will affect the existing name.

Apply digits before or after your image names to keep versions separate.   Type a new name here.

FIGURE 3-7   Rename your image entirely or add a prefix or suffix to the existing name.

(you can retype it), along with options for adding to the existing name rather than replacing it outright, as shown in Figure 3-7 (above). You can add digits to your image names, which makes it easy to keep track of image versions—before and after editing, versions in black and white vs. color, or different-sized versions.

Sharing Images via Email

If you want to send an image to someone via email, you can do it through the Picture Library by following these steps—you'll be able to pick the image to share, decide how the image will appear within, or attached, to the email, and click a button to create the message that will whisk your image to the recipient of your choice:

1. Click the Email Pictures link on the Home panel (right side of window) to open the tools for sending the image via email.

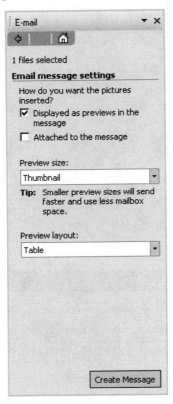

2. Select the images you want to send. You can press the SHIFT key and click multiple images in the same folder, or you can click a single image to send just one.

3. Choose the way you want the image(s) to accompany the message—simply as an attachment or with a preview within the body of the message.

4. Choose the size of the preview. Thumbnail is the default.

5. Choose the Preview Layout setting. Table is the default, but you can choose 1 Per Line. Of course, you only need to think about this if you're attaching multiple files.

6. Click the Create Message button. A message window opens, with the image(s) attached or included as a preview within the body. You can address the image(s) to any recipients you desire and then click Send.

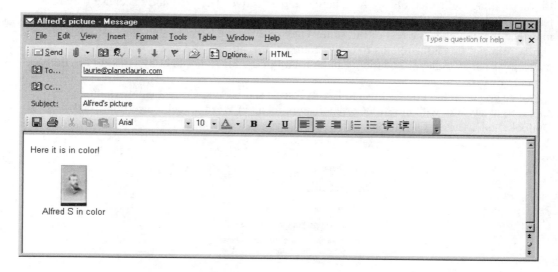

How to ... Export Pictures for Use in Other Documents and Applications

You can also export your images, choosing the format to export in and renaming the files as needed. Click the Export Pictures link under the Sharing section of the right-most panel in the Picture Library window and then use the offered options to select the file to be exported (the open image is assumed to be the one you're exporting, but you can choose another). Then rename the file and choose a format for the file. When you're exporting images for use on the web or to be viewed online, JPG is a good format for photos, and GIF is a good choice for clip art and other simplistic images.

Editing Your Digitally Captured Images

Going the very rudimentary editing tools in the Picture toolbar one better, the Picture Library's image editing tools are both handy and effective. They're handy because they're part of Office, and they're displayed in a fashion you're used to—through a comfortable interface that matches the rest of the suite. They're effective because they give you the ability to make fine adjustments to color, contrast, brightness, and size, and even repair problems such as red eye. The tools can be found in the far right panel by clicking the Edit Pictures link.

Once you click the Edit Pictures link, you'll see a single Auto Correct button (not to be confused in any way with the AutoCorrect feature found in Word, Excel, PowerPoint, and Outlook) and a series of six links:

The Auto Correct tool makes an allover adjustment to various attributes of the image, such as brightness, contrast, and color levels. You'll probably like the results, but if you want to tweak just one or two of the image attributes, you can use the task-specific links found in the Picture Correction Tools section of the task pane.

This list of six links works by displaying task-specific tools. If you click the Brightness & Contrast link, for example, tools for changing the amount of light and the intensity of lights and darks in the image are displayed.

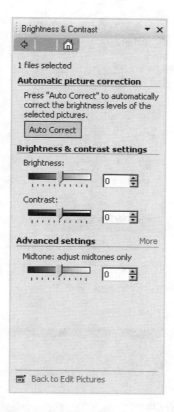

If you click the Color link, you can adjust the hue and saturation (the amount of color) in the image. The Crop, Resize, and Rotate & Flip commands are also offered through the Picture toolbar (discussed earlier in this chapter), but you'll see that the tools are a bit more comprehensive here (Figure 3-8 shows the Crop tools).

Fixing red eye requires clicking the Red Eye link and then clicking over the pupil(s) to be fixed. A targeting circle appears (see Figure 3-9), and you can click to position a small eye icon over the offending pupil. Then click the OK button to get the red out!

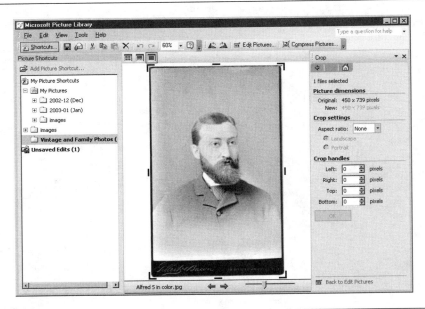

FIGURE 3-8   Use the handles (lines and corner brackets on edges of image) to crop the image, or enter numbers in the right-hand panel's text boxes.

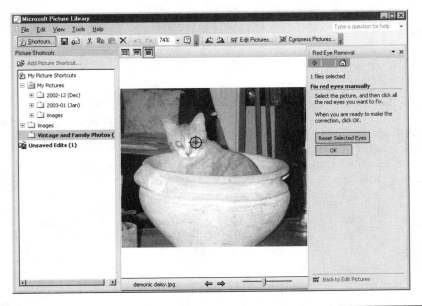

FIGURE 3-9   No more demonic-looking subjects, thanks to the Picture Library's Red Eye tools.

Part II

Creating Documents with Word

Chapter 4

Building a Basic Document

How to...

- Start with a new, blank document
- Start a new document from a template
- Move around in a Word document
- Select text with the keyboard and mouse
- Enter, edit, and rearrange text efficiently

Of the entire Office suite, Word is the most often-used application. Why? Because no matter what you do at work or in your personal life, you need to write. If your writing primarily consists of email and you use Outlook, chances are Word is your email editor, so you're *still* using Word several times a day. If you're like most people, whose correspondence and documentation needs are more varied, you need to write letters, memos, notes, stories, poems, grocery lists, and even manifestos. Whatever you need to write, Word has tools that can take thoughts currently residing in your head and help you transfer them to the computer, where they can end up on paper or even on the web. In this chapter, you'll learn the basics of entering and editing text in the Word workspace and how to efficiently move around in a Word document, making your entry, editing, and formatting tasks much easier.

Getting Started in Word

When you open the Word application, you're faced with a blank slate—a big white space, awaiting your text. This white area (also known as the *document window*) is surrounded by tools. You'll find toolbars, menus, a task pane, a status bar, and lots of tools and features to empower you as you write your letter, memo, report—whatever it is you're creating. As shown in Figure 4-1, it's a busy but logically constructed workspace.

The blank page also contains a *cursor*, also known as an insertion point. Whenever the document is active, the cursor will be blinking, waiting for you to type. The fact that the cursor greets you when you open a new Word document is further proof that you don't need to know much about Word to create a document. Just start typing at the cursor, and Word's default settings for text handling and formatting will do much of the rest.

The Not-So-Blank Document

The blank document that Word offers up when you first open the application isn't really blank. I know it looks blank (all except for that blinking cursor), but it isn't. There's a lot going on, and a lot of settings are in place to help you build a document without too much planning or effort. Your blank document is based on something called the *Normal template*, a cookie cutter of sorts that dictates some basic features of a new document:

- **Font**   Already decided for you, Times New Roman, in 12 points, is the default font for new documents. It's a font that's acceptable in business and personal documents; it's highly legible, photocopies well, and is *web-safe*, meaning that browser software (Internet Explorer or Netscape) happily displays it.

Toolbars   Menus   Access to Help   Task pane

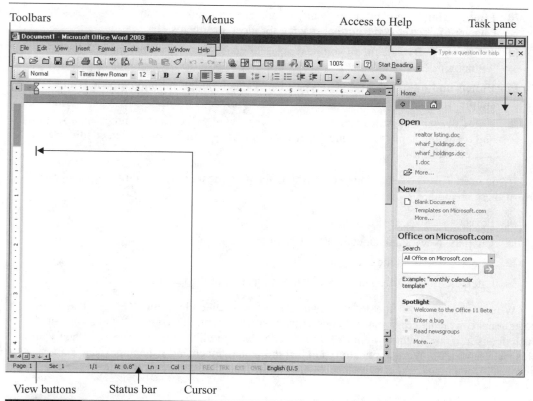

View buttons   Status bar   Cursor

FIGURE 4-1   Tools are found above, below, and in the task pane on the right.

■   **Margins**   Default margins are set at 1 inch from the top and bottom, and 1.25 inches from the left and right sides of the paper. This is standard for business and personal correspondence. In Print Layout view (View | Print Layout), you can see your top and left margins represented by gray areas on the ruler, as shown in the following:

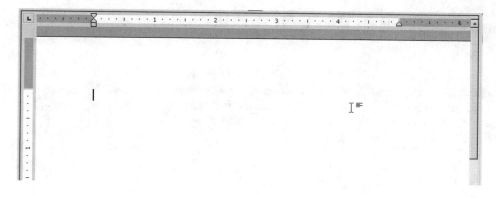

- **Line spacing**   Single spacing is the default, and although you can change it (see Chapter 6), it's set to the normal spacing for most documents.
- **Alignment**   By default, all your text is left aligned, meaning it lines up with the left margin.
- **Bullets and numbers**   Need to type a list? Default bullets for unordered lists and simple Arabic numerals for ordered lists are ready and waiting.
- **AutoCorrect and AutoFormat**   As you type, Word will correct common misspellings and typos and apply formatting (such as automatic list numbering) when conditions seem to call for it.

If you need to start a new, blank document again after opening Word, you can do so using any of these methods:

- Press CTRL-N.
- Click the New Blank Document button on the Standard toolbar.
- Choose New from the File menu.
- Click the Blank Document link in the New section of the task pane.

When you open Word, the document you get at first is called Document1. Any subsequent documents you create are numbered consecutively—Document2, Document3, and so on—and each opens in its own window and is represented by an individual taskbar button. When you close and reopen the Word application (not just individual documents), the numbering starts over with Document1.

Starting with a Template

Word comes with a large selection of document templates that go the blank, Normal template one better. Rather than being blank with some defaults set for a vanilla document, these templates have common elements—headings, paragraph text (in some cases), forms, graphics, and color—

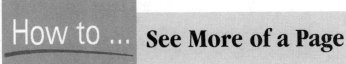 **How to ... See More of a Page**

Want to see more of the page while you work? Reduce the Zoom percentage. Click the Zoom button on the Standard toolbar (it appears as a percentage) or choose View | Zoom. A zoom such as 50 or 75 percent will show you more of the page from side to side and from top to bottom. You can also choose Page Width or Whole Page if you're in Print Layout view (View | Print Layout).

that every document based on the template in question will require. There are web page templates, legal-pleading templates, letter templates, fax coversheet templates, memo templates, and templates for a variety of reports and publications. You can access them through the File | New command or by clicking the On My Computer link in the Other Templates section of the New Document task pane (it appears when you choose File | New). Figure 4-2 shows the Templates dialog box that appears when you click that link.

TIP   *You can also search the web for templates by typing a keyword in the Search box in the Templates on Microsoft.com section of the New Document task pane. This requires that you be online, of course, and goes to a store of templates at Microsoft's website.*

4

When you start a new document based on a template, you're not opening the template. Instead, you're using the template as a foundation for the new document. The new document will start its life with everything the template had, and then it's up to you to fill it. As shown in Figure 4-3, the Contemporary Report template provides a coversheet with a heading, space for your organization's name, and other text that you can replace with your own information for your report's cover page.

Templates help maintain consistency in an office. If everyone uses the same memo template, everyone's memos will look the same. Templates also speed the process of building a document by inserting much of the content and formatting for you, so all that's left to do is fill in specific text and information. Any changes made to the template-based document do *not* affect the template itself. It will remain in its original condition for the next time you use it.

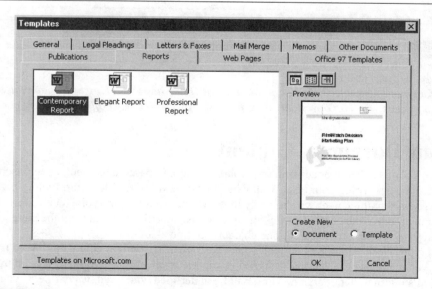

FIGURE 4-2   Choose from several template categories, each represented by a tab in the Templates dialog box.

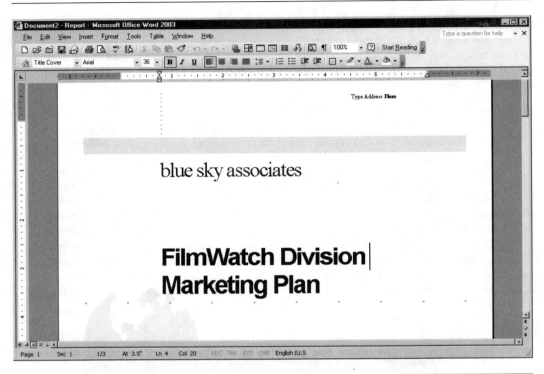

FIGURE 4-3   Enter your own information to replace the instructional text, and you have a cover sheet for your report.

Want more templates? If you don't think that Office has enough installed templates for your needs, you can download more from Microsoft—just visit office.microsoft.com.

Typing Your Document Content

So you have your new, blank document, or perhaps a template-based document, open onscreen and you want to start typing your text. Well, what are you waiting for? Just start typing. As long as you can see a blinking cursor, you're ready to go. If you want to start typing at a different spot in the document, move the cursor by clicking your mouse in a different place on the page, or use the arrow keys to reposition the cursor one character or line at a time.

As you type, Word might interact with you. Those smart tags might chime in if Word thinks it can help you make use of what you've typed in another application. If you type a word that isn't in Word's internal dictionary, the word will be underlined with a red, wavy line. If you make mistakes that Word has stored in its collection of common errors and corrections, it will fix your

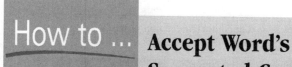

How to ... Accept Word's Suggested Completions

As you're typing, Word may take a guess as to what you're trying to say. For example, if you start typing "Sept" (the beginning of the word September) and it happens to *be* September at the time, Word will assume that you're trying to type the date and will offer up the system date in a ScreenTip, just above your text. If that's what you want to type, just press ENTER, and the date is inserted automatically. Word makes other guesses, such as To Whom It May Concern (if you type "To" in the salutation spot in a letter). If you don't want what Word is suggesting, just keep typing and the ScreenTip will go away—but if you do like the suggestion, take it!

mistake for you, working so fast that you might not even notice it happening. You'll find out how to deal with spell checking and other proofing tools in Chapter 5.

TIP *Find out more about the corrections and changes that Word makes automatically and learn to control when and how those corrections are made in Chapter 5.*

Working with Word Wrap

As you type your text, it's important that you really just type. Don't worry about your margins or press ENTER in anticipation of running into the right margin. Word will automatically flow your text from one line to the next, using a feature called *word wrap.*

Word wrap only works if you let it. If you press ENTER at points other than the end of a paragraph or between items in a list, you'll be preventing word wrap from working, and you'll also be breaking your paragraphs into smaller paragraphs than you want to. As shown in Figure 4-4, a paragraph that is allowed to flow naturally will break at the right margin on its own, and the text will flow onto the next line.

However, if you press ENTER at the right margin, your paragraph is broken into several paragraphs (each a single line), and it will be impossible to set indents and other paragraph formats for the entire paragraph because Word sees it as several small paragraphs instead. To see if your document contains any of these unnecessary breaks, click the Show/Hide button on the Standard toolbar.

Working with Paragraph and Line Breaks

When you do want to break a paragraph, you can press ENTER. This should only be done at the end of a paragraph or at the end of each item in a list. It's important to understand that every time you press ENTER, you're creating a paragraph and inserting a paragraph code (those backward "P" characters that display when you click the Show/Hide button). That means that in a letter,

Paragraph marks indicate that the ENTER key was pressed.

The Show/Hide button displays even hidden characters and codes.

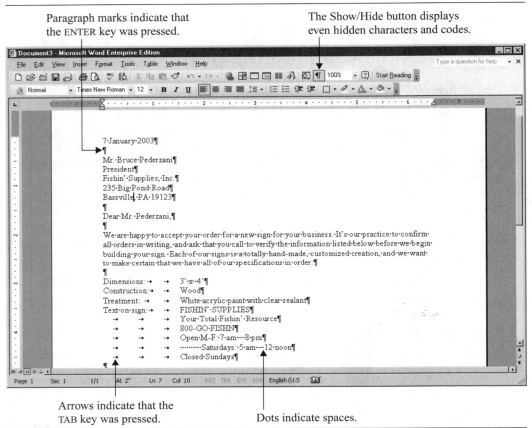

Arrows indicate that the TAB key was pressed.

Dots indicate spaces.

FIGURE 4-4 It might sound like advice found in a self-help book, but you really should let your words flow.

the date is a paragraph, each line of the recipient address is a paragraph, and even the salutation "To Whom It May Concern," is a paragraph.

If you don't want to break a paragraph and insert a paragraph code, you can create a line break instead. This forces text (beginning at the current cursor position) onto the next line but doesn't create a paragraph break. The result? You can format the entire paragraph, the text before and after the line break included, because Word will still see the text as one paragraph. This can make it faster and easier to apply paragraph formats such as indents, alignments, and styles that are paragraph oriented. You'll learn about all sorts of formatting options, including those applicable only to paragraphs, in Chapter 6.

To insert a line break, press SHIFT-ENTER. As shown in the following illustration (Show/Hide is on), the resulting line break code looks different from a paragraph code and behaves differently

4

How to ... Create Consistent Indents

As with ENTER, another key you should use judiciously is the SPACEBAR. Don't use the SPACEBAR to indent a paragraph or items in a list. Instead, use TAB when you need to indent. The only time you want to press the SPACEBAR is to insert a space between words or sentences, or after commas. Why? Because for all non-monospace fonts, Word is typesetting your text as you type, creating effective spacing between characters (a process also known as *kerning*), spreading your text across the page for maximum legibility. If the font has the word "monospace" in its title, the space between all characters typed in that font will be uniform, and therefore kerning is neither possible nor necessary. For the vast majority of fonts, however, the width of a space is based on the width of the characters before and after it—so unless every indented paragraph or list item starts with the same character, they'll never line up vertically because the spaces in front of them won't be the same width. A tab is based on measurement (by default, a half-inch per TAB press), so the text has no impact on the depth of an indent created with TAB.

as well. The paragraph remains intact, despite this interruption in the natural flow of text, as indicated by the paragraph code that appears at the true end of the paragraph.

When·a·sign·is·ordered,·50%·of·the·purchase·price·is·paid,·the·remainder·to·be·paid·when·the·sign·is·completed·and·installed·at·the·customer·site.·The·customer·has·48·hours·to·report·any·problems·with·the·sign,·including,·but·not·limited·to,·the·following:↵
↵
Misspellings↵
Wrong·typeface/font↵
Wrong·colors·used↵
Sign·installed·improperly·or·in·the·wrong·location¶

Navigating a Word Document

It's a rare document that is typed from top to bottom, saved, printed, and closed, without the author ever having to reposition the cursor within previously typed text. I'd be willing to say that I've never typed a document that I didn't have to move around in during and after the original composition process, and I would hazard a guess that you won't either. With this inevitable need to move around in a document in mind, it's important to understand the best ways to get from where you are now to where you want to be.

Word provides two methods for navigating a document: via the keyboard, using your arrow keys and a few easily remembered keyboard shortcuts, and via your mouse. You can use whichever method suits a particular situation; sometimes using the keyboard and mouse in concert will have the appropriate navigational effect.

Moving Around with the Mouse

Because Word invites you to work with your mouse to click toolbar buttons, access menus, and click links in the task panes, you probably have become very mouse oriented in your communication with the computer. If using the mouse is your default tool for invoking commands, you'll like these navigational techniques:

- Click to position your cursor anywhere in the text.

- If you want to position your cursor on a blank page, look for the Click and Type mouse pointer. Click and Type allows you to place your cursor anywhere on a blank page, even below the last blank line inserted by ENTER. Double-click to position your cursor.

- Drag the scroll bar. As you drag the scroll box up and down within the scroll bar, the page numbers appear in a ScreenTip. When the page you want appears in the tip, release the mouse. This technique is especially effective when you're in Print Layout view.

- Use the Next Page and Previous Page buttons at the foot of the vertical scroll bar. If the triangles on the buttons are blue (not their default, black), click the Select Browse Object button and choose Browse by Page from the palette of objects. (For more on documents that have many pages, see Chapter 7.)

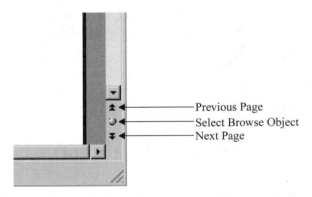

Previous Page
Select Browse Object
Next Page

> **TIP**   *If you want to move through your document by something other than pages, use the other Browse By options in the Select Browse Object palette. You can leaf through a document by tables, sections, comments, pictures, fields—anything. The safest choice for basic documents is by page, however, because your document might not contain many of the other Browse By elements.*

Keyboard Navigation Techniques

Even for the most mouse-oriented user, it's very quick and easy to move around in your document using the keyboard. Consider the following keyboard shortcuts to take your cursor from point A to point B in no time at all:

- CTRL-HOME moves your cursor to the very beginning of the document.

- CTRL-END takes you to the very end of your document.

- HOME takes you to the beginning of the line you're on. Note that I didn't say beginning of the *sentence*, but the beginning of the line.

- END takes you to the end of the line you're on.

- Use the LEFT ARROW and RIGHT ARROW keys to move one character at a time, left and right.

- Press CTRL as you press the LEFT ARROW and RIGHT ARROW keys, and you'll move word by word instead of character by character.

- Use the UP ARROW and DOWN ARROW keys to move one line at a time, up and down in the document.

- Press CTRL as you press the UP ARROW and DOWN ARROW keys, and you'll move by paragraph instead of by line. Of course, if you have blank lines between paragraphs, created by pressing ENTER, this keyboard shortcut will stop on those individual blank lines because they're each, technically, a paragraph.

- Press PAGE UP to move up one screenful of text.

- Press PAGE DOWN to move down one screenful of text.

- Press CTRL-G or F5 to open the Find and Replace dialog box with the Go To tab in front (see Figure 4-5). This allows you to enter a page number to "go to" in the Enter Page Number text box. Enter a number and press ENTER, and your cursor goes to the top of that page. The dialog box stays open, and you can close it when you don't need it anymore by pressing ESC (escape). This is probably the longest way around the barn for short documents, but if you want to go from page 5 to page 55, it's probably the most efficient way to get there.

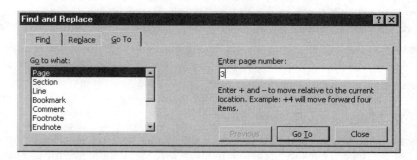

FIGURE 4-5   Type a page number in the Enter Page Number box and press ENTER to go to that page.

Selecting and Working with Text

Before you can do anything with the text in your document—delete it, edit it, copy or cut it to another file, or format it—you need to select it. If you're not a big fan of the mouse, relax; you can use keyboard techniques instead. If you love the mouse and rarely let go of it except to type content into your document, you'll be happy to know that there are quick and easy ways to use the mouse to select text and that you can combine the keyboard and the mouse to make and adjust text selections. Your options are virtually unlimited.

Selecting Text via the Keyboard

Just as you can move your cursor with the keyboard, you can select text with the keyboard, too. The key that takes you from moving to selecting is right there, under your finger: SHIFT! Try these techniques for selecting text with your keyboard:

- Press and hold SHIFT as you click the arrow keys. If you're using the UP ARROW and DOWN ARROW keys, you'll select lines of text. If you're using the LEFT ARROW and RIGHT ARROW keys, you'll select text letter by letter. Press CTRL at the same time to accelerate the process: You can select whole paragraphs (CTRL-SHIFT-UP/DOWN ARROW), or whole words (CTRL-SHIFT-LEFT/RIGHT ARROW).

- To select the rest of your document (from the cursor to the end), press CTRL-SHIFT-END.

- To select the previous portions of your document (from the cursor to the beginning), press CTRL-SHIFT-HOME.

- Press SHIFT-END to select the line you're on, from the cursor to the end of the line.

- Press SHIFT-HOME to select the line you're on, from the cursor to the beginning of the line.

- SHIFT-PAGE UP will select from the cursor to the top of the page you're on.

- SHIFT-PAGE DOWN will select from the cursor to the end of the page you're on.

- To augment an existing selection (whether it was selected by keyboard or mouse), press and hold SHIFT and click with your mouse after the last word that should have been included in your selection.

- To reduce an existing selection, press and hold SHIFT and click where the selection should have ended.

- Press CTRL-A to select the entire document.

Using Your Mouse to Select Text

The mouse can be used to drag through text if you want a phrase within a sentence or a sentence within a paragraph. You can click to place your mouse where you want to begin your selection and then drag to the end, or you can work backward, starting at the end. It's your call, and it all depends on what's the most comfortable and effective method for you. As shown here, you can select anything from a single character to a long string of text.

Dear Mr. Pederzani,

We are happy to accept your order for a new sign for your business. It's our practice to confirm all orders in writing, and ask that you call to verify the information listed below before we begin building your sign. Each of our signs is a totally hand-made, customized creation, and we want to make certain that we have all of our specifications in order:

4

> **TIP** *Word won't let you start or stop your selection in the middle of a word or just select the first letter? If so, choose Tools | Options, and on the Edit tab of the Options dialog box, turn off the When Selecting, Automatically Select Entire Word option by clicking the check box next to it to remove the check mark. This option is on by default, but it's one of the first things I turn off when I install Word.*

What happens if you drag and get more or less than you wanted? It's very common, especially when selecting within a paragraph, to accidentally get the line above or below the text you wanted, or to select text beyond where you wanted to end your selection. It's also possible to let go of the mouse button too soon and not get everything you wanted. In that last sentence is the solution to this problem, no matter how it manifests itself: Don't let go of the mouse until you have the exact selection you want.

If you're dragging through a paragraph to select a couple of sentences, it's very easy to stray up or down slightly with your mouse and suddenly have selected lines or even paragraphs above or below what you wanted. When this occurs, simply leave your mouse button depressed and drag back into the range you wanted, even going back to the beginning of the intended selection and starting your selection process over. As long as you don't let go of the mouse button, the selection will follow you, increasing or reducing the amount of text selected as you drag your mouse left or right, up or down.

Sometimes, the amount of text you need to select lends itself to some very convenient mouse alternatives to the dragging technique. Here's a list:

- To select a single word, double-click the word.
- If you want to select an entire paragraph, triple-click anywhere within the paragraph.
- Double-click in the left margin next to any paragraph you want to select. As shown here, when you're in the left margin for the purposes of text selection, your mouse will turn to a right-pointing arrow.

Dear Mr. Pederzani,

We are happy to accept your order for a new sign for your business. It's our practice to confirm all orders in writing, and ask that you call to verify the information listed below before we begin building your sign. Each of our signs is a totally hand-made, customized creation, and we want to make certain that we have all of our specifications in order:

- Triple-click in the left margin anywhere in your document to select the entire document.

Editing Your Text

Nobody's perfect. Let's get that stated now. No matter how fast and accurate a typist you are, you're going to make mistakes. Even if you don't make any on your own, you may find out that what you typed isn't what was wanted, or that the paragraph on page 3 belonged on page 5, and the man's name on page 7 isn't spelled the way you were told it was. If you're like I am, you probably make a lot of mistakes on your own, transposing letters, leaving out words, repeating words, even finding stupidly complex ways to explain something simple. All these things will require editing, whether you're lucky enough to have a proofreader or you go back over your text later to check it.

Editing text is easy enough, using what you've learned earlier in this chapter about selecting text with the keyboard and mouse and adding BACKSPACE and DELETE to your repertoire. Here are some editing techniques to master (don't worry, they're simple):

- To replace a word with another word, double-click the existing word and type the new word. No need to delete the first word and then type its replacement. Whatever's selected when you start typing will be replaced by what you type. It doesn't matter if the original word and its replacement are of different lengths.

- To change the case of text (for example, UPPERCASE, Title Case, Sentence case, or lowercase), select the text and press SHIFT-F3. As you hold down SHIFT and press F3, your text will cycle through various cases. When the case you want is applied, release SHIFT. You can also choose Format | Change Case after selecting the text you want to change. The resulting dialog box appears:

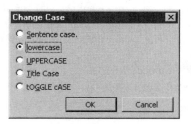

- To get rid of text, select it and press DELETE.

- To make minor changes within a word or phrase, use BACKSPACE and DELETE. Remember that BACKSPACE goes back through your text, removing text to the left of the cursor. DELETE removes text to the right of your cursor, one character per keypress.

- If you want to get rid of text one word at a time, use CTRL plus BACKSPACE or DELETE. You'll delete whole words at a time to the left of the cursor (CTRL-BACKSPACE) or to the right of the cursor (CTRL-DELETE).

Rearranging Words, Sentences, and Paragraphs

One of Word's most convenient tools is Drag and Drop. As mentioned in Chapter 2, Drag and Drop makes it possible to avoid the whole cut-and-paste process and simply drag something from where it is to where it should be. The only limitation? It works best when both the current location and the desired location are both visible at the same time (on the same page or section thereof). If you want to move something from page 2 to page 5, it's better to use Edit | Cut to remove it and Edit| Paste to put it where it belongs.

To use Drag and Drop, follow these steps:

1. Select the text to be moved. You can select it with the mouse or the keyboard.

2. If you used your mouse to select the text, make sure to release the mouse button after finishing the selection.

3. Point back to (but don't click) the selection. Your mouse pointer turns to an arrow:

now is the time

4. Depress and hold the mouse button and then drag the text to the desired location. A small vertical line (the Drag and Drop cursor) will follow you as you drag:

now is the time

5. When the Drag and Drop cursor is where you want to insert the dragged text, release the mouse.

There are times when you want to repeat text in several spots on the same page and you want a quick method (quicker than Edit | Copy and repeated Paste commands, anyway) to make sure the same text appears in each spot. You can use Drag and Drop in these situations as well, with one minor adjustment: Press CTRL as you drag, and release the mouse before you release CTRL. A plus sign (+) will follow as you drag, and as long as you don't release CTRL before you release the mouse (when you've reached the desired location to drop the text), you'll deposit a copy. You can also skip using CTRL by dragging the selection with the right mouse button. When you release the mouse at the desired spot, a shortcut menu appears, as shown here. Choose Copy Here from the menu, and the copy appears in place.

TIP   *If your document is more than one page long, you wouldn't consider it to be a long document, but it becomes a candidate for page numbers (on the second and any subsequent pages) and possibly headers and footers. To find out more about such things, check out Chapter 7, which covers several topics related to longer documents and their special needs.*

Chapter 5

Proofing, Printing, and Saving Documents

How to...

- Check and correct spelling errors as you type
- Run a full spelling and grammar check on your document
- Print your entire document
- Print specific pages and ranges of your document
- Save a file for the first time
- Resave a file to change its name or location
- Save a document as a template to use in building future documents

Nobody's perfect. You're going to misspell words, transpose letters in words, leave words out of sentences, and generally mess up as you type your documents. (I once ended a letter with, "If you have any questions, please hesitate to call.") Word will waste no time pointing out your errors. It checks your spelling and grammar as you type and gives you quick and easy ways to fix them, or to skip its suggestions if you know you're right. Word's spelling- and grammar-checking tools aren't always perfect, though. Therefore, you may want to make them match your needs more exactly by customizing the way they work.

In this chapter, you'll learn to proof your documents, and once they're as perfect as they can be, to print and save them. You'll also learn how to save certain documents as templates, which will help you consistently and quickly create similar documents in the future.

Proofing Word Documents

The most obvious thing about Word's proofing tools is that they're working all the time. As you build your document, if you type a word that's not in Word's internal dictionary (really just a list of letter combinations that we think of as words, nothing like the dictionary we'd use to look up word definitions), it is immediately underlined with a red, wavy line.

Notice that little book icon down on the status bar? It only appears when there's text in your document, and it either has a red check mark or a red X on it. When the book has a check mark on it, the document contains no spelling errors or the user has directed Word to ignore any errors found. If a red X appears on the book, the document contains unresolved spelling errors. You'll see the book's pages flipping as Word checks the text as you type, looking for errors in the text you're adding to or editing in the document.

Green, wavy underlines indicate a grammatical error, which is more often than not an extra space between words or a missing period at the end of a sentence. It doesn't always mean you've committed some egregious error such as saying "nobody got none." If you want to ignore the grammatical error indicators, too, you can. Word will stop and deal with each one later if you decide to run the spelling and grammar check.

It's important to remember that not everything that's underlined in red or green is really a mistake. It could be Word's mistake in flagging the item. Word could be applying too formal a set of standards to your document, or in the case of spelling, the word in question could be someone's name or an esoteric term that Word just doesn't have in its internal dictionary.

Handling Errors as You Type

As stated, Word is checking your text as you type it, looking for misspellings and grammatical errors. This feature is on by default but can be turned off. I don't recommend turning it off, however, because one of the best reminders to run the main spelling and grammar check is the sight of red or green wavy underlines in your document; it will keep you from printing and perhaps mailing a document containing errors.

If you choose to resolve the errors as they're pointed out, it's easy to do so. Right-click the underlined text and view Word's suggested corrections on the shortcut menu that appears. Here are examples of spelling and grammar errors.

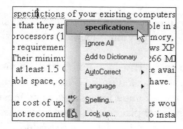 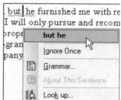

In the case of some spelling errors, Word will make multiple suggestions based on the spelling you typed. For example, if you type "ogrange," Word will suggest "orange," "grange," and "oranges." These alternatives are based on the number of letters, starting letters, and letter combinations in the word as you spelled it. If the word you wanted to type (in this case, orange) appears in the list of suggestions, click it and Word will replace your error with that word. Here are some other options offered through the shortcut menu:

- If you know that the word is spelled correctly—perhaps it's a name or term—you can choose Ignore All from the shortcut menu.

- Ignore All is good only for this document and for this round of spell checking. If you know the word is spelled correctly and don't want to be flagged for using it in future documents, click Add to Dictionary to add it to the list of words that Word uses to verify the spelling in your document.

- If the word you typed is in a foreign language (for example, if your default language is English, you might be flagged for typing *muchas gracias* instead of "thank you," or *ciao* instead of "good bye." If you're not sure of your spelling of the foreign word(s), you can switch to another language and verify (or correct) the spelling by choosing Language | Set Language. In the resulting Language dialog box (see Figure 5-1), scroll to select the language you want to do your spell check in and click OK. Once you've checked the foreign word (using the same spell-checking procedures used for your default language), repeat this process to return to the language the rest of your document is typed in.

FIGURE 5-1 Want to make sure your spelling is *muy bien*? Switch to Spanish and verify your spelling of a foreign word or words in your document.

■ If you'd prefer to have Word show you each error in a dialog box, choose Spelling from the shortcut menu. The Spelling and Grammar dialog box opens offering you the options Ignore, Ignore All, Add to Dictionary, and Change for a selected suggested correction. If you feel you've made the same mistake in other places in the same document, click Change All to fix all instances without having to stop and deal with them individually.

Running the Spelling and Grammar Check

The full spelling- and grammar-checking process is invoked by choosing Tools | Spelling and Grammar or by clicking the Spelling and Grammar button on the Standard toolbar. You can also press F7 to start it if you like to use keyboard shortcuts.

Once the spelling- and grammar-checking process begins, any errors in your document (or errors as perceived by Word) will appear in the top text box in the Spelling and Grammar dialog box (see Figure 5-2). If the error involves spelling, the error will appear in context, with the error itself in red. If the error is grammatical (or a problem with spacing or capitalization), the error will appear in green.

As you deal with each presented error (by clicking the Ignore, Add, or Change button), Word will move through the document, until no more errors are found. When there are no more errors, a prompt appears, telling you that the spelling and grammar check is complete.

It's best to start your spelling and grammar check at the beginning of your document (with your cursor at the top of the first page) so that you know the entire document is checked and Word doesn't have to ask if you want to check the whole thing. For example, if you have text selected at the time you issue the command to start the check, Word will check the selected section and then display a message box asking if you want to continue checking the rest of the document.

Another good reason to start your check with your cursor at the top of the document is that working from start to finish makes it easier for you to make judgment calls depending on where the error is in the document.

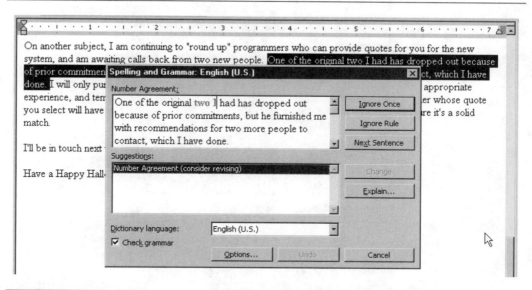

FIGURE 5-2   The Spelling and Grammar dialog box shows errors, in context, so you can see where and how you used a word or phrase before deciding how, or if, to correct it.

Making Automatic Corrections

One of the options in both the shortcut menu you see when you right-click an underlined word and in the Spelling and Grammar dialog box is AutoCorrect. AutoCorrect is an extremely powerful and convenient feature, and it's available in Word, Excel, and PowerPoint, so your actions within Word (customizing its use, adding to its tasks) will affect the way it works in the other applications as well.

Along with the spelling and grammar checking that occurs as you type, AutoCorrect is working as you enter your document text, fixing common misspellings and transpositions, and turning combinations of punctuation marks into symbols. For example, if you type "adn," Word will automatically change it to "and." If you type a colon, a hyphen, and a right parenthesis (in that order, with no spaces between them), Word will change it to a smiley-face symbol. You can view all the AutoCorrect actions and settings by choosing Tools | AutoCorrect Options. Here's a list of some other things that AutoCorrect does for you, as shown in Figure 5-3.

- ■ **Corrects two initial capitals**   If you hold down SHIFT too long when capitalizing the first letter of a word, "THank you" becomes "Thank you."

- ■ **Capitalizes the first letter of sentences**   If you often forget to capitalize your sentences, this feature will be a real timesaver. Word assumes you're starting a new sentence whenever you type a period followed by a space, press ENTER, or begin typing on a brand new document.

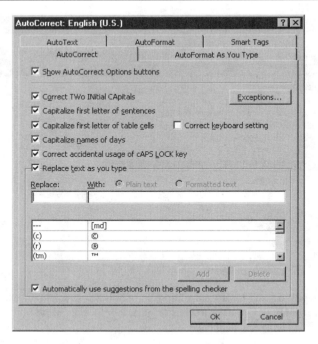

FIGURE 5-3 All the AutoCorrect actions are on by default, but you can turn any of them off if they're inconvenient.

- **Capitalizes the first letter of text in table cells** Because each table cell's first word is normally the beginning of a sentence, Word assumes you want these words capitalized.

- **Capitalizes the names of days of the week** People often forget that the days of the week should be capitalized, but Word won't forget.

- **Corrects accidental use of CAPS LOCK** If you press CAPS LOCK and then SHIFT while typing the next word in your document, Word will assume you didn't mean to be in CAPS LOCK mode and will reverse all the upper- and lowercase letters in that word.

The option Show AutoCorrect Option Buttons appears at the top of the AutoCorrect dialog box and refers to the little blue icon that appears whenever AutoCorrect makes a correction. If you put your mouse over the icon, a drop-down arrow button appears. If you click it, you can choose to undo the correction (as shown next) and turn off any automatic corrections related to the text that was corrected. You can also choose Control AutoCorrect Options to open the AutoCorrect dialog box.

Chris further states that the cost of upgrading your machines would be more than the cost of new workstations, so he does not recommend that you attempt to install new processors or more RAM. As you know, we have no vested interest in how many computers you buy, so this is a completely unbiased...

> Change back to "teh"
> Stop Automatically Correcting "teh"
> Control AutoCorrect Options...

In any case, this information should allow you to determine the number of workst... Dell—all but the current standalone PC will have to be replaced. If you have any...

Creating AutoCorrect Entries

Beyond the built-in list of hundreds of common misspellings and transposition errors, AutoCorrect can be made more powerful by you adding your own entries—words you misspell, letters you transpose frequently, and abbreviations for things you get tired of typing in their full form. For example, I often type "int he" instead of "in the." I got tired of having the error flagged as a spelling error every time, so I added the incorrect version ("int he") to AutoCorrect, paired with the correct spelling of the pair of words. Now whenever I make the mistake, Word has fixed it before I even realize I've made the error.

Storing abbreviations is a great way to use AutoCorrect. I've built in several that help me write books, such as the one you're reading now. For example, I built in "db" to be replaced by "dialog box," and "rc" becomes "right-click."

TIP   *Make sure your AutoCorrect trigger (the misspelling or abbreviated form) isn't a real word or an acronym/abbreviation that you may want to use in that form in the future. For example, if your name is Ann Smith, you don't want your trigger to be "as", because that's a word. If you're building in an abbreviation that you'd also like to be able to type as initials (such as PETA, which would flesh out to People for the Ethical Treatment of Animals), build your entry as "PETA1," and only that will trigger the whole organization name.*

To create an AutoText entry, follow these steps:

1. Choose Tools | AutoCorrect Options. The AutoCorrect dialog box opens (refer to Figure 5-3).

2. Your cursor should be blinking inside the Replace text box by default, but if it isn't, click inside that box.

3. Type the error you want fixed or the abbreviation you want fleshed out.

4. Press TAB to move to the With box, or just click inside that box to position your cursor.

5. Type the correction or full version of the abbreviation. Be sure to type it exactly as you want it to appear in the document. Make sure you spell it correctly and use the capitalization you want Word to use.

6. Click Add.

7. Repeat steps 1 through 6 for any other entries you want to build. Then click OK to close the dialog box.

If you want to add a misspelling to AutoCorrect, creating an instant pairing of the error and its suggested creation, choose AutoCorrect from the shortcut menu that appears when you right-click a flagged (underlined in red) word. When you choose AutoCorrect from the shortcut menu, a submenu appears offering the same suggested corrections seen in the main shortcut menu (shown here). When you make a selection from this AutoCorrect submenu, the selection and the error it corrects are automatically stored as a new AutoCorrect entry and will be used the next time you make the same error.

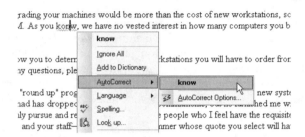

Editing and Removing AutoCorrect Entries

Imagine you've built an AutoCorrect entry that you now want to change. You can edit the entry you made or you can delete the entire entry and start over. Deleting is also handy if you want to get rid of an entry—maybe you realize the trigger is a word you need to be able to type without Word tinkering with it.

To edit an AutoCorrect entry, follow these steps:

1. Choose Tools | AutoCorrect Options.

2. In the AutoCorrect dialog box, type the first letter of the "replace" text (your error or trigger), and the list of stored entries moves to the first one starting with that same letter. Scroll around to find your entry and select it, or continue typing until the entire entry appears in the box. Its correction appears automatically in the With box.

3. In the Replace and/or With box, edit the entry to meet your needs.

4. Click the Replace button.

5. A prompt appears, asking you to confirm your intention to redefine the entry. If you want to do so, click Yes.

6. Repeat steps 1 through 5 for any other entries you need to edit.

7. Click OK to close the dialog box.

Deleting an AutoCorrect entry uses the same procedure, except that in step 4, you click the Delete button. There is no confirming prompt to make sure you want to make the deletion, so be sure you've selected the right entry before you click the Delete button.

Customizing the Proofing Tools

Word's proofing tools aren't any more perfect than you are. Yes, the spell checker will infallibly check every word you type against its internal word list, but words might not be on that list because they're legal, medical, or some other industries' terminology. The grammar checker sometimes makes suggestions for changing a word or rearranging your text that would completely change the meaning of your text—and not for the better. In these cases, you can ignore the suggestions, or if this happens too frequently, you can adjust the proofing tools to better meet your needs.

When it comes to spelling, you can add words to the dictionary. When you add a word, you're storing it in your personal dictionary, a separate word list that is built by your additions. This list is checked, along with the main dictionary, against all text in your document. Of course, to add to this list, click the Add to Dictionary button in the spelling shortcut menu or the Spelling and Grammar dialog box.

Customizing the Spell-Checking Process

Word's spelling tools can also be customized by using the Spelling and Grammar Options dialog box. Choose Tools | Options and click the Spelling and Grammar tab in the Options dialog box. You can also click the Options button in the Spelling and Grammar dialog box. In either case, the options shown in Figure 5-4 appear, and you can turn them on and off to customize when and how Word checks your text for spelling errors.

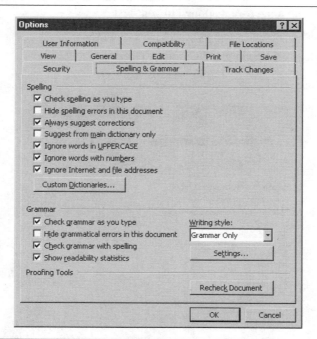

FIGURE 5-4   The settings shown here are the defaults. You can change them as needed by removing check marks next to any unwanted actions.

Adjusting the Standards for Grammar Checking

If you work for a very conservative, formal organization or write to clients who might fall into the "serious" category, your grammar checking should be very thorough, allowing no colloquialisms, fragments, run-on sentences, or uses of any inappropriate tense to make it through the grammatical filter. You shouldn't be allowed to end a sentence with a preposition or use a split infinitive without the error being flagged.

On the other hand, if you work for or write to a more informal crowd, where comfort and clarity is more important than absolute correctness, you might want to loosen the grammatical grip Word has on your text and allow a few errors to slip under the radar. Whether you want Word to be more informal or more exacting in its grammar checking, the customization steps are as follows:

1. Choose Tools | Options and click the Spelling and Grammar tab. You can also click Options in the Spelling and Grammar dialog box.

2. In the Grammar section of the dialog box, click the Settings button to bring up the Grammar Settings dialog box (see Figure 5-5).

3. Adjust the Writing Style option in the resulting Grammar Settings dialog box to check your grammar only or to check your grammar and style.

4. Scroll through the Grammar and Style options and turn on any desired options and turn off any that you no longer want applied to your text.

5. Click OK to close the dialog box and save your changes.

6. Click OK to close the Spelling and Grammar Options dialog box.

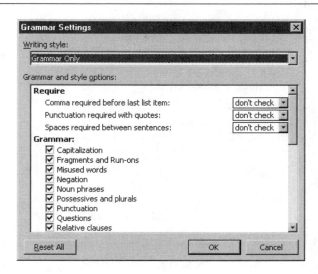

FIGURE 5-5   See just what sort of grammatical rules Word is applying to your documents.

Turning As-You-Type Proofing On and Off

If you find the red and green underlines annoying to look at and know you'd never forget to run the full spelling and grammar check in their absence, you can turn them off. You can turn either or both of them off, or you can simply hide the errors in a particular document but leave the checking on and visible in all other documents.

To adjust how (or if) the spelling and grammar checking is performed as you type, choose Tools | Options and then click the Spelling and Grammar tab in the Options dialog box. You can also click the Options button in the Spelling and Grammar dialog box.

- If you want to turn off the Check Spelling as You Type option, click the check box to remove the check mark.

- If you want spelling to be checked as you type but want to hide the underlines in the active document, click to place a check mark in the box next to Hide Spelling Errors in This Document.

- If you don't want grammar to be checked as you type, click to remove the check mark next to Check Grammar as You Type.

- If you want grammar checking to continue but don't want to see the green underlines in the active document, leave Check Grammar as You Type on but place a check mark next to Hide Grammatical Errors in This Document.

Once you've made your choices, click OK to save your changes and close the dialog box.

Viewing Your Document's Readability Statistics

If you're writing to a particular audience and you know the educational level of that audience, you can view your readability statistics at the end of each spelling- and grammar-check session.

Readability is measured by three standards: how easy the document is to read, at which grade level it is written, and the number of sentences in the passive voice ("When you click OK, a dialog box will open" rather than "Click OK to open the dialog box"). The readability statistics are based on existing measurement tools, developed to help writers match their style to their audience. You needn't be an expert in this topic to use the statistics—suffice it to say, the lower the level of education your audience has, the lower the statistic numbers should be. For example, if your audience contains many people who are not well educated, you want to aim for a Flesch-Kincaid Grade Level below 9 so that people who didn't attend high school (or the equivalent) won't have problems with your text.

To view a document's readability statistics, choose Show Readability Statistics in the Grammar section on the Spelling and Grammar tab of the Options dialog box and then click OK. The next time you run a full spelling and grammar check, the process will end with a display that shows the word, character, paragraph, and sentence counts, as well as the average number of sentences per paragraph, words per sentence, and characters per word, which can indicate complex sentences and long words. The statistics for a sample document are shown in Figure 5-6.

5

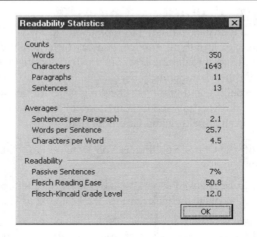

FIGURE 5-6   Don't talk down to a well-educated audience or over the heads of an audience who might not be familiar with your topic.

Printing Your Document

Despite the fact that more and more documents are viewed onscreen and online rather than on paper, you will need to print a document from time to time. I find it easier to read longer documents on paper and to do my final proofing on a printed version of my document rather than reading and looking for errors onscreen. I'm not sure why this is, but I'm not alone. Whether you're printing out a document for review, to send to someone, or for photocopying purposes, Word makes the printing process quick and easy. You have three alternatives, most of which work interchangeably:

- ■ *Click the Print button on the Standard toolbar*. With no questions asked, Word will print one copy of every page of the active document, sending the job to the printer currently set as your default device. If you don't know which printer is set as the default or if you definitely don't want the job to go to one of the printers to which you can potentially print, you might want to skip this method.

- ■ *Choose File | Print*. Misleadingly, this menu command is accompanied by a picture of the Print button from the toolbar. The command and the button don't work exactly the same way, however. When you choose File | Print, the Print dialog box opens (see Figure 5-7), through which you can choose a different printer, set the number of copies to print, and choose to print only certain pages of the document.

- ■ *Press CTRL-P*. This keyboard shortcut is the equivalent of the File | Print command and opens the Print dialog box.

Obviously, the Print button is only a good alternative if you have a very short document (and therefore don't mind printing all the pages) or if no matter how many pages your document has,

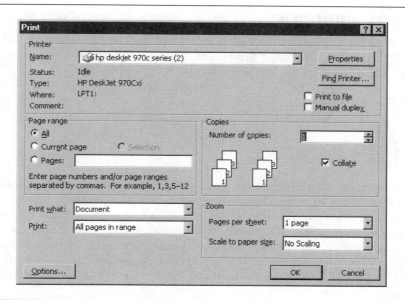

FIGURE 5-7   Control everything from the number of copies to the selection of pages printed through the Print dialog box.

you want to print one copy of each one. If you want to control the print job in any way, you need to work with the Print dialog box. Here are some controls to consider:

- **Printing only selected text**   If you select the text you want to print—say, a series of paragraphs that span two pages—before opening the Print dialog box, you can click the Selection option in the Page Range section. The only thing to print will be the text you selected prior to issuing the File | Print command.

- **Printing only odd or even pages**   If you're going to print on both sides of the paper and bind the document, you can choose to print just the odd pages and then put them back in the printer and print the even pages. Click the Print drop-down list in the lower-left corner of the dialog box and choose Odd Pages or Even Pages.

- **Printing more than one page per sheet**   If you want to print several pages on a single sheet of paper—perhaps for the purposes of reviewing the layout of multiple pages—click the Pages per Sheet drop-down list in the Zoom section of the dialog box. Bear in mind that you might end up with tiny text that no one can read, but printing multiple pages per sheet will allow you to review the layout of your document on one handy sheet.

> **TIP**   *If your printer doesn't do duplex printing (printing on both sides of the paper automatically), you can click the Manual Duplex option in the Printer section of the Print dialog box. After the odd-numbered pages have been printed, Word will prompt you to refeed the paper upside down so that the even pages can be printed.*

Saving Word Documents

There are two words you need to remember with regard to saving your documents: early and often. Save your documents as soon as you get started, and continue saving every five or ten minutes. In fact, you should save your document after each of the following events:

- Checking the spelling
- Formatting the document text
- Editing
- Typing more than a couple of sentences

Now, you're probably wondering why on earth you'd need to save so often, and why I'd possibly suggest something so potentially time-consuming as a frequent action. The answer is to save you from losing your work. The time it takes to save your document is miniscule compared to the time you'll waste rebuilding a document that you lose to the application crashing, your computer shutting down, or a power failure. If you've been typing, formatting, and editing for an hour without saving, or if the computer or Word shuts down before you have a chance to resave, you'll lose that hour's worth of work, and it invariably takes more than an hour to remember what you did and to do it again.

Remember, too, that the process of saving is only time-consuming the first time you do it. The first time you save a document you have to give it a name and choose where to store it. Subsequent saves simply update that file, and it only takes a second—literally—to do it.

TIP *You might have heard about Word's Auto Recovery feature or the "background saves" that Word does every ten minutes by default. These features do not eliminate the need for you to save early and often. If your power goes out or your computer crashes, a recovered version of the file might be available when you reboot and restart Word, but the file will only contain your work as of the last background save, which could have been long before the crash or power outage occurred.*

Performing a First-Time Save

The first time you save a file, by using either the File | Save or File | Save As command (or by clicking the Save button on the Standard toolbar), the Save As dialog box opens. As shown in Figure 5-8, the dialog box defaults to saving your file in the My Documents folder (assuming you haven't changed the default file location setting) and will save your document as a .doc file, the default Word format.

When the dialog box opens, the current document name (the name Word assigns it temporarily, until you give it a name and save it) appears in the Filename box, and is highlighted. To give the file its real name, simply type the name. There's no need to delete the temporary name or click in the File Name box. Because the current generic name is highlighted, the very next thing you type will replace that name. After naming the file, you can choose to save it somewhere other than the My Documents folder. This can be an entirely different folder or a folder within the My Documents

Create New Folder

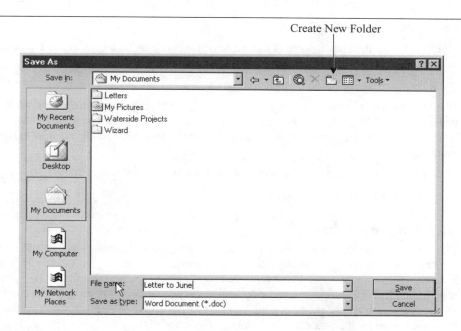

FIGURE 5-8 Word makes it easy to save your file by assuming where you want to store it.

folder. You can also create a new folder to house this document. To save to a different location, follow these steps:

1. In the Save As dialog box, click the drop-down triangle at the end of the Save In text box. A directory of all the possible locations, from your desktop to any network drives you might be attached to, is displayed.

2. Click the drive you want to save to. If you want to save your document to your local hard drive, click C:.

3. When the folders within the selected drive appear in the dialog box, double-click the one you want to save to.

4. If you haven't already named your document, do so now by selecting the name in the File Name box and typing the new name.

5. Click the Save button in the lower-right corner of the dialog box. The file is saved, and the name you've given it appears on the title bar.

To create a new folder for your document, follow these steps:

1. Choose File | Save As. In the Save As dialog box, move to the drive or folder the new folder should be stored in. For example, if your new folder will be a subfolder of My Documents, make sure it says My Documents in the Save In text box.

2. Click the Create New Folder button.

3. The New Folder dialog box opens. Type the name for your new folder (up to 255 characters) in the Name box.

4. Click OK to close the New Folder dialog box.

5. Word automatically creates the new folder and puts your file in it, displaying the new folder in the Save In text box. This is because Word assumes your reason for creating the folder was to save the new file into that folder, so it saves you the step of selecting the new folder manually.

6. If the file is as yet unnamed, type a new name for it in the File Name box.

7. Click the Save button to save the new file into the new folder.

Updating a Saved File

After a file is saved for the first time, each subsequent save is just an update of that file, to add any new text or other content, include any edits or formatting, and generally make sure the file stored on your computer is the same as the one you're looking at onscreen. No dialog box opens, no prompt appears. The file is simply resaved, overwriting the previous version, and you can continue to work. To perform such an update save, simply press CTRL-S. You can also choose File | Save or click the Save button on the Standard toolbar, but I recommend the keyboard shortcut, even to people who aren't normally keyboard-shortcut oriented. It allows you to save your file *and* keep typing so you don't lose your momentum, you don't waste any time, and you don't risk losing your work.

Saving a Document with a New Name

After the first-time save, most documents require only update saves—the saves that update the file to include changes as you continue to work—and that's it. The file is never moved to a new folder, never renamed. This is the ideal situation, of course, because it eliminates extra work, and there's never any doubt what a file is called or where to look for it.

Remember, however, I said "most documents." There are situations where a file needs a new name or needs to be stored in a new place, perhaps an additional location, leaving the original file where it was saved the first time. Perhaps you need to create a second version of the file for someone else, and you want to keep your version for your own use and let the other person do as they please with their version. Perhaps you want to save the file to a network drive so other people can get at it, but you want to leave the original file on your local hard drive for your own use.

Whatever your motivation, it's easy to resave an existing, saved file and give it a new name and/or save it to a new place. Follow these steps:

1. From within the file to be renamed or relocated, choose File | Save As. The Save As dialog box opens, displaying the file's current name and location.

2. To rename the file, simply type a new name in the File Name box. The current name should be highlighted when the dialog box opens, so all you have to do is start typing the new name.

3. To save the file to a new place, click the Save In drop-down list and pick a new drive. If you want to save to the same drive but to a different folder, click the Up One Level button until you're back to the root of the C drive and then select the folder you want to save the file in.

4. With the new location and/or new name displayed in the Save In dialog box, click the Save button. The original file will close, and the new version will remain open for your use until you close it.

If, after creating the new version, you want to go back to the old one, simply close the new version and reopen the old one (it should be the first one listed in the Most Recently Used file list at the foot of the File menu, or on the task pane). The new version can be emailed to the person who needs it, or you can let that person know which network drive the file can be found on. You'll be able to continue working with your own version of the file, unaffected by anyone's use of the new version.

> TIP
>
> *It's a cruel and complicated world at times—power goes out, computers crash, and files get lost. I like to store copies of the final version of important files in a special folder. This gives me a single location to find important documents and makes it easy to back up these documents. I just drag the folder to the Zip drive (using the Windows Explorer or My Computer window), and the folder and all the documents in it are backed up to my Zip disk. You can do the same thing with a floppy disk, if the files don't exceed disk capacity, or if you have a writeable CD drive, you can write the folder and its files to a CD for safekeeping.*

Creating Document Templates

Templates are perhaps the most underused part of Word's considerable power. People spend hours (probably days or weeks when all the time is added up) creating documents from scratch when a template could have saved them as much as 90 percent of the time spent entering and editing text and then formatting their documents. Templates, if used properly, can also help maintain consistency across a group of people so that the documents created in a single department or throughout an entire company are similar in important ways—fonts, layout, and content.

So what are these wonderful things, these templates? Templates are like cookie cutters for documents. They help you create many similar (or perhaps identical) documents from a single mold. Common examples of templates include fax cover sheets, memos, proposals, reports, and letters. Just about any kind of document can be a template, becoming the foundation for future documents.

Building Template Content

Word allows you to turn any document into a template, simply by choosing the Document Template format for the file when you save it. That's all you need to do. If you choose that format for a document, Word automatically saves the file to a Templates folder, making the resulting template file accessible for use in building new documents later. The process is very simple. Just follow these steps:

1. To build a template from a new document, start with a blank document and build the content and apply the formatting that every document based on this template will need. Don't add anything that's specific to one particular document, such as the date or reference to a particular product or client. Figure 5-9 shows the content you'd want to include in a memo template.

2. Choose File | Save As. In the resulting Save As dialog box, click the Save As Type drop-down list at the bottom of the dialog box and choose Document Template (.dot) from the list of formats. When you select the document template format, Word automatically changes the Save In location to the Templates folder, where existing templates that came with Word are already stored.

3. In the File Name box, type a name for the template that will help you choose it for specific uses later, such as "Standard Memo" (rather than plain old "Memo") or "Quarterly Report" (as opposed to "Report," which isn't very specific).

4. Click the Save button to create the template and close the Save As dialog box.

The template file remains open onscreen, and you can continue to edit and format it as needed. Continue to resave it (in the .dot format) as you make changes and then close the file.

TIP   *Never save the template to a folder other than Templates, and to the Templates folder where Word automatically takes you when you choose the Template format. If you save a template to any other folder, it won't be available to you when you choose File | New or click the On My Computer link in the task pane. At most, save the template to one of the Templates folder's subfolders or create your own subfolder within the Templates folder, such as "My Templates." If you create your own subfolder (within the Templates folder), it will appear as a tab in the Templates dialog box, and on that tab you'll find the template you created.*

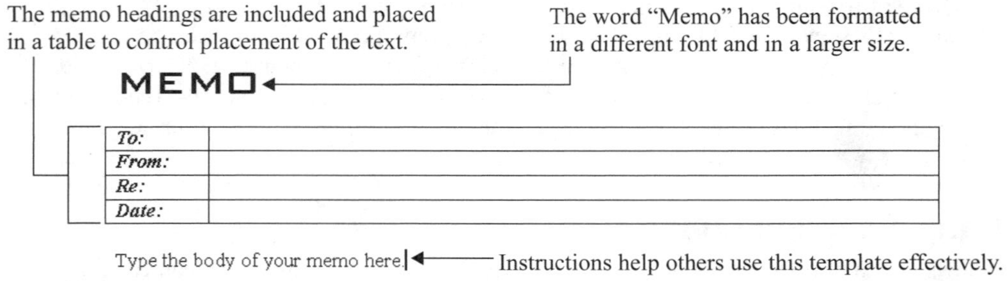

The memo headings are included and placed in a table to control placement of the text.

The word "Memo" has been formatted in a different font and in a larger size.

MEMO◄

To:	
From:	
Re:	
Date:	

Type the body of your memo here ◄——— Instructions help others use this template effectively.

FIGURE 5-9   Think about the future documents you'll create based on this template and only include the text and formats those documents will need.

Creating New Documents from Your Templates

To use the templates you create, simply choose File | New. You can also click the On My Computer link in the task pane to open the Templates dialog box. Within that dialog box, the General tab will contain the templates you've created. Double-click the template you want to use, and a new document opens, containing the content and formatting that was included in the template file. You'll note that the name of the new document is DocumentX (where "X" is the consecutive number assigned to all new documents in Word). Word doesn't open the template itself but rather a new document *based* on that template.

Template Tips and Techniques

The most useful piece of advice I can give you when it comes to templates is to make a lot of them. Any document you create more than once is a good candidate for a template. For example, if you write more than one report per month, you need a template for that report. Why? Because using a template will save you setting up the things that all your reports have in common, such as the name, the layout, the formatting, even some of the data that doesn't change or that changes only slightly.

When building template content, stick to text and other elements (such as tables and graphics) that every document you build based on the template will need. For example, if you're building a memo for meeting agendas, include the headings for each section (for example, Date, Attended By, Topics, Actions, and Follow-Up) but don't type anything specific to any particular or actual meeting. The more generic you can make the content, the more applicable the template will be for future agenda documents. Using tables in a template helps to structure the document by providing cells into which data and text can be entered. (For more on tables, see Chapter 8.) Styles, covered in Chapter 6, can be used to customize the templates' tables.

Another useful feature to build into a document is instructions, which are particularly helpful if people other than you will use your template. This can be as simple as "type your name here" or as detailed and specific as "please enter full department names and avoid using abbreviations whenever possible." The instructions should be obvious, however, so that people see them and replace them with their text, or delete them if they don't have text to insert in that part of the template. Preceding instructions with the word "NOTE" in all caps can help draw attention to instructional text and prevent it accidentally remaining in the document after the user has filled in the parts they need.

TIP   *Word comes with an extensive selection of templates, ready for your use. Most of them contain instructions, some use self-running Wizards that coach you through the process of filling in user-specific parts of the template, and some of the templates contain automated features such as fields (for making choices, inserting data). They're all available through the File | New command or by clicking the On My Computer link on the task pane. The templates are divided into several categories, designated by tabs in the dialog box, to help you find the one you need.*

5

Chapter 6

Effective Document Formatting

How to...

- Change the appearance of text by applying fonts and font sizes
- Use styles to make multiple changes to the appearance and placement of text
- Adjust alignment settings to position headings and justify paragraphs
- Format paragraphs to control the placement and flow of blocks of text
- Adjust margins, paper size, and page orientation
- Use default tabs to create simple column lists
- Create custom tab stops throughout a document

Your document can be formatted on three levels: character formatting, which works with your document at an almost atomic level; paragraph formatting, which works with large sections of text and deals with them as blocks; and page formatting, which allows you to control the appearance of the document as a whole. In this chapter, you'll learn to approach the formatting of your document on all three levels, using easily accessed toolbar buttons, dialog boxes that offer greater levels of control, and keyboard shortcuts to speed the process along. You'll also learn to structure your text with tabs, using both the default tab settings that are part of the Normal (blank document) template and custom tabs that you can set for specific layout requirements.

Changing the Appearance of Text

Text formatting is rather limited. You can change the font (or *typeface*) of text, the size of it, and the color of it. You can make it thicker (bold), you can make it italicized, and you can underline it. Beyond that—indents, margins, and bulleted lists—you're talking about paragraph and page formatting. The formatting of characters is limited to what you can change about the way individual letters and numbers look.

Although what you can change is limited, the ways to make those changes are not. You have the Formatting toolbar, nearly half of which is devoted to character formatting, you have the Font dialog box, and you have keyboard shortcuts. Figure 6-1 shows the Formatting toolbar, with the character-formatting tools individually identified.

The most important thing to remember before making any changes to the appearance of text is that you need to have the text in place and selected (highlighted) before applying any formatting. If you don't have text selected, Word assumes you want the format(s) to apply to the next thing you type at the cursor.

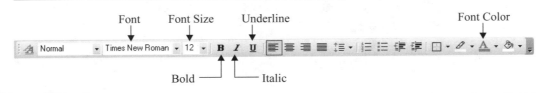

FIGURE 6-1 Pick a font, size, and color, and use the B, I, and U buttons to add emphasis.

You can cut your formatting efforts in half by applying formatting after all the text is typed rather than turning the formatting off and on as you go.

Choosing the Right Font and Size

What's the "right" font and size for your text? That's a subjective question. There are some basic rules for maintaining legibility and an overall pleasing design, but other than that, the choice is up to you.

- For business documents, 12-point text is best. It's large enough to be read, yet it's not so big that it wastes space.

- Times New Roman is clear onscreen and when printed on paper. It's the traditional favorite for business documents and is much clearer and easier on the eyes than Courier (which looks like an old typewriter was involved), and it photocopies better than Arial or Helvetica (which can cause unwanted letter combinations, such as an *r* followed by an *i* looking like an *n*).

- Try not to use more than two fonts per document, and when using two fonts, pick one from each font type. The two types are *serif* and *sans serif.* Serif text has flourishes on the ends of the letters, and sans serif (literally, "without serifs") does not have flourishes. Times New Roman is a serif font; Arial is sans serif.

- If you must use a very fancy font (from the pool generally referred to as *artistic* fonts), use it sparingly, and only on a heading or title.

To adjust the font and size of your text, use the Font and Font Size buttons on the Formatting toolbar. When you click the Font drop list, a list of fonts appears, each graphically represented so you know what the font looks like before you apply it to your text. The most recently used fonts appear first, followed by an alphabetical list.

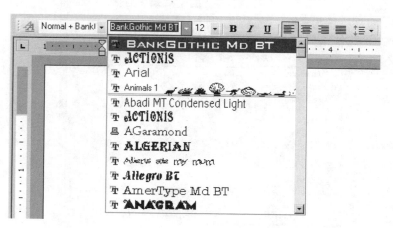

When you click the Font Size drop list, a series of numbers, representing sizes from 8 to 72 points appears (you have to scroll to see all the sizes). To select and apply a size, all you need to do is click the size you want to apply. You can also click in the button and type a new size, if you want one that's not represented in the list. After entering the number, press ENTER to apply it to your selected text.

Using the Font Format Dialog Box

Although the Font and Font Size buttons on the Formatting toolbar are easy to use, they don't give you as many options for formatting text as you'll find in the Font dialog box. To use it, select the text you want to format and then choose Format | Font. The dialog box appears in Figure 6-2.

If you would like to change Word's default of 12-point Times New Roman, make your selections and then click the Default button in the Font dialog box. A prompt will appear, asking if you really want to make your choices the default for all new documents based on the Normal template. Ideally, you want the font and size you've set as the new default to be appropriate for 99 percent of your documents; otherwise, you could be creating more formatting work for yourself.

Applying Text Color

Available through the Font dialog box and from the Formatting toolbar is the ability to change the color of text. By default, text is set to Automatic, which is the color set as your text color

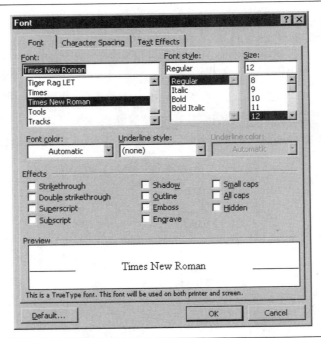

FIGURE 6-2   The Font dialog box provides one-stop shopping for your character-formatting needs.

through the Windows Display Properties. For most users, this means Black. You can change your text to any color of the rainbow, using the palette of 40 different colors that appears when you click the Font Color button on the toolbar or the Font Color drop list in the Font dialog box.

You can choose More Colors from the palette to open the Colors dialog box, which allows you to choose from more than 100 different colors, plus several shades of gray, or you can click the Custom tab and create your own colors by adjusting the levels of colors within the color model that you select. You can click anywhere on the spectrum shown on the tab, and then raise or lower the brightness (amount of white or black) and tweak the color levels by using the spinner triangles for each color level.

Applying Special Text Effects

Accessible only through the Font dialog box, you can change the spacing between letters (known as *kerning* when you're adjusting the space between two characters, and as *tracking* when you're adjusting space throughout a word or sentence) and apply fancy-schmancy text animations.

Why change character spacing? For the sake of legibility—sometimes very small text is easier to read if you add a little space between letters—and for graphic effect. Imagine spreading a title across a page rather than leaving the letters of a word or phrase clustered in the middle of the page. You can spread text out over the width of the page or any portion thereof, or if you need to tweak the space between letters so that something will fit "just so" on a line, you can reduce the spacing between letters as well. The Character Spacing tab is shown in Figure 6-3.

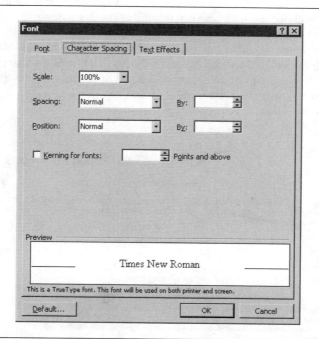

FIGURE 6-3   Adjust the space between, and vertical position of, characters in your document.

6

Another thing you can do on the Character Spacing tab has nothing to do with the spacing between letters, but with the spacing between the text and the *baseline*. The baseline is the invisible foundation each line of text sits on; the descenders of letters such as *y, g, p, q* dip below that line. The Position option (also shown in Figure 6-3) in the Character Spacing tab allows you to adjust the distance above or below the baseline that your selected text should be. You can choose Raised or Lowered and then set the point distance you want the text moved up or down.

The Text Effects tab offers six different animations—from a flashing background to sparkling confetti—and allows you to preview the selected effect before you apply it to your text. Of course, the animations show only in documents onscreen, because printing can't capture motion.

Altering Text Position and Flow

In a new document based on the Normal template, text flows (thanks to *word wrap,* discussed in Chapter 4) from line to line, and only when forced line and paragraph breaks are inserted, does that flow change. If left to its defaults, a Word document's text will follow the block letter format—text aligned to the left side of the page, with no indents for the first line of paragraphs and no other indents from the left or right side of paragraphs.

Changing Paragraph Alignment

The simplest, most commonly performed paragraph formatting is a change in paragraph alignment. As previously stated, the default for all document text is left alignment, meaning the text flows out from the left side of the page, and the text is flush with the left margin. The right margin text is ragged, with the distance between the end of the line and the margin varying on each line because of the length of words and how they fit (or don't fit) on the lines.

Not all text in a document should be left-aligned, however. Headings and titles can be centered (or even right-aligned) to change the visual layout of the page, indicating a change in topic. As you can see here, simply changing the alignment of a series of headings makes a rather boring-looking document look a little more interesting.

MARKETING STRATEGIES

Meeting Agenda

The meeting, scheduled for February 5, 2003, will be attended by the Marketing, Sales, and Operations department heads, managers, and directors. Attendance by staff within the departments is at the discretion of the directors.

Topics for discussion:

New products
Response to winter programs
Spring marketing plans
Budgetary concerns

It is hoped that everyone who will be at the meeting will review this agenda and make note of their questions, concerns, and any information that pertains to the topics that will be discussed. This will save time during the meeting, and will make the meeting more effective and productive.

Full justification is left alignment with a twist. Instead of the right margin being ragged as word wrap forces words of varying length onto the next line, the right margin is straight, just like the left. This effect is achieved by Word increasing and decreasing the size of the spaces between letters and words throughout the lines of a paragraph until the block effect you see here is achieved.

> ¶
> As· we· discussed· in· our· conversation· yesterday,· we· will· require· certificates· of· completion· for· these· students,· as· they· are· working· through· an· in-house· certification· program—proof· of· their· having·attended·and·passed·this·course·is·required·for·them·to·receive·their·certificates·and·move· on·with·the·program.·I·understand·that·there·are·also·Continuing·Education·Units·(ceu)·available· for· this· course,· and· we'd· like· to· have· these· attributed· to· the· students· as· well.· Whatever· documentation· you· have· pertaining· to· this· will· be· greatly· appreciated,· and· can· be· faxed· or· emailed·to·me.¶
> ¶

6

TIP   *Full justification makes it easier to read snaking columns of text that wrap vertically on a page, such as in newspaper columns. More on this is in Chapter 7.*

Remember that alignment is a paragraph format. If you select an individual word inside a paragraph and change the alignment, the entire paragraph's alignment will change. Therefore, unless you're changing the alignment of a series of consecutive paragraphs, you don't need to select a paragraph to align it. Just leave your cursor in the paragraph and then employ one of the following techniques to change the alignment to suit your needs:

- ■ *Click the Alignment buttons on the Formatting toolbar.* There are four of them: Align Left, Align Center, Align Right, and Justify.

Left Alignment   Right Alignment

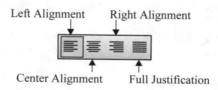

Center Alignment   Full Justification

- ■ *Use keyboard shortcuts.* These are CTRL-L for Left, CTRL-R for Right, and CTRL-J for Justify. The only surprise? CTRL-E for Center. (CTRL-C was taken by the Copy command.)
- ■ *Choose Format | Paragraph.* In the Indents and Spacing tab, click the Alignment drop list and choose Left, Centered, Right, or Justified. Figure 6-4 shows the Paragraph dialog box, and a variety of paragraph formats that it allows you to apply.

Indenting Text

The quickest way to indent a paragraph is to press TAB before you start typing the first word in the paragraph. An instant half-inch indent will be applied to the paragraph's first line, and as word wrap kicks in, the next line of the paragraph will run back to the margin, unindented. This is the most common form of indent and the easiest to apply.

Using the Increase Indent button on the Formatting toolbar you can achieve a quick indent from the left, in half-inch increments, for the entire paragraph containing the cursor. The Decrease

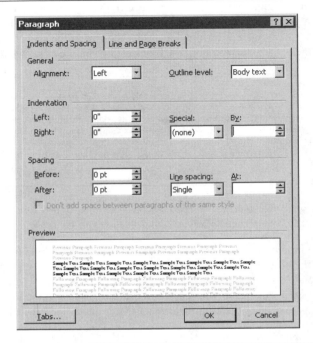

FIGURE 6-4   Using the Paragraph dialog box for alignment takes longer, but it contains many other formatting features that aren't represented elsewhere.

Indent button works in reverse. As shown in Figure 6-5, there are a variety of indent effects you can achieve.

Setting Indents from the Keyboard

Word offers a series of keyboard shortcuts designed to allow you to indent your text as you type—no need to even remove your fingers from the keyboard to reposition your text:

- CTRL-M indents text from the left, one half of an inch.
- CTRL-SHIFT-M reduces the left indent by a half an inch.
- CTRL-T creates a hanging indent.
- CTRL-Q removes all paragraph formatting, including indents.

 *Be careful when using the CTRL-Q shortcut to remove your indents. If your text is bulleted or numbered as well, that formatting will also be removed.*

Indenting Text via the Ruler

First, make sure your ruler is displayed. If it's not, choose View | Ruler. With your ruler in place, stop to identify the indent markers on the ruler, as shown here. The triangles represent the

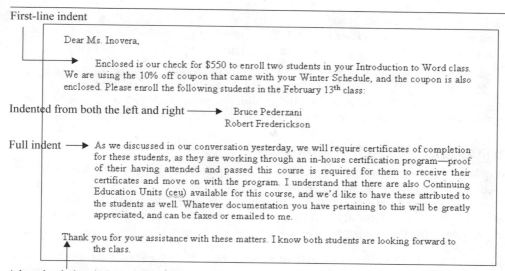

First-line indent

Dear Ms. Inovera,

Enclosed is our check for $550 to enroll two students in your Introduction to Word class. We are using the 10% off coupon that came with your Winter Schedule, and the coupon is also enclosed. Please enroll the following students in the February 13th class:

Indented from both the left and right ⟶ Bruce Pederzani
Robert Frederickson

Full indent ⟶ As we discussed in our conversation yesterday, we will require certificates of completion for these students, as they are working through an in-house certification program—proof of their having attended and passed this course is required for them to receive their certificates and move on with the program. I understand that there are also Continuing Education Units (ceu) available for this course, and we'd like to have these attributed to the students as well. Whatever documentation you have pertaining to this will be greatly appreciated, and can be faxed or emailed to me.

Thank you for your assistance with these matters. I know both students are looking forward to the class.

A hanging indent indents the body farther than the first line.

FIGURE 6-5   Between the Paragraph dialog box, the toolbar, the ruler, and the keyboard, you can set a wide assortment of indents.

positions of paragraph text on the left and right. Once you've spotted the tools, you can use them (by dragging them with your mouse) to adjust the indent of selected text.

Left first-line indent   Left indent   Right indent

Drag the box to adjust both the first line and body of a paragraph.

Although it isn't the fastest way to set an indent, using the Paragraph dialog box is the most accurate method. Choose Format | Paragraph to open the dialog box, then refer to the Indentation section to set left and right indents, as well as special indents, such as a first-line indent or a hanging indent.

Adjusting Line Spacing

By default, text in a document based on the Normal template is single-spaced. You can also set line spacing to double or to one-and-a-half line spacing using these methods:

■ *Use the keyboard.* Select your text and then press CTRL-2 to change to double spacing, CTRL-5 for one-and-a-half line spacing, or CTRL-1 for single spacing. You want to use the numbers above the alphabetical keyboard, not the ones found on the numeric keypad.

- *Click the Line Spacing button on the Formatting toolbar.* The button has a drop-down triangle and offers line-spacing options of 1, 1.5, 2, 2.5, and 3. If you click the More option, the Paragraph dialog box opens, and you can set spacing to any number of lines there.

- *Use the Paragraph dialog box.* Choose Format | Paragraph and, in the Line Spacing section of the dialog box, click the drop list and choose from six different spacing options. If you choose At Least, Exactly, or Multiple, you need to use the At box to the right to enter the measurement (in points) or number of lines (for Multiple).

Understanding Text-Flow Controls

Word wrap keeps your text flowing from line to line within paragraphs so that as soon as your text exceeds the width of the page within the margins, the text is forced onto the next line. Text flow between pages is also something that occurs naturally. As soon as your text exceeds the height of the page within the top and bottom margins, a page break is inserted automatically, and your text flows onto the next page—with a few minor exceptions:

- Word won't leave a single sentence from a paragraph back on the previous page if the rest of the paragraph is being forced onto the next page. It will force the entire paragraph to the new page rather than leave that sole sentence behind.

- If the opposite occurs—all but the last sentence of a paragraph fits on a page, but that last sentence is forced onto the next page—Word will keep the entire paragraph on the previous page rather than send a lone sentence on ahead.

The technical terms for these straggling sentences are *widows* and *orphans*. Widows are the single sentences sent ahead to the next page while the rest of the paragraph remains on the previous page. Orphans are the sentences that are left behind when the rest of the paragraph has flowed to the next page. This sort of flow control is also called *pagination*, and it is by this term that Word refers to text flow from page to page. To access all of Word's pagination controls, choose Format | Paragraph and click the Line and Page Breaks tab in the Paragraph dialog box (see Figure 6-6).

The other pagination options allow you to control the relationship between two or more contiguous paragraphs and to make sure a selected paragraph is always at the top of a page, no matter what happens in your document. The remaining three pagination options are described in the following list:

- **Keep Lines Together**   Selecting a paragraph and then turning on this option prevents the paragraph from ever being split up by a page break.

- **Keep with Next**   If it's important that a pair or series of paragraphs remain together and never be separated by a page break, select them, and then turn this option on. If keeping the reader's attention and preventing the physical break in concentration caused by turning the page or scrolling down in a document to read the next page are important, you'll like this option. The following illustration shows the small black boxes in the left margin that indicate two paragraphs (and the blank line between them) are set to be kept together.

> ¶
> • As· we· discussed· in· our· conversation
>   these· students,· as· they· are· working· t
>   having· attended· and· passed· this· cours
>   on· with· the· program.· I· understand· tha
>   for· this· course,· and· we'd· like· to· h
>   documentation· you· have· pertaining·
>   emailed· to· me.¶
> • ¶
> • Thank· you· for· your· assistance· with· th
>   the· class.¶
>   ¶

■ **Page Break Before**   Normally applied to headings, this pagination option forces a page break before a selected paragraph. The result of this action is that no matter how much text you add before the paragraph—which might push it to the middle or bottom of a page—Word will keep the paragraph at the top of a page, tying the paragraph to the page break preceding it.

TIP   *If you insert a page break (by pressing CTRL-ENTER), Word will ignore the pagination settings and allow a page break to occur between paragraphs or lines set to be kept together.*

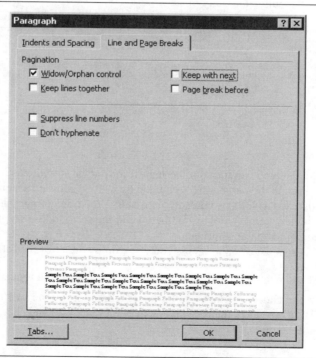

FIGURE 6-6   Turn Word's pagination options on or off to suit the needs of your document.

The remaining two options in the Line and Page Breaks tab pertain to text as it appears in lines rather than how text is handled across naturally occurring page breaks. Suppress Line Numbers will prevent selected lines from being numbered if you apply line numbers to a series of lines or an entire document. The Don't Hyphenate option will prevent a selected, longer word from being broken at the right margin and hyphenated.

Creating Lists

This book is full of lists—lists of features, bulleted to indicate that each paragraph represents a separate point in a series of related points, and numbered lists that indicate the order in which steps are to be performed.

When creating bulleted or numbered lists, it's important that you type the lists first and *then* apply the list formatting. Why? Because it saves a lot of work—about 50 percent of the labor. If you decide to bullet or number as you go, you'd have to turn the bulleting or numbering on, type the list, and then turn bulleting or numbering off before continuing to type in the document.

Numbering a List of Steps

By default, numbered lists are numbered with Arabic numbers (1, 2, 3, and so on), and each number is followed by a period. Numbered steps that exceed a single line wrap so that the subsequent lines left-align under the first word in the first line, and the ruler indent markers indicate the location of the bullet and body of step.

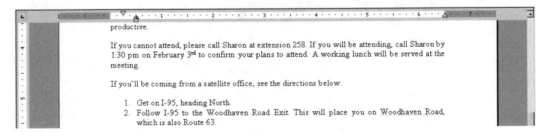

After you number a list, you can turn numbering off for one or more items in the list, or you can delete items in the list and the numbering within the list will be adjusted accordingly. You can also add items to the list, and as long as you add them before the final paragraph mark for the final item in the list, the new item(s) will be numbered and the surrounding numbered items will be renumbered to accommodate the addition.

To apply numbering to a list of paragraphs, you can employ either of the following methods:

- Select the text and click the Numbering button on the Formatting toolbar.

- Select the text and choose Format | Bullets and Numbering. In the resulting Bullets and Numbering dialog box, click the Numbered tab (see Figure 6-7) and choose the numbering style you want to apply.

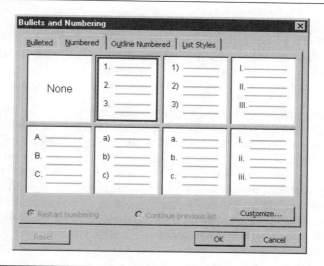

FIGURE 6-7   There are eight main numbering styles, including None.

Turning off numbering for a selected series of paragraphs is just as simple. You can either toggle the Numbering button while the list is selected or choose Format | Bullets and Numbering and on the Numbered tab choose the None style and click OK.

> **TIP**   *If you have more than one numbered list in your document, Word might need to make one a continuation of the other. If this need arises (say, a list of four steps following a list of five steps on a previous page starts with the number 6), select the incorrectly numbered list and open the Bullets and Numbering dialog box. Select the Numbered tab, click the Restart Numbering option, and then click OK. The list will be renumbered, starting with 1.*

Creating a List of Points

When you have a list of words, phrases, or paragraphs that don't need to be in any particular order, or that don't represent instructions or a prioritized list of terms or concepts, you want to use bullets for each item in the list. Again, you also want to select the list before applying the bullets so that Word knows which text to bullet. The default bullet is a large black dot to the left of each item in the list:

> **Topics for discussion:**
>
> - New products
> - Response to winter programs
> - Spring marketing plans
> - Budgetary concerns
>
> It is hoped that everyone who will be at the mee
> their questions, concerns, and any information th

You can apply bullets in one of two ways:

- Select the text and click the Bullets button on the Formatting toolbar.
- Select the text and choose Format | Bullets and Numbering. On the Bulleted tab (see Figure 6-8), choose the bullet style you want to apply by clicking in one of the seven boxes (other than None). Click OK to apply the selected bullets to your list.

To turn off bulleting for one or more (or all) of the items in a list, you can click the Bullets button, which will toggle off the bulleting, or choose Format | Bullets and Numbering. In the Bulleted box, click the None box and then click OK to remove the bulleting from selected text.

Don't like any of the seven bullet styles? You can apply virtually any character or picture to your list, turning the image into a bullet. In the Bullets and Numbering dialog box (on the Bulleted tab), click any one of the offered styles. Note that the Customize button becomes available. Click it. In the resulting Customize Bulleted List dialog box you can click the Font, Character, or Picture button to access various font libraries, symbols, or graphics to serve as your bullet. You can also set indents and the distance between text and bullets.

Working with Styles

A *style* is a collection of formats you can apply to individual characters and entire paragraphs to change the appearance of the text in several ways, such as changing the font, size, or position and making the text bold or italic. Any formatting you can apply to text can be made part of a style, and when that style is applied to the text, the associated formats are applied as well.

Why use styles? For two main reasons: speed and consistency. Imagine you have a document that's divided into chapters, each of which starts with a title. Imagine further that you have formatted

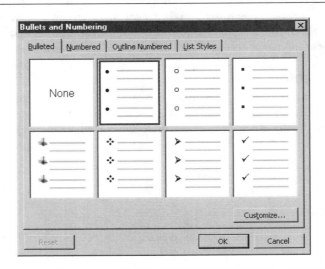

FIGURE 6-8   Eight options (including None) are offered for bulleting your selected list.

the first of those chapter titles in a very specific way. You've chosen a font, size, and color; changed the alignment of the title text; and added paragraph formatting to insert extra space after the titles. That's five different formats applied to the chapter titles. By creating a style for the chapter titles, you can apply all five of the formats with one action, which will take much less time than applying the formats to each title individually, and it will eliminate the possibility of one title looking different from another.

Of course, Word comes with a long list of styles built in, and the ones you'll see when you start a new, blank document are the styles that are part of the aforementioned Normal template. There are heading styles, styles for paragraph text, and styles for bulleted and numbered lists. You can apply these styles from the Style drop list (on the Formatting toolbar) by simply selecting the text the style should apply to and then clicking the desired style in the drop list. You can also display the Styles and Formatting task pane (see Figure 6-9) to view and apply the available styles from there.

6

If you're using other templates, you may find additional styles appearing in the Style drop list or on the Styles and Formatting task pane.

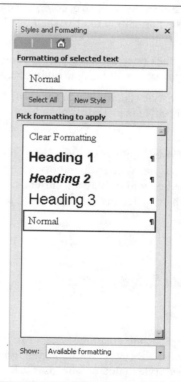

FIGURE 6-9   The Styles and Formatting task pane offers a list of styles and access to tools for creating new styles.

Creating Styles

You can easily build your own styles and make them available in specific documents or in all existing and future documents. There are two methods for creating new styles: by example, in which you format and select text to serve as a sample of the new style's formatting, and through the New Style button on the Styles and Formatting task pane. The latter approach provides a dialog box through which to create the style, and it allows you to apply the style to the Normal template, which will make the style available to all documents based on the Normal template. If you don't opt to make the style part of the template, the style will be available only in the document in which the style was created. Styles made "by example" are available only in the current document.

Creating Styles by Example

The fastest way to create a style is to base the new style on existing text, following these steps:

1. In the document where you want the new style to be available, select some text to which the style should be applied.

2. Format the text as desired. Select the font, size, color, alignment, and any other formats that are available through the Formatting toolbar, the Font dialog box, or the Paragraph dialog box.

3. With the text still selected, click once on the displayed style in the Style box on the Formatting toolbar. The style name will become highlighted.

4. Type the name for your new style (the name you type will replace the highlighted style name) and press ENTER. The style is instantly created and can be applied throughout your active document.

You can create as many styles-by-example as you need in a given document, and you can create multiple versions of a single style. When you modify a style (using the by-example method discussed earlier), the Style box will display the current style followed by a plus sign (+) and the changed format, as shown here. Click the style name and press ENTER to create the new version of the original style.

Changed style

Building a New Style

If you prefer a more methodical approach to creating styles, or if you want more control over the way a style will work, you can use the New Style button in the Styles and Formatting task pane. When you click the button, the New Style dialog box opens, as shown in Figure 6-10. You can name your style, choose the type of style (character, paragraph, table, or list), choose a style to base the new style on, and select what style will be applied to text in the next paragraph. All the

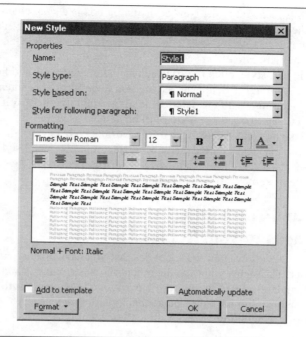

6

FIGURE 6-10   Create a new style from scratch, controlling every aspect of the character and paragraph formatting that the style will apply.

formatting tools you'll need for font, size, color, alignment, spacing, and indents are available in the dialog box.

If you want the style to be available beyond the active document, click the Add to Template check box. This will make the style a part of the Normal template, and any documents created based on that template (which includes all new, blank documents) will contain your style in the Style drop list. If you don't check this option, the style will be available only in the active document.

The Automatically Update option is a trickier one. If you turn this on, any time you make any formatting change to text that is formatted with a given style, all text formatted with that style will be changed to match whatever formatting change you've applied. For example, if you create a Title style that's Times New Roman, 20 points, blue text, bold, and centered, then later you left-align some text that's been formatted with the Title style, all the other Title-formatted text will become left-aligned. You can imagine the negative impact of such a sweeping change, so use this option with great care!

Editing and Deleting Styles

To edit any style—one that came installed with Word, one that you created by example, or one you built from scratch in the New Style dialog box—simply click the drop list on the style in the Styles and Formatting task pane and choose Modify from the resulting menu. The Modify Style dialog box opens, which is identical to the New Style dialog box. You can change any aspect of the style, including the name if you want to make a new style that's based on the one you're editing. Doing so will leave the selected style intact and create a new style. Once your changes are made, click OK to put them into effect.

If you want to get rid of a style, click the style's drop list in the Styles and Formatting task pane and choose Delete. A prompt will appear, asking you to confirm your intention to delete the style. Click Yes to go through with the deletion. It's important to note that if you delete a style that other styles are based on, those styles will be deleted as well.

There are some styles you can't delete, such as the Normal style because it's the basis of all Word's built-in styles. You also can't delete the built-in Heading 1, 2, and 3 styles, although any of them can be modified. If you do choose to modify these installed styles, be sure your changes will be appropriate for the vast majority of your documents.

Locking Styles and Formatting to Prevent Changes to Your Templates

A new feature of Office 2003 allows you to lock styles that you have created, preventing anyone from changing them later. This helps you keep documents consistent and is a great tool when you're using styles in templates. After all, the whole purpose of a template is to make it possible to create documents quickly and to have the documents look the *same*, every time.

To lock your formatting (including styles), follow these steps:

1. In the document that you want to control, display the Document Protection task pane.

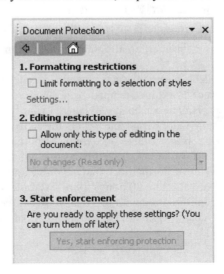

2. Use either or both of the first two formatting controls: Formatting Restrictions and Editing Restrictions.

3. If you're using the first control (Formatting Restrictions), click the Settings link. This opens the Formatting Restrictions dialog box, which displays a list of styles that are editable. If you don't want any of your styles changed, make sure all of them are checked in the list.

4. Click OK to return to the document.

If you'd like to start using the protections you've applied, click the Yes, Start Enforcing Protection button in the third section of the Document Protection task pane. Once you click that button, no one using the document will be able to make changes to the formatting—unless, of course, they turn off the controls using the same task pane you use to turn them on.

Customizing Page Layout

The third level of formatting for any document is page formatting. Placing it third in this chapter and in discussions of the types of formatting one can do in Word (character, paragraph, and page formatting) does not imply that page formatting should be done last or that it is of less importance than character and paragraph formatting. Rather, if you think of formatting as a building process, you're working from the inside out, starting at an atomic level with character formatting, then dealing with text in larger pieces through paragraph formatting, and culminating the formatting process with changes to the document as a whole.

Page formatting includes adjusting margins, changing the paper size, and turning the paper in another direction, also known as changing the *page orientation*. These changes can affect the flow of text, because changes in the margin will increase or decrease the amount of the paper text can be printed on. Changing the paper size can have a similar effect. For example, if you make your paper size larger, even if your margins don't change, the amount of the page you can print on will change. Page orientation can also affect the flow of text because the width and height of the paper will be changed, going from 8.5 inches wide by 11 inches tall to 11 inches wide by 8.5 inches tall.

Whenever you change page formatting, you have the opportunity to choose how much of the document is affected by your change. If you choose to apply the changes to anything less than the entire document, a section break will be inserted, essentially saying that the document is now broken into two sections—a section where one set of page formats are in use, and another where a different set of page formats are applied. This shouldn't affect your document building and editing process in any significant way because things such as page numbers and headers and footers will span section breaks and flow consistently throughout the document by default.

Setting New Page Margins

By default, your page margins are 1 inch on the top and bottom, and 1.25 inches on the left and right. This is fine for most business documents, but you might want to change them for certain documents or reset them for all documents by changing the default to some new set of margins.

To change the margins for the active document, choose File | Page Setup. In the resulting Page Setup dialog box (see Figure 6-11), click the Margins tab and view the Top, Bottom, Left,

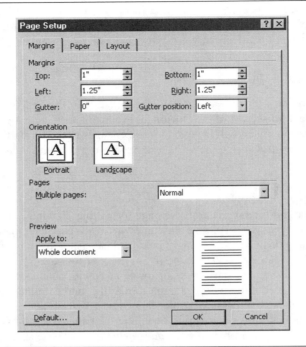

FIGURE 6-11   Change one or more of the four margins for your page.

and Right margin settings. You can increase and decrease them individually by typing new numbers in each box or by using the spinner triangle buttons on each of the margin boxes.

The gutter options apply to documents that will be bound. The gutter is the extra space you'll want to have in the margin so your text won't be cut off by the binding. By entering a gutter measurement (it's 0 inches by default), you add to the margin for that side of the page (left for odd pages, right for even pages). Use the Gutter Position setting to choose the side of the document that will be bound: Left for book-style binding or Top for easel-style binding.

Adjusting Page Orientation

The Margins tab is also the home of the Orientation setting, giving you a choice between Portrait or Landscape orientation for your paper. By default, all document pages are in Portrait mode, but you might need to apply Landscape orientation to documents that contain wide content—tables that need more columns than Portrait mode will accommodate—or if you want to print a sign or banner. When you change the Orientation setting, you'll notice that the current margins for the left and right are swapped with the margins for top and bottom. The preview also changes in the Page Setup dialog box to show the new orientation you've selected.

Changing Paper Size

You can also change the size of your paper using the Page Setup dialog box, through the Paper tab, as shown in Figure 6-12. You can click the Paper Size drop list to choose from a variety of preset paper sizes, or you can enter custom width and height measurements if you're using paper that isn't found on the list.

Also found in the Paper tab on the Page Setup dialog box is the ability to control which printer tray paper is drawn from for your first, and subsequent, document pages. Of course, if your printer has only one tray, this might be a moot point. If, on the other hand, your printer has two or more trays or has a tray and a manual feed slot, you can specify which tray to access for the first page of a document (typically to be printed on letterhead) and which tray contains the blank sheets for the rest of the document.

What About the Layout Tab?

I'm not ignoring the Layout tab, but for a basic document, you won't need to tinker with this tab. You can use the Layout tab to set up different headers and footers for the odd and even pages within your document (if you'll be printing on both sides of the paper) and to change the vertical alignment of text. This can be handy for a title or cover page, where you want the text to start in the vertical middle of the document, rather than at the top, which is the default. The Section Start option dictates where section breaks (changes in page layout for certain pages within a document) will occur.

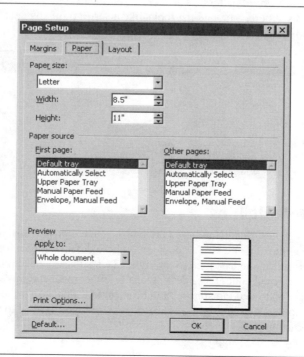

FIGURE 6-12 Letter is the default paper size for users in the United States, whereas A4 is the default for most of Europe.

You can also click the Line Numbers button if you're creating a legal document (such as a pleading) or for some other reason need each line of your document numbered.

Working with Tabs

Whenever I teach computer classes to people who have never used a typewriter (electric or manual), I find that I have to explain the use of TAB. On a typewriter, TAB is used to indent text and to create column lists, and it serves as the only way to adjust the horizontal position of text without using the SPACEBAR or changing the margins. The same is true when it comes to word processing. TAB on a computer keyboard is also used to indent the first line of a paragraph and to move text across the page, creating lists of evenly spaced columns. Although Word's Table features (discussed in Chapter 8) are more effective for setting up column lists and structuring document layout, there are some situations in which TAB is just what you need to control the horizontal placement of text quickly and easily.

Creating a Tabbed List

A tabbed list is a series of paragraphs, each containing two or more words or numbers separated by tab codes—the information added to a paragraph by pressing TAB. The information included in the tab code varies depending on the position and alignment of the tab. Each place where TAB is pressed is known as a *tab stop*. The term is also used to indicate a place where a custom tab has been set. As you can see here, a tabbed list looks like a series of neatly spaced columns, with each column's text falling under a tab stop.

Using Word's Default Tabs

When you press TAB in any new document based on the Normal template (I make this qualification in case you're working with someone else's document, where defaults might have been reset), you will see your cursor move one half inch to the right. Each subsequent TAB press moves you another half inch. The text typed under these default tabs is left aligned, and this alignment cannot be changed because there is no real tab stop set and no vehicle for changing the alignment of the text. If you need to set up tabs that are right-aligned or centered, you'll need to use the ruler or Tabs dialog box to set custom tabs.

It can be helpful to turn on Word's Show/Hide feature when creating a tabbed list. Just click the Show/Hide button on the Standard toolbar. As shown here, each tab code is represented by an arrow, and it's easy to see how many tabs were pressed between each item on each line in a tabbed list. Once your list looks and prints as it should, you can turn off Show/Hide.

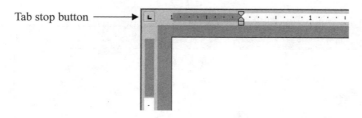

6

Setting Tabs from the Ruler

When you need tabs that don't fall neatly on each half-inch mark on the ruler, you can use custom tabs. Custom tabs can be set from the ruler or by using the Tabs dialog box, or a combination of both tools. The ruler is probably the easiest tool to use for building custom tabs, but it does have some limitations. You can't set up *leaders,* the characters that lead up to a tab, such as dots (periods), dashes, or underscores. You also can't set very specific, accurate measurements on the ruler, simply because of the way it's calibrated onscreen. If you need a tab stop at precisely 1.6 inches, the Tabs dialog box is your best bet. If you'd be just as happy with a tab set at approximately an inch and a half, then the ruler method is for you.

Of course, to use the ruler to set tabs, the ruler must be displayed. If it isn't, choose View | Ruler. Further, you might wish to switch to Print Layout view (View | Print Layout), and you might even want to reduce your Zoom setting to Page Width so you can see the entire width of the page.

Choosing Tab Alignment

The first step in setting tabs on the ruler is to choose the alignment for the first tab you're going to set. At the junction of the vertical and horizontal rulers (both rulers are visible when you're in Print Layout view) is a tab stop button:

Tab stop button ——————▶

To change to a different tab alignment, click the tab stop button. Each successive click changes the alignment, cycling through Left, Center, Right, Decimal, and Bar. You can also click to display additional first-line and body indent symbols (the triangles used to set indents, discussed earlier in this chapter). For our purposes here, however, we'll stick with the tab stop alignment options. They're represented by the following symbols:

| Left | Center | Right | Decimal | Bar |

Positioning Tab Stops

Once you've chosen a tab stop alignment, you need to place that stop on the ruler. To do so, simply click the ruler below the calibrations (clicking above them will have no effect). A vertical line helps you place your tab stop, especially if your document already has text in it.

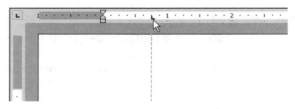

You can continue to place tab stops on the ruler, placing as many as you need. At each click the ruler will place a new tab stop at the currently selected alignment. If you want to place a stop that's aligned differently, go back to the tab stop alignment button and click it until the desired alignment is displayed, and then click the ruler to place the next stop.

Creating Bar Tabs

When it comes to word processing, the term *bar tab* doesn't refer to money you owe a bartender. Rather, it refers to tabs that create vertical lines between tabbed columns. Positioning bar tabs is done in much the same way as positioning tab stops. The only procedural difference is in your choosing where to place the bar tabs. As shown here, the bar tabs are placed between the regular tab stops, carefully centered between the regular tab stops so that the bars aren't any closer to one column than another.

Using the Tabs Dialog Box

The Tabs dialog box provides a complete set of tools for creating tabs at any position on the ruler (see Figure 6-13), aligned to the left, center, right, or a decimal point in your content. You can also set bar tabs, choose a leader character to lead up to tabbed content (thus the term *tab leader*), and reposition or delete existing tabs.

To open the Tabs dialog box, choose Format | Tabs. From within the Tabs dialog box, follow these steps for creating tab stops:

1. Click in the Tab Stop Position text box and type the ruler position (for example, type **1.75** for an inch and three quarters).

2. Choose the alignment you want for the tab. If you're creating a bar tab, you'll find this within the Alignment options, even though it isn't technically an alignment.

3. Select a leader. None is the default, but you can also choose dots, dashes, or underscores.

4. Click the Set button. The tab stop appears in the white box below the Tab Stop Position field.

5. Repeat steps 1 through 4 for as many tabs as you need to set.

6. When you've set up all the tab stops you need, click OK to close the dialog box and return to the document, with your new tab stops in place on the ruler.

Within the Tabs dialog box, you'll notice the Default Tab Stops field, which displays 0.5" by default. If you want to have default tabs at, say, every inch (instead of every half inch), click the

6

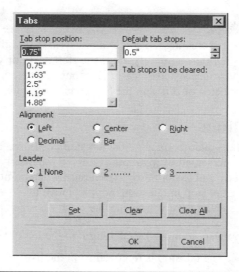

FIGURE 6-13   Set the ruler position and alignment and choose a leader, if needed, for your custom tabs.

spinner triangles until 1" appears in the box. You can increase or decrease the default as desired, and as soon as you click OK, the setting is in effect for the active document.

Setting Up Multiple Tabbed Lists in a Single Document

As with nearly all formatting, tabs are in effect from the point where the cursor was when they were created to the end of the document. For example, if you start a document with a series of paragraphs and then you want to set up some custom tabs two lines below the last of the paragraphs, the tabs will only be in effect from that point on in the document. You can type the tabbed list you want and then return to typing paragraph text, but the custom tab stops you created will remain on the ruler, and any TAB press will place your cursor under one of those custom stops.

This doesn't mean that you can set tabs only once in a document. You can set as many sets of tabs as you'd like, conceivably having a different set for every line of the document. To create a new set of tabs in a document that already has custom tabs set, position your cursor where the new tab settings should begin to take effect and then choose one of these methods for setting the new stops:

- Using the ruler, remove the existing tab stops and create new ones. To remove the existing stops, click and drag them down off the ruler. Don't worry about the text you typed under these stops elsewhere in the document. The only place that's affected by removing the stops is text at the current cursor position.

- Using the Tabs dialog box, click the Clear All button and see that the listed tab stops are removed from the box. Create new tab stops using the dialog box, or click OK and go back to the ruler to set up your new tabs.

Editing Tab Settings

The same techniques you used for creating tab stops can be used to edit them. If you want to move a tab stop, you can use the ruler to literally move the stop itself, or you can use the Tabs dialog box and edit the ruler position. When you edit tab stops, the text typed under those stops is only affected if the text is selected or if it's on the line containing your active (blinking) cursor.

Adjusting Tab Positions

You can use the ruler or the Tabs dialog box to adjust tab stop positions. To move them on the ruler, simply drag the stops (represented by symbols discussed previously) with your mouse. Be careful to keep the mouse steady and to not release the mouse when pointing above or below the ruler. To do so will remove the tab stop in question, not just move it.

If you prefer to use the Tabs dialog box, you can change a tab's position by following these steps:

1. Select the tab stop you want to move by clicking it in the list of tab stops.
2. Click the Clear button. The tab stop is removed from the list.
3. Click in the Tab Stop Position box and type the new position for this tab stop.
4. Choose an alignment and, if needed, a leader for the tab being moved.

5. Click the Set button.

6. Click OK. Even though you've removed the tab and re-created it in a new position, the text at the cursor or any selected text will simply be moved when the Tabs dialog box closes.

Changing Tab Stop Alignment

If you like the position of your tabs but need to change their alignment, you can use the ruler or the Tabs dialog box to make the change. As with any tab creation or change, be sure to select the text that you want to realign before tinkering with the ruler or opening the Tabs dialog box.

To adjust a tab alignment from the ruler, you'll need to remove the misaligned tab stop entirely and re-create it at the same location, following these steps:

1. Drag the misaligned tab stop off the ruler, pulling it down from the ruler with your mouse. The text typed under that tab will fall into place next to any text typed under adjacent tabs. Don't worry if your document looks messed up. You'll be putting things back together in the next step.

2. Click the tab stop alignment button until the desired alignment is displayed.

3. Click the ruler where the removed tab stop was and then replace the misaligned stop with a properly aligned one. The text that had been typed under the removed stop will now fall into line below the new stop, aligned as desired.

The Tabs dialog box makes it a bit easier to realign tab stops. Rather than removing the misaligned tab and re-creating it with the proper alignment, all you have to do is select the misaligned tab stop from the list and click a different Alignment option. Click Set to confirm the change and then click OK to put it into effect. The text typed under the realigned tab never moves or falls out of line; it is simply realigned when you click OK to close the dialog box.

6

Chapter 7

Working with Long Documents

How to...

■ Add page numbers to long documents

■ Use headers and footers to provide consistent page and file information throughout a document

■ Break a document into distinct sections

■ Build a table of contents

■ Turn boring paragraph text into a newsletter with columns

■ Search for and replace content throughout a long or complex document

A document that exceeds two pages is considered long, in that it may require page numbers, it could need additional information to appear at the top and/or bottom of all the pages, and if it's a very long document—ten pages or more—you may need to add a table of contents to help people find specific information within the document. Another problem that a longer document presents is editing—what if you need to find every occurrence of a particular name, date, or term? You could wade through manually, or you could ask Word to find all the occurrences and change them for you—to some other name, date, or term, or to eliminate them altogether.

These challenges presented by a longer document are all easily handled with Word's considerable array of page-numbering, section-handling, and indexing tools. In this chapter, you'll learn to take a long document and turn it into a professional-looking, easily navigated work of word processing art.

Inserting and Formatting Page Numbers

Any document that exceeds a single page needs page numbers. Even a two-page letter should have a "2" on the second page (never put a number on the first page of business or personal letters). Longer documents need numbering for reasons that go beyond tradition and good correspondence etiquette—imagine that you have a six- or seven-page document in your hand and drop it on the floor. When you gather up all the pages, how would you put them back in the right order (without reading the text and piecing it together that way, which would take a long time)? You'd hope that the pages were numbers so you could easily re-collage the stack.

Inserting page numbers in Word is very easy. Simply choose Insert | Page Numbers and use the Page Numbers dialog box to choose where the numbers will appear, and whether there should be a number on the first page.

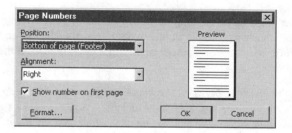

If you click the Format button in the Page Numbers dialog box, the Page Number Format dialog box opens, enabling you to customize the type of numbers (Arabic, Roman, or letters) used to number your pages, add chapter numbers (such as 1-5 for Chapter 1, page 5), or change your starting page number. For typical business and personal letters, you probably won't need any of these options, but for long documents, especially those that combine multiple documents into one or that contain several chapters or sections, these options can be invaluable.

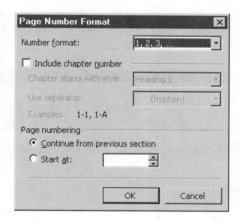

Working with Headers and Footers

The headers and footers on a document are any text that's repeated across the top or bottom (respectively) of all the pages in that document. Typical header and footer content includes page numbers, document names, copyright information, chapter titles, or the date or time that the document was created or last edited. Long documents don't have to have headers or footers (beyond the default use of them incurred by using the Insert | Page Numbers command), but they can come in handy if you have chapters or sections within your document, or if, for example, you want to make sure your name, as the author, appears on every page.

The header and footer are on a layer separate from the text of your document. Any document, whether or not page numbers are ever applied, has two layers—the Header and Footer layer and the Document layer. Figure 7-1 shows the active header in a document, and the Document layer is dimmed.

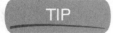

You can adjust the distance between the header or footer and the edge of the paper by using the Page Setup dialog box. Choose File | Page Setup and click the Layout tab. In the From Edge section, adjust the measurement (half an inch, by default) that determines the distance for header and/or footer placement.

Inserting Header and Footer Content

To view and edit the Header and Footer layer in your document, choose View | Header and Footer. This displays the Header and Footer toolbar and displays the first Header layer. By "first Header layer" I mean that if you have page numbers already inserted in the header (on the top of the

Toggle to view the Header or Footer layer.

The Header and Footer toolbar appears when these layers are active.

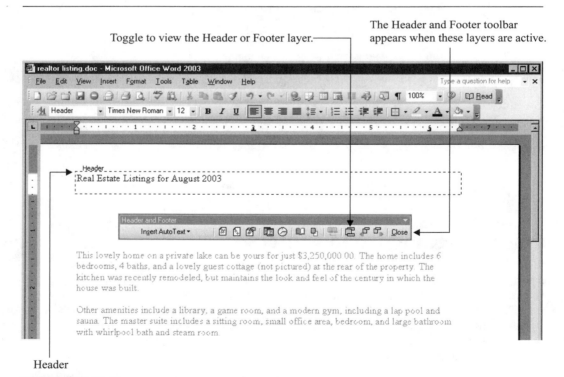

Header

FIGURE 7-1 Apply or edit header and footer content using the Header and Footer layer of your document.

page) and have opted to not include them on the first page, you'll see that you have a First Page header, followed by a regular Header section. Using the buttons on the Header and Footer toolbar (see Figure 7-1), you can move from header to header and switch to your footers.

Once the Header and Footer layer is displayed, you can begin typing in either the header or the footer—simply go to the one you want to work with first and click inside the dashed box. The font and size of text is determined by the template in use—if it's the Normal template, Times New Roman in 12 points is the default. Your text is automatically left-aligned, but you'll see on Word's ruler that there are two tabs set. This allows you to have content on the left, in the center, and on the right side of the header or footer section. If you use the tabs, you'll find that your text typed under the center tab is center-aligned, and the text typed under the right tab is right-aligned.

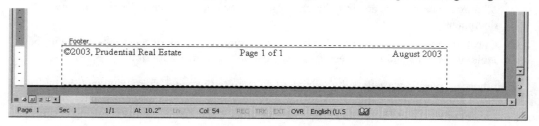

Once header and footer content is entered, you can edit it at any time by double-clicking it (while in the document layer) or by reselecting View | Header and Footer.

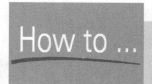

Use Section Breaks in a Long Document

Section breaks are like page breaks, except that they don't necessarily force text onto a new, following page. They are used primarily to "change the rules" in a document, allowing a variety of header or footer settings throughout (whereas there'd only be one set of headers and footers in an entire document) or to allow for multiple documents to be combined into one (and for each one to retain its own formatting, page numbers, and so on). To insert a section break, choose Insert | Break, and in the Section Break Types portion of the resulting dialog box, choose the type of break you need—Next Page (to insert a page break *and* a section break in one fell swoop), Continuous (to insert a break in the middle of a page without inserting a page break, too), Even Page (so that all even-numbered pages will be in one separate section), or Odd Page (so that all odd-numbered pages are in one separate section). Once there is a section break inserted, you'll see it reflected in the Header and Footer layer, as you'll have a separate header or footer for each section within the document.

Creating a Table of Contents

So you've got a document that's so long people need help navigating it or finding specific information within it. To help them, you can add a table of contents, created automatically by Word, to your document. It's a pretty simple process that requires just a few preparatory steps:

- Make sure you've applied the Heading 1 style to all the section headings you want to appear in your table of contents. For lower-level sections that you want to appear in the table of contents, use Heading 2 and Heading 3 styles and so on.

- Have your page numbers already inserted. This makes it possible to verify that the table of contents entries are accurate in terms of the page numbers that will print on your document.

- Check the wording of your section or chapter headings. Think of their appearance in the table of contents and try to keep them as clear and concise as possible.

With these preparations made, all you have to do is go to the page where you want the table of contents to appear (usually a blank page after the cover page and before the first page of the body of the document) and choose Insert | Reference | Index and Tables. In the resulting dialog box, click the Table of Contents tab (see Figure 7-2) and customize your table of contents using the options available.

TIP *Although the Heading 1, 2, and 3 styles are the default styles used to build table of contents entries, you can establish other styles and include them.*

Once your choices are made, click OK, and the table of contents appears before you, as shown in the following illustration, on the page where your cursor was blinking when you started the procedure. You can edit the table of contents as desired, or if you've made changes to your document and want to update the table of contents, select the entire table of contents and press F9—this "refresh" command causes the table of contents to be rebuilt, based on your original formatting, but with changes in content and page numbers to reflect the changes within your document.

TABLE of CONTENTS

Finding the Right Realtor for You 3
   Researching Area Realtors 4
   Should You Work with Multiple Realtors? 4
Finding Your Dream Home 6
   Listing Your Dream Home's Qualities 6
   Finding the Best MatchPurchasing a Home 6
   Purchasing a Home 7

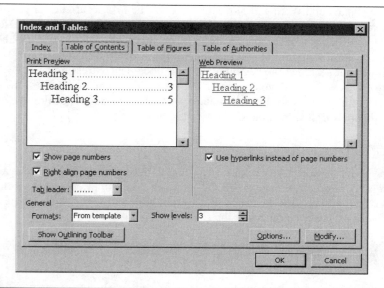

FIGURE 7-2 Make selections that will dictate the appearance of your table of contents.

Searching for and Replacing Document Content

Imagine this: Your company's 35-page employee manual contains several references to the Human Resources Director, Fred. That'd be great, except for the fact that Fred left three months ago, and now Julius is in charge of HR. What to do? Well, you could scroll through the document, page by page, looking for any text that mentions Fred directly, or you could let Word do the work for you.

Using Find to Move Through a Document

If all you want to do is go right to a particular reference in your document, choose Edit | Find to bring up the Find and Replace dialog box. In the Find What box on the Find tab, type what you're looking for:

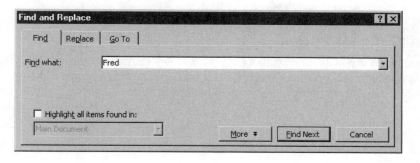

Click the Find Next button and Word will move the cursor to the first occurrence of your Find What entry. If the entry appears more than once in the document, subsequent clicks of the Find Next button will show each one in succession. If there are no more occurrences of the entry (or if there were none to begin with), Word will prompt you that it can't find what you're looking for.

It's best to start your search at the beginning of your document. (Pressing CTRL-HOME moves your cursor there.) This will enable you to search the entire document, and not risk missing any occurrences of the item you seek to find and replace. Note that you can reposition the cursor even if you have already opened the Find and Replace dialog box.

Replacing Text

If, after finding what you wanted, you want to replace it with something else, Word makes this easy and relatively foolproof, too. Instead of Edit | Find, choose Edit | Replace, or while in the Find and Replace dialog box, click the Replace tab. From within this tab, you can type an entry to be inserted instead of any occurrences of the found content.

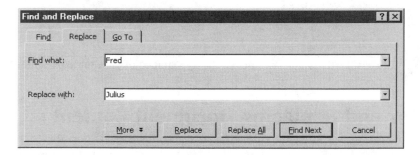

The Replace feature can be used in one of two ways: item by item, deciding to replace or skip each occurrence as you come to it (the Replace button), or globally, where you let Word change all occurrences without any further intervention or guidance from you (the Replace All button). When you use the Replace All feature, Word prompts you with the number of replacements it made, and you can click OK to accept them.

TIP *Replace All is a relatively drastic measure. If you realize after doing it that you shouldn't have, press CTRL-Z or choose Edit | Undo (or click the Undo button) to revert all replacements to their pre-Replace All status.*

Replacing Special Codes

The letter, number, and punctuation/symbol keys on your keyboard aren't the only ones that add content to your document. Every key you press adds something, either characters that you can read and print, or codes that tell Word how to position or format the content of your document—

Refine a Search

The Find and Replace dialog box gives you the ability to control the scope and results of your Find or Replace activities. Click the More button to access these options. You can use Match Case (which controls what's found or replaced, restricting it to occurrences that match the case of what you type in the Find What and/or Replace With boxes) or Find Whole Words Only, which will, for example, eliminate "Fred" being found if you're looking for "red." The Use Wildcards option allows you to type an asterisk (*) to represent the unknown. For example, if you want to find every date reference in your document that starts with January, type **January*** in the Find What box. The Sounds Like option will look for "Cathy" even if you typed "Kathy" in the Find What box, and Find All Word Forms will find run, running, and ran, no matter what form of the verb "run" you've entered for your Find What criteria.

7

you can see virtually all of them if you turn on Show/Hide (by clicking the Show/Hide button on the Standard toolbar). These codes (among others) can be found and replaced as needed, with just a step in addition to the ones you use to find and replace text:

1. With your cursor in the Find What box, click the More button. This button changes to a Less button, and the dialog box expands to offer more options, as shown in Figure 7-3.

2. When the dialog box expands to display more options, click the Special button. A list of document codes appears.

3. Click the special code(s) you want to search for. This could be two or more consecutive spaces, extra tabs, or perhaps two consecutive paragraph marks indicating excessive use of ENTER.

4. Click in the Replace With box and click the Special button again.

5. Select the special code the found codes should be replaced with.

6. Click Replace All to do a global replacement with no interaction from you, or use the Find Next and Replace buttons as needed to move through the document, replacing each found code with the established replacement code.

Working with Columns

If you've ever read a newspaper, you've seen columns—the text that flows vertically, in narrow strips. Placing text into columns gives you more layout options and makes it easier to integrate

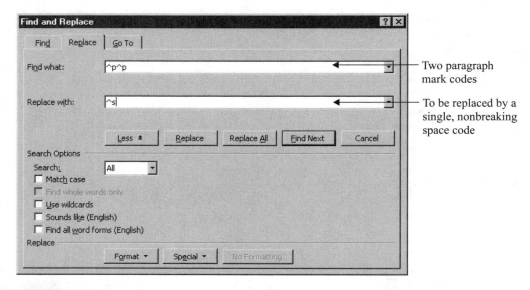

Two paragraph mark codes

To be replaced by a single, nonbreaking space code

FIGURE 7-3 Expand the capabilities of Find and Replace by viewing more options.

graphics into the document's design. As shown in Figure 7-4, text and graphics are much more interesting to look at when placed into columns.

Building a Newsletter Document

To build a newsletter or other columnar document, you have two choices: You can type the text first and then apply the column formatting to the existing text, or you can set up the columns and then type the text. Your preference between these two options depends on several factors:

- Proofreading text is easier if the text is not in columns, because the eye can flow across single paragraphs that span the width of the page.
- If you type the text first, you can more easily select which text will be turned into columns. For example, you can leave the headline or newsletter title out of the column formatting by selecting the text that comes after it before setting up the columns.
- If you set up columns before typing the text, you can see your text flow into the columns as you type. For some users, this is helpful.
- Columns appear as they'll print only if you're in Print Layout view. If you prefer to type and edit in Normal view, you won't be able to see column-formatted text in snaking columns as you type.

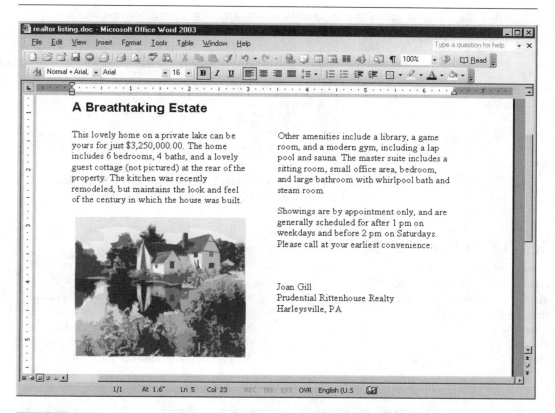

FIGURE 7-4   When text is placed in columns, the graphics, headlines, and body of articles are more interesting to look at.

Applying Columns to Existing Text

The process of converting existing text to columns is actually quite simple, and it's the same procedure—except for one step—that you'd employ to set up columns before typing. Here goes:

1. Select the text to be formatted in multiple columns. Be sure to select only the text and paragraph marks at the end of paragraphs that should be in columns, and not any that should not fall into columns.

2. Turn on columns using one of two methods outlined in the following steps.

3. Click the Columns button on the Standard toolbar and drag through the resulting palette to select the number of columns to apply. The palette and a three-column configuration being selected is shown here:

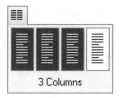

4. Choose Format | Columns. In the resulting dialog box (see Figure 7-5), click the box for the number of columns desired and then click OK. By default, the columns will be of equal width.

Setting Up Columns Before Typing

If you prefer to see your text flow into columns as you type it, you can set columns at the current cursor location, then type the text that will flow into those columns as you've set them. You can do this the same way you'd set up columns for existing text, except that instead of selecting text first, you'll just click to position your cursor where the columns should begin going into effect. Then use the Columns button on the Standard toolbar, or use the Format | Columns dialog box, to set up the number of columns you want, and exactly how they should look. Once that's done, you can start typing and watch your text fill up the first column, flow into the second, and so on.

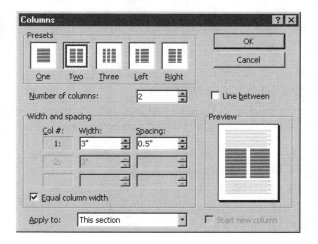

FIGURE 7-5   Use the Columns dialog box to take a more methodical approach.

Customizing Columns

When you use the Columns button on the Standard toolbar, you don't have much choice in how the columns are set up. You can choose how many columns you'll have, but their width will be equal and dictated by the width of your page within the left and right margins. If you've set up columns using this button, you aren't stuck with their settings. Similarly, if you used the Columns dialog box but simply chose the number of columns and clicked OK without making any adjustments, you don't have to live with their settings. You can change the number of columns, adjust column width, and even add a vertical line between columns. How? Try the following techniques.

To change the width of columns, use the ruler. With your cursor inside column-formatted text, look at the ruler and note the gray sections between the white sections. These gray portions represent the space between columns, as shown in Figure 7-6. You can resize these portions by dragging their ends with your mouse. When your mouse turns into a two-headed arrow on either end of the gray section, drag it and release it when you've achieved the desired column width. You might have to do this to both columns if you want to change both.

Using the ruler really requires adjustments be made "by eye." If you want to make changes more exact, use the Columns dialog box. Through this dialog box you can pick a new number of columns, set the width of all the columns to a new uniform width, or make an individual column different from the others. You can also add a vertical line between columns, which can be helpful on a crowded page if you think people's eyes might wander instead of following the vertical flow of the columns.

If you want to make adjustments to more than one column, select all the columns you want to deal with through the Columns dialog box. If your entire document is set to the same column

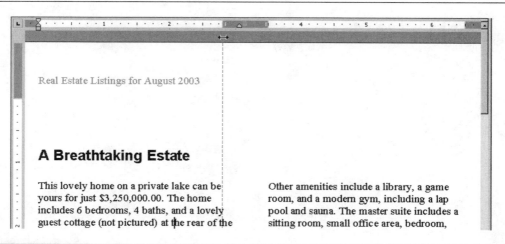

FIGURE 7-6   For quick column-width adjustments, use the ruler and your mouse.

format, press CTRL-A to select everything, or use your mouse to drag through the columns on one page to make sure your changes will apply only to a specific range of text.

Setting Up Multiple Column Configurations in One Document

There's no rule that says if you have two columns on page 1 that you must have two columns throughout your document. You can have a different number of columns on each page of your document, or even on a single page. The key to setting up columns throughout your document is to make it clear to Word where your various settings begin and end. Of course, this is much easier if your text is already typed, because having existing text makes it possible to select just the text you want in two columns (for example) and leave out the text that should stay as it is.

To indicate that a paragraph or series of paragraphs should be formatted with columns, select the text, then apply the column formatting. If the next paragraph or series of paragraphs should be in a single column (we think of that as *no* columns), you can leave that text as is. If the next text should be in three columns, select it and apply three columns to it. It's really that simple, and the only possible problem you'll run into is selecting the wrong text or applying a number of columns you didn't want.

TIP

Paragraph marks are important when you're selecting text to be placed in columns. Why? Because the paragraph mark at the end of a paragraph holds all the formatting information about the text that precedes it; therefore, if you want to place a paragraph in columns, you need to select the paragraph mark at the end of that text before you set up the columns or make changes to the existing column configuration. To be sure you're selecting the paragraph mark along with the text, click the Show/Hide button on the Standard toolbar.

Chapter 8

Structuring Documents with Tables

How to...

- Build a uniform table grid to house text and graphics
- Structure a document with table columns and rows
- Format a table with borders and shading
- Draw a free-form table
- Nest a table inside another table's cell

Here's a strong statement: Tables might be the most powerful feature in Word. Why? Because you can use them to do everything from building simple column lists to laying out an entire document, eliminating the need to set and maintain tabs and indents. From a basic letter that contains a multicolumn list to an elaborate document such as a resume or report, tables make setting up, building, and controlling the placement of text on a document easy, and they give you considerable power over the appearance of your document.

Structuring Documents and Text with Tables

Tables are containers for your text and graphics. Rather than typing in the open territory of a blank line, you can house your content in a table's *cells*. The size of the cell controls the flow of text (especially effective for paragraphs), and the placement of the cell controls the location of the table content. As shown in Figure 8-1, a table makes it possible to not only structure a document (a resume, in this case) but to place text and graphics side by side and to control the size and shape of paragraph text.

Word gives you two ways to build a table: You can create a uniform grid or a freeform cluster of cells, as shown in Figure 8-2. You can even create a single table cell to stand on its own using either method. I'll start by showing you how to create the uniform table, because it's the most commonly used table feature, and you'll find it applicable in most situations. Freeform tables will be covered later in the chapter.

Building a Uniform Grid

You can build a uniform grid in two ways—using Word's Insert Table tool on the toolbar or using the Insert Table dialog box. Which one should you use? The end result is the same, so it's your procedural preference that matters. The toolbar method is quick and easy, but the dialog box provides additional tools for customizing the way the table looks.

Inserting a Table from the Toolbar

The Insert Table button presents a grid that you drag through with your mouse. As shown in the following illustration, you drag across the grid to indicate the number of columns your table needs, and you drag down to set the number of rows.

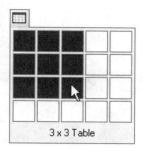

The grid expands as you drag, so you're not restricted to a 5×5 table. As soon as you release your mouse, the tool's grid disappears, and a table appears on your page, at the cursor.

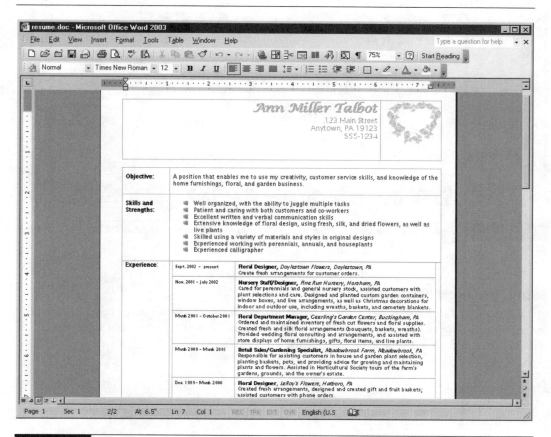

FIGURE 8-1   Build a grid that suits the needs for a selected portion of your document content.

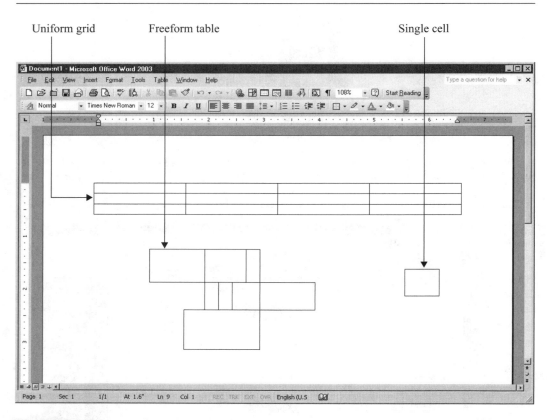

FIGURE 8-2   Word's table features enable you to make layout choices you never thought possible.

Using the Insert Table Dialog Box

To use the Insert Table dialog box, choose Table | Insert | Table. The dialog box, shown next, provides options for setting the number of columns and rows, as well as for controlling the relative size and position of those table elements.

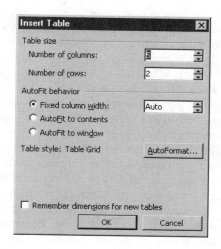

Your table options in this dialog box are as follows:

- ■ **Table Size**   Using the Number of Columns and Number of Rows boxes, enter the dimensions of your table.

- ■ **AutoFit Behavior**   You have three options here: Fixed Column Width, which you can set to Auto or any measurement you want; AutoFit to Contents, which will cause the table cells to grow and shrink to match the width and height of the text and graphics you place in them; and AutoFit to Window, which is especially useful for documents that will be viewed onscreen rather than on paper.

- ■ **Table Style**   The table style is Table Grid by default, and you can click the AutoFormat button to open a dialog box filled with preset table formats—border styles, shading colors, fonts, and table layouts.

- ■ **Remember Dimensions for New Tables**   Click this check box to save your current settings, making them the default for each new table created with the Insert Table dialog box.

Entering Table Content

Now that you have a table, it's time to put things in it, such as text and graphics, and fill its cells with the document content you need to control. To begin entering your table content, click inside the first cell you want to fill with content and begin typing or use the Insert menu's commands to add graphic elements.

8

If you're typing paragraph text, just keep typing in the desired cell, allowing the text to wrap within the confines of the cell. You can adjust the cell's width or height later, and you can even adjust the internal cell margins if you want to. To get started, just get the content into the cell and worry about formatting later. You can type in a table cell just as you would on the page, except the text will wrap to the table's walls, rather than to the page margins.

When you're ready to begin entering content in the next cell, press TAB to move to that cell. Continued pressing of TAB will move you from cell to cell, going left to right within the current row. When you get to the end of the current row, TAB will take you to the first cell in the next row. If you're in the last cell of the table, TAB does a very cool thing: It gives you a new row! It's that easy to add rows to your table. Just go to the last cell and press TAB. You'll learn more about using this technique and others for changing the dimensions of your table later in this chapter.

You can also click in a particular cell with your mouse, or while the cells are empty, you can use the arrow keys to move around—up, down, left, and right. Once the cells have content, the arrow keys will move among the text first, then only when you've gone to the beginning or end of the text will the arrow keys move you out of the current cell.

> **TIP** *Because TAB works differently when you're in a table, if you need to insert an actual tab (say, to indent the first line of a paragraph in a table cell), press CTRL-TAB.*

Navigating a Table

Yes, TAB is the primary tool for moving around in a table, but there are some other navigational techniques you might find handy:

- To move backward (right to left), press SHIFT-TAB.
- To move to the first cell in a row, press ALT-HOME.
- To move to the last cell in a row, press ALT-END.
- To move to the first cell in a column, press ALT-PAGE UP.
- To move to the last cell in a column, press ALT-PAGE DOWN.

Selecting Table Columns, Rows, and Cells

To enter table content, you need only be in the cell, you don't need to select it. If, on the other hand, you want to format a particular cell or specify a column, row, or contiguous group thereof, you'll need to select them. Try these techniques:

- Select a cell by pointing to the lower-left corner of the cell. Your mouse turns to a right-pointing arrow. Click your mouse, and the cell is selected.
- Select an entire column by hovering your mouse above the column, just outside the table. When you point just above the column's top cell wall, your mouse pointer turns to a black, down-pointing arrow. Click your mouse, and the entire column is selected.

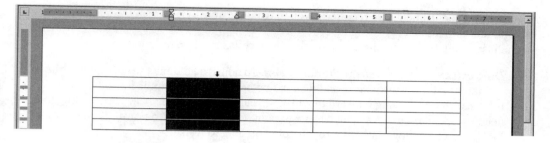

- Select an entire row by pointing to the left side of the first cell in the row (in the left margin). When your mouse turns to a right-pointing arrow, click, and the entire row is selected.

- To select a block of cells, click inside one of them and drag through the rest until the desired block is selected.

- To select multiple columns or rows, follow the instructions for selecting a single column or row. With your mouse in position for a single column or row selection, drag left or right to select more columns, or up or down to select more rows.

- To select the entire table, choose Table | Select | Table. Your cursor must be in the table in order for this command to work. You can use the Table | Select submenu to select columns and rows, too.

Formatting Tables

As I've said, you can apply any formatting you want to the text in your table. Use the Formatting toolbar and the Font and Paragraph dialog boxes to manipulate the appearance of your text, just as you would when formatting text that's not in a table. When it comes to formatting the table itself, however, there are some task-specific tools you should be aware of:

- **The Table menu**   This menu contains all the tools, commands, and submenus you need for changing the size, dimensions (number of columns and rows), and appearance of your table and its cells.

- **The Shading tool**   Found on the Formatting toolbar, use this tool to shade individual cells, entire rows or columns, or the whole table.

- **The Borders tool**   This tool is also found on the Formatting toolbar. By default, your table has a hairline black border. You can turn borders off and turn borders back on for specific cells.

- **The Borders and Shading dialog box**   Choose Format | Borders and Shading to open this dialog box. Assuming you're in the table when you do so, any changes you make within the dialog box (using its Shading and Borders tabs) will apply to the table.

Resizing Columns and Rows

Most tables need a little tweaking in terms of the width of columns or cells or the height of rows. You should do most of your sizing after entering or inserting the content, however, if only so that you can see what adjustments are required—you may not be able to tell when the table is empty or only partially filled.

To adjust your table's columns, rows, or individual cells, try these techniques:

■ *Drag column and row walls with your mouse.* To adjust a column's width, point to the column's wall (as shown here) and then drag when your mouse turns into a horizontal two-headed arrow. Drag outward to widen the cell or inward to narrow it. Adjusting row height works the same way, but be sure to point to the top or bottom wall of the row and look for a vertical two-headed arrow before you drag to resize.

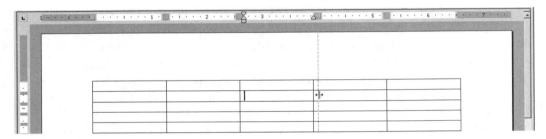

■ *Set a specific measurement through Table Properties.* Select the column or row that you want to resize (drag through the cells in that column or row) and choose Table | Table Properties. In the resulting dialog box, click the appropriate tab—Column or Row. These tabs allow you to set specific measurements by typing or using the spinner triangles.

Yes, there's a Cell tab in the Table Properties dialog box, but if you make adjustments to an individual cell, the entire row and/or column containing that cell will be adjusted as well—unless you have that cell selected. If your cursor is merely in the cell, then the column and/or row will be adjusted, too.

Restoring Table Defaults and Uniformity

If you've resized your columns and rows and wish you could go back to the uniform grid where all your cells were the same size and/or the columns and rows were the same width and height, you can undo your resizing actions by using the Undo button, or you can choose Table | AutoFit. From the AutoFit submenu, choose from the same automatic sizing options you saw in the Insert Table dialog box. You can make the table fit the contents or fit the page, or you can enter a fixed width for all the columns (rows, as I said, will size to fit the amount of text typed into them). You can also choose Distribute Columns Evenly or Distribute Rows Evenly, which will make all the columns or rows the same size across the entire table. The uniform size will be based on the cell with the most content. That cell will be sized to fit what's inside it, and the other cells will be resized to match it, even if they're empty.

Setting Cell Margins and Spacing

Cell margins can be set for your entire table, making it easier to create distance between cell content and the cell's walls—especially important if you have borders turned on. Choose Table |

Table Properties and click the Table tab. On that tab, click the Options button to set margins for all four sides of the selected cell(s), as shown in Figure 8-3. You can also set spacing between cells, which will create an interesting effect if you shade your cells or apply borders to them later.

NOTE   *Whatever selections you make in the Table tab of the Table Properties dialog box or through the Table Options dialog box will affect your entire table. Don't use these dialog boxes to make changes to individual cells. If you need to treat a section of a table differently in terms of margins or spacing, consider nesting a table inside another table's cell. The technique for this approach is discussed later in this chapter.*

Adding and Deleting Columns and Rows

Just as your table cell dimensions might not be right for your table content, the table dimensions might need some tweaking after you've built the table. The most common problem you'll run into is not having enough columns, normally due to forgetting one of the data categories you wanted to store in the table. You can choose from these methods to make the changes you need:

■ Select the column to the right of where you want a new column and click the Insert Column button on the Standard toolbar and a new column is added to the *left* of the selected column. (You'll notice that the Insert Table button changes to an Insert Column or Row button depending on what you have selected.) To insert a row with this method, select the row below where you want the new row, click the Insert Row button, and a new row is added *above*.

■ Click in a cell in the column to the right of where the new column should be or in the row below the spot where a new row is needed. Choose Table | Insert and then from the submenu choose Columns to the Left, Columns to the Right, Rows Above, or Rows Below.

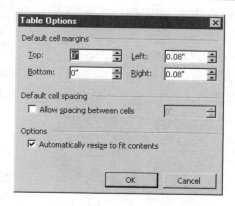

FIGURE 8-3   The Table Options dialog box allows you to set margins and spacing between table cells.

■ To insert multiple columns or rows, you can repeat either of these methods until the desired number of columns or rows is added, or you can select a number of existing columns or rows equal to the number of new ones you need before inserting the new columns or rows.

Deleting parts of your table is just as easy as adding columns and rows. To get rid of a column, just select it or be in any cell within that column. From the Table menu, choose Delete | Columns. You can do the same thing for rows. Click in any cell in the row, or select the entire row, and then choose Table | Delete | Rows. To delete multiple columns or rows, select them first and then issue the Table | Delete command.

When you delete individual cells, a dialog box opens, asking what you'd like to do with regard to any surrounding content. Your choices are to shift the cells up, down, left, and right. The choices offered will depend on the position of the cell being deleted and the table that will remain after the deletion. You can also choose to delete the entire row or column containing the cell, which you might decide to do if the shifting options will create chaos in your table.

While a column or row is selected, right-click any cell in the selected block and choose Insert Columns or Insert Rows from the resulting shortcut menu. You can also choose Delete Cells, which opens a dialog box of deletion options. You can delete an entire table by clicking in any cell of the table and choosing Table | Delete Table.

Splitting and Merging Cells

Another way to change your table's dimensions is to split and merge its cells. As the terms indicate, splitting a cell takes a single cell and breaks it into two or more cells, whereas merging cells takes two or more cells and joins them into a single cell.

When splitting cells, you can select a single cell by clicking inside it, or you can select an entire row or column. If you select an entire row or column, every cell in it will be split into the number of cells you specify. Merging cells can be performed only if two or more contiguous cells are selected before you issue the command. In fact, the Merge Cells command will be dimmed in the Table menu if you don't have two or more cells selected.

Splitting Cells to Increase Table Dimensions

Splitting cells is quite simple. Just click inside a single cell or select a row or column and then choose Table | Split Cells. The Split Cells dialog box opens, as shown here:

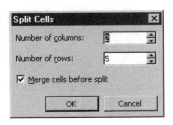

By default, the Merge Cells Before Split option is selected in this dialog box. This means that if you have more than one cell selected (a block, column, or row), the cells will be merged into one cell and then split into the number of columns and rows you specify. The following shows a three-column, two-row table with one of the rows split into three rows and four columns.

Merging Cells to Consolidate Table Structure

When you merge cells, you're combining them. To merge cells, simply select the cells you want to merge and then choose Table | Merge Cells. Much simpler than splitting, the merge process does one thing: It creates a single cell where there were multiple cells. This command is extremely handy when you need a title row for a table, as shown in the example here. This two-column table's first row was merged into one long cell, a perfect home for the text that identifies the table's purpose.

Table Title			

Applying Borders and Shading

When you use tables purely to provide a grid structure for your text or to lay out a document, you won't want to call attention to the table itself. You won't want to include borders, and you won't want any color in the table cells. If your document will be viewed onscreen, you can turn off the guidelines that indicate that a table's in use, too.

If, on the other hand, you want to take full advantage of the table's existence and apply borders and even shading to all or some of the table, you can easily do so, turning the table into a graphical element as well as a structural device. Figure 8-4 shows two tables—one with borders, and one without. In the table with borders and shading, these formatting elements have been placed strategically to enhance the document's usefulness and to make it more visually appealing.

Turning Borders On and Off

By default, all tables start out with a hairline border. You can turn this border off entirely, or you can turn it off for portions of the table, leaving it on in other portions. You can also apply different

Upcoming Courses

Course Name	Date and Time
Introduction to HTML	5/15/03, 6 pm – 9 pm
Photoshop for Web Designers	6/03/03, 9 am – 4 pm
Designing Websites with Dreamweaver	7/5/05 and 7/6/05, 9 am – 4 pm
Creating Flash Movies	8/15/03 & 8/16/03, 9 am – 4 pm

Course Evaluation

Your Name				
Date of Course				
Name of Course				
Instructor's Name				
Overall Rating (circle one):	Excellent	Good	Fair	Poor
Rate the Instructor (circle one):	Excellent	Good	Fair	Poor
Materials (circle one):	Excellent	Good	Fair	Poor
Facilities (circle one):	Excellent	Good	Fair	Poor
Would you take a course from this instructor again?	Yes	No	Maybe	

FIGURE 8-4   The content and nature of your table will dictate whether to use borders and shading.

border colors and thicknesses to some or all of your table. Word gives you several tools to control the placement and appearance of table borders:

- **The Border tool on the Formatting toolbar**   Click the drop-down triangle next to this button to see a palette of borders—top, bottom, left, right, inside, outside, and even diagonal.

- **The Borders and Shading dialog box**   This dialog box provides "one-stop shopping" for all the things you can do with, or to, a border.

Obviously, it's very easy to turn borders off or to turn them all on for the entire table. What might be a little more difficult the first time is applying or changing borders for a specific part of a table. The key is to turn off all the borders on the table and then go back and turn them on for selected cells. This enables you to consider each cell individually and choose the appropriate border. It can be very confusing to leave borders on and turn them off in certain areas, so try what might seem like a backward approach. You should find it to be quite effective.

TIP   *It can be hard to tell which borders are on and which are off if the table gridlines (nonprinting cell wall indicators) are on. To turn them off, choose Table | Hide Gridlines; however, if you find (as I do) that having the gridlines hidden makes it hard to locate and select individual cells or find cell walls in order to resize columns and rows with your mouse, you can turn them back on by choosing Table | Show Gridlines.*

Shading Table Cells

Shading draws attention to particular cells, or in the case of forms it can warn users away from filling in certain parts of the document. Shading adds color, or at least shades of gray (if you're printing in black and white), so it adds visual interest to a table. You can add shading to an individual cell or any selected block of cells, including individual columns and rows. To add shading to a table, choose either of the following methods:

- Click the Shading Color button on the Formatting toolbar and choose a color from the resulting palette. You can access additional colors and color-creation tools by clicking More Colors at the bottom of the palette.

- Choose Format | Borders and Shading and click the Shading tab. On this tab, you see the same palette as offered through the Shading Color tool, plus you can choose from a variety of patterns—from shades of gray to striped and dotted fills.

SHORTCUT *A quick way to select the whole table is to hover your mouse above and to the left of the first cell. When a block with a four-headed arrow appears, click that block, and the entire table is selected. Once the whole table is selected, any formatting you apply will apply to the entire table.*

8

Drawing a Freeform Table

What if you need the structure that a table offers, but you don't want the uniformity of a grid? You could manipulate a uniform table and end up with a table that's anything but uniform, but that can require a lot of effort—merging and splitting cells, adjusting the dimensions of individual cells, and so on. If you have a mental picture of the sort of table you need—perhaps one with one long cell across the top and several columns beneath it, each with a different number of cells in it—you can easily draw it using Word's freeform table tools, eliminating the need to change a uniform table into something else. The tool also makes it easy to create single-cell tables, useful when you need a block in which to confine text and/or graphics within your main document text. When you use Word's freeform table tools, you'll be starting with the table that you need!

The Draw Table button was on the Standard toolbar in Office XP, but in Office 2003 it has been relegated to the Tables and Borders toolbar, which you can display by right-clicking any toolbar or menu and choosing Tables and Borders from the shortcut menu. When you click the button, your mouse pointer turns to a pencil, and you can draw your table, cell by cell, adding rows and columns, even stray cells that aren't part of a column or row, all by dragging your mouse on the page.

Drawing Table Cells

To draw a table cell, simply click and drag to draw a rectangle where you want your first cell. A dashed line, forming a box, will follow your mouse as you draw. You can draw more cells attached to that first cell by dragging to draw more boxes alongside the first cell or by subdividing the first cell into smaller cells. Figure 8-5 shows a freeform table in progress.

Draw Table

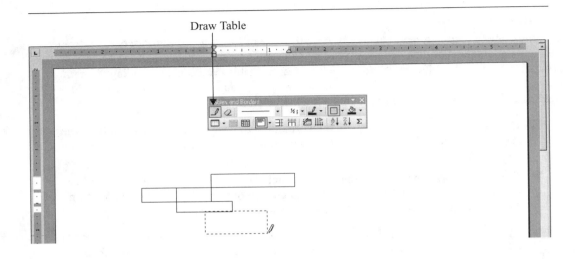

Draw the cells you want, in the configuration and size you need.

Erasing Table Cell Walls

Unlike the menu commands required to reduce the number of columns and rows in a uniform grid table, you can simply erase walls and cells within a freeform table by using the Eraser tool on the Tables and Borders toolbar. You can use it to literally scrub out existing cell walls. This can simulate a merge, removing a wall between two cells and turning them into one larger cell, or it can remove an entire row or column, depending on how many cell walls you erase.

Eraser

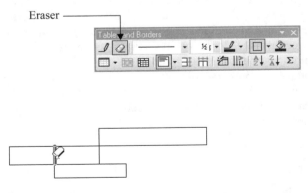

You can also use the Eraser to remove borders. Drag the Eraser along a wall, and the border will disappear. You might find in your clicking and dragging of the Eraser that you've removed a wall when you wanted to get rid of just its border, or that you've removed a border when you really wanted to get rid of a wall. Mastering the use of the Draw Table tool and its companion, the Eraser, is a matter of understanding table structure. You can't remove a wall if it's shared by other cells that have not yet been removed. Inner walls that simply break a single cell into multiple cells can be removed, but an outside wall of an otherwise intact cell cannot be erased. Using the Eraser on such a wall will remove only its border.

 *Be sure to turn the Eraser off after you're finished using it. If you don't click it again to toggle it off, you risk erasing large portions of your table as you attempt to select cells or drag through text with the intention of formatting it.*

Working with the Tables and Borders Toolbar

Once you've created a table, either through the Insert Table tool or dialog box, or by drawing a free-form table with the Draw Table tool, you can use the Tables and Borders toolbar to customize it. You can change the line-style and thickness of your table borders, apply colored fills, change column width and row heights, sort your table's content, and even perform calculations using numeric content within your table's cells.

Applying Border Styles

For quick application of border styles and thicknesses, you can use the Tables and Borders toolbar to draw new borders onto an existing table. On a document with a table, display the Tables and Borders toolbar and use the Line Style and Line Weight buttons to choose the type of line (thick, dashed, double) and how thick it will be. Once your selections are made, your mouse pointer turns into a pencil, and you can drag over the cell walls (or existing borders) to draw the new format directly onto the table. You can also change the color of borders by clicking the drop-down triangle next to the Border Color button.

When applying color to existing borders, simply select a color and with your pencil mouse pointer (it should appear as soon as you've made your color selection) click the cell walls you want to color. This can be somewhat time-consuming, especially if you want to apply the same color to all the borders in your table. It's a great approach for coloring some of your table's borders, but if you want to color the whole table, click once on the Border Color button (not on the drop-down triangle), and the Borders and Shading dialog box opens, with the Border tab in front.

To pick a single color for all your table's borders, click the Color option, choose a color from the palette, and then click OK. The color will be applied to the entire table—to every wall of every cell that currently has a border displayed.

Changing Table Size, Dimension, and Alignment

The Tables and Borders toolbar offers tools for changing the number of cells, columns, and rows in your table, as well as the ability to alter the width of columns and rows and change the way text or graphic content is aligned within them. These tools are detailed in Table 8-1.

The Tables and Borders toolbar includes a button that looks like an A on its side; this is the Change Text Direction button. If your column headings (or row labels) are too wide for the width

8

Button	Function
	Select two or more contiguous cells in the table and click this button to merge the cells.
	Select a single cell and click this button to break it into two or more cells. You can also select a block of cells and use the resulting dialog box to choose how many rows and columns to create from your selected table cell(s).
	This button makes all your columns the same width. No need to select the columns—just put your cursor anywhere in the table.
	If you need all your rows to be the same height, place your cursor anywhere in the table and click this button. As with creating uniform columns, the standard size will be based on the cell with the most content.
	Click this button's drop-down triangle to see a palette of horizontal alignment options. There are nine options in all, from Top (vertical) Left (horizontal) to Bottom Right.

TABLE 8-1   Tables and Border Toolbar—Tools for Altering Table Size, Dimension, and Alignment

of the columns (or the height of the rows) that you want in the table, you can turn the text so that it reads straight up and down instead of side to side. Click the button to cycle through the options—vertical text facing left, vertical text facing right, and then back to horizontal text.

Sorting Table Content

For tables that house data—such as lists of names, products, classes, recipes, and books—you might have the need to put the items in order. Although this need might drive you to store your list in an application such as Excel or Access, if you don't do much more than read the list, there isn't any need to do so. Further, if you do keep your list in Excel or Access and you paste it into a Word document, it will appear as a table, and you'll have to deal with it in that form anyway. Here's an example of a typical list found in a Word document, currently not in any useful order.

First Name	Last Name	Department	Extension
Jean	Bowling	Marketing	245
Nan	Stickney	Sales	320
William	Fuller	Operations	410
Samantha	Frankenfield	Sales	350
Gary	Thomas	Marketing	262
Mark	Chambers	Operations	430
Shane	Weller	Sales	330
Nick	Fabiano	Marketing	275
Kaitlin	Patrick	Operations	440

It's assumed that your list will contain a row (preferably the top row) that labels each column. In the table shown here, the top row identifies each column (First Name, Last Name, Department, and Extension). These column labels are seen as *fields* in the table so that the rows can be sorted as though they're data. Word will see this top row as a *header row*, and only the rows beneath it will be sorted.

To sort your table, simply click to place your cursor in any cell in the column you want to sort by. In our example table, to sort by Department, click in any cell in the Department column. Next, using the Tables and Borders toolbar, click either the Sort Ascending (A-to-Z) or Sort Descending (Z-to-A) button. You can also choose Table | Sort and use the resulting dialog box to choose which column to sort, potentially sorting by up to three columns, as shown in Figure 8-6.

TIP *When sorting by more than one column, start with the one that has the greatest number of duplicate entries in it, such as State in a name and address list, or Department in an employee list. The last column you sort by should be the one with the least duplicates, such as Last Name. The first sort puts the list in groups, and then the subsequent columns place those groups in an order that makes sense for you.*

Here are some troubleshooting tips for building and sorting a list inside a Word table:

■ Don't leave any blank rows in your table. They'll be sorted along with the rows containing data and will appear before the data-bearing rows if you perform an ascending sort.

■ Don't worry about individual cells that are left empty—they're not a problem, and it's not uncommon to have less data for one record than another.

8

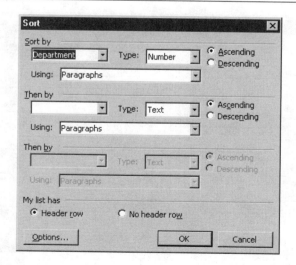

FIGURE 8-6 The Sort dialog box gives you the ability to sort by one, two, or three columns in your table.

■ Word will sort by the first letter or number in the cell. For example, if you're sorting by address, "123 Main Street" will come before "246 Apple Lane," even though Apple comes before Main when listed alphabetically. The sort will be done on the numbers because they come first.

■ Break your data into as many columns as you can to give yourself more sorting possibilities. In a name and address list, for example, don't just have a Name field with each person's full name. Rather, have two fields, First Name and Last Name, and perhaps a field titled Middle Initial.

Nesting Tables

A nested table is simply a table inside another table. To create one, simply click inside any cell in an existing table and use the same techniques you used for building the first table. Choose Insert | Table or click the Insert Table button and choose the dimensions (number of columns and rows) for the nested table. The new table will live inside another table's cell, but you can format it separately, sort data within it, even perform calculations on numbers inside the nested table, all without any effect on the surrounding table or its content. Figure 8-7 shows a nested table that provides a way to potentially break down the data in the main table.

Course Evaluation				
Your Name				
Date of Course				
Name of Course				
Instructor's Name				
Overall Rating (circle one):	Excellent	Good	Fair	Poor
Rate the Instructor (circle one):	Excellent	Good	Fair	Poor
Materials (circle one):	Excellent	Good	Fair	Poor
Facilities (circle one):	Excellent	Good	Fair	Poor
Would you take a course from this instructor again?	Yes	No	Maybe	
How can we make this course better?				

Make it longer	Agree	Disagree	Don't Know
Offer it in both day and evening sessions	Agree	Disagree	Don't Know
Reduce the number of students per class	Agree	Disagree	Don't Know
Add more exercises	Agree	Disagree	Don't Know
Your other comments:			

FIGURE 8-7 By nesting a table, you're able to deal with its contents separately from the main table's data.

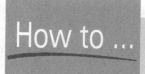

Sum a Row or Column of Numbers in a Table

Word also allows you to "do the math" when it comes to numeric content in your tables. You can perform any sort of calculation you need, but the simplest (and most commonly performed) is an AutoSum. An AutoSum quickly sums (adds) a column or row of numbers. To perform an AutoSum, click in the cell that should contain your total, the result of the AutoSum. Then, click the AutoSum button (the last button on the bottom row of buttons in the Tables and Borders toolbar). The total of the adjoining cells (the numbers in the cells above if you're totaling a column, or the numbers to the left if you're totaling a row) appears in the cell. If you later change any of the numbers in the cells that are included in the total, simply click once on the total and press F9 to update it. You can also reclick the AutoSum button on the Tables and Borders toolbar to achieve the same goal.

Or another quick method is to paste a section of an Excel worksheet into your Word document. This creates a table and builds in Excel's formula functionality all in one fell swoop. Just select the block of cells in Excel, press CTRL-C (Copy), switch to Word, and then press CTRL-V (Paste). Voilà!

8

Chapter 9

Creating Form Letters, Envelopes, and Labels with Mail Merge

How to...

- Merge data with documents
- Create a form letter for mass mailings
- Print labels and envelopes from a database of addresses
- Sort and query a database to refine a mail merge

The term *mail merge* really says a lot about itself. When you perform a mail merge with Word, you're merging (combining) data and a document for the purpose of a mailing. The document can be a letter, a label, or an envelope, or you can use the same database to create all three items—imagine a sales letter going to potential customers, where you insert the recipients' name, address, and perhaps even the name of the product you expect them to purchase. After merging the form letter with your database of potential customers, you need to mail those letters, so you merge again to create envelopes for the letters, re-grabbing the name and address information from the database. If you prefer to place labels on envelopes, that's doable, too—instead of merging the database with envelopes, you can merge it with a table of labels, printing one label for each record in the database. Word's mail merge tools allow you to customize your merge so that you only get the records you want, and so that the records you do get are in the order you need them. It's a powerful set of tools, and in this chapter, you'll learn to harness them.

Starting the Mail Merge Process

Of course, before you invoke Word's mail merge tools, you need a plan, or an idea of what you want to do. You should know what data you want to use for your merge, what kind of document you want to merge with that data, and how you'll use the merged documents. If you're going to create a form letter, you should know what the letter will say, or already have the body of the letter typed. You'll be adding content to any existing letter later, inserting places for data to be added to the letter's text—names, addresses, and so on.

Once you have those basics covered, you can start the mail merge process. Choose Tools | Letters and Mailings | Mail Merge. The Mail Merge task pane appears. Through this task pane you can perform the mail merge, step by step, telling Word what you want to do and how you intend to do it. In the first pane that appears, you select the type of document you are working on: Letters, E-mail messages, Envelopes, Labels, or Directory.

Creating a Form Letter

For our example, we're going to create a form letter, so choose Letters in the first pane of the Mail Merge panel. After you've made your selection, click the Next: Starting Document link at the bottom of the task pane—this moves you to the next step in the process, which is selecting the starting document. Choose the Use the Current Document option to begin building the form letter on the new, blank document that's already open, or choose Start from a Template if you have one ready.

If you already typed your form letter earlier and just need to convert it to a form letter with places in it for the data to go, choose Start from an Existing Document. (In these latter two scenarios, you'll be presented with a dialog box from which you can select that document/template.) When you click Next: Select Recipients at the bottom of the task pane, you'll move to the next step in the process.

At this point, you have to tell Word where your database is—is it an existing list (stored in Excel or Access in tabular form), or do you want to use your Outlook contacts database? In the absence of either of those options, you can choose to create a new list for this particular mailing, but that will require a lot of data entry on your part—at least one record for every letter you need. Assuming you have a list ready to go, choose Use an Existing List (this is the default).

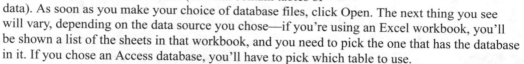

Now you need to tell Word where the list is. Click the Browse link and the Select Data Source dialog box opens, through which you can navigate to the drive and folder that contains your database. The dialog box is set to search for all known database formats—including Access tables, Excel workbooks, and Word documents (that can contain tables of data). As soon as you make your choice of database files, click Open. The next thing you see will vary, depending on the data source you chose—if you're using an Excel workbook, you'll be shown a list of the sheets in that workbook, and you need to pick the one that has the database in it. If you chose an Access database, you'll have to pick which table to use.

Once you've specified the worksheet or table that contains your data, that list, in tabular form, is presented. You can choose which records will be merged with your letter (all of them are selected by default), and you can sort the records by clicking the field names at the top of the columns (see Figure 9-1).

9

> **TIP** *If you click the drop list on a particular field, you can choose Advanced to filter for particular records, using tools similar to the filtering tools in Excel and Access.*

Now you're ready to build your form letter—to type it from scratch if you chose to use the current document back in the second step of the mail merge process, or to add *merge fields* to an existing letter. If you're typing from scratch, you can leave spots for the merge fields (instructions for Word to tell it where to insert the data) and just type the letter itself. Click the Next: Write Your Letter link at the bottom of the task pane, and after you've written the body of your letter, use the links—Address Book, Greeting Line, Electronic Postage, Postal Bar Code, or More Items— to access the list of field names from your chosen database, each of which becomes a potential merge field to be added to the letter.

> **TIP** *Don't forget to type punctuation and spaces as needed before and after merge fields (for example, using a space between the First Name and Last Name fields) so that the letter's text flows normally.*

Click the field name button to sort by that field in ascending order.

Click the drop list to choose to see specific records.

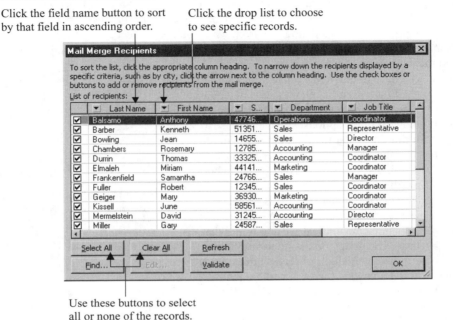

Use these buttons to select all or none of the records.

FIGURE 9-1 Got the right data? If so, and if you want to use all the records, click OK to proceed.

With the body of your letter typed, position your cursor at any spot where you want Word to insert data—it can be after the word "Dear" in the salutation, or below the date, where you may want to insert the recipient's name and address. Depending on your database and the purpose of the letter, you may have other data that can be inserted, as shown in Figure 9-2.

When you're finished inserting merge fields, click the Close button in the Insert Merge Fields dialog box. In the task pane, click the Next: Preview Your Letters link to preview the selected records from your database merged with the letter you just created. As shown in Figure 9-3, you can scroll through the letters (there will be one for every record you selected), and you get another chance to eliminate people from your mailing—click the Exclude This Recipient button to get rid of a particular merged letter.

When you like what you see, click Next: Complete the Merge. This performs the actual merge, and you can choose to have the letters go directly to the printer (click the Print link) or you can create a new document that's made up of all the letters you created by merging your database with the form letter (click the Edit Individual Letters link). If you choose the latter option, you can edit particular letters, customizing one or more for specific recipients, make changes to all the letters (using Find and Replace, for example, to replace something in the body of the form letter), or just to give yourself another chance to proof the letters before potentially wasting several sheets of letterhead if it turns out you missed a typo.

The merge field appears where your cursor was when you chose a field.

Notice the space between names is included here.

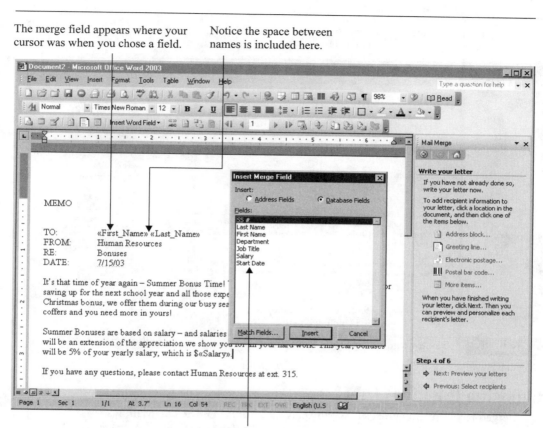

Pick a field from this box and click the Insert button.

FIGURE 9-2 Your database fields are now insertable merge fields that show Word where to insert data into your letter.

Creating Mailing Labels

Now that you've created your letter, you may want to mail or otherwise deliver it. The internal memo created in the previous section of this chapter would be delivered to employees, probably in individual envelopes, for security—after all, salary information is included in the memo. Such delivery—whether executed internally or via postal mail—requires either envelopes with names and addresses printed on them, or labels to be applied to blank envelopes. In this section, we'll create labels—a process very similar to merging names and addresses with envelopes, but more effectively shown within the context of this book's illustrations.

The First Name and Last Name fields
brought the employee name in here.

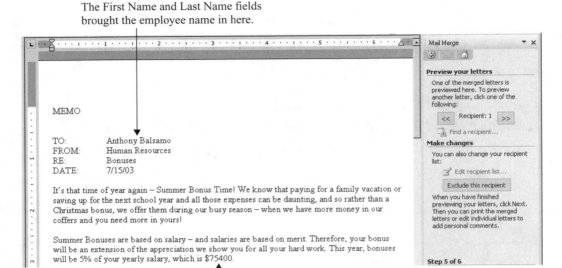

A reference to the employee's
salary is included here.

FIGURE 9-3 Preview your letters, one for each record you chose to include from the selected database.

Choosing the Right Label

The merged label-creation process starts by choosing Tools | Letters and Mailings | Mail Merge. In the first Mail Merge task pane, select Labels from the Select Document Type list, and then click the Next: Starting Document link at the bottom of the pane. This makes a new pane available, including a Label Options link—click this to choose the labels you'll be printing on. You want to make this selection now so that the labels you go on to build are set up for the dimensions of the specific labels you're intending to use. The Label Options dialog box, shown in Figure 9-4, gives you a choice of printers (dot matrix or laser/inkjet), a choice of label manufacturers (Avery is the default), and a list of the selected manufacturers' label product numbers. For the purposes of this demonstration, I'll be using Avery's 5160 label, a 1"×2.63" label.

TIP *If the label you have isn't on any manufacturer's list, create a new label by clicking the New Label button in the Label Options dialog box. You can enter the dimensions of the labels, how many there are per sheet, and the margins around and between the labels. You can name the custom label for future use, and you will be able to find it later in the manufacturer list by choosing Custom.*

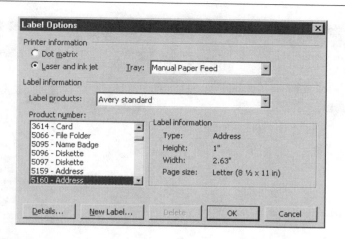

FIGURE 9-4   Select your label manufacturer and product number, and click OK to set up a sheet of blank labels awaiting your merge instructions.

Selecting Your Data Source

Your sheet of blank labels can now be fleshed out by clicking the Next: Select Recipients link at the bottom of the task pane. As with form letters, you can use an existing list (an Excel worksheet, Access table, or other database) or create a new list from scratch (Type a New List), or you can use your Outlook contacts as the source of your recipients' list. For this demonstration, as we've already seen the process of using an Excel worksheet as our data source, we'll use my Outlook address book, clicking the Select from Outlook Contacts option in the Select Recipients section of the task pane (see Figure 9-5).

Click the Choose Contacts Folder link (which appears after you've designated Outlook as your data source) and choose a profile name in the resulting Choose Profile dialog box. The profile is the name by which Outlook stores your contacts and other information—you can have multiple profiles, and therefore multiple sets of contacts.

After you choose a profile and click OK, the Select Contact List dialog box opens, showing you the contact lists associated with that profile. Choose the one you want to use and click OK—the Mail Merge Recipients dialog box appears next, showing you all the people and organizations in your Outlook contacts list. All the recipients are selected, which you can accept, or you can go through the list and uncheck those for which you don't want to print a label (as shown in Figure 9-6).

Merging Data with Your Labels

Assuming you want all the recipients in the list to get a label, click OK to accept them. Then click Next: Arrange Your Labels from the bottom of the task pane. As we did with the form letter, it's now time to insert the merge fields that tell Word which pieces of information from the selected data source (your Outlook contacts, in this case) to include in the label, and in which order they should appear. Because we're printing an address label, you can click the Address Block link,

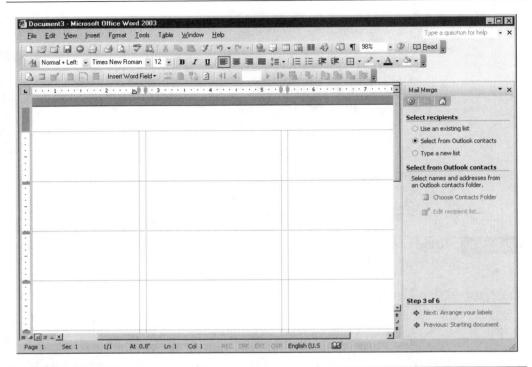

FIGURE 9-5 Your blank labels will cease to be blank after you've chosen a data source in the task pane and told Word which pieces of data to place on the labels.

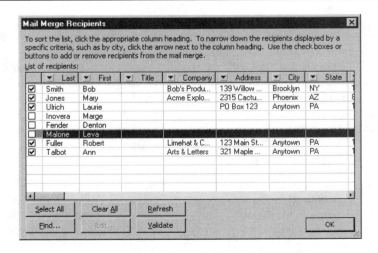

FIGURE 9-6 Choose who will and won't get a label from your list of potential recipients.

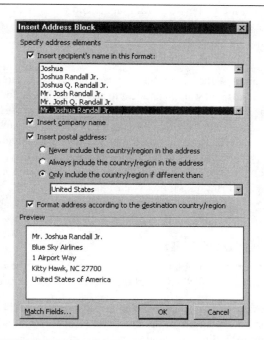

FIGURE 9-7   Assuming you've built your contacts list to include full names and complete addresses, you can use the Address Block method of fleshing out your labels.

which shows you a default address setup, as shown in Figure 9-7. You can also click More Items to open the Insert Merge Field dialog box, from which you can select only the fields you want to use.

After inserting the <<Address Block>> code into the first label, click the Update All Labels button at the foot of the task pane—this places the <<Address Block>> code in each of your labels. Click the Next: Preview Your Labels link to see how your contact list records look:

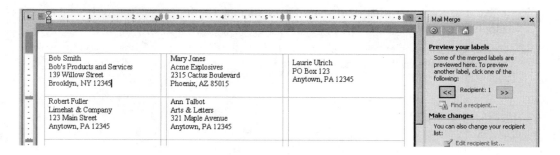

Then to perform the actual merge between your labels and your contact list click the Next: Complete the Merge link.

Printing Labels

When you click the Next: Complete the Merge link, the task pane changes to offer you two choices: Print and Edit Individual Labels. If you want to add text to any of the labels, format the labels (maybe choose a different font for the whole sheet of labels), or do anything else to the labels before printing, choose Edit Individual Labels. If they look fine as they are and you're ready to print them, click the Print link. This opens the Merge to Printer dialog box, where you can choose to print all records, the current record (whichever cell in the table of labels contains your cursor), or a range of records using the From and To boxes. Choosing All is your best option in most cases, so leave that selected and click OK. The Print dialog box opens, and you can then choose a printer and how many copies of the labels to print.

Mail Merge Troubleshooting

A lot of variables can contribute to a problematic mail merge. Most of them can be alleviated by doing some research and planning before you start the literal mail merge process:

■ Make sure you know where your database is—which Excel workbook, Access database, or other source—and make a note of the drive and folder on which it's stored. This will save you scrambling to find it when you get to the point in the mail merge process where you have to tell Word where your list of recipients is.

■ Check your database before you use it. If, for example, you intend to use an Outlook contacts list, make sure the vast majority of your records are not just names and email addresses or names and phone numbers. Many people build a contacts list through receiving emails and don't have actual mailing addresses for everyone on their list. If you need to use the contacts list and find that full addresses are not included for many of the records, now is the time to go get that information and flesh out the records so they can be used for labels or envelopes.

■ Make sure you know what label you'll be printing on. Don't just guess—go check the supply cabinet now.

■ If you're printing on envelopes, check your printer settings ahead of time so you know how to insert the envelopes and how the feeder on your printer works, if there is one.

Part III

Crunching Numbers and Keeping Lists with Excel

Chapter 10

Building and Formatting Worksheets

How to...

- Start a new workbook
- Work with Excel worksheets
- Enter text and numbers
- Adjust column widths and row heights
- Apply fonts and font sizes to text and numbers
- Use borders and shading to add visual interest
- Save workbook files

Excel is Office's application for storing and manipulating numbers and data in spreadsheets. If you think you don't know anything about spreadsheets, you're probably wrong. Ever created a table in Word? Ever written a list? Ever balanced your checkbook? Well, then you've already worked with a rudimentary spreadsheet. Excel calls them *worksheets* and stores them in groups called *workbooks*, but other than that, the concept is the same: rows and columns of numbers and text, stored in a logical fashion. Excel adds the ability to perform calculations and to sort and filter the data automatically, and you'll learn all these things in this and the subsequent chapters.

Touring the Excel Interface

The Excel application window looks a lot like the Word application window. You'll see a lot of the same toolbars and buttons, and the menu bar is virtually identical. There's a task pane on the right side of the window (the first time you open Excel, anyway) and a status bar across the bottom of the window. This, however, is where the similarity ends in terms of onscreen features. Because Excel is a spreadsheet program, the workbook window (Excel's equivalent of the Word document window) is a set of three worksheets, each containing 256 columns and 65,536 rows, which means each sheet has 16,777,216 cells. As shown in Figure 10-1, depending on your monitor size and resolution (we're using 1024×768 resolution), you may only be able to see a handful of columns and rows at once. You'll probably never use all 16,777,216 cells, but they're there if you need them. This grid is the workspace you'll use in Excel, typing numbers and text into the individual cells.

Starting a New Workbook

When you first open Excel, you're given a blank, new workbook file. As with all new blank workbooks, three worksheets are already in place: Sheet1, Sheet2, and Sheet3 (see Figure 10-1). You can change this as needed by choosing Tools | Options and on the General tab changing the Sheets in New Workbook option to the number of sheets you need.

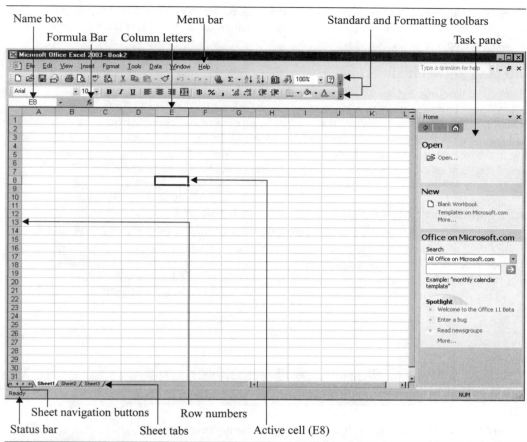

Name box   Menu bar   Standard and Formatting toolbars

Formula Bar   Column letters   Task pane

Sheet navigation buttons   Row numbers

Status bar   Sheet tabs   Active cell (E8)

FIGURE 10-1 The Excel workbook window offers a grid and tools for storing text and numbers, plus a lot of the features you'll recognize from Word.

Understanding Worksheets

As stated previously, each worksheet contains 256 columns and more than 65,000 rows. Where these columns and rows intersect, you have *cells*, and you have more than 16 million per sheet. Each cell's address is its column letter and row number. If you're in cell E8, for example, you're in column E and row 8. The first cell in any worksheet is A1, and the last is IV65536. Figure 10-1 shows an active cell and the column letter and row number for that cell in the Name box. You'll also notice that the column letter and row number are highlighted for the active cell, making it easy to see where you are when you click inside a cell.

Of course, you can be in a cell that's not visible onscreen. If you click cell Z100 and then use the scroll bars to scroll up and left to look at cell A1, you're still in Z100, but that cell doesn't show onscreen at the same time as A1. That's where the Name box comes in handy. No matter which cell you're in, that address (or name, if you've named the cell, and you'll learn how to do that later) will appear in the Name box.

Switching Between Sheets

When you're working in a workbook, you might use only one of the sheets. Many users never venture beyond Sheet1 unless they're creating several related worksheets and want them in one workbook but on separate "pages" of that book. The process of switching between sheets is very simple—just click the tab for the sheet you want to switch to. On the keyboard, press CTRL-PAGE UP to move to a sheet to the left of your currently active sheet or CTRL-PAGE DOWN to move to a sheet to the right of the active sheet. When you're on the desired sheet, release CTRL. The active sheet tab turns white, and cell A1 in the active sheet becomes the active cell.

Adding and Deleting Worksheets to a Workbook

What if you need a new worksheet in the current workbook? Simply click the sheet that should be to the right of the new sheet and choose Insert | Worksheet. The new sheet appears to the left of the active sheet and becomes the new active sheet. Of course, once you've added sheets, you might need to rearrange them. To move sheets, just drag the sheet tabs with your mouse. Here you can see a new Sheet4 being dragged to the right so that it comes after Sheet3.

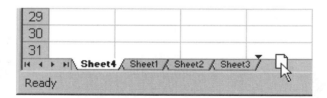

You can also create duplicate sheets by dragging them. Press and hold CTRL as you drag a sheet tab, and you'll drag a duplicate of that sheet, leaving the original in place. A plus sign will appear in the small sheet graphic that accompanies your mouse pointer as you drag.

Deleting sheets is also quite simple but should be done with great care, especially if there's data on them. If you realize you have an unnecessary sheet in the workbook after entering data onto the sheet, you'll want to make sure that data isn't essential to the workbook (the data will be deleted along with the sheet) or that you've copied it to another sheet in the workbook for safekeeping.

To get rid of a sheet, click its tab and choose Edit | Delete Sheet, or you can right-click the tab and choose Delete from the shortcut menu. If there is no data on the sheet, the sheet disappears immediately. If there is any data—even a single character in a single cell—Excel will prompt you that there might be data lost if you proceed.

Naming Sheets

As easy as it is to insert, delete, and rearrange sheets, it's even easier to rename them. Double-click the tab, and when the existing name turns black, simply type the new name and press ENTER or click in a cell on the sheet when you're finished typing the name. Here you can see Sheet1 is being renamed:

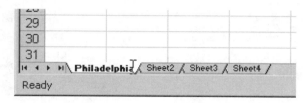

If in the renaming, your sheet tabs no longer fit within the space allocated for them on the bottom of the window, you can use the sheet-navigation buttons to move to a sheet with a tab that's not currently visible, clicking the appropriate button to move to the first tab in the book, the last tab in the book, or between the next and previous sheets.

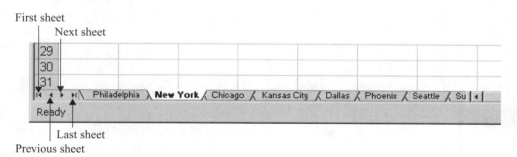

Grouping and Ungrouping Sheets to Create Identical Worksheets

If your workbook will contain two or more sheets that have common layouts and content, you can save yourself a lot of time by grouping the worksheets before entering any data into them or applying any formats. Once the sheets are grouped, anything you do in any one of the sheets in the group is done to all of them. This includes entering text and numbers, creating formulas, applying any formatting, and changing column and row dimensions. For this reason, don't group the sheets until you're ready to build the content and formatting that are common to all the grouped sheets. You'll want to plan ahead of time. Think about the layout and content and know what you want before you start typing and applying formats to the worksheets.

To group sheets in your workbook, simply press CTRL, and while the key is pressed, click the tabs of the sheets you want in the group. If the sheets are in a series (say, sheets 1, 2, and 3), press and hold SHIFT, click the first tab in the group, and then click the last tab in the group. All

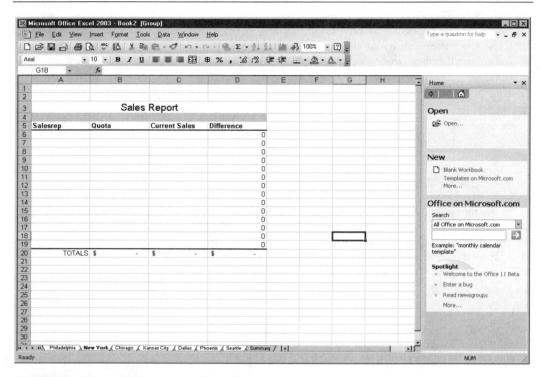

FIGURE 10-2   The Sales Report format shown here on the New York tab also appears on the other sheets that are grouped with it (indicated by the sheet tabs that are white).

the sheets between and including the first and last tabs you click will be grouped. Figure 10-2 shows a group of sheets, and because they're grouped, all the tabs in the group are white.

To ungroup a group of worksheets, click any tab outside the group or right-click the grouped tabs and choose Ungroup Sheets from the shortcut menu. Once the group is broken, each sheet returns to an independent status, and entries in a single sheet remain in that sheet, affecting none of the other sheets in the group—unless you've linked cells through pasting or formulas, and then only those cells will be affected.

Navigating Worksheets

With a worksheet of more than 16 million cells, it's important that you know how to get around quickly and easily. Nothing would waste more of your time using Excel than to have to scroll endlessly in a large worksheet, looking for the cell you want, or to have to use your mouse every time you wanted to select a different active cell. Excel makes it easy to use your mouse, the keyboard, and even a simple menu command to move from place to place in a worksheet. The following table lists these techniques:

Command or Action	Navigational Result
CTRL-HOME	Moves you to cell A1 and makes that the active cell.
CTRL-END	Moves you to the last cell in the worksheet that contains data.
PAGE DOWN	Moves you one screen-full of rows down the worksheet. The number of rows per screen varies by each user's monitor dimensions and the resolution the monitor is set at.
PAGE UP	Moves you one screen-full of rows up the worksheet.
ALT-PAGE DOWN	Moves you one screen-full of columns to the right.
ALT-PAGE UP	Moves you one screen-full of columns to the left.
CTRL-PAGE UP	Moves you one sheet to the left of the currently active sheet. If you're on Sheet2 when you press this key combination, you move to Sheet1.
CTRL-PAGE DOWN	Moves you one sheet to the right of the currently active sheet. If you're on Sheet2 when you press this key combination, you move to Sheet3.
CTRL-UP ARROW	Moves you to the top of the column you're currently in.
CTRL-DOWN ARROW	Moves you to the bottom of the column containing the active cell.
CTRL-LEFT ARROW	Moves you to the end of the row you're in at the time.
CTRL-RIGHT ARROW	Moves you to the first cell in the row containing the active cell.
CTRL-G	Opens the Go To dialog box, where you can enter a cell address and click OK to go to that cell.
Choose Edit | Go To	Open the Go To dialog box and enter a cell address to go to. In the resulting dialog box, enter the address and then click OK to move to that cell.

To make small moves—for example, going from cell B5 to C10—you can easily click in the target cell with your mouse or use the arrow keys on your keyboard. You can also press TAB to go from cell to cell, moving one cell to the right of your current location. To move one cell to the left of your current location, press SHIFT-TAB. If you press ENTER, you'll go to the cell directly below the current cell.

 *Want to go from the end of one row to the beginning of the next one down? Press ENTER then HOME. This makes entering several rows of data go much faster.*

Entering Worksheet Content

Typing text and numbers into a worksheet is very simple. Just click in the cell and start typing. There's no limit to what you can enter into a single cell, and you can format cells to wrap text, which gives you the ability to type paragraph text into a cell. Most worksheets, however, don't contain paragraph text. They normally contain heading and label text (at the tops of columns and at the beginning of rows) to identify the rest of the worksheet's content, whereas the cells within the worksheet contain numbers and short strings of text. The following shows a typical worksheet that stores sales figures for a series of products.

When you type numeric content into a cell, the numbers are automatically right-aligned as soon as you press ENTER. Click the Enter button (the green check to the left of the Formula Bar), or move to another cell. When you type text or any combination of text and numbers, the content is automatically left-aligned.

If the content you type exceeds the width of the cell, one of three things will happen, depending on what you've entered (text or numbers) and what's in the cell to the right of the cell with more content than width:

- ■ If you enter more text than will fit into a cell, the extra text will overlap the cell to the right but won't actually fill that adjoining cell. It will simply appear on top of it, unless that cell has content already.

- ■ If the adjoining cell has content, the overflow will be truncated (cut off) at the end of the cell. This illustration shows both text that overlaps the adjoining empty cell and text that's cut off because the next cell already has content of its own.

No text on the right lets this text display fully.

Content in cell B10 truncates this product name.

- ■ If you enter numeric content into a cell and the cell isn't wide enough to accommodate it all, a variety of results can occur:

■ If you've already adjusted the column width, which tells Excel you have a specific
width in mind, the numbers will be displayed as pound signs, rather than just cutting
off what doesn't fit (so you don't think a cell contains 10,000 when it really contains
100,000!).

■ If the column width has never been manually adjusted, the column will automatically
widen to accommodate the full number, unless the number is more than 11 digits long.
If it is, an exponent is displayed, such as E+16.

No matter what you enter into a cell and no matter what happens to the entry in terms of its
display in that cell, the entire entry will always show in the Formula Bar. If your text is being cut
off by the adjoining cell's content, you can still see the whole string on the Formula Bar. Even if
your numbers are displayed as pound signs, you can see the entire number, string of text, or the
formula that gives you the result that should appear in the cell.

Editing Cell Content

Nobody's perfect. Even with the most thorough preparation and impeccable typing skills, you're
bound to enter the wrong thing into a cell or the right thing into the wrong cell, or you'll misspell
something or transpose some numbers. Luckily, correcting mistakes is very simple. Here are
some tips:

■ To replace the content of a cell, click in the cell and begin typing the replacement
content. The very first keystroke after you click in the cell removes the current content
and begins the replacement.

■ To edit the content of a cell, click in the cell and press F2 or double-click to activate the
cursor in the cell. Use LEFT ARROW and RIGHT ARROW to move among the characters/
digits in the cell, and make your corrections using BACKSPACE or DELETE to remove
unwanted text or numbers.

■ You can always edit cell content on the Formula Bar. Click once in the cell to be
corrected and then go to the Formula Bar. Your mouse pointer appears as an I-beam,
as though you were on a page in a Word document. Click to place your cursor in the
content and make your corrections.

After making your corrections, press ENTER to confirm, or click the Enter button on the
Formula Bar. You can also confirm a cell's entry by clicking in any other cell on the worksheet.
If you want to reverse your correction, returning the cell to its original content, press ESC or
click the Cancel button on the Formula Bar. This works only if you haven't pressed ENTER
or clicked the Enter button yet. Once you've confirmed a cell's entry or correction, the only
way to go back to previous content is by clicking the Undo button. Bear in mind that Excel
gives you only 16 levels of Undo—far fewer than the 100 levels that Word gives you.

10

Selecting Cells, Blocks, Columns, and Rows

A quick way to enter a series of column headings is to select the block of cells that will contain them and then begin typing. If, for example, your headings will be in cells B3 through E3, you can select that range of cells and then type your first heading. Press ENTER, and you're automatically taken to the second cell in the range (C3, in this example), and so on. By selecting the block of cells, you're telling Excel where you're going to be working. The order you selected the cells in (dragging from B3 to E3) indicates the direction the entries will follow.

There are other reasons to select individual cells and blocks of cells, of course. You click in a particular cell to make it the active cell, at which point you can enter content or make a correction. Selecting blocks of cells enables you to apply formatting to several cells at once or to make a large-scale deletion. If you need to cut or copy content from your worksheet, selecting the cells that contain that content is the first step in the process.

Selecting a Block of Cells

To select a block of cells, click in the first cell in the range of cells you want to select. Press and hold the mouse button and then drag up or down and left or right through the adjoining cells you want to include in your selection, as shown here. This range (from A4 through G10) was started in A4 and ended at G10. Because the selection began in A4, that cell remains white.

You can also select cells using the SHIFT key. Activate the first cell in the intended block of cells and then press SHIFT. With SHIFT pressed, click the arrow keys, and the selection will grow, following the direction of the arrow keys you press. When your selection is complete, release SHIFT and don't press the arrow keys again until you're ready to move away from and deselect the range.

Selecting Multiple Cell Ranges

You can also select multiple blocks and random individual cells by pressing CTRL as you gather selections. For example, you can select a range—A6 through G6—and then select the individual cells A8 and A10, then another range, such as G7 through G10, as shown here. By keeping CTRL pressed while the cells were clicked (for the individual cells) and dragged through (for the ranges/blocks), the selections were accumulated instead of each successive selection canceling out the previous one.

	A	B	C	D	E	F	G
	G7		f_x				
1							
2							
3							
4	First Quarter Sales by Product						
5							
6	Product Name	Product Number	Unit Price	Units Sold	Total Sales	Last Month	Comparison
7	Gunpowder Bird Seed	GP357	17	105789	$ 1,798,413.00		
8	Giant Sling Shot	SL172					
9	Anvil-on-a-Rope	AN948					
10	Jet-Powered Roller Skates	JP753					

TIP *You can't use the Cut or Copy command on nonconsecutive selections. If you select noncontiguous cells and then try to issue the Cut or Copy command, an error message appears, indicating that the command cannot be used on multiple selections.*

Selecting Entire Columns and Rows

Another powerful selection method results in entire columns and rows being selected—very handy if everything in a given column or row should be formatted the same way or needs to be cut, copied, or deleted. To select an entire column, click the column letter once. Similarly, if you want to select an entire row, click the row number. When you make such a selection, the entire column or row is selected—all 256 cells in the row, or 65,536 cells in the column. To select multiple columns or rows, simply drag through the column letters (to select two or more contiguous columns) or the row numbers (to select several contiguous rows).

Inserting Rows and Columns

Just as you might forget a column heading or row label, you might completely forget an entire section of your worksheet—a whole column of numbers, a series of names, or a product that should have been added to a list of sales figures. It's very simple to insert the blank space you need to add the content that you forgot.

To insert a column, simply select the column to the right of the spot where the new column should be and then choose Insert | Columns. The new column appears, and everything to its right is moved over one column. You can insert multiple columns in one step by selecting a number of existing columns equal to the number of new columns you need and then choosing Insert | Columns. The new batch of columns appears to the right of the first column in the series you selected.

Inserting rows is just as simple and requires nearly an identical procedure. To insert a row, select the row beneath where you want the new row to appear and choose Insert | Rows. As the plural command name would imply, it's also possible to insert multiple rows all at once—just select the same number of existing rows as you want to insert and choose Insert | Rows. The existing content is moved down to accommodate the new blank rows.

Saving Workbook Files

Probably the most important step in the process of building a workbook is saving it. If I accomplish one thing with this chapter, I hope it's to keep you from having to redo hours of work because you didn't save early or often enough. To protect yourself, make File | Save (or the CTRL-S shortcut) your first action after starting a workbook, and your repeated action during the process of building your worksheets.

Saving a New Workbook

After you've started a new workbook and done about five or ten minutes of work, you should save the file. Some people save the file immediately, giving it a name and choosing where to save it so that all they have to do is keep resaving it periodically as they work.

To save a file, you can pick one of the following methods: choose File | Save, press CTRL-S, or click the Save button on the Standard toolbar.

The *first* time you save the file, no matter what method you use, will bring up the Save As dialog box, which is virtually identical to that in Word, PowerPoint, and Access. There you have to choose what to call the workbook and where to store it. (You can also choose File | Save As for the first save.) It's after the first-time save that it matters which method you use. If you choose File | Save for a file that has already been saved, you'll update the file by resaving it to include your latest changes and additions, and no dialog box will appear. If you choose File | Save As in a previously saved file, the Save As dialog box opens, and you have the chance to save the file with a new name or to a new place, thus protecting the current version and creating a new version of the file.

Saving a Workbook as a Template

Just as grouping worksheets and then building a series of identical worksheets saves time and achieves greater consistency within a workbook, a template saves you time and assures you greater consistency among workbooks. Every worksheet based on a particular template will look and work the same way. Figure 10-3 shows a sales report template that would enable you to build the same report every time—from the headings, to the formatting (fonts, shading, and borders), to the formulas that tally the sales.

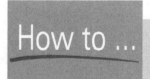 **How to ...** **Password-Protect Your Sensitive Worksheets**

If you really want to protect the original from any changes, don't just save it with a new name. Instead, save it with a password. In the Save As dialog box, click the Tools button and choose General Options from the resulting menu. In the Save Options dialog box, enter a password to protect the file from being opened or modified. Only people who know the password you set up will be able to open or save the file with changes. Of course, make sure it's a password you can never forget, because there's no way to retrieve the password (or open the file) if you forget it.

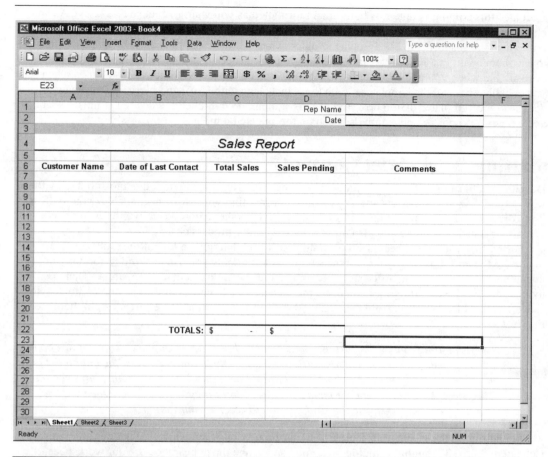

FIGURE 10-3 A template contains the basic structure, content, and formatting that each new workbook based on it should have.

The most important step in creating a template is planning. You want to be sure that the only content in the template-to-be is the content you want in every file that's created based on the template. For example, if you're creating an expense report template, you don't want specific expenses in the report. You want only the column headings, the row labels, and the formulas that total the columns and rows in the report.

> **TIP**
>
> *If you want to use an existing, data-filled worksheet as a template, simply save the workbook as is and then remove the unique content—the data that you wouldn't want in other workbooks created based on this workbook. Then choose File | Save As, which you now know will open the Save As dialog box and close any existing version of the file, protecting it from changes.*

Once this common content is built in and formatted as you want it, choose File | Save As and click the Save As Type drop list. From the list of file formats, choose Template (.xlt). You are immediately transported to the Templates folder, where all template files must be saved in order to use them again in the future. Name the file and click the Save button. The template will now be available when you click the On My Computer link on the New Workbook task pane. When you click that link, all the templates—both those that came with Excel and those you've created—appear in the Templates dialog box. To use one of them, double-click the desired template's icon, and a new workbook is opened that's based on the selected template.

Formatting Worksheet Content

Despite the old saying, "You can't judge a book by its cover," people do judge most things by the way they look, and worksheets are no exception. Formatting your worksheet enables you to dress it up, draw attention to important data, and make the worksheet more visually interesting overall. Good worksheet formatting can also make your data-entry process easier.

Formatting your worksheet is simple, and you'll find that quite a few of the tools you use to change the appearance of your worksheet are the same tools you use in Word to format your documents. There are some differences, though, and these are immediately apparent when you look at the Excel Formatting toolbar. Tools for currency style, percentage style, and comma style as well as tools for increasing and decreasing the displayed decimal places are all right there (see Figure 10-4).

> **TIP** *The formatting tools work just as you'd assume, based on what you already know about Word—select the content the formatting should apply to and then click the button for the formatting you want. But, unlike the Bold, Italic, and Underline tools, however, the Currency, Percentage, and Comma Style tools don't toggle on and off. Once you've applied them, you must use the Undo button to reverse your action.*

In addition to the Formatting toolbar is the Format | Cells command, which opens the Format Cells dialog box. Through this dialog box, you can change the appearance of your worksheet content—be it text or numbers—in many ways. The Format Cells dialog box contains tabs for Number, Alignment, Font, Border, Patterns, and Protection options that affect virtually every aspect of a cell's appearance—from the font, to the color of the cell, to the way the content is aligned.

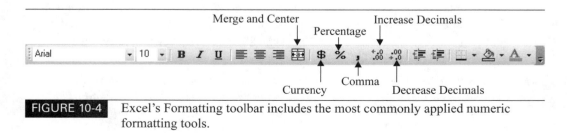

FIGURE 10-4 Excel's Formatting toolbar includes the most commonly applied numeric formatting tools.

Of course, as with the toolbar buttons, you should have the cell or block of cells the formatting should apply to selected before opening this dialog box. You want Excel to know which cells you want to format. You can select entire rows or columns and apply formatting to them, which is very useful if every cell in a given column or row should be formatted the same way. It saves you time selecting smaller blocks repeatedly, and it helps you make certain that every cell in a given row or column will look as it should.

Applying Numeric Formats

When your worksheet contains numbers, it can be helpful to format them appropriately, if only so that people viewing your worksheet know that, for example, the numbers represent sales dollars and not units sold, or that the figures are percentages of another number on the same worksheet. Using the Formatting toolbar or the Format Cells dialog box, you can apply the formats that will help you and others quickly and easily interpret your numeric data.

To apply numeric formatting, you have several options:

- Use the Currency, Percentage, and Comma Style buttons on the Formatting toolbar.

- Adjust the number of displayed decimal places with the Increase Decimal and Decrease Decimal buttons.

- Choose Format | Cells, click the Number tab, and choose from a variety of number formatting options—for everything from money (Currency) to dates and times.

10

NOTE
The Increase and Decrease Decimal buttons don't work if you have anything other than numeric content selected. If you select a block of cells and even one of the cells contains text, the buttons won't work when you click them.

Most of the categories and the formatting options within them are fairly self-explanatory. One, however, is quite powerful, and maybe a little enigmatic for the first-time user. The Custom category allows you to build your own formats for specialized numbers, such as serial numbers, phone numbers, and dates, and combinations of text, symbols, and numbers that you might enter into your worksheet. As shown in Figure 10-5, plenty of Custom formats are built in, and a text box is provided for you to type your own into.

For example, imagine your company has product numbers such as 5-43489.2—a single digit followed by a dash, followed by five numbers, followed by a decimal point, then another number. This sort of number is ripe for typos. Another problem with a number like this is that Excel will see the dash and think you're trying to do some math. Creating a Custom format will eliminate this problem for the selected cells.

This Custom category is also great for creating date formats other than those offered by the Date category. You can set up any combination of date components: d for day, m for month, y for year. If, for example, you want the year first, with four digits, then the month, followed by the day, you could create the custom format yyyy-mmm-dd. (By using three m's, you're telling Excel you want the three-letter abbreviation for the month rather than the number of the month.)

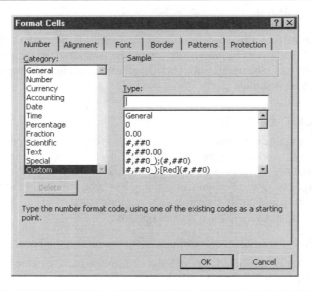

FIGURE 10-5   Need a special number format? Create it yourself in the Custom category.

Changing Fonts and Sizes

By default, Excel uses the Arial font, in 10-point size. This is a very legible font, and virtually every computer has Arial on it, which means you can share your worksheet with just about anyone and know that it will look the same for that person as it does for you. You can tell which font and size is in use for any cell in your worksheet by clicking that cell and viewing the displayed Font and Size settings on the Formatting toolbar.

When a block of cells is selected, the font and size of the first cell in the selected range (the cell you started your selection from) is what appears on the toolbar. This can be deceiving, especially if there is a different font or size applied to some of the cells in the selected range. For this reason, if you want to be certain which font or size is in use in a particular cell, be sure only that cell is selected when you view the toolbar's display.

Of course, not everyone likes the way Arial looks, and sometimes you need to change the fonts in your worksheets to make them match other documentation (such as an accompanying report, done in Word, in Times New Roman), to create a certain look or feeling, or to draw attention to titles or headings.

If you want to change the fonts on your worksheet, it's very quick and easy to do. Select the cells you want to format (press CTRL-A if you want to set a single font for the whole worksheet), then either use the Font and Size buttons' drop lists on the Formatting toolbar or choose Format | Cells. In the resulting Format Cells dialog box, click the Font tab and make use of the tools for selecting a font, size, style, and color. You can also apply special effects, such as strikethrough, to indicate content that is to be deleted or ignored.

When choosing a font, be sure that the one you choose makes both text and numbers legible. Some fonts are great on text but render numbers completely illegible. The script and artistic fonts are a perfect example. Further, if you know your worksheet will be photocopied or might be reduced to fit on one page when printed, pick a font that's clear even when small. To test this, reduce the Zoom setting on your page and see if you can still read the content. You can do this by choosing View | Zoom or clicking the Zoom button on the Standard toolbar. Choose 75 or 50 percent as the magnification level and test the legibility of your fonts and sizes.

Applying Color to Text and Numbers

If you choose to apply color to your fonts, pick a color that looks good both onscreen and when the worksheet is printed. Some colors look fine onscreen but wash out too much on paper. Also, you won't know for sure if everyone who's printing your worksheet has a color printer. For example, bright blue can become a very light gray when printed on a black-and-white printer. To apply color to your content, you can use the Font Color button on the Formatting toolbar, or you can use the Color option on the Font tab in the Format Cells dialog box.

Resetting the Default Font and Size for All Workbooks

If you absolutely hate Arial or must have 12-point text and numbers in your worksheets, you can change the default from Arial 10 to anything you want. Choose Tools | Options, and on the General tab change the Standard Font setting. From that point on, all worksheets will use your new setting as the default. Make any changes to the default with care. You could end up picking something that other users don't have on their computers (and their computers will make a potentially unappealing substitution) or that other people simply don't like. If you work with others who'll use your worksheets, use discretion when changing any of your Excel defaults.

Aligning Worksheet Content

By default, text is left-aligned in your worksheet cells, and numeric content is right-aligned. Nothing is centered by default. You can change the alignment of all or some of your worksheet content, however, simply by clicking the Alignment buttons on the Formatting toolbar or by using the Alignment tab in the Format Cells dialog box to change the way text is horizontally oriented in your worksheet cells.

Changing the Angle of Text

The Alignment tab in the Format Cells dialog box (choose Format | Cells to open the dialog box) provides more than simple left, right, and center alignment tools. You can also rotate your text on anything from a 90-degree to a minus-90-degree angle, as shown in Figure 10-6. This can be very handy for longer column headings. If you don't want to use space from left to right to accommodate a long heading, rotate the heading text so that it appears on an angle. It will take up less space from side to side, and you can keep your columns narrower and still display the entire column heading.

You can set the orientation by clicking the half-circle (it looks like a clock), or you can enter a specific number of degrees in the box below it. Either way, the bar in the half-circle shows how the text will appear at the selected angle: tilting down or up, or running straight up and down.

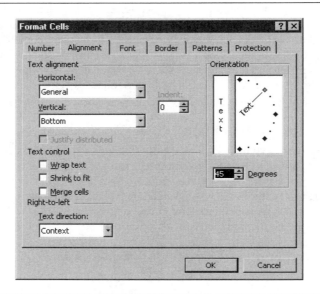

The Alignment tab allows you to control the horizontal placement of content within worksheet cells.

Wrapping and Shrinking Text to Fit

Other options in the Alignment tab include text controls. These settings allow you to have text wrap within a cell, making it possible to type paragraph text or longer column or row headings in a cell. You can also have the text shrink to fit within the confines of the cell, which would be determined by the column width and row height—but be careful that this doesn't make your text too small to read! You can also merge cells, which takes two or more cells and turns them into one larger cell—one that can easily house a long worksheet title or some instructional or explanatory text.

Using Merge and Center

The Formatting toolbar has a fourth alignment option: the Merge and Center button (refer back to Figure 10-4). This alignment option is especially useful for worksheet titles, because it allows you to center a title over the width of the worksheet data and merge the title into a single cell so it's truly centered.

To merge and center a worksheet title, select the cell containing the title as well as all the cells on either side of it, for the span of the worksheet's data. After selecting the cells, click the Merge and Center button. The selected cells are merged into one long cell, and the title text is centered within that single cell. After making this alignment change, you can tinker with it through the Format Cells dialog box using the Alignment tab.

Shading Worksheet Cells

Adding color to a worksheet can be done through the color of text and numbers and by changing the background color of worksheet cells. Color makes parts of the worksheet stand out, and it can also help you match your worksheet to folders, binders, and other materials that might accompany your printed worksheet. If your worksheet will be part of a visual presentation—perhaps shown on a big screen or over the web—you can use colors in your worksheet that will match the slides and graphics included in that presentation.

Applying color to worksheet cells is done in one of two ways:

- Use the Shading Color button on the Formatting toolbar.
- Choose Format | Cells and click the Patterns tab.

If you use the Shading Color button, you can pick from a palette of 40 colors. This palette looks just like the one you see if you use the Font Color button discussed earlier in the "Applying Color to Text and Numbers" section. Be sure to pick a color that won't make the cell content illegible. A very dark shading with black text will be hard to read, as will a light shading with light text. Try to remember, too, that what looks good onscreen might not look good on paper if someone prints the worksheet, and that not everyone has a color printer. For example, bright yellow cells might look great onscreen, but they're light gray on a black-and-white printer.

If you use the Patterns tab (so named because you can apply patterns as well as solid colors), you can choose from the same palette of 40 colors, plus a group of custom colors (if you've ever created custom colors using any of the other Office applications) and a series of 18 patterns, including no pattern, which reverts to a solid color.

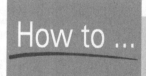

Apply Formatting Based on Cell Content

If you need to apply shading to cells, color to cell content, font formatting, borders, or any other visual formatting to parts of your worksheet and want the content of the cells to dictate which formatting is applied, you can use Excel's Conditional Formatting tools to make it happen. With these tools, for example, you can shade every cell that contains a number higher or lower than a number you specify, or place a thick cell border around every cell containing a particular word or phrase. To access the Conditional Formatting tools, choose Format | Conditional Formatting, and use the Condition 1 box to choose how the worksheet content is analyzed and used to apply formatting you specify in the three adjacent text boxes/drop lists. You can set multiple conditions (click the Add >> button), applying a format to numbers below a certain level but above another level. After setting the criteria (the Conditional part of the process), click the Format button inside the Conditional Formatting dialog box to make your formatting selections for the cells that will meet your conditions.

Applying Borders

Borders break your worksheet into visual sections. By default, the gridlines on your worksheets don't print (you can set them to print, as discussed in Chapter 14), so borders are a great way to make it clear where one part of your worksheet ends and another begins. For example, if you have several columns of numbers and each one is summed at the bottom, you can place a dark or double border beneath the last numbers in each row.

To apply a border, you can use either of two methods:

■ *Use the Borders tool on the Formatting toolbar.* You can turn on borders on any side of the selected cell or range, and you can choose from a variety of border styles and thicknesses.

■ *For more options, including border color, choose Format | Cells and click the Border tab.* On this tab you can turn borders on and off on all sides of the selected cell(s) and also choose from different border styles. There are more options here than offered through the Borders button. To apply a colored border, click the Color drop list and choose a color from the palette that appears. Once your settings are complete, click OK to apply them and close the dialog box.

A third way to create cell borders is draw them with your mouse. To access this tool, choose Draw Borders from the bottom of the Borders button palette. When you make this selection, your mouse pointer is turned into a pencil and the Borders floating toolbar appears (see Figure 10-7).

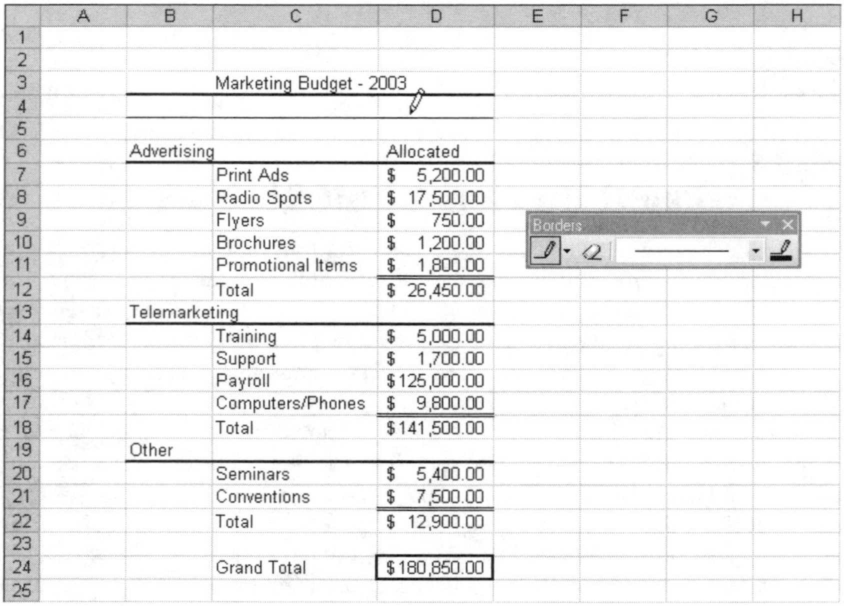

FIGURE 10-7 Click a cell wall to apply a border to it.

To apply a border in this fashion, choose a line style and a line color from the Borders toolbar—the styles range from solid lines to dashed or dotted lines—and then click the borders of cells to which you want to add that particular type of border. You can also click the Eraser button (it looks just like the eraser from Word's Tables and Borders toolbar) and delete cell borders. Just click the border with your mouse, and it disappears.

Copying Cell Formats

Whatever the formatting you've applied to a cell, you can use the Format Painter to apply it to other cells, saving yourself the time and trouble of repeating all your formatting steps. Simply select the cell or range thereof that has the formatting attributes you want to use elsewhere on the worksheet. Then, click the Format Painter on the Standard toolbar (shown in Figure 10-8) and notice that as soon as you do, your mouse pointer has a paintbrush on it. Next, click in the single cell or drag through the range of cells that should be formatted to match your sample cell(s). After you release the mouse, the Format Painter is automatically turned off. If you want to copy your formatting to several locations on the same worksheet, double-click the Format Painter button to turn it on. It will remain on until you click it to turn it off or until you press ESC.

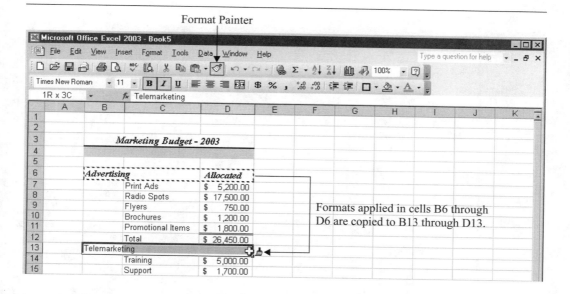

FIGURE 10-8   The Format Painter copies formatting from one cell to another.

Chapter 11

Working with Formulas and Functions

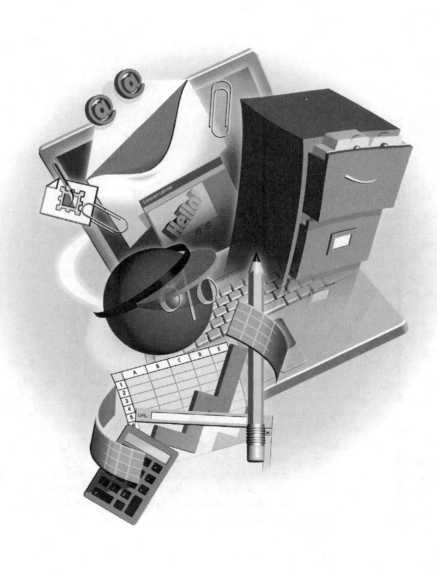

How to...

- Quickly sum a series of cells with a single toolbar command
- Build any formula from scratch
- Control the order of formula operations to make sure the right result is achieved
- Copy your formulas to multiple locations, making your worksheet more consistent throughout
- Use Excel's built-in functions to perform a variety of calculations, from averaging to calculating a loan payment

The benefits of using an electronic spreadsheet program rather than working with pencil, paper, and a calculator are well known. You can give the command to total a series of numbers (or perform any other type of calculation, including built-in operations, called *functions*), and the result appears automatically. If one of the numbers contributing to that total changes, the total changes automatically. No writing, no erasing. Further, Excel makes it possible to copy a formula from point A to point B and have the formula work in both places, referring to different cells in each place. Pretty slick, eh?

Understanding Spreadsheet Calculations

Performing mathematical operations in Excel is pretty simple, and even the more complex calculations can be performed with functions, built by tools that guide you through the process of "doing the math." For formulas you create from scratch, however, you need to know the math behind the operation. If you want to figure out the difference between last year's sales and this year's, you need to know how to structure that formula—is it this year's minus last year's or last year's minus this year's? Once you know how the math should go, however, constructing the formula is easy, and Excel will perform the calculations flawlessly. And unlike your speedy fingers on a calculator, Excel won't make a mistake.

When it comes to calculations on an Excel worksheet, they're generally performed by telling Excel to take one cell's numeric content and add it to, subtract it from, multiply it by, or divide it by another cell's content. For example, if the number 50 is in cell B5 and the number 72 is in cell C5 and you want to multiply them, the formula should multiply B5 times C5, not 50 times 75. Why? So that if you change the number in B5 to 60, the result changes automatically. If you use the actual numbers in the formula, you have to redo the formula from the beginning, editing the formula within the worksheet to recalculate with new numbers. By using cell addresses in the formula, whatever's in the cell is used in the formula, and changes need only be made in the cell in order to see them reflected in the formula result.

Excel has some basic structural requirements for formulas. First, the formula goes in the cell where the result should be, not in any of the cells that contribute to the formula. As shown next, the formula that calculates the difference between two years' sales goes in the Difference column, and it refers to cells in the 2001 Sales and 2002 Sales columns.

	SUM	▾	X ✓ *fx* =C7-B7		
	A	B	C	D	
1					
2					
3					
4		**Sales Analysis**			
5					
6		2001	2002	Difference	
7	Philadelphia	5,246,780.00	5,321,100.50	=C7-B7	
8	New York	14,895,630.00	14,534,810.62		
9	Chicago	1,089,540.00	1,904,657.62		
10	Kansas City	914,578.00	1,037,717.60		
11	Santa Fe	2,578,964.00	2,312,882.58		
12	San Diego	13,789,512.00	13,432,011.27		
13	Seattle	8,650,124.00	6,153,295.78		
14	*Totals*				

The second requirement is that all formulas begin with an equal sign. Why? Think of it this way: "This cell is EQUAL to..." as you click in a cell to start a formula. If you think of each formula as simply a sentence, expressed mathematically, you won't forget the equal sign, and it can also help you organize your formula in your head before you begin to create it.

Performing Quick Addition with AutoSum

One of the simplest formulas is an AutoSum. It's "Auto" because it's automatic—it seeks out the cells near to the cell containing the AutoSum formula and automatically sums them. It's "Sum" because it's adding up a series of cells. As shown in this example, the columns in this worksheet need to be totaled. Each quarter's sales can be totaled at the foot of each column, and each regional office's individual sales can be totaled as well, in the last column of the worksheet.

	B13	▾	*fx*			
	A	B	C	D	E	F
1						
2						
3		**Quarterly Sales by Division**				
4						
5		Q1	Q2	Q3	Q4	TOTALS
6	Philadelphia	1,344,612.50	1,204,500.30	1,371,337.45	1,400,650.25	5,321,100.50
7	New York	3,975,700.25	3,426,200.40	3,875,125.35	3,257,784.62	14,534,810.62
8	Chicago	525,781.00	574,126.00	478,961.62	325,789.00	1,904,657.62
9	Kansas City	245,712.35	250,462.00	315,793.00	225,750.25	1,037,717.60
10	Santa Fe	625,796.25	715,987.40	345,951.78	625,147.15	2,312,882.58
11	San Diego	3,772,700.35	2,428,200.40	3,975,326.85	3,255,783.67	13,432,011.27
12	Seattle	1,825,612.70	1,304,705.30	1,721,357.43	1,301,620.35	6,153,295.78
13	TOTALS					
14						

Of course, you could do that by typing a long formula (starting with an equal sign, of course) that takes one cell plus another cell plus another cell and so forth, but that would take forever and increases the margin for error significantly. Using AutoSum simplifies, speeds, and streamlines the process of performing the most common of worksheet calculations: the summing of a row, column, or other range of numbers.

11

Using the AutoSum Function

To perform an AutoSum, simply click in the cell where the sum result should appear and then click the AutoSum button on the Standard toolbar. As soon as you click the AutoSum button, Excel looks at the cells surrounding the active cell and when it sees two or more cells with numbers in them, it assumes those are the cells you want to sum. It then places a dashed border around the cells to be summed and puts the AutoSum formula in the cell, awaiting your approval.

	SUM	▾ ✕ ✓ ƒ×	=SUM(B6:B12)			
	A	B	C	D	E	F
1						
2						
3		**Quarterly Sales by Division**				
4						
5		Q1	Q2	Q3	Q4	TOTALS
6	Philadelphia	1,344,612.50	1,204,500.30	1,371,337.45	1,400,650.25	5,321,100.50
7	New York	3,975,700.25	3,426,200.40	3,875,125.35	3,257,784.62	14,534,810.62
8	Chicago	525,781.00	574,126.00	478,961.62	325,789.00	1,904,657.62
9	Kansas City	245,712.35	250,462.00	315,793.00	225,750.25	1,037,717.60
10	Santa Fe	625,796.25	715,987.40	345,951.78	625,147.15	2,312,882.58
11	San Diego	3,772,700.35	2,428,200.40	3,975,326.85	3,255,783.67	13,432,011.27
12	Seattle	1,825,612.70	1,304,705.30	1,721,357.43	1,301,620.35	6,153,295.78
13	TOTALS	=SUM(B6:B12)				
14		SUM(**number1**, [number2], ...)				

Assuming the range of cells to be summed is correct, you can press ENTER or click the AutoSum button again to tell Excel to proceed with the formula and place the result in the active cell. If the range isn't right, you can take your mouse and drag through the correct range of cells. Just click in the first cell of the desired range and then drag through the adjoining cells that should be summed. You can also use the CTRL key to click in two or more nonadjacent cells, resulting in a sum of several random cells. This allows you to add up cells from all over a worksheet, or even cells on different worksheets in the same workbook—just keep the CTRL key pressed as you gather the cells to be summed, and you're in business.

It's important to note that the range that Excel selects (or that you drag to select) is represented by the first cell address in the range, followed by a colon (:), followed by the last cell in the range. This literally means "this cell through this cell." For example, A5 through A10 is expressed as A5:A10. If you've selected individual, nonadjacent cells to be summed, they'll appear with commas between them, as in =SUM(F10, J15,G3). Once you've pressed ENTER or clicked the AutoSum button to perform the calculation, the *formula* appears only on the Formula Bar. The *result* appears in the cell.

Pasting the AutoSum Function

As quick and easy as AutoSum is, so is the process of pasting one AutoSum formula to other columns or rows nearby. Rather than repeat the process of building the AutoSum formula for a series of columns or rows, you can simply paste the AutoSum from the first column (or row) across the foot of all the other columns (or up or down all the rest of the rows) that need to be summed.

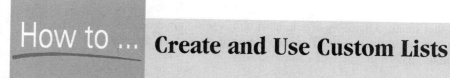

How to ... Create and Use Custom Lists

You can use the paste process to copy any cell's content to adjoining cells or to create a list of consecutive items, such as days of the week, months of the year, or numeric patterns. If you want to repeat a name, number, or even fill in a series, all you need to do is drag the first cell through the adjoining cells. Excel will fill in the cells you drag through based on what was in the starting cell. Excel's custom lists can be pasted and filled in by typing the first (or any) item in the list. View the complete list of automatic custom lists and create your own by choosing Tools | Options and clicking the Custom Lists tab. To create a list of numbers following a pattern, establish the pattern in the first two cells and then select them both before pasting from the lower-right corner of the second cell—the cells to which you paste the content will perpetuate the pattern you established.

Pasting works for any calculation, not just AutoSum. To paste a function, click in the cell that contains the formula you want to use in the adjoining cells. When the cell containing the formula is active, point to the lower-right corner of the cell (look for the small black box in the corner). Your mouse turns to a black cross, and at that point you can drag your mouse through the adjoining cells, as shown here. When you've dragged through all the cells that should contain the formula, release your mouse, and the formulas are pasted. The results appear in the cells to which the formula was pasted.

B13		f_x =SUM(B6:B12)			
	A	B	C	D	E	F

	A	Q1	Q2	Q3	Q4	TOTALS
3		**Quarterly Sales by Division**				
6	Philadelphia	1,344,612.50	1,204,500.30	1,371,337.45	1,400,650.25	5,321,100.50
7	New York	3,975,700.25	3,426,200.40	3,875,125.35	3,257,784.62	14,534,810.62
8	Chicago	525,781.00	574,126.00	478,961.62	325,789.00	1,904,657.62
9	Kansas City	245,712.35	250,462.00	315,793.00	225,750.25	1,037,717.60
10	Santa Fe	625,796.25	715,987.40	345,951.78	625,147.15	2,312,882.58
11	San Diego	3,772,700.35	2,428,200.40	3,975,326.85	3,255,783.67	13,432,011.27
12	Seattle	1,825,612.70	1,304,705.30	1,721,357.43	1,301,620.35	6,153,295.78
13	TOTALS	12,315,915.40				

Of course, you might be thinking that Excel is going to copy the formula from the first column or row to all the other columns or rows and you'll somehow have to update those copied versions to sum the columns or rows where they now appear. Wrong! Thanks to a concept called *relative addressing*, the formulas will update themselves to sum the cells relative to their new

11

position. A formula that summed numbers in column A will now sum numbers in column B, C, and so forth. As you can see in the Formula Bar shown next, the AutoSum that was pasted from column B is now summing cells in column C, automatically.

	A	B	C	D	E	F
3		Quarterly Sales by Division				
5		Q1	Q2	Q3	Q4	TOTALS
6	Philadelphia	1,344,612.50	1,204,500.30	1,371,337.45	1,400,650.25	5,321,100.50
7	New York	3,975,700.25	3,426,200.40	3,875,125.35	3,257,784.62	14,534,810.62
8	Chicago	525,781.00	574,126.00	478,961.62	325,789.00	1,904,657.62
9	Kansas City	245,712.35	250,462.00	315,793.00	225,750.25	1,037,717.60
10	Santa Fe	625,796.25	715,987.40	345,951.78	625,147.15	2,312,882.58
11	San Diego	3,772,700.35	2,428,200.40	3,975,326.85	3,255,783.67	13,432,011.27
12	Seattle	1,825,612.70	1,304,705.30	1,721,357.43	1,301,620.35	6,153,295.78
13	TOTALS	12,315,915.40	9,904,181.80	12,083,853.48	10,392,525.29	44,696,475.97

C13   fx =SUM(C6:C12)

Creating Simple Formulas from Scratch

Imagine you want to take the sales total for a given sales rep and compare it to another rep's total, or maybe you need to show the total expenses for a department as a percentage of the company's total expenses. How would you do that? If you know how to do it on a calculator, you can do it in Excel.

Building formulas is very simple, assuming you stick to the rules: Place the formula in a cell on its own, start it with an equal sign, and press ENTER at the end to confirm the formula and perform the calculation. The other thing to remember is that Excel uses four simple operators for the main mathematical operations it performs:

+ (plus sign)	Addition
– (minus sign)	Subtraction
* (asterisk)	Multiplication
/ (slash)	Division

If the numbers you want to calculate are in the worksheet, refer to them by their cell addresses. Also, try to get into the habit of using your mouse to click cells that you want to include in the formula rather than typing the addresses on the keyboard. It will save you time and reduce the margin for error, and you can construct formulas more logically, building them cell by cell, the way you think about the calculation that you're setting up. For example, if you want to take one division's first quarter sales (in cell B6) and figure out what percentage of the entire company's sales they represent (the total sales for all the divisions for Q1 is in B13), you would type =, then click in cell B6, type / (to divide), and then click in cell B13. The formula =B6/B13 is created, but you were able to build it by thinking "Divide Philadelphia's sales by the total of all the divisions' sales to see what portion of the total its sales represent."

Editing Formulas

As with any cell, if you want to replace the content, simply click in the cell and start typing the replacement content. In the case of a formula, if it's so out of whack that you want to start over completely, this is probably your best bet. Click in the cell, type an equal sign, and start all over again.

If your formula is salvageable—maybe you just need to change a single cell address, operator, or number—you can edit it in one of three ways:

- ■ Click in the cell, then go up to the Formula Bar, position your cursor, and start editing, just as you would a cell containing text or numbers.

- ■ Double-click the cell and edit the formula right within the cell. The formula won't appear in the cell unless you double-click it.

- ■ Press F2 to activate the cursor in the cell and display the formula there as well. You can edit the formula right inside the cell.

When you're finished editing, press ENTER to recalculate with your changes in place.

TIP   *You might notice that when you edit a formula, each cell address in the formula turns a different color, and the cells on the worksheet that were used in the formula change to colors that match their cell references in the formula. This color-coding helps you figure out where all the parts of the formula came from and assists you in editing the formula.*

Understanding Relative vs. Absolute Addressing

You've seen relative addressing at work. When you paste an AutoSum formula from one cell into another, the formula updates relative to where you've pasted it. The opposite of this default behavior is called *absolute addressing*. Absolute addressing is a state in which one or more of the cells in a formula do not update, no matter where you paste the formula. Looking back to our worksheet with sales reps' totals and the percentage of the total sales represented by each, this is a perfect opportunity to save time with the paste function procedure, but to do so requires the use of absolute addressing.

Take the formula for Philadelphia's percentage of the total sales, =B6/B13. If you paste that formula down the column for the other divisions, the formula will update each time, becoming =B7/B14 for the next division, =B8/B15 for the division after that, and so on. Each time the formula moves down, the cell addresses will increment by one cell, following the rules of relative addressing. If, however, we instruct Excel to "always go back to cell B13 for the total sales," we can take the formula that calculates Philadelphia's percentage and paste it down the column to get the percentages for each individual division, as compared to the one total for everyone's sales.

So how do we tell Excel to use absolute addressing rather than relative? With the F4 key. Continuing to use Philadelphia's percentage formula as an example, when you click cell B13, press the F4 key. Figure 11-6 shows the result of our doing so: Dollar signs appear before the B and the 13 in the Formula Bar, indicating that the B (column location) and 13 (row location)

11

should remain fixed (or absolute)—when the formula is copied to columns C, E, G, and I, B13 will remain in the formula.

SUM	▾ X ✓ ƒx	=B6/$B$13										
	A	B	C	D	E	F	G	H	I	J	K	
1												
2												
3					Quarterly Sales by Division							
4												
5		Q1	% of Total Sales	Q2	% of Total Sales	Q3	% of Total Sales	Q4	% of Total Sales	TOTALS		
6	Philadelphia	1,344,612.50	=B6/$B$13	1,204,500.30		1,371,337.45		1,400,650.25		5,321,100.61		
7	New York	3,975,700.25		3,426,200.40		3,875,125.35		3,257,784.62		14,534,810.62		
8	Chicago	525,781.00		574,126.00		478,961.62		325,789.00		1,904,657.62		
9	Kansas City	245,712.35		250,462.00		315,793.00		225,750.25		1,037,717.60		
10	Santa Fe	625,796.25		715,987.40		345,951.78		625,147.15		2,312,882.58		
11	San Diego	3,772,700.35		2,428,200.40		3,975,326.85		3,255,783.67		13,432,011.27		
12	Seattle	1,825,612.70		1,304,705.30		1,721,357.43		1,301,620.35		6,153,295.78		
13	TOTALS	12,315,915.40		9,904,181.80		12,083,853.48		10,392,525.29		44,696,476.08		
14												

TIP   *A great way to make use of the absolute reference is to place a multiplier or divisor in a cell, intended for use as an absolute reference. Imagine a series of products, and you want to calculate a price increase, but you're not sure if you want to increase prices by 15 or 18 percent. If you place the multiplier (0.15 or 0.18) in a cell and then refer to that cell and turn it into an absolute reference, you can increase all the prices on the worksheet with one formula, pasted down the list of products.*

Controlling the Order of Operations

Left to its own devices, Excel will perform the calculations in your formula in order—from left to right if all the operators are the same, or in order based on the operators if they vary throughout the formula. The operators-based order can be used to your advantage, enabling you to control the order of operations by using certain symbols in your formula. Without attempting to control the order of operations, you risk getting a wrong answer to your formula. Using real numbers to make the concept clearer, imagine this formula:

$5 + 3 \times 10 = 80$

Five plus three is eight, times 10 is 80, right? If you typed the formula =5+3*10 into a cell on an Excel worksheet, however, the answer would be 35. Huh? Well, because of the order of operations, the multiplication would be performed first, then five would be added to that. Three times 10 is 30, add five, and you get 35. If you wanted to get the correct answer, you'd have to construct the formula as follows:

$(5 + 3) \times 10 = 80$, or in Excel's format, =(5+3)*10

The parentheses tell Excel to perform the addition first, then to take that result and multiply it by 10. To help you remember and utilize the order of operations, remember the phrase "Please My Dear Aunt Sally," where the first letters stand for the order of operations—Parentheses, Multiplication, Division, Addition, Subtraction.

Using 3-D Formula References

References to worksheets or workbooks other than the one that contains your formula are called *3-D* (three-dimensional) because they add depth to your formula. Instead of operating solely on the flat surface of a single active sheet, a formula that references a cell in another worksheet in the active workbook or that refers to a cell in another workbook entirely is creating a connection to data outside the current worksheet, and it's therefore considered 3-D.

The scenarios that require pulling cells from other worksheets and workbooks are limited only by the scope of the data you have stored through Excel. Imagine that you want to project sales or productivity for the new year or an upcoming month, and you want to base the projection on data from the past. If that past data is in another worksheet, you need to reference the cell or cells containing it rather than reenter that data into your active sheet. Referencing the external cell is much less labor intensive than copying the external data to your active worksheet, and it reduces the margin of error.

Combining Worksheets in a Formula

Building a formula that references a cell in another worksheet (a worksheet within the same workbook as the formula) requires nothing more than your knowledge as to which worksheet contains the cell or cells you want to reference. Your 3-D formula starts just as any other formula does—type an equal sign and begin entering your formula. At the point where the external cell is required, simply click the sheet tab for the worksheet containing the desired cell, and when that sheet is displayed, click in the cell. The formula will now include the sheet name, followed by an exclamation point and then the cell address, as in =F3+Sheet2!C6.

In this example, cell C6 is in Sheet2, and it is being added to what's in cell F3 on the active sheet (the sheet containing the formula). Obviously, having sheets that are named to indicate their content ("Sales" instead of "Sheet2") would be a big help so you know which sheet tab to click as you build your 3-D formula.

Combining Workbooks in a Formula

When you know your formula will require references to cells in another workbook, open that workbook before you begin building the formula. You can use the taskbar to switch between workbooks when the time comes to select the cell from the external workbook, or you can use the Window menu in Excel to switch between workbooks.

Including a cell from another workbook is just as simple as including a cell from another worksheet in the same workbook. It's just a matter of switching to the sheet (now found in

11

another workbook) that contains the cell you need and then clicking that cell. The following shows a formula that contains information inserted from another workbook—note the workbook name in brackets, followed by the sheet name (with an exclamation point), followed by the cell address from the external workbook.

	J15	▾	*fx* =J13/'[Projected Sales.xls]2002 Projections'!$B$7						
	C	D	E	F	G	H	I	J	
4									
5	% of Total Sales	Q2	% of Total Sales	Q3	% of Total Sales	Q4	% of Total Sales	TOTALS	
6	11%	1,204,500.30	12%	1,371,337.45	11%	1,400,650.25	13%	5,321,100.84	
7	32%	3,426,200.40	35%	3,875,125.35	32%	3,257,784.62	33%	14,534,811.61	
8	4%	574,126.00	6%	478,961.62	4%	325,789.00	3%	1,904,657.76	
9	2%	250,462.00	3%	315,793.000	3%	225,750.25	2%	1,037,717.67	
10	5%	715,987.40	7%	345,951.78	3%	625,147.15	6%	2,312,882.73	
11	31%	2,428,200.40	25%	3,975,326.85	33%	3,255,783.67	33%	13,432,012.15	
12	15%	1,304,705.30	13%	1,721,357.43	14%	1,301,620.35	13%	6,153,296.20	
13		9,904,181.80		12,083,853.48		10,392,525.29		44,696,478.97	
14									
15							Projection Comparison:	107%	

When you've selected your external cell, press ENTER if that cell is the last component of the formula, or if the formula is not yet complete, switch back to the workbook containing the formula or switch to yet another workbook or worksheet to gather more cells for your formula.

 *3-D references needn't include actual formulas that perform mathematical operations. If you simply want data from another worksheet or workbook's cell to appear (typically, for quick visual reference) in your active sheet, just type an equal sign in the cell that should contain the externally referenced cell's content and then go click in the cell that contains the data you want. Press ENTER to confirm, and the number (or text content, whatever's in the referenced cell) will appear in your active sheet.*

Using Excel's Built-in Functions

If you've used the AutoSum button, you've already used one of the built-in functions. The button invokes the SUM function—just one of more than 100 mathematical, statistical, and analytical functions, all ready and waiting to help you do things such as calculate the payment on a car loan or figure out how much an investment will be worth in 20 years.

The rest of Excel's functions can be invoked by using the Insert Function button (found on the Formula Bar, just to the left of the box where you enter/edit cell content) or by typing the function name after the equal sign and building the formula from there. Of course, the latter approach assumes you know the structure of the formula (which cell goes where within the formula, which operators to use, and any numeric or text content to include), but for functions such as SUM and AVERAGE (simple mathematical operations that most people know how to construct), you can usually forgo the Insert Function button.

For example, if you know you want to average the numbers in cells B6 through B12, you can simply type **=AVERAGE(B6:B12)** in the cell that should contain the average, and the result will appear when you press ENTER. If, on the other hand, you want to calculate a loan payment based on interest rates, down payments, length of the loan, and other variables, you'll want to use the Insert Function dialog box to select the appropriate function (PMT, in this case) and click OK.

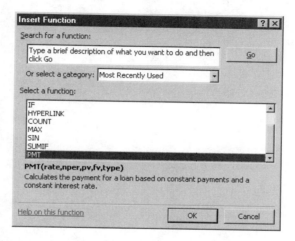

In the Function Arguments dialog box that appears, you then build the function one component at a time, by entering arguments (cell addresses, text, or numbers). The results are shown in the Formula Result field at the bottom of the dialog box, and the Formula Bar shows the function.

11

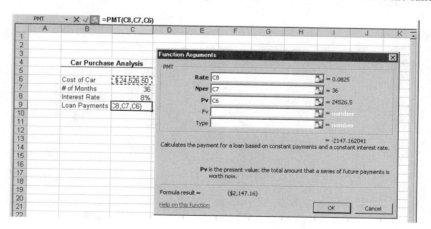

Chapter 12

Building and Maintaining List Databases

How to...

- Create a useful list database in Excel
- Avoid common pitfalls in database construction and data entry
- Put your database in any order you need it
- Search for records and query your database
- View your data from a variety of perspectives

Excel isn't just an application for storing your budget reports and maintaining accounting information. That's just half the story! You can also use Excel to store data—lists of records that can be sorted, queried, and used to create a variety of interesting reports. Although Access is touted as the database application within the Office suite, Excel's database features enable you to store your lists in a perfect environment for them—a worksheet. With 65,536 rows in an Excel worksheet, you can store up to 65,535 pieces of information (save one row for the labels that identify the information), and with 256 columns, you can break that information down into 256 parts.

Understanding Database Concepts

What is a database, exactly? It's a collection of information. The Rolodex on your desk is a database, as is the phone book. When you call a store to ask if something's in stock, they're checking their database to find out. A list of people you're inviting to your wedding, even if it's written on a sheet of paper, is a database.

Database Terminology

Before you begin the process of building a database in Excel, it's important that you understand some database terms and commands. As with any field of endeavor, getting a handle on the language is key to your success, and it will help you navigate Excel's database tools:

- **Fields and records** Remember how I said each piece of information could be broken down in to as many as 256 parts? Well, each piece of information is technically known as a *record*. Thinking again of the phone book, each listing in the phone book is a record. Also, each part of each record is a *field*. Records are broken into two or more fields, and each field is given a name. Again thinking of the phone book as a database, the field names would be Last Name, First Name, Address, and Phone Number. Figure 12-1 shows an employee database with several records (the rows), each broken into a series of fields (the columns).

- **Sorting** One of the first things most people want to do with a database is put the records in a specific order. That's called *sorting* the database. If you need to put a name and address list in alphabetical order by the Last Name field, or if you need to put a list of merchandise in alphabetically ordered groups by Product Type and also in numerical order by Product Number, Excel provides tools for sorting a database on one or more fields.

■ **Filtering** The process of viewing only certain records that meet a set of criteria is known as *filtering*. For example, if you have a list of customers and need to see only those who are in a certain state or who have a certain representative assigned to them, you can filter for records accordingly—say, for all the records with "PA" in the State field, or "Bob Smith" in the Sales Rep field.

Each row is a record.   Each column is a field and the column labels are the field names.

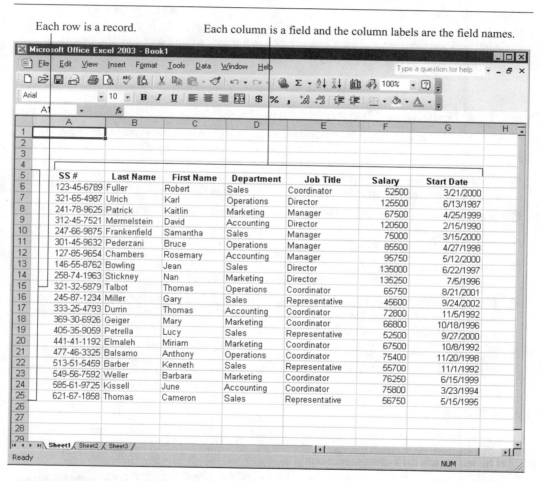

SS #	Last Name	First Name	Department	Job Title	Salary	Start Date
123-45-6789	Fuller	Robert	Sales	Coordinator	52500	3/21/2000
321-65-4987	Ulrich	Karl	Operations	Director	125500	6/13/1987
241-78-9625	Patrick	Kaitlin	Marketing	Manager	67500	4/25/1999
312-45-7521	Mermelstein	David	Accounting	Director	120500	2/15/1990
247-66-9875	Frankenfield	Samantha	Sales	Manager	75000	3/15/2000
301-45-9632	Pederzani	Bruce	Operations	Manager	85500	4/27/1998
127-85-9654	Chambers	Rosemary	Accounting	Manager	95750	5/12/2000
146-55-8762	Bowling	Jean	Sales	Director	135000	6/22/1997
258-74-1963	Stickney	Nan	Marketing	Director	135250	7/5/1996
321-32-5879	Talbot	Thomas	Operations	Coordinator	65750	8/21/2001
245-87-1234	Miller	Gary	Sales	Representative	45600	9/24/2002
333-25-4793	Durrin	Thomas	Accounting	Coordinator	72800	11/5/1992
369-30-6926	Geiger	Mary	Marketing	Coordinator	66800	10/18/1996
405-35-9059	Petrella	Lucy	Sales	Representative	52500	9/27/2000
441-41-1192	Elmaleh	Miriam	Marketing	Coordinator	67500	10/8/1992
477-46-3325	Balsamo	Anthony	Operations	Coordinator	75400	11/20/1998
513-51-5459	Barber	Kenneth	Sales	Representative	55700	11/1/1992
549-56-7592	Weller	Barbara	Marketing	Coordinator	76250	6/15/1999
585-61-9725	Kissell	June	Accounting	Coordinator	75800	3/23/1994
621-67-1858	Thomas	Cameron	Sales	Representative	56750	5/15/1995

FIGURE 12-1   Logical layout is the key to an effective database.

12

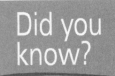

Relational vs. Flat File Databases

The Office 2003 suite provides two different types of database tools. Access, which is a *relational* database, allows you to set up multiple database tables that can be related to each other by one or more common fields, such as a table that lists customers, and another table that lists customer credit limits. The two tables with this customer data in them can be linked by the common Customer Name or Customer Number field, and reports can then be created that draw data from both tables. Excel, which is a *flat file* database, allows you to build as many databases as you want, but each one is an island. Flat file databases can't be linked to each other, even if there's a great deal of overlap in the information stored within them.

Excel List Database Requirements

As simple as Excel is to use in building and maintaining a database, it does have some rules. If you don't follow them, your ability to sort, filter, and report on your data will be compromised:

- *Always set up your database horizontally.* The field names (column heading) should be in the first row of the database (though not necessarily the first row of the worksheet).

- *You can have only one row of field names.* If you need more than 256 fields (the total number of columns available in a single worksheet), you need to use Access instead of Excel to store your data.

- *Leave no blank rows within the database.* Any blank rows can make sorting difficult, because blank rows can prevent the entire database being sorted.

- *Use consistent spelling.* If you're entering a list of employees and the departments they work in, and some of the Department fields contain "Acctg." and others have "Accounting," a sort by department won't work properly.

- *Break the records into as many fields as possible.* The more fields you have, the more sorting and filtering options you'll have.

Building a List

With the rules for database setup in mind, you're ready to build the list. The building process consists of two steps: setting up the column headings (which are the field names) and entering the records. To begin entering the records into your list, simply click in the first cell of the first blank row under your columns headings and start typing the data for the first record. When you get to the end of the first record, press ENTER, then press HOME. This keyboard progression will take you to the first cell in the next row, where you can begin entering the second record in your

How to ... Freeze Your Database Field Names

As you're entering records, you will eventually reach a point where if you go to the next row, the column headings will no longer show onscreen. This can be confusing for you as you continue to enter records. The answer? Keep your column headings onscreen by freezing the row that contains them. Select the row beneath your column headings and choose Window | Freeze Panes. The column headings (your field names) will now remain onscreen no matter how many rows of data you enter.

database. Remember, it's not important that you enter your records in a particular order. You can always sort them later, by any field in the database.

> **TIP**   *To speed your data entry, Excel's AutoComplete feature will try to guess what you're going to enter into cells in each field, based on previous entries in the same field. For example, if you're entering a list of employees and the Job Title field contains "Coordinator," simply typing "Co" will signal AutoComplete to fill the field with "Coordinator." If you also have "Consultant" in one or more of the cells in that same column/field, the guess won't be triggered until you type "Con" or "Coo." Once the guess appears, if it's correct, press TAB to accept it and move to the next field. If it's not correct, ignore it and keep typing the desired entry.*

Sorting by a Single Field

A single-field sort is very simple to do. Just click in any cell in the column that you want to sort by and then click either the Sort Ascending or Sort Descending button on the Standard toolbar. Once you've sorted by a single field, you can do subsequent single-field sorts by clicking in any other column and using the Sort buttons again. If the field(s) you've previously sorted by don't conflict with the new sort, the original order will be maintained. For example, in a list of employees, if you just sorted by Last Name, a sort by Department will list the employees by department, but for each department, the employees will remain in Last Name order.

Sorting by Multiple Fields

For larger databases, multiple-field sorts can turn your database into a series of groups of records, each group further sorted by an additional field or two. Using the employee list example, a logical multiple-field sort might include sorting by Department, and within that sort, sorting by Job Title, then by Last Name. The result? All the people in each department would be grouped, then within those Department groups, the records would be in order by Job Title. If there are two or more people in any department who have the same job title, those records would be in Last Name order.

12

To perform a multiple-field sort, choose Data | Sort. In the resulting Sort dialog box, you can choose the first field to sort by, then up to two subsequent fields by which to sort. When selecting fields, always start with the one that has the most duplicate entries; otherwise, there won't be enough records in the first sort-created group to sort by the remaining field(s).

As you can see, the Sort dialog box contains an option regarding a "header row" in your database. The *header row* is the row that contains your field names. If instead of seeing your field names in the Sort By and Then By text boxes you see Column A, B, C, and so on, make sure that the Header Row option is selected—this tells Excel to look to that row for your field names. If the option is selected and you're still not seeing your field names, click Cancel and go back to your worksheet. Make sure that the active cell is within the data portion of the sheet (not on a field name or a blank row below the rows of data) and then reopen the Sort dialog box.

Creating a Subtotal Report

Subtotal reports take your sorted list and perform calculations on each group created by the sort, be it a single-field sort that breaks one column into groups, or a multiple-field sort that creates several groups within the data. The calculations performed on each group in the sorted list can be any of 12 listed functions, but you'll find that SUM, AVERAGE, and COUNT are the most useful. Using our Department/Job Title/Last Name sort, we can SUM the Salary field for each Department grouping so that you can see how much is spent on payroll for each department.

If you also want to COUNT the people in each department, you'll need to repeat the following procedure, preserving the first report and adding to it. Before any subtotal report is created, you need to perform the sort that will put the database in the proper order, an order that breaks your data into the groups that will be summed, counted, averaged, or otherwise calculated. After your sort is completed, choose Data | Subtotals. In the resulting dialog box (shown here), follow these steps:

CHAPTER 12: Building and Maintaining List Databases **215**

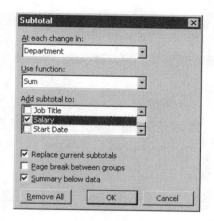

1. Click the drop list for the At Each Change In option and choose the field you sorted by that created the largest groups of records.

2. In the Use Function list, select the calculation you want to apply.

3. From the list of fields in the Add Subtotal To option, place check marks in the fields the selected function should apply to. For example, if you chose SUM, you would choose fields that contain numeric data; if you chose COUNT, you can choose any field, because Excel will literally count how many records fall into the sort-created groups.

4. By default, Replace Current Subtotals is checked, which means that if you had already created a subtotal report on this database, it would be removed in favor of the one you're creating now. Uncheck this option if you're adding a new level (further subtotaling) to the existing report.

5. Click OK to create the report. Figure 12-2 shows a subtotal report that includes total salary paid to each department's staff.

So what do you do with all those number buttons on the left side of the worksheet? You can use them to expand and collapse sections of the report. If you want to see all the details of the report—every record and all the subtotals—click the 3 button. If you want to see only the subtotals, as shown next, click the 2 button. If you want to see only the grand total and no supporting information at all, click the 1 button.

F10	▼	fx	=SUBTOTAL(9,F6:F9)					
	A	B	C	D	E	F	G	H
5	SS #	Last Name	First Name	Department	Job Title	Salary	Start Date	
10				Accounting Total		$ 364,850.00		
16				Marketing Total		$ 413,300.00		
21				Operations Total		$ 352,150.00		
29				Sales Total		$ 473,050.00		
30				Grand Total		$1,603,350.00		
31								

12

Use these buttons to expand or collapse sections of the report.

	A	B	C	D	E	F	G
4							
5	SS #	Last Name	First Name	Department	Job Title	Salary	Start Date
6	333-25-4793	Durrin	Thomas	Accounting	Coordinator	$ 72,800.00	11/5/1992
7	585-61-9725	Kissell	June	Accounting	Coordinator	$ 75,800.00	3/23/1994
8	312-45-7521	Mermelstein	David	Accounting	Director	$ 120,500.00	2/15/1990
9	127-85-9654	Chambers	Rosemary	Accounting	Manager	$ 95,750.00	5/12/2000
10				Accounting Total		$ 364,850.00	
11	441-41-1192	Elmaleh	Miriam	Marketing	Coordinator	$ 67,500.00	10/8/1992
12	369-30-6926	Geiger	Mary	Marketing	Coordinator	$ 66,800.00	10/18/1996
13	549-56-7592	Weller	Barbara	Marketing	Coordinator	$ 76,250.00	6/15/1999
14	258-74-1963	Stickney	Nan	Marketing	Director	$ 135,250.00	7/5/1996
15	241-78-9625	Patrick	Kaitlin	Marketing	Manager	$ 67,500.00	4/25/1999
16				Marketing Total		$ 413,300.00	
17	477-46-3325	Balsamo	Anthony	Operations	Coordinator	$ 75,400.00	11/20/1998
18	321-32-5879	Talbot	Thomas	Operations	Coordinator	$ 65,750.00	8/21/2001
19	321-65-4987	Ulrich	Karl	Operations	Director	$ 125,500.00	6/13/1987
20	301-45-9632	Pederzani	Bruce	Operations	Manager	$ 85,500.00	4/27/1998
21				Operations Total		$ 352,150.00	
22	123-45-6789	Fuller	Robert	Sales	Coordinator	$ 52,500.00	3/21/2000
23	146-55-8762	Bowling	Jean	Sales	Director	$ 135,000.00	6/22/1997
24	247-66-9875	Frankenfield	Samantha	Sales	Manager	$ 75,000.00	3/15/2000
25	513-51-5459	Barber	Kenneth	Sales	Representative	$ 55,700.00	11/1/1992
26	245-87-1234	Miller	Gary	Sales	Representative	$ 45,600.00	9/24/2002
27	405-35-9059	Petrella	Lucy	Sales	Representative	$ 52,500.00	9/27/2000
28	621-67-1858	Thomas	Cameron	Sales	Representative	$ 56,750.00	5/15/1995
29				Sales Total		$ 473,050.00	
30				Grand Total		$ 1,603,350.00	
31							
32							
33							

FIGURE 12-2   Sorting the records (shown earlier in Figure 12-1) by one or more fields makes it possible to perform calculations on the groups created by the sort.

The plus and minus sign buttons on the left allow you to expand and collapse parts of the report. If, for example, you've elected to see only the subtotals and no per-record detail, you can expand one of the subtotals to see its detail, leaving the other groups collapsed. Click the plus sign next to the subtotal you want to expand, and it turns to a minus sign, which indicates that all the detail that's available is already displayed.

TIP *To remove the Subtotal Report from your database, simply choose Data | Subtotals and click the Remove All button in the dialog box. The dialog box immediately closes, and the subtotals are removed from the database.*

Searching for Specific Records

Nothing's worse than staring at a list of several hundred records and not being able to find the one you need. When this happens, you can use either of Excel's two features for filtering a database. First, there's AutoFilter, which enables you to select certain criteria for one or more fields in your database and see only the records that meet that criteria. Second, there's the Advanced Filter feature, which allows you to set up a sample record and to execute a search for all records that match the example.

Using AutoFilter to Locate and Display Records in a List

AutoFilter is simply an automatic tool for filtering an Excel database. To use this feature, follow these steps:

1. Click in any cell in your database and choose Data | Filter | AutoFilter. As soon as you choose this command, your database field names acquire drop lists, as shown here:

E7		*fx*	Representative						
	A	B	C	D	E	F	G	H	
1									
2									
3									
4									
5	SS #	Last Name	First Name	Departmen	Job Title	Salary	Start Date		
6	477-46-3325	Balsamo	Anthony	Operations	Sort Ascending	$ 75,400.00	11/20/1998		
7	513-51-5459	Barber	Kenneth	Sales	Sort Descending	$ 55,700.00	11/1/1992		
8	146-55-8762	Bowling	Jean	Sales	(All)	$ 135,000.00	6/22/1997		
9	127-85-9654	Chambers	Rosemary	Accounting	(Top 10...)	$ 95,750.00	5/12/2000		
10	333-25-4793	Durrin	Thomas	Accounting	(Custom...)	$ 72,800.00	11/5/1992		
11	441-41-1192	Elmaleh	Miriam	Marketing	Coordinator	$ 67,500.00	10/8/1992		
12	247-66-9875	Frankenfield	Samantha	Sales	Director	$ 75,000.00	3/15/2000		
13	123-45-6789	Fuller	Robert	Sales	Manager	$ 52,500.00	3/21/2000		
14	369-30-6926	Geiger	Mary	Marketing	Representative	$ 66,800.00	10/18/1996		
15	585-61-9725	Kissell	June	Accounting	Coordinator	$ 75,800.00	3/23/1994		

2. Select the field you want to filter your data by, click the drop list next to that field's name, and choose from one of three options (All, Top 10, and Custom) or pick one of the listed entries for that field.

After distilling the list based on the first filter, you can filter additional fields. The subsequent filters can reduce the list, potentially reducing the list to one record, or even to no records if none of the records match the criteria you've chosen. Note that your AutoFiltered list is in a temporary state:

■ To refilter or unfilter a field, simply click the filtered field's drop list again and choose All from the list to bring back all the records that were hidden by filtering that field, or choose different criteria from the list.

■ To bring back all the records and unfilter all the fields in one fell swoop, choose Data | AutoFilter | Show All. The AutoFilter drop list remains onscreen for each field, but all the records are shown.

12

■ To remove the AutoFilter feature from your worksheet, choose Data | Filter | AutoFilter. Select it to turn the feature on, select it again to turn it off.

Setting Up Advanced Filters

Within the Data | Filter submenu is the Advanced Filter command. This particular filtering tool allows you to set up an example that is compared to the database, and only those records that match it are displayed. To perform an Advanced Filter operation, follow these steps:

1. Create a space above your database on the same worksheet with your data by using the Insert | Rows command to add three or four rows above column headings.

2. Copy your field names to the top row of the sample area you've created.

3. Type the sample data in the cell(s) under one or more of the sample field names.

4. Click in any cell within your database and choose Data | Filter | Advanced Filter. The Advanced Filter dialog box opens.

5. In the Action section of the dialog box, choose where the results of your filter will appear: in place or copied to another area. If you choose to copy it to another location, you'll have to specify where.

6. Click the Criteria Range box and move the dialog box aside so you can select the cells that contain the sample area. This should include the copied column headings and the sample data entered below one or more of the field names.

7. Click OK. The criteria range (your sample area) is compared to the main database, and any matching records are displayed.

Figure 12-3 shows a sample area on the employee worksheet and the matching records displayed within the main database.

TIP *If you perform an advanced filter and no records appear, check for typos in your field names and sample data—this is the most common reason that filters don't work.*

For numeric data, you can use > and < symbols within the sample data to refine the filter.

	A	B	C	D	E	F	G	H
1								
2	SS #	Last Name	First Name	Department	Job Title	Salary	Start Date	
3				Accounting	Coordinator	>65000		
4								
5	SS #	Last Name	First Name	Department	Job Title	Salary	Start Date	
10	333-25-4793	Durrin	Thomas	Accounting	Coordinator	$ 72,800.00	11/5/1992	
15	585-61-9725	Kissell	June	Accounting	Coordinator	$ 75,800.00	3/23/1994	
26								
27								
28								

FIGURE 12-3 Set up your example and compare it to the database to find records that match the criteria.

PivotTable Basics

The term "PivotTable" isn't exactly self-explanatory. What *is* a PivotTable and what does it do? The best and simplest explanation I can give you is that a PivotTable is a report that allows you to turn (pivot) your data and view it from a variety of angles. The process of building a PivotTable is somewhat lengthy, but not terribly complex, and can be used to create a unique view of a database, such as our employee list, as shown in Figure 12-4.

Building a PivotTable

Once you've decided what you want to see on your report, it's time to build it:

1. Click in any cell within your database and choose Data | PivotTable and PivotChart Report. Step 1 of the wizard appears.

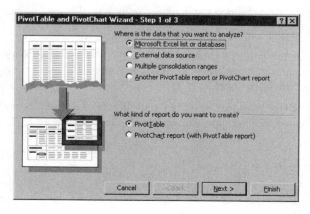

Job Title data is in rows so that each title can be analyzed.

Choose a department from this drop list.

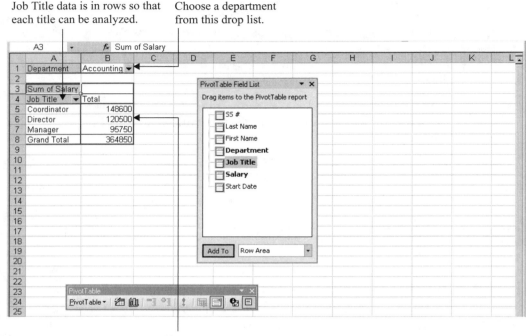

The Salary field is viewed here, where it can be summed, averaged, or counted.

FIGURE 12-4 More intuitive than a sort or subtotal report, the PivotTable report gives you the ability to create unique perspectives on your data.

2. Stick with the defaults. You're intending to analyze Microsoft Excel List Database, and you just want a PivotTable, so click Next to move to Step 2.

3. In Step 2 of the wizard, confirm where the data you want to work with is located. The wizard should have selected your entire database, including the column headings. If this didn't happen, drag through the database to include the headings and all the rows.

4. Click Next to move to Step 3.

5. In Step 3 of the wizard, indicate where you want your report to appear—in a new worksheet or on the same worksheet as the data. Again, stick with the default here and choose the New Worksheet option.

6. Click Finish. The wizard closes, and the empty PivotTable report, a toolbox listing your fields, and a floating toolbar appear onscreen, as shown in Figure 12-5.

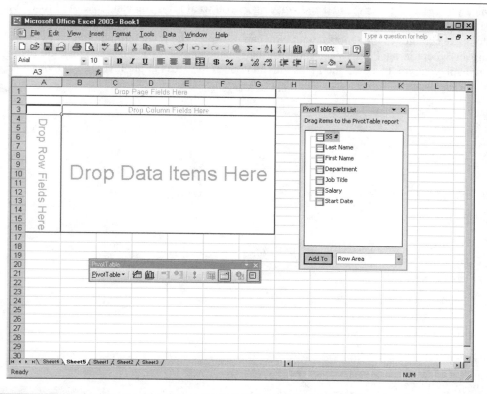

FIGURE 12-5 The basic layout of a PivotTable appears in four graphical boxes, along with a list of your fields and tools for customizing your PivotTable.

7. Move your field names from the PivotTable Field List into the empty sections of the PivotTable report by dragging the field names with your mouse.

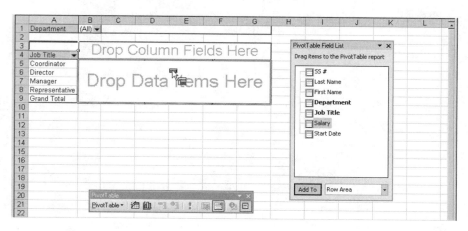

Once your PivotTable is created and working as you want it to, you can close the PivotTable Field List box and PivotTable toolbar so that there's nothing cluttering your workspace. If you need to make changes to the report layout, you can redisplay the PivotTable Field List by right-clicking anywhere in the PivotTable report itself and choosing Show Field List. Once the field list is redisplayed, you can drag the fields into and out of the areas in the PivotTable, redesigning your report as desired.

Chapter 13

Charting Excel Data

How to...

- Understand chart types and charting terminology
- Choose the right type of chart for your data
- Build a useful and attractive chart
- Format charts for dynamic visual effects

If a picture's worth a thousand words, a chart is worth at least that many numbers. Worksheet cell after worksheet cell filled with numeric data can be mind-numbing to look at and very difficult for others to understand. One look at many worksheets and you might have absolutely no idea what the worksheet data means. What does it say? What does it prove? What message or information should you take away from looking at the worksheet? If you need to express a simple concept through your worksheet data (one division's sales are down, productivity is up in a certain part of the organization, more people like chocolate than vanilla), converting that data to a chart might be the way to go.

Using Charts to Enhance Worksheets

Although a chart will never replace your worksheet, it can be a significant enhancement. An Excel chart can be on the same worksheet with the data that created it, or the chart can be on its own sheet in the same workbook. An Excel chart can also live in an entirely different workbook, in a Word document, or in a PowerPoint presentation. The visual impact of a chart is useful just about anywhere that the plotted data will be displayed, discussed, or simply referred to. Figure 13-1 shows an Excel worksheet with a chart accompanying it.

Excel charts are free-floating objects appearing on top of the worksheet, not within any particular cell. Charts are linked to the data that was used to create them, so if the data is updated, the chart updates as well. The only time this isn't the case is if you paste an Excel chart into a Word document or PowerPoint presentation. When using a chart outside of the worksheet containing the charted data, you must use the Paste Special command to create a link between the chart and the Excel data if you want updates to occur in the pasted location. Chapter 2 discusses in detail the process of building these links.

Understanding Chart Types

Several major chart types are offered through Excel's charting tools. Each type of chart will express data differently, creating a different picture of your data. Figure 13-2 shows data from the same worksheet charted using three different chart types.

How do you know which type of chart to use for your data? Think about your goals for the chart. What story do you want to tell? To whom are you telling the story? If your goal is to show several groups of the same type of information and show how each group is different, you want a chart that shows *comparisons*. If you want to show how something is going, how progress is being made from one or more perspectives, you want a chart that shows *trends*. If you want to reflect the amount of something—"Yes" answers to a survey question, for example—you probably want a

Click the Chart Wizard tool to create a chart
based on the selected worksheet content.

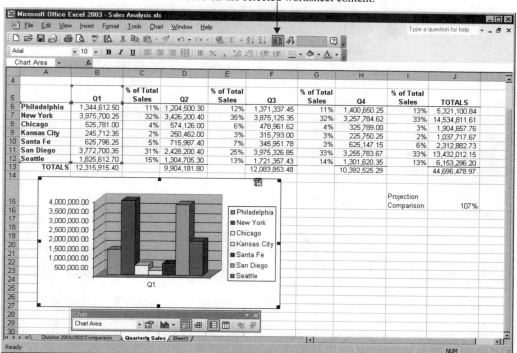

FIGURE 13-1   The data in the worksheet is clear enough, but the trends and comparisons it
reveals are much clearer in the chart.

chart that shows *frequency*. You may also, however, want to see comparisons on a frequency
chart—to see how many "No" answers (and "Don't Know" responses) were given to the same
question. Can a single chart type do both things? Sure it can. Consider these charting goals and the
charts that will help you achieve them:

- Line charts and column charts are good choices for showing trends.

- Pie, bar, column, doughnut, and area charts are best for showing comparisons.

- Column charts can be used to show frequency. You can also use scatter charts, where
  each dot indicates a response or an occurrence of an event.

TIP   *If you want to suggest a trend at the same time that you're showing a comparison, use
the Drawing toolbar's Line or Arrow tools to draw one or more lines that indicate the
direction things are headed. If your columns are generally getting higher over the course
of time represented by the chart, draw a line (with an arrowhead) above the columns' tops
that emphasizes this "onward and upward" trend.*

The data, including data labels from row and column headings, that makes up the chart

Column chart

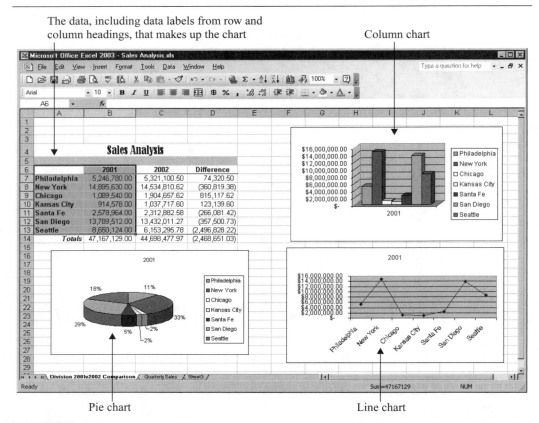

Pie chart

Line chart

FIGURE 13-2   Use different types of charts to tell very similar stories in very different ways.

Understanding Chart Elements

Each row or column label and each piece of data in the area of your worksheet designated for charting creates a piece of the chart. Within the chart, the various parts have names, and it's important to learn them so that you can choose the right tools to adjust them later and also understand how they work together:

- **Data points**   Each number in your worksheet—the total sales for a given location or the number of products sold in a given time period—is a *data point*.

- **Data series**   Each logical collection of related data points is called a *data series*. If your chart contains the sales for January, February, and March for two sales divisions, one data series would be three month's worth of sales for one of the divisions. Another data series would be one month's worth of sales for both divisions.

> **NOTE** *A pie chart can show only one data series at a time. If you want the look of a pie but need to plot more than one series, use a doughnut chart. Each concentric ring of colored sections is a different series.*

- **Chart axes** Your chart's data is plotted along a vertical *value axis* and a horizontal *category axis*. The value axis is used to determine the value each column represents, and the category axis helps indicate the nature of the data being plotted.

- **The legend** A legend further explains the data represented, and normally appears on the right side of the chart, matching the colored bars/slices/lines with specific data series.

- **Titles** You can add a chart title and a title for each axis on your worksheet. Titles can be helpful to people who aren't familiar with the information included in your chart.

- **Gridlines** Typically running horizontally behind columns, bars, or lines on a chart, the gridlines help you visually connect the data points with a number on the value axis.

- **Plot area** This is the portion of the chart where the data is plotted. Legends and titles are not part of the plot area. You can resize the plot area (shown encompassed in a gray border on the active chart in Figure 13-3) within the chart object itself, or you can move the plot area so that the chart is no longer centered within the chart object.

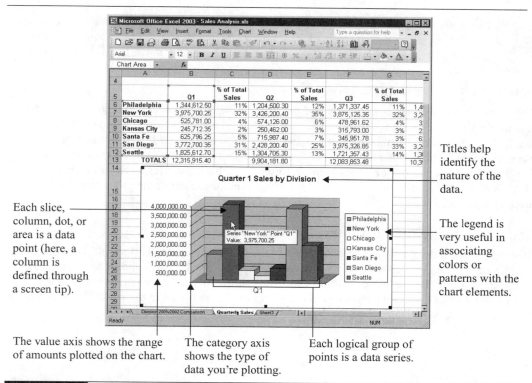

Each slice, column, dot, or area is a data point (here, a column is defined through a screen tip).

Titles help identify the nature of the data.

The legend is very useful in associating colors or patterns with the chart elements.

13

The value axis shows the range of amounts plotted on the chart.

The category axis shows the type of data you're plotting.

Each logical group of points is a data series.

FIGURE 13-3 All your chart's data is within the movable and resizable plot area.

Building a Chart

The process of building a chart is relatively simple, thanks to the Chart Wizard, which appears as soon as you click the Chart Wizard tool. This wizard coaches you through the process of selecting a chart type, confirming which data to chart, applying any desired chart formats, and positioning your chart on the active worksheet or on a sheet all its own. Don't worry about all the choices you make through the wizard. Although planning is a good first step—best taken before you even open the Chart Wizard—you won't necessarily know everything your chart will need or how it will look best until you've actually created the chart in the first place, and at that point, you can go back and make changes.

Selecting Data for Charting

When you begin a new chart, the first step is to select the data that will be charted. This sounds easy enough, and it is—with one small caveat: It's very important to omit things that might make the chart confusing, such as the worksheet title and any cells with content unrelated to the chart's data. You also want to avoid selecting columns or rows of totals, averages, or other formulas that operate on the data you're charting—if you accidentally include them, they can be mistaken for the core data.

TIP   *Your selection needn't be one contiguous range of cells. If you want to chart one column of numbers, select the row labels for as many cells in the column as you want to plot and identify. Then, with CTRL pressed, select the column with the data you want to plot.*

Setting Up a New Chart

Once the data and headings are selected and the Chart Wizard is invoked, you're guided, step by step, through the logical steps in building a chart. Each of these steps is handled in a new dialog box, and virtually all of them contain two or more tabs. You don't need to delve into each tab for every chart you build, but there are plenty of options to play with should you need or want to. You'll use the Next and Back buttons to move forward and backward (respectively) within the wizard's dialog boxes, and of course, the Cancel button bails you out of the process without building the chart.

Step 1: Choosing the Best Chart for Your Data

Your choice of chart type should be based on the kind of message your chart should convey—trends, comparisons, or frequency. This will mean choosing between two- and three-dimensional charts, and various chart subtypes that meet specific charting needs, as shown here. The chart type you choose will affect the choices offered in the subsequent steps in the wizard. To proceed to the next step in the wizard, click the Next button.

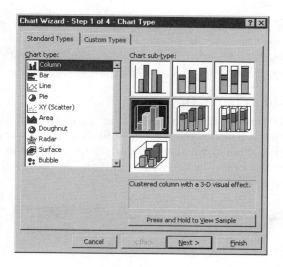

Step 2: Confirming the Data to Chart

This wizard dialog box shows you your selected range of cells, expressed as a range or series of ranges, and displays a very rudimentary example of how that data will be charted with the chart type you selected in the previous step. As you can see here, you can also choose to plot the data series in columns or rows—this will determine which data goes into the category axis and which data goes into the legend. To see how this will affect your chart, experiment by clicking the Rows radio button and then switch back to Columns (the default). When you like what you see, click Next to move to Step 3.

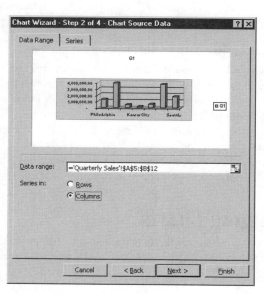

13

 *If you don't want one or more of your chart's series to be included after all, click the Series tab and select the series to remove. You can also add series by entering a Value range and clicking the Add button. To designate a Value range, simply move the dialog box aside so you can see the desired portion of your worksheet.*

Step 3: Setting Up Your Chart's Options

This step in the Chart Wizard process offers six tabs: Titles, Axes, Gridlines, Legend, Data Labels, and Data Table. For most charts, you won't have to tinker with the options in all six tabs, but you might want to customize your chart's titles, reposition or remove the legend, or change the style and frequency of the chart's gridlines. To view the options in each of these areas, click the corresponding tab.

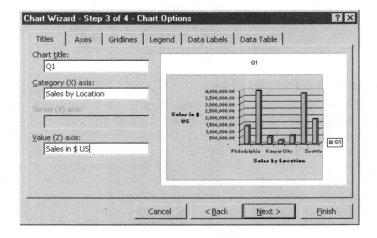

Step 4: Selecting a Home for Your Chart

Here, you have two choices for where to place the chart you've just built: on the active sheet or on a new sheet entirely devoted to the chart. In the former case, the chart will be a floating object that can be moved anywhere on the sheet (or on any other existing sheet in the workbook, selected by clicking the drop list for this option). In the latter case, the chart will be a full page in size and cannot be moved. It becomes the entire sheet itself rather than being a movable graphic object. To name the new chart sheet, type a name in the As New Sheet text box.

When your chart's name and/or location have been established, click Finish. The chart appears as you've created it, on the sheet you chose for its final location.

Updating and Changing Charts

If you want your chart to update whenever the data on which it is based is changed, you're in luck. This is what happens automatically, whether your chart is on the sheet with that data or on a sheet all by itself in the same workbook. If you don't want the chart to update—perhaps to freeze the chart's data in time while the worksheet goes on to be continuously updated—you can store the chart and a copy of the original data on a separate sheet and allow the original worksheet to continue being updated as needed. The chart will remain intact because the duplicate version of the data it is based on will remain unchanged.

If you need to change the range of cells included in your chart, select the chart and choose Chart | Source Data. The Source Data dialog box (see Figure 13-4) shows the current range of cells in the chart, and you can select a new range by moving the dialog box aside and dragging through a new range of cells.

> **TIP** *If you want to add to the existing range, choose Chart | Add Data. You can type an added range (including any headings or labels you want to include) or move the resulting Add Data dialog box aside and drag through the range to be added. Click OK to add the range to your chart.*

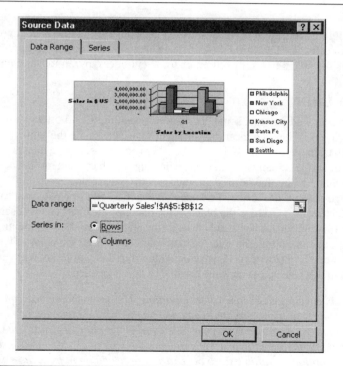

FIGURE 13-4   View and edit the chart's existing data range in the Source Data dialog box.

13

Changing Chart Types

To change from the type of chart you chose originally to a different chart type (or between 2-D and 3-D versions of the same chart type), click the Chart Type button on the Chart toolbar while your chart is selected. As you can see here, a palette of 18 choices appears when you click the button.

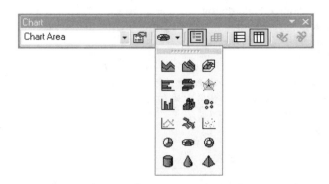

The first two columns represent the 2-D and 3-D varieties of five different chart types, and the third column offers five additional chart types. The options on the bottom row are the different 3-D shapes for use in bar and column charts—cylinders, pyramids, and cones.

Formatting a Chart

Although your chart may be fine as is, some charts need tweaking. Excel offers very simple tools for making changes in your chart's appearance, most of which resemble the same tools you used when building the chart in the first place. Excel also offers context-sensitive menus—on the menu bar and in the form of shortcut menus—that make selecting the chart element that needs changing or reformatting and then making the desired alterations very easy to do.

To take advantage of these tools, just click once on the chart element you want to change and choose Format | Selected _____, where the blank is the name of the chart element selected. You can also right-click any selected element and choose Format from the shortcut menu. The resulting dialog box offers options for editing the selected chart element—from the color of bars or slices, to the size and font of the axis or title text. The options offered in the dialog box will vary, depending on the chart element that's selected at the time the dialog box is opened.

TIP *With your chart selected, choose Chart | Options. The same dialog box you saw in Step 3 in the Chart Wizard will open, and you can use the tabs to make changes, add new elements, and remove things from your chart that you no longer want. The Chart Options dialog box that appears will vary depending on the type of chart you have selected. For example, the options available for a pie chart are very different from those you'd see for a column chart.*

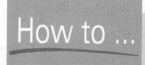

Reposition Slice Values and Names on a Pie Chart

If you want to move a category name on a pie chart, click once on any of the names and then click once more on the individual name you want to move. The individual name acquires handles, and if you point to the border between the handles and drag, you can move the entire name anywhere you want on the chart. Note that if you drag a pie slice label (the category name or the percentage, for example) away from the slice, a line appears between the name and the slice so that it remains clear that the label pertains to that particular slice of the pie.

Editing Chart Text

To edit the text in a chart or axis title, just click twice on the text—these are two distinct clicks, not a double-click. On the first click, the title is selected, and on the second, your cursor is activated in the text box right on the chart. At this point, you can use the arrow keys to move within the text for editing it, or while the text is selected, you can retype the text to replace it entirely. If you open the Chart Options dialog box (Chart | Chart Options), you can edit your chart titles right within the dialog box rather than on the chart itself.

Resizing and Moving Charts

When a chart is an object on a worksheet—as opposed to being a sheet unto itself—you can move and resize it as you would any graphic element. When you click a chart object, handles appear on the four corners and in the middle of each side. These handles can be used to resize the chart, making it taller, wider, narrower, shorter, or some combination thereof. Figure 13-5 shows a selected chart and a handle in use—the dashed border shows how big the chart will be when the mouse is released.

Deleting Charts

To delete a chart object on any worksheet, just click the chart to select it (make sure the handles are on the perimeter of the chart, not on an element within the chart object) and press DELETE. You can also right-click the chart and choose Clear from the shortcut menu. If your chart is on a chart sheet all by itself, you need to delete the sheet. In so doing, you get rid of the chart as well. To delete the sheet, right-click the sheet tab and choose Delete from the shortcut menu.

13

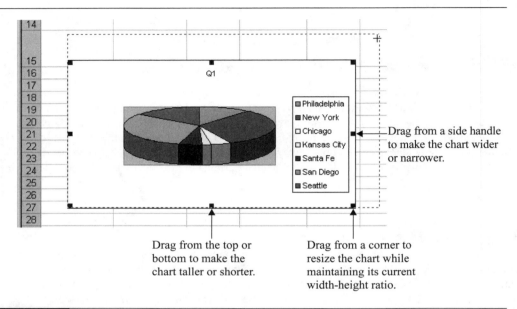

Drag from a side handle to make the chart wider or narrower.

Drag from the top or bottom to make the chart taller or shorter.

Drag from a corner to resize the chart while maintaining its current width-height ratio.

FIGURE 13-5 Choose a handle and drag it to resize the chart.

Chapter 14

Printing and Publishing Worksheets

How to...

- Print a selection, one or more worksheets, or an entire workbook
- Control how many sheets of paper your printout requires
- Customize the appearance of a printout
- Publish worksheet content to the web

More and more often, the worksheets we create are viewed only onscreen. Whether opened after being sent as an email attachment or viewed through a website, when you need to show someone else your worksheet, you don't necessarily need a printer to do so. So why even talk about printing? Because Excel offers so many options for printing that even if printing worksheets is something you rarely do, you'll want to know how to control your printout and make sure your printed worksheet makes a good impression. Another focus of this chapter is the publishing of Excel content to the web—saving a worksheet in HTML format and making the worksheet an interactive part of a web page.

Printing Workbooks and Worksheets

Printing a workbook or worksheet is extremely easy. Simply choose File | Print or click the Print button on the Standard toolbar, and after you click the OK button in the resulting Print dialog box (see Figure 14-1), your worksheet prints out. This simple procedure and result are just the tip of

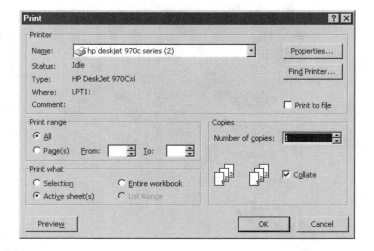

FIGURE 14-1 Choose your printer, which sheets to print, and how many copies to generate—all within the Print dialog box.

How to ... **Control Your Print Area**

The CTRL-P keyboard shortcut sends a default print job (one copy of every page in the active sheet) to the default printer (or the printer you last used in the current Excel session), offering no dialog box for you to use in customizing the print job. To get around this, you can set a print area for your worksheet so that you can use CTRL-P to do a quick print of a section of your worksheet. Select the area to be printed and then choose File | Print Area | Set Print Area. Until you clear the print area (File | Print Area | Clear Print Area), the designated print area will be what's printed if you press CTRL-P.

the iceberg, however. For example, what if you only want to print part of your worksheet? Or if your worksheet is large, what if you need it all to fit on one sheet of paper? Excel makes it possible to customize your printout to meet your needs.

The first thing to know: By default, when you choose to print (by choosing File | Print or by clicking the Print button on the toolbar), the active worksheet is printed. If you want to print more than one of your sheets or only some of the pages in a particular sheet, or if you want to print the entire workbook (all the sheets), you have to request it through the Print dialog box.

The second, and perhaps the more important thing to know: By default, Excel will print your worksheets on as many sheets as it needs to. If, based on the amount of content and your formatting, a worksheet spans four pages, your worksheet will print on four sheets of paper, the breaks between them indicated by dashed lines running along certain columns and rows on your worksheet.

Printing an Entire Workbook

What if you want to print all the worksheets in the active workbook? Easy enough—just click the Entire Workbook option in the Print dialog box. Many people are surprised by how many pages even a smallish worksheet can require when printed. You can find out how many pages your printout will require before actually sending the workbook to the printer by previewing the print job. To do this, choose File | Print and click the Entire Workbook option in the Print What section of the resulting Print dialog box. Then, click the Preview button in the lower-left corner of the dialog box, and the Print Preview window will open. When you view the preview, you'll see your active worksheet's first page, and by using the Next button at the top of the window, you can move through the workbook, page by page, worksheet by worksheet. The Zoom button lets you toggle between full-page and close-up views of your worksheet(s). To immediately find out how many pages the printout will require, look in the lower-left corner of the Preview window— the page count and the number of the current page are displayed.

Assuming all's well with the preview, you can go right to the printer by clicking the Print button in the Print Preview window, or you can close the preview and go back to your active worksheet and print later.

14

 *Why not choose File | Print Preview or click the Print Preview button on the Standard toolbar? Because without first specifying that you want to print the entire workbook, the preview will only show you the default—the pages of the active worksheet.*

Printing Individual Worksheets

If you want to print one or more individual sheets in a workbook, you can do so through the Print dialog box. To print multiple sheets, you'll want to group the worksheets to print before opening the Print dialog box. Then, using the Print What section of the dialog box, click the Active Sheet(s) option.

If you want to print only certain pages within the active worksheet, make sure the desired sheet is the active one and then choose File | Print. In the Print dialog box, enter the page numbers you want to print. Unlike in Word, where you can print ranges and individual pages in the same print job, in Excel you're limited to printing ranges (1 to 5, for example).

Printing a Range of Cells

So you can print an entire workbook, a particular worksheet, or even a group of worksheets. What if you want to print just part of a worksheet? You can select as little as one cell or a large range of contiguous and noncontiguous blocks of cells on a single worksheet and print them. This is rather convenient if you want to print and share part of your worksheet with someone but don't want him or her to see the whole thing.

To print part of a worksheet, follow these steps:

1. Select the cell or range of cells that you want to print.
2. Choose File | Print. The Print dialog box opens.
3. In the Print dialog box, click the Selection option in the Print What section.
4. Click OK to send the print job to the printer.

Controlling Page Breaks and Page Count

Thus far, all the printing we've discussed has been based on using the default settings—letting the printout flow as it wants to, using as many sheets of paper as it wants to. That's fine for many print jobs, but there will be times when you want to control how many sheets of paper are used for a print job. To achieve this control, you have several choices. You can specify the number of pages you want and force Excel to shrink or expand your printed content to fit, or you can tinker with the worksheets' margins, paper size, and paper orientation to achieve the printout you need. You might find that using one or more techniques together will give you the exact printout you're looking for.

Adjusting Margins

Just as in a Word document, your worksheet has margins—space on the four sides of the page where no printing can occur. You can reduce or enlarge them in one of two ways:

■ Choose File | Page Setup. On the Margins tab, enter the desired top, bottom, left, and right margins. You can also set header and footer margins. These represent the space set aside for things such as page numbers, your name, copyright information, or the date and time.

The smallest margin you can set for any side of the page, or for your header/footer margin, is .25 inches.

■ Choose File | Print Preview (or click the Print Preview button on the Standard toolbar) and click the Margins button in the preview window. This displays the margins for your pages as vertical and horizontal lines on the page, and you can drag the lines with your mouse to adjust them. Figure 14-2 shows the margins for a page, with one of the margins being adjusted (note the two-headed arrow on the right margin line).

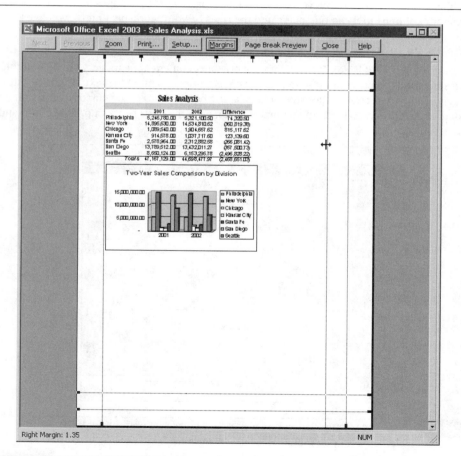

14

FIGURE 14-2   The Print Preview Margins view shows both page and header/footer margins.

Changing Paper Orientation and Size

Adjusting the size of your paper and how your printout is oriented (turned) on the page is easily done through the Page Setup dialog box's Page tab, shown in Figure 14-3. If your worksheet content is wider than it is tall, choose Landscape. If the worksheet is longer than it is wide, choose Portrait. While you're on the Page tab, you can also choose your paper size. Click the drop list next to that option and choose the size of the paper you intend to use for your printout.

Scaling the Printout

When all else fails to fit your worksheet on the number of pages you want, get tough and set some limits. On the Page Setup dialog box, click the Page tab and use the Scaling section (refer to Figure 14-3) to reduce or expand the number of pages in your printout. The Adjust To option allows you to reduce your printout to a percentage of the default 100 percent—be careful such a reduction doesn't render your content too tiny to read. Alternatively, you can use the Fit To option and enter the exact number of pages you want, such as 1 page wide by 2 pages tall. Such a setting will force your columns to fit on one page, and the rows of your worksheet onto two pages.

Working in Page Break Preview

If you choose View | Page Break Preview, your worksheet content appears very small, and thick blue lines appear on the page along with graphic page numbers behind the text. The blue lines, both dashed and solid, represent the page breaks, and when you hover the cursor over them, a two-headed arrow appears, which signals that you can drag the page breaks up, down, left, and

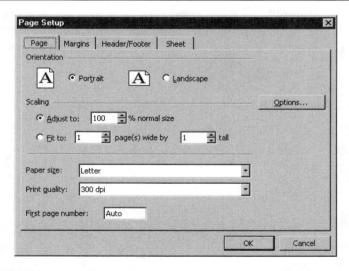

FIGURE 14-3   The Page Setup dialog box's Page tab gives you options for what page elements will be included in your printout.

right, moving them to just about anywhere you want them. After you've completed your page break adjustments, you can return to a normal view of your worksheet by choosing View | Normal.

	F5	▾	*fx* Q3						
	C	D	E	F	G	H	I	J	K
4									
5	% of Total Sales	Q2	% of Total Sales	Q3	% of Total Sales	Q4	% of Total Sales	TOTALS	
6	11%	1,204,500.30	12%	1,371,337.45	11%	1,400,650.25	13%	5,321,100.84	
7	32%	3,426,200.40	35%	3,875,125.35	32%	3,257,784.62	33%	14,534,811.61	
8	4%	574,126.00	6%	478,961.62	4%	325,789.00	3%	1,904,657.76	
9	2%	250,462.00	3%	315,793.00	3%	225,750.25	2%	1,037,717.67	
10	5%	715,987.40	7%	345,951.78	3%	625,147.15	6%	2,312,882.73	
11	31%	2,428,200.40	25%	3,975,326.85	33%	3,255,783.67	33%	13,432,012.15	
12	15%	1,304,705.30	13%	1,721,357.43	14%	1,301,620.35	13%	6,153,296.20	
13		9,904,181.80		12,083,853.48		10,392,525.29		44,696,478.97	
14									
15							Projection Comparison:	107%	

Working with Print Options

When you print a worksheet, the default settings don't include the gridlines, column letters and row numbers, or page numbers. For the times that you do want gridlines, column and row headings, and/or page numbers, it's easy enough to include them. You simply need to open the Page Setup dialog box and choose the options on the Sheet tab, shown in Figure 14-4.

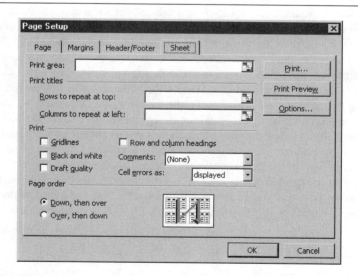

FIGURE 14-4 The Sheet tab allows you to control what's included in your printed worksheet.

In addition to turning on gridlines or setting your printout to black and white, you can use this tab to customize the following aspects of your printout:

- ■ **Print Area**   This option allows you to type or select a region of your worksheet to be designated as the area to print.

- ■ **Print Titles**   If you want your column headings or row labels to appear on each page of the printed worksheet, type the cell addresses where these headings and/or labels can be found, or move the dialog box aside and select the range with your mouse. This feature can be especially helpful when you're printing out a database with many, many rows of records.

- ■ **Print**   This section gives you the choices to print gridlines, to print in black and white, to print in draft quality, and to include the column letters and row numbers from the worksheet. You can also choose whether or not any cells with comments in them are printed, and if so, where they appear.

- ■ **Page Order**   By default, pages print down, then over, and the dialog box itself shows how this works with a graphical explanation. You can switch to Over, Then Down, which can be a good choice for worksheets that are much wider than they are tall.

Setting Up Headers and Footers

For printouts that have more than one page, it's a good idea to include page numbers on the second and subsequent pages, just as you would include them on a long letter or report done in Word. To add page numbers (or any other header or footer content), you need the Page Setup dialog box again. From within the dialog box, click the Header/Footer tab and view the current header or footer content in the large white boxes. By default, there is no header or footer content, but if you're working with a worksheet created by someone else, there might already be content there.

If you want to add or change header and/or footer content, use the Custom Header and Custom Footer buttons on the Header/Footer tab. The dialog box opened by either button (the Header dialog box is shown in Figure 14-5) gives you the ability to type your own text into the header or footer and to insert automatic data—the filename, the date, the time, the page number, and even the total number of pages, which is very handy for long printouts.

As you click the buttons to insert information, the insertions appear as fields, with symbols and names relevant to Excel's programming. For example, if you click the Date button, &[DATE] appears in the active section of the header or footer. The actual date will appear only on the printed worksheet or in the Print Preview window. Be sure to press SPACEBAR between inserted pieces of data (and any extra text you add manually) so that the text and numbers don't run together when printed. Click OK to apply your header or footer to the worksheet.

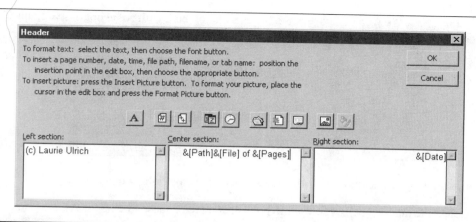

FIGURE 14-5   Use this dialog box to create custom headers; there's a similar one for footers.

Publishing Excel Content to the Web

Imagine that you're presenting a new commission plan to your company's sales reps or that you're instituting a new retirement plan. You've created a worksheet—perhaps one that contains charts—that shows how the new plan will work, and you'd like anyone who's interested to be able to view and even play with the sheet to see what his or her new commission or pension will be under a variety of different circumstances. Perhaps the best way to share the worksheet and give people the chance to play with it is to save it as HTML and post the worksheet to the web, adding the ability for people to interact with the data—adding, deleting, changing, even performing their own calculations on it through a mini version of the Excel toolbars. Page visitors will be able to locally save their version of the worksheet content as an Excel file, while the version on the web page remains intact for each new site visitor.

TIP   *See Chapters 26 and 27 to find out how to use FrontPage to create web pages that can house any kind of information—text, numbers, and images—and to post that information to the web.*

14

Saving Your Worksheet as a Web Page

The process of saving a worksheet as HTML is surprisingly easy. You can save a portion of a single worksheet, an entire worksheet, or a group of sheets, or you can publish an entire workbook.

Choosing File | Save As Web Page opens the Save As dialog box, with some options you don't see if you simply choose File | Save As:

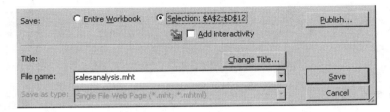

To save your worksheet as an HTML file for use on the web, follow these steps:

1. Select the range of cells you want to publish and then choose File | Save As Web Page.

2. Type a filename for the HTML file. It should be short, and you should use only lowercase letters, and no spaces. The .htm extension will be added automatically, or the .mht (Microsoft's proprietary format) extension will be applied if you choose Add Interactivity (see Step 4 of this procedure).

3. Choose what you want to publish—the entire workbook or a selection. The Selection option will list the range you selected prior to opening the dialog box.

4. Click the Add Interactivity check box if you want people to be able to work with the data online.

5. Click the Publish button. The Publish as Web Page dialog box opens. You can verify your selection in the Item to Publish section, and choose to preview your page right after publishing by checking the Open Published Web Page in Browser option. Checking the AutoRepublish option keeps the web content up-to-date.

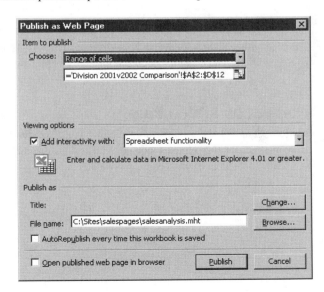

6. Click Publish to complete the process of saving your worksheet as an HTML file. Here is the resulting page, including interactivity tools.

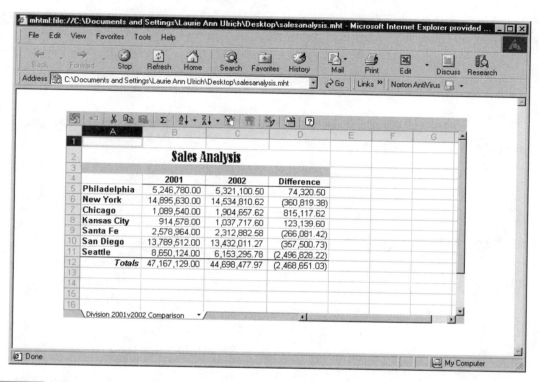

NOTE
Be sure to use the Open Published Page in Web Browser option so that your new page opens immediately in an Internet Explorer window. If you used the Change Title option, the title you gave the document appears on the browser's title bar.

14

Part IV

Creating Presentations with PowerPoint

Chapter 15

Planning and Building a Presentation

How to...

- Plan your presentation topics
- Select the appropriate presentation template
- Develop an effective presentation outline
- Build text slides
- Format slide text
- Save and print a presentation

PowerPoint is an appropriate name for the presentation application within the Office suite. It really does enable you to make your point, and to make it powerfully. It's a feature-rich application, yet easy to use—as you'll discover in this introductory chapter. From tools for choosing a template that supplies a visually pleasing backdrop for your presentation, to an onscreen environment for building a presentation outline, PowerPoint helps you every step of the way. In this chapter, you'll learn to plan your presentation and get started on the right foot, and wrap up by saving and printing your slides, each containing text that conveys your message through its content and appearance.

Planning Your Presentation

The first step in any successful venture is planning, and your PowerPoint presentations are no exception. Planning consists not only of mapping out what your presentation will say, but how it will be said—the text you need, the data you want to display, and the images you need to tell your story. Planning also consists of deciding on a look, a feel, and a tone for your presentation. To help you turn the plan in your head into a presentation onscreen (or later, on paper, transparencies, or 35mm slides), consider these questions:

- *Do I know what I want to say?* This means more than what information you'll be providing. It also refers to your "message." If you're giving a presentation on sales to your board of directors, it's a much different presentation than the one you'd give to your sales reps on the same topic. Think about what the audience cares about, what will interest them most, and what their background with the topic is, and plan accordingly.

- *Do I have all the information I need?* Make sure any files, facts, figures, statistics, and terms are at your fingertips before you sit down to build your slides.

- *Do I have all the images I need?* Gather all the graphics you need to use and make sure they're accessible while you're working on the presentation. It's a good idea to make sure they're all good quality images, too—if a faded photo or a graphic with choppy edges is displayed on a wall or large monitor, the problems will be magnified.

■ *Do I know where the presentation will be given?* If you aren't sure where the presentation will take place, find out now. Why does this matter? Because your presentation should be aimed at the lowest common denominator. This means it has to be legible to the person seated farthest from the screen or monitor, and it must be audible to the person in the back of the room with the worst hearing. This is more of a challenge in a large hall than in a reasonably sized conference room. It's also a good idea to test all your projection equipment prior to the presentation, for obvious reasons.

Organizing Your Presentation Content

You'll want to finish the planning phase with a list of the slides you imagine producing—you can write it or type it, but take the time to list all the points you intend to make and major pieces of information you intend to impart. The items in the list will become your slides, starting with a title slide—something that tells the audience what's happening. It can be the title of the seminar you're about to give, the name of the event, or the name of the person giving the presentation. The next slide is normally a list of the major topics that will be covered, or stages that the presentation will go through. This slide is important in any presentation because it sets the audience's expectations and provides some structure for the event. From there, the slides should cover the points listed in the second slide (one or more slides per topic listed in that second slide), preferably in the same order.

The PowerPoint Environment

The PowerPoint application window that appears when you start the program provides nearly all the tools you'll need to build any presentation. There are alternative views you can work in for specific tasks, but the Normal view you start out in (see Figure 15-1) is a very comprehensive work environment. From the Outline and Slides panels on the left, to the task pane on the right, you've got a full set of slide-creation and formatting features at your fingertips.

You can dive right in to the presentation by typing your list of headings (slide titles) into the Outline tab. The headings you type in this panel will become slide titles automatically, but you can edit them later, as I've said. If you opted to write your list on paper, you can build your slides one at a time, entering a title (derived from your written list) and building the slide content for each slide, one at a time.

After typing the titles for the slides in your presentation, all that's left to do is flesh out each of the slides by cleaning up the titles as needed, adding bullet and paragraph text where desired, and inserting graphics and charts. That might sound like a lot of work left to do, but once the flow of the presentation is created by building the slide titles, the rest of the process goes rather quickly—assuming you've prepped adequately by gathering all your data, text, and graphics beforehand!

15

Thumbnails of slides appear in the Slides panel.

Choose a template for your presentation.

The first slide appears here, with instructions for adding text to it.

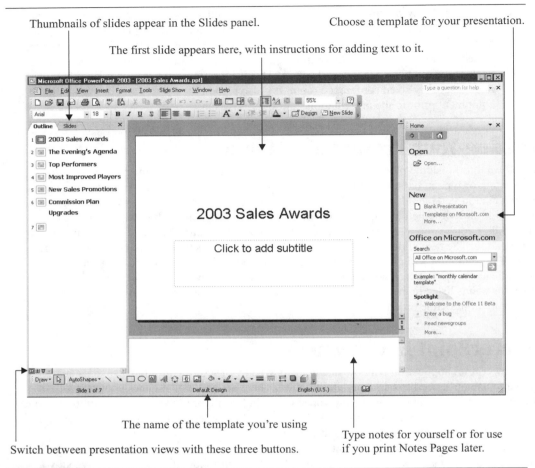

The name of the template you're using

Type notes for yourself or for use if you print Notes Pages later.

Switch between presentation views with these three buttons.

FIGURE 15-1   PowerPoint's Normal view gives you everything you need to build your presentation.

Deciding on a Presentation Template

The next step in building a presentation is applying a template. A template inserts a background color or image, chooses fonts and text colors, and even dictates the default colors of columns and pie slices in any charts created in the presentation. You can forgo the template-selection process and stick with a simple black-and-white slide, but your audience is likely to fall asleep without the added stimulation of color and pictures.

You might be wondering why the template needs to be chosen before the slides are filled in with more text, graphics, charts, and so on. The reason is that the template helps to set the overall tone of the presentation by means of providing background content, fonts, and colors. It's much easier to build your slides' individual content if you can also see these other slide elements onscreen. As shown here, a template background imposes itself (in a good way) in the slides. Your choices and placement of clip art and chart colors can be affected by the template you choose.

It's important to note that you can change to a different template later, and that you can also tweak the template you've chosen by editing the presentation *master* for one particular presentation. The manipulation of the presentation master is covered in Chapter 17. To change to a new template, simply repeat these steps for selecting one in the first place:

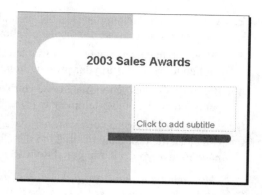

1. Click the Design button or choose Format | Slide Design. The task pane appears (or changes, if it was already displayed) and offers a series of templates, as shown in Figure 15-2.

FIGURE 15-2 Choosing a template for your presentation.

15

2. Scroll through the templates in the Available for Use list. Those used recently and any template already in use are displayed above this in the task pane.

3. When you find a template that looks interesting, click it once. The template is automatically applied to the slides in your presentation.

4. If you don't like the template once you've seen it on a full-size slide, go back to the task pane and click another template to try a different one.

5. When you settle on a particular template, simply go on building your presentation. You can close the task pane by clicking the Close button (x) in the upper-right corner of the pane to give yourself a larger slide workspace.

Most templates have two different layouts: one for title slides, and one for the rest of the slides. It's a good idea to check the first slide in your presentation (which is a title slide, by default) and one of the other slides (any of the nontitle slide layouts will do) to make sure you like the template in both of its forms.

Choosing Slide Layouts

As you work with the slides, you will probably want to change slide layouts. A slide's layout dictates what can be placed on the slide, and PowerPoint offers more than 20 different layouts for text slides, graphical slides, chart slides, and several miscellaneous layouts. By default, each of the slides after the first (title) slide in your list is a Title and Text slide, which includes a title text box and a box for typing a bulleted list. If any of your slides need to contain a chart, a table, or a graphic, you'll want to change to a layout that's conducive to that.

To change a slide's layout, follow these steps:

1. Using the Slides panel to select and make active the slide you want to change, click the slide you want.

2. Click the drop list on the task pane's title bar and choose Slide Layout, or choose Format | Slide Layout. Either action displays the Slide Layout task pane, as shown in Figure 15-3.

3. Scroll through the slide layouts and apply the one you want by clicking the layout itself. If you click the triangle to the right of the layout image, you should choose Apply to Selected Slides.

Inserting New Slides

Even if you created the most comprehensive slide list when you built your outline, chances are you're going to need to add a slide. It's very easy to add a new slide to an existing presentation:

1. To control where the new slide appears within the existing list of slides, select the slide that should appear before the new one by clicking it in the Slides panel.

2. Click the New Slide button. The task pane automatically appears, offering slide layouts for the new slide.

3. Your new slide is set up as a Title and Text slide (title and bulleted text) but will change to whichever layout you click, should you need to change it.

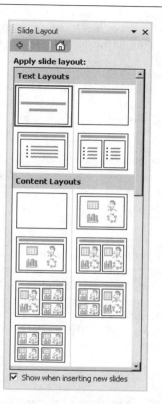

FIGURE 15-3 Choose from several different layouts for slides with text, graphics, charts, or a combination thereof.

Oops! What if you inserted the new slide in the wrong place? You can rearrange your slides easily in the Slides panel. Click and drag the slide that's in the wrong place, releasing your mouse when the horizontal line, shown here, is in the spot where the selected slide should go.

Deleting Slides

Getting rid of a slide is perilously easy. Using the Slides panel, right-click the unwanted slide and choose Delete Slide

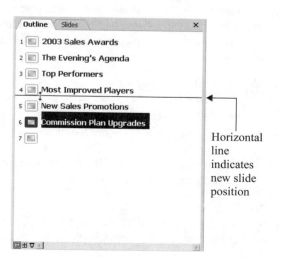

Horizontal line indicates new slide position

15

from the shortcut menu. With no fanfare, not even a prompt that asks you to confirm your intentions, the slide you right-clicked is removed. Of course, if you deleted the wrong slide, you can undo the action by pressing CTRL-Z (the universal Office Undo shortcut) or choosing Edit | Undo.

To delete a series of slides, you need to select them as a group. To select a series of contiguous slides, click the first one in the series and press SHIFT. With SHIFT pressed, click the last one in the series. All the slides between, and including, the first and last slide are selected, and whatever you do next will apply to the selected slides. Use this technique with great care when deleting slides.

> **TIP** *If you need to select random, noncontiguous slides (for deletion, rearrangement, or to copy and paste them into another presentation), use CTRL instead of SHIFT. With CTRL pressed, click the slides you want to select.*

Inserting Slide Text

If you built your series of slide headings through the Outline tab, your slides already have their titles. You'll probably need more text on each slide, of course, and there will be slides you add to the presentation without working through the Outline or Slides tab, so you'll want to type their titles directly on the slide. Inserting slide text is quite simple, and each new slide comes with instructions, in the form of the Click to Insert text boxes on the slides themselves. Each slide layout—Title, Title and Text, Title Only, and so on—will offer different sets of instructional text boxes.

Working with Bulleted Text

A list of bulleted items—single words, short phrases, or entire paragraphs—is probably the most common element seen in a presentation. The second slide in most presentations includes a bulleted list that tells the audience what to expect in the presentation—topics that will be covered, an agenda, the time that various events will take place. Throughout the rest of your presentation, you'll want to include bulleted lists whenever you have a series of points to discuss. Each bullet point should introduce a topic, in a very brisk, clean way.

Here are some tips for effective lists:

- *Avoid using complete sentences, and stick to short, punchy phrases whenever you can.* The surest way to bore your audience to tears is to fill your slides with long sentences and paragraphs.

- *Don't cram too many bullet points onto a single slide.* The maximum you should have? Four or five, depending on length—four if any of the points wrap to two lines, or five if they're all single lines. If you have more than four or five things to say about a given topic, spread them over two slides.

Typing a bulleted list is easy. Just click inside the text object and start typing. The bullet is there automatically, and your text will wrap within the text box, creating a hanging indent. You'll remember hanging indents from Chapter 6, where the formatting and indenting of paragraphs were discussed. In a bulleted list with a hanging indent, the bullet remains on the left margin of the text box, and both the first line and body of the paragraph (if any) indents.

Using Multiple Bullet Levels

As you're typing, if you have a series of bullet points that have subpoints, such as lower-level topics in an outline, you can indent these subpoints further, as shown here, by using TAB at the beginning of the line. Pressing TAB *demotes* the bullet point, and the bullet character changes. When you press ENTER at the end of the bullet point, you'll get another bullet of the same rank. If you want to *promote* the next bullet point back up to first-level status, press SHIFT-TAB.

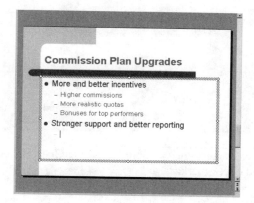

Formatting Bullet Characters

The template you chose for your presentation will control which bullet characters you get for first-, second-, third-, and fourth-level bullet points. Even if you're working with the Blank Presentation template, you get a particular bullet (the very generic large dot). You can change this, for one bullet point in a list or for the entire list:

1. Click inside the bulleted list and select the bulleted lines you want to reformat. Note that if your list has subpoints, you'll have to repeat these steps for individual bullet points rather than select a series that includes the subpoints. Otherwise, all the bulleted levels will have the same bullet character.

2. Choose Format | Bullets and Numbering. You can also right-click the selected text and choose Bullets and Numbering from the shortcut menu. As a result, the Bullets and Numbering dialog box opens, as shown in Figure 15-4.

3. Choose one of the bullet characters from the array of seven options (choosing None will remove the bullet).

4. As needed, pick a color for the bullet by clicking the Color drop list. The shades offered first are those that go well with your current template, but you can choose More Colors to pick from the entire spectrum.

15

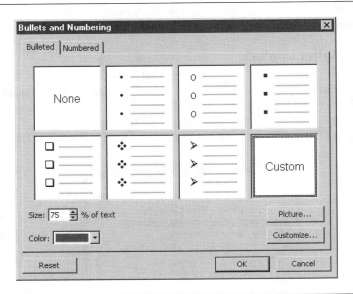

Six basic characters are available for bulleted lists, including dots, circles, boxes, and check marks.

5. If none of the basic bullet characters are appealing, click the Customize button to choose a character from various font libraries (such as Wingdings or Monotype Sorts) or click the Picture button to choose from a collection of graphic bullets.

6. Click OK to apply the selected character or picture, and the dialog box closes.

You can repeat these steps for individual bullets, enabling you to choose a different bullet for second-level bullets in your list or to choose different bullets for each item in your list, regardless of rank. Try to pick characters that match your template color scheme and the overall tone of your presentation—you want your bullets to stand out but not to overwhelm or clash with the text and other elements on the slide.

Typing Paragraphs

Although it's generally a no-no to have full paragraphs on a presentation slide, there will be times that you have to type full paragraphs with complete sentences. Quoting a policy manual, customer testimonial, set of instructions, mission statement, or inspirational speech requires that you break from the preferred quick, short phrases and actually type paragraphs.

Even though you risk boring your audience with a long paragraph, PowerPoint supports you as you type, allowing text to wrap naturally within the confines of the active text box. Just as you would in a Word document, you can type one or more paragraphs, letting the text wrap at the margin (the margin is the edge of the text box), and press ENTER when you're ready to add a blank line or start a new paragraph.

If you need to type a paragraph into a slide that's set up for a bulleted list, click in the bulleted text box and then turn off the bullets from the Formatting toolbar. You can then type regular paragraph text without bullets popping up whenever you press ENTER. If you've already typed the paragraph and it has a bullet, just click inside the paragraph (no need to select it, just make sure your cursor is inside it) and click the Bullets button to remove the bullet format from the paragraph.

Inserting Extra Text Boxes

Sometimes the slide layout you have doesn't offer all the text objects you need. Maybe you need a title or subtitle, a bulleted list, or a small paragraph at the bottom or off to the right side of the slide. When none of the preset slide layouts offer the number or type of text boxes you need, what can you do? The answer is simple: Go to the Drawing toolbar and use the Text Box button.

As shown here, drawing a text box is simple. Just click the Text Box button and move your mouse onto the slide. Click and drag diagonally away from your starting point to draw a box on the slide in the size and position you need for the text you want to add to the slide. When the box dimensions seem right for the text you want to type, release the mouse. There's no need to be exact in the sizing or position, though, because it's easy to resize and move text objects, as you'll discover later in this chapter. Once the text box is drawn, a cursor appears inside it, and you can just start typing. The font will be dictated by the template you're using for the presentation.

TIP   *You'll learn more about the rest of the Drawing toolbar in Chapter 16.*

15

Formatting Slide Text

With a template in place, or even if you're working on a plain, black-and-white slide based on the Blank Presentation template, fonts and font sizes are chosen for you. The titles of each slide will appear in a particular font, at a particular size, and this might be the same or different from the font and size applied automatically to any bulleted list or paragraph text you type on those same slides.

The fonts and sizes chosen are part of the total "look" of the template you've chosen, but they aren't carved in stone—you can change them easily. Even if you're using the Blank Presentation template, you don't have to stick with the default Arial font or the sizes that are applied to titles and bullet text automatically. When changing fonts, consider these points:

- Choose a font that's appropriate for the presentation you're giving. You don't want to use something festive and fun for a serious presentation on life insurance, for example.

- The other thing to consider is legibility. Don't use fonts that are too fussy or ornate, because they might be too hard to read at a distance. Crisp, clean fonts are your best choice.

 Formatting your text in PowerPoint is no different procedurally from formatting text in Word or Excel. You have a Formatting toolbar, complete with Font, Size, and alignment buttons, and you can use them to change the font, size, and position of your text, just as you would in a document or worksheet. The only significant tools that are unique to PowerPoint's default Formatting toolbar are the Increase Font Size and Decrease Font Size buttons (shown here). With text selected or your cursor within a word you want to adjust, simply click the appropriate button. Each click will adjust the size of the text, and you can do this "by eye"—just keep clicking until you like the size you see.

When formatting text in PowerPoint, you can select some of the text in a text object, or you can select the entire object and reformat all the text in that object. The trick to controlling how much text is affected lies in your selection method:

- To select text within a text object, click inside the object and use your mouse to drag through and select only the text you want to reformat. After selecting the text, whatever formats you apply will affect only the selected text.

- Click anywhere within a text object to activate it, then click the object's border. This selects the entire object and enables you to format all the text within it in one step. Here you can see an entire text object selected.

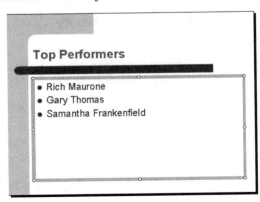

Repositioning Text Objects

If your slides follow their layouts, there should be no need to move anything, because the layout itself provides the most efficient and visually balanced placement of the individual text objects.

You might need to move something, however, if you've added a text box or inserted a graphic (more on that in Chapter 16) that's not part of the slide layout, or if you've typed an excessively long list of bullet points and the last one is too close to the bottom of the slide. If you need to move objects up, down, left, right, or a combination thereof, try these techniques:

- Click the object to be moved and pass the mouse over its border. When your mouse pointer turns into a four-headed arrow, drag the object with your mouse. You can drag it in any direction, for any distance—just don't drag it off the slide. It's also not a good idea to place objects right on the edge of a slide because this can reduce legibility, and if the slide will be printed, the content might be cut off on the edge.

- Click the object, then click its border to select it. Using the arrow keys on your keyboard, move the object up, down, left, or right. This technique is great for preventing unwanted changes in one aspect of the object's current position. Imagine that you like where the object is horizontally, but you want to move it up. If you use your mouse, the lack of precision in human hand movement will not allow you to move the object up without risking side-to-side movement as well. If you use UP ARROW, however, the object remains in its current horizontal position but is moved up, in tiny increments, each time you press the key.

Aligning Text Objects

One of the keys to any good composition is balance. You'll notice that in the preset slide layouts, everything is lined up. If the slide title is centered, so is the text in the subtitle box below it. If there are two bulleted lists side by side, they're aligned by their tops so that they both begin at the same level on the slide. This is important because you don't want the eyes of the audience distracted by subtle mismatches—items you've added or moved that are now just slightly out of alignment or bear no consistent placement at all. If you want the audience to read your content without thinking about anything else, make sure everything is tidy, with items aligned to the same side of the slide, and related items lined up with each other:

- To change the alignment of text within a text box, click inside the box to position your cursor and use the Left, Center, or Right alignment button on the Formatting toolbar. The keyboard shortcuts are CTRL-L, CTRL-E, and CTRL-R, respectively.

- If you want to line up two separate text objects, select them by clicking the first one and then pressing SHIFT as you select the second (and third or fourth) object. Next, click the Draw button on the Drawing toolbar and choose Align or Distribute. From the resulting shortcut menu, pick the alignment you need (Left, Center, Right, Top, Middle, Bottom) or the distribution method (Horizontally or Vertically) you want.

Resizing Text Objects

The primary motivation for resizing a text object is to redirect the flow of text, causing more or less text wrap in a paragraph or series of bullet points, or to create or eliminate text wrap on a title. Text objects are sized to control the flow or wrap of text within them. Typically, the text boxes that are part of a slide's original layout are sized to accommodate the expected amount of text for the particular object. A text box that will house a title is sized to hold from two to

15

five words at the designated font size, whereas a box intended for a bulleted list is much wider and grows to the height needed to accommodate as many bullet points as the user types within the confines of the slide.

To resize a text box, click once on it to select it, then point to one of the resulting handles. The side handles (on the center of the top, bottom, left, and right sides) will enlarge or reduce the box in one direction, and the corner handles will resize it in two directions at once.

TIP *If you want to enlarge or reduce the size of a text box yet maintain its current proportions, use a corner handle and press SHIFT as you drag it. Be careful to release the mouse before SHIFT when you've achieved the desired box size so that the proportions are maintained. If you release SHIFT first, the box will snap to the dimensions it would have been had you not pressed SHIFT at all.*

If it's important to you that you achieve a very specific text box size, you can use the Format Text Box (or Format AutoShape) dialog box to set the width and height. Click the box in question, then right-click it's border. From the resulting shortcut menu, choose Format Text Box or Format Placeholder (it will appear as the latter if the text object is part of the slide's original layout). You can also click in a box and choose Format | Text Box from the menu. In the resulting dialog box (see Figure 15-5), click the Size tab and enter the desired width and height for the selected text

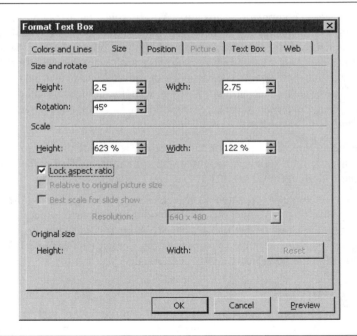

FIGURE 15-5 Enter a specific width and height for the text box.

box. Through this tab, you can also rotate the box by entering the degrees to turn it, and you can click the Lock Aspect Ratio option to make sure that whenever the box is resized, it maintains its current width-to-height proportions.

Saving a Presentation

The process of saving a presentation is no different from saving a Word document or an Excel worksheet. If it's the first time the presentation has been saved (and hopefully you're doing so early in the development of the presentation), choosing File | Save, File | Save As, pressing CTRL-S, or clicking the Save button on the toolbar will open the Save As dialog box. From within this dialog box, you can name the presentation and choose a drive and folder to save it in. The .ppt extension will be applied automatically, so all you need to do is type a file name for the presentation and click the Save button.

Because PowerPoint is a highly graphical application—with lots of pictures and visual effects onscreen all the time—it uses a great amount of system resources. Because PowerPoint is a big user of memory, it's a good idea to save early and often as you're creating a presentation so that any application crash (in PowerPoint or another application that runs out of memory) won't result in you losing your work. A good way to keep from putting off saving is to commit the CTRL-S method to *your* memory. Pressing the keyboard shortcut is faster than using the toolbar or menu, and you're less likely to delay saving if you can issue the command without taking your hands off the keyboard as you type your slide text.

> TIP   *You can also save your PowerPoint presentation as a web page, generating an interactive web page from your slides, each in its own frame, with navigational tools for the page visitor to use in moving through the presentation online. The use of the File | Save As Web Page command and the whole concept of publishing your presentation as a web page is covered in Chapter 17.*

Printing Your Slides

Despite the fact that most presentations are shown on a large monitor or projected onto a wall or screen, there will be times that you need to print your slides. You can print on sheets of clear plastic that can be used in your laser or inkjet printer or generated from your PowerPoint file by a professional printing company, or you can print on plain paper. PowerPoint supports the printing of presentations as a series of slides, in the form of pages with speaker's notes, or as groups of slides (from two to six per page) to serve as audience handouts.

The Print command is issued in PowerPoint just as it is in Word or Excel. You can choose File | Print or press CTRL-P. The Print button will send a print job directly to your default printer, one slide per page, no questions asked. The former methods will open the Print dialog box, through which you can customize the print job, controlling the number of copies printed, what's included in the printout, and how the printout looks. Figure 15-6 shows the PowerPoint Print dialog box.

15

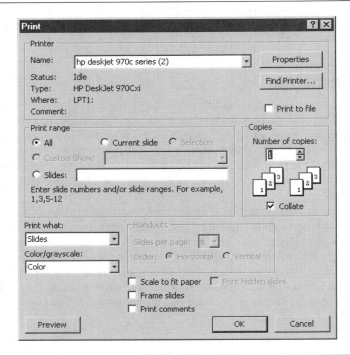

FIGURE 15-6 Choose which slides to print and how many copies to generate.

The top half of the Print dialog box looks very much like the Print dialog box found in Word or Excel. You can choose a different printer, pick which slides to print, and set the number of copies to be printed. The lower half of the dialog box is where the PowerPoint-specific printing options are found. You can choose what to print—slides, speaker's notes, audience handouts— and how to print them—in color, black and white, or grayscale. You also have options for making oversized slides fit onto your paper and for putting a frame (thin line border) around each of your slides.

Printing Color Options

Obviously, you can print in color only if you have a color printer. If you don't have one, printing in color will result in a printout that uses shades of gray to approximate the color in your slides. If you do have a color printer, you might want to print in color so you have a tangible record of exactly how your slides looked, or to generate color transparencies. Your other color choices are as follows:

■ **Grayscale**   This option results in something very similar to printing in color on a black-and-white printer, because your slides' colors are interpreted as shades of gray.

■ **Pure black and white**   If you choose this option, everything that has a color fill is turned to black or white, depending on the intensity or darkness of the color. For example, royal blue would be printed as black, but yellow or pink would be printed as white.

Creating Notes and Audience Handouts

In the Print What section of the dialog box, Slides is the default. This means that each of your slides will print on a single page, in the color you chose, and with or without a frame, depending on your use of the options at the bottom of the Print dialog box. If you're printing on paper that's smaller or larger than the slides, you can also choose to scale the slides to fit on the paper. This generally results in larger slides because each slide is only 7.5 by 10 inches, and letter-size paper is 8.5 by 11 inches, with a quarter-inch edge that can't be printed on if you're using a standard laser or inkjet printer.

In addition to printing one slide per page, you can take advantage of the following Print What options:

■ If you opt to print handouts, the Handouts section of the dialog box becomes available, and you can choose how many slides will print per page, and with choices ranging from 1 to 9 (stick to 3 or fewer so that the slides don't become too small to read). You can also choose whether to arrange the slides on the page horizontally or vertically.

■ Notes Pages is intended for use in creating speaker's notes for the presentation. A small (but entirely legible) image of the slide appears at the top of the page, and any notes typed in the Notes panel during presentation development appear on the page with the slide. I like to use Notes Pages view for my audience handouts, because the slide is large enough to be read later, and my notes remind the reader what was said while that slide was onscreen.

■ Outline prints the titles, subtitles, and bullet text from each slide and obviously omits any graphics, charts, or extra text boxes you added. This is a good view to print if you want someone to review your presentation content, but you don't want to invite his or her comments on your color choices or layout.

15

CAUTION   *Unless you absolutely have to, don't hand out your audience handout until after the presentation. Why? Because the audience will be reading it while you're talking and jotting notes instead of listening (another reason to hand out the Notes Pages view, which already has your notes on it).*

Chapter 16

Enhancing a Presentation with Graphics and Charts

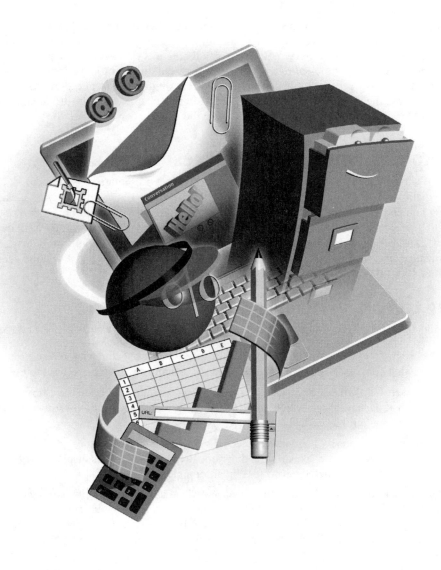

How to...

- ■ Insert and customize graphics
- ■ Add drawn shapes and lines to your slides
- ■ Create a PowerPoint chart to display numeric data
- ■ Build an organization chart
- ■ Create a diagram to depict concepts or procedures

The whole point of an electronic presentation is to grab and maintain the attention of an audience, be it a handful of people clustered around a monitor or a huge group of people seated in an auditorium. How is that goal achieved? By using small amounts of text and lots of graphics and color to convey one or more messages throughout the presentation. Nothing bores an audience faster than a text-heavy presentation, so you need to rely on graphics—photographs, clip art, charts—to express the information you have to share. In this chapter, you'll learn to add graphic content of all kinds to your presentation and to make the graphic content work for you.

Using Graphics Effectively in a Presentation

Although it's important to use more pictures and less text in a presentation, is there a risk of using too many graphics? Certainly. Just as too much text can be a bore, too many images can be distracting and confusing. One image per slide is a good rule of thumb. Don't pack two or three charts onto a single slide; instead, spread them out over two or three slides. Don't try to fit everyone from the CEO down to the guy who stocks the snack machine onto the organization chart. Break the organization into sections and show each one on a separate slide. No one will mind seeing a whole lot of slides if none of the slides are boring and/or confusing.

Adding Clip Art and Photographs

You can add a graphic image—clip art, a photograph, or a drawing—to a slide in one of three ways:

- ■ Choose Insert | Picture from the File menu to open the Insert Picture dialog box. From within this dialog box, navigate to the drive and folder containing the image you want to use.

- ■ The Insert Clip Art button (found on the Drawing toolbar) will open the Clip Art version of the task pane, through which you can select a graphic, searching by keyword for just the right image for a particular slide.

- ■ As shown in Figure 16-1, if you've selected a slide layout that includes graphic content—a clip art image, a picture, a chart, or a diagram—a palette of icons is displayed within that object placeholder. Click the icon for clip art or a picture.

- ■ Once inserted, the graphic can be moved or resized as needed, just as you would resize and move it within a Word document or an Excel worksheet (you read all about the use of images in Chapter 3). One minor difference: If you insert the graphic through an icon within a graphic placeholder, the image will appear within the placeholder. If you add a

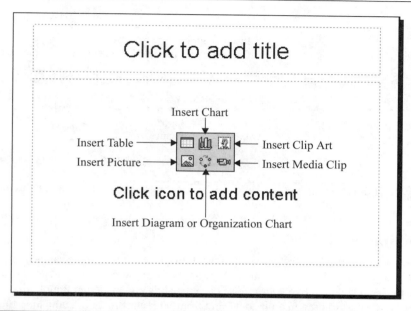

Click to add title

Insert Chart

Insert Table ——————→ Insert Clip Art

Insert Picture ——————→ Insert Media Clip

Click icon to add content

Insert Diagram or Organization Chart

FIGURE 16-1   The possible choices for content are represented by icons inside the content placeholder.

graphic to a slide without such a placeholder, PowerPoint will attempt to place the graphic in a logical spot, and it might even change the size and placement of an existing text object to accommodate the new graphic.

NOTE   *Graphic placement and selection is really an art unto itself, but it's one you can learn. Good composition—the effective, balanced placement of elements on a slide—requires a good eye and the ability to distribute elements—text blocks, titles, graphics—so that the viewer's eye is drawn to what's important without ignoring everything else. You want to position all your slide elements carefully, spacing and sizing them so that no one item overwhelms another. Each item should stand out on its own yet work as part of the group.*

Drawing and Manipulating Shapes and Lines

The Drawing toolbar (see Figure 16-2) offers tools for creating shapes and lines, and for applying color and fills to them. You can even apply shadows and 3-D effects to your drawn items, and spin them on any axis you dictate. The Draw Menu button provides access to grouping, alignment, and repositioning commands, and the AutoShapes button offers several palettes of categorized shapes. You can use all these features to enhance PowerPoint slides, emphasizing important text, creating your own drawings, and designing logos and symbols to create graphic effects that you may not have found represented in your clip art selection.

16

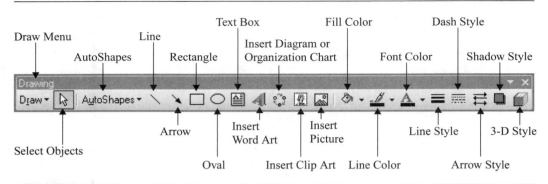

If the Drawing toolbar isn't displayed, choose View | Toolbars | Drawing.

Drawing Shapes

To draw shapes, you can use the Rectangle and Oval tools, or click the AutoShapes menu and select a shape category and then choose one of the shapes from the resulting category palette. Once a shape tool is selected, move your mouse onto the slide and click and drag to draw the shape. Generally, it's best to drag in a diagonal line from your starting point, adjusting the angle of your dragging to adjust the proportions of the resulting shape. If you want to draw a very long, slim arrow, drag in a more horizontal direction. You can also use SHIFT as you draw to create a shape that has equal height and width—perfect for drawing squares and circles using the Rectangle and Oval tools, respectively.

> **TIP** *Make it easier to position items on the slide, especially if vertical or horizontal alignment is important. Display the grid (click the Show/Hide Grid button) to provide a series of horizontal and vertical lines that help you place items in a straight or diagonal line.*

Drawing Lines and Arrows

Drawing a line or an arrow (a line with an arrow head or other graphical endpoint) is done in much the same way as drawing a shape. Simply turn on either the Line or Arrow tool and click to establish a starting point. Then, drag away from that point in the direction the line should go. By default, the lines and arrows you draw with these tools are straight, despite any jagged look they might have onscreen. When printed, the lines will be smooth. You can control the angle of the line, constraining it to 45 or 90 degrees, by holding down SHIFT as you drag to draw the line or arrow.

>  *If you need two or more of a particular shape or line, draw it once, and while it's still selected, press CTRL-D. This duplicates (thus the D in the shortcut) the selected object. You can use this command on text objects, drawn shapes and lines, clip art and pictures, and even on slides in the Slides panel. It's a very powerful shortcut!*

Formatting Graphic Elements

Once you've drawn your shapes and lines, you may want to make changes—choosing a different fill color for shapes, making a line or arrow thicker, or rotating a shape. These changes are easy to make, and the tools for performing them can all be found on the Drawing menu or on the shape or line itself.

Applying Fills and Outlines

When you draw a shape, the outline color and fill color are applied, dictated by the template in use. You can change these colors easily, however, and even apply patterns, textures, and picture fills to the shape. To apply a fill, use the Fill Color tool. The palette displayed when you click the drop arrow to the right of the tool offers a series of colors that match the current presentation template, but you can select More Colors to access a complete palette of colors, or you can click Fill Effects to access fill options such as patterns, textures, and picture fills (see Figure 16-3).

To apply color to a line or to change the outline color of a shape, use the Line Color tool. Again, as in the case of the Fill Color tool, colors that complement your current presentation template are offered first, but you can venture beyond them (carefully, don't pick colors that clash) by choosing More Colors. You can also apply patterns to create the look of dashed or dotted lines.

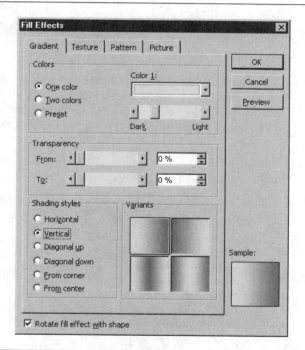

16

FIGURE 16-3   Click the Gradient, Pattern, Texture, or Picture tab to access options for filling your shape with an interesting effect rather than a solid color.

TIP

Moving shapes and lines is done using the same method you'd use to move a graphic—click it to select it and then drag it with your mouse. To resize a shape or line, drag from the handles, and in the case of shapes, use SHIFT to control the width-to-height ratio.

Typing in Shapes

If left to their own devices, most users imagine that to put text inside a shape (such as placing the word "Wow!" inside a star or sunburst shape) they'd have to draw the shape, then place a text box with no colored fill on top of it and type the word into the text box. Not so! PowerPoint makes it much easier to add text to a shape. Just click the shape to select it and begin typing. The text is automatically centered within the shape and appears in a font dictated by the template in use. If you want a short phrase or sentence to wrap within the shape, right-click the shape and choose Format AutoShape. In the resulting dialog box, click the Text Box tab and turn on the Word Wrap Text in AutoShape option.

Rotating Shapes and Lines

Although not of much use for circles, the rotation of other shapes can create interesting effects. Stars can stand on one point instead of two, boxes can appear to be tumbling, and the arrow shape you drew can be turned to point in a different direction. Note that you don't need to use the Rotate feature to redirect drawn lines or arrow lines, because simply grabbing one end handle and dragging in a different direction will redirect the line or arrow.

To rotate a shape, you have two options:

- Set a specific angle of rotation in the Format AutoShape dialog box. To access this dialog box, click to select the shape, choose Format | AutoShape, and then on the Size tab enter the rotation angle by typing a new number or use the spinner arrows to increase or decrease the current number. Note that if your shape contains text, the text will rotate with the shape.

- Click the Rotation handle on the shape (it's a green circle connected to the top-side handle, as shown here) and drag it in the direction the shape should be rotated.

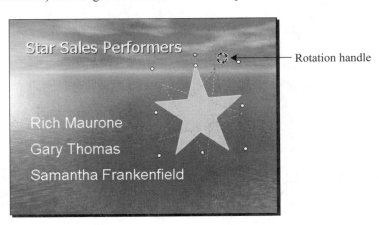

Rotation handle

Aligning Graphic Objects

If you have two or more drawn shapes or lines that need to be aligned or distributed relative to either the slide or each other, you need the Align or Distribute command found in the Draw menu. To use this command, select the shapes or lines to be aligned/distributed and then choose Draw | Align or Distribute. The choices in the submenu are illustrated by tiny icons and are self-explanatory.

The trick to using this feature is to select multiple shapes or lines before issuing the Align or Distribute command. If you don't have two or more items selected, the submenu will be dimmed. To select multiple objects, click the first one and then hold down SHIFT as you click and select the rest of the objects to be aligned or distributed.

Changing the Stacking Order of Graphics and Drawn Objects

As you add graphics, shapes, and lines to your presentation, their stacking order is determined by the order in which the objects are added. The last one added will appear on top of those added before it. For objects that don't overlap, this isn't an issue. If, on the other hand, you want to put a shape behind an existing piece of clip art, or you want to restack a series of overlapping shapes and/or lines, you need to use the Draw | Order command. The Order submenu offers four options:

- **Bring to Front**   This takes the item from wherever it is in the current stacking order and puts it on top, as though it were the last item added to the slide.
- **Send to Back**   If you want to place a recently added object behind the rest of the slide content, choose this command.
- **Bring Forward**   With this command, you can reshuffle a stack of items, bringing the selected item forward one layer at a time.
- **Send Backward**   If you want to move the selected item down in the stack, use this command. Send Backward and Bring Forward can be used repeatedly until the proper position in the stack is achieved.

Grouping and Ungrouping Objects

To group a series of shapes and/or lines, select them with SHIFT and choose Draw | Group. The entire group is then selected, with one set of handles for all the objects in the group. If you move or resize one of the objects, the rest of them move and resize in tandem. The same goes for changing fill colors, outline colors, and resizing: If you click the group and apply any formatting, the change applies to every object in the group. If you find that you've inadvertently included an unwanted object in the group, you can use the Draw | Ungroup command, followed by the Regroup command once you've selected the appropriate objects. If you no longer want your objects grouped at all, click the group and choose Draw | Ungroup.

Creating a PowerPoint Chart

As you learned in Chapter 13, the Office 2003 suite already has Excel, an excellent tool for turning data into charts. So why also offer charting tools through PowerPoint? By building a chart in PowerPoint, you're able to take advantage of important tools for animating the chart (having chart elements appear one at a time, so you can talk about each one individually during

16

the actual presentation), and you're able to work with a very scaled-back worksheet environment and simple charting tools, which is handy for those people who don't use Excel much or at all.

 *If you're comfortable with Excel and its charting tools, why not create charts in Excel and just paste them into your PowerPoint presentation? Well, you can, and you can use the techniques for using the Clipboard discussed in Chapter 2 to do it.*

To create a PowerPoint chart, you should convert the active slide to one of the layouts that include a placeholder for charts. These are found on the Slide Layouts task pane. After converting to the proper layout, click the Insert Chart icon on the slide. This will open PowerPoint's charting tools (many of which you'll recognize from Excel), plus a small worksheet (called the *datasheet*) and a chart, based on sample data already in the datasheet.. As shown in Figure 16-4, everything you need to build your chart is there. All you have to do is replace the sample data with your data and—voila!—you have a chart.

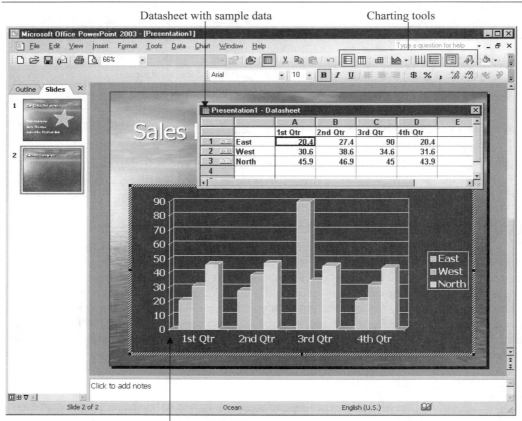

Datasheet with sample data   Charting tools

Chart based on the sample data

FIGURE 16-4   The chart you start with reflects the sample data in the datasheet.

To replace the sample data in the data sheet with your data, select the sample data by clicking in any cell in the datasheet and pressing CTRL-A. With every cell in the datasheet selected, press DELETE. Now you have an empty datasheet and can start entering your own data, or even paste data from an Excel worksheet or Word table. Whether you're typing your data manually or you're pasting from another source, note that there is a blank first column (the datasheet doesn't start with column A, as it does in Excel), and this is where your row labels should go—not in column A, where your first data should appear. As you type or after you paste your data, a new chart forms on the slide.

CAUTION   *If you click anywhere outside of the datasheet or the chart object on the slide, the datasheet will disappear, and so will all the charting tools and related features. Don't panic—you've merely deactivated the chart. To reactivate the chart and redisplay all the related tools, including the datasheet, double-click the chart object.*

Selecting a Chart Type

The default chart type for any new PowerPoint chart is a column chart. It's the default because it's easy to assemble and format, and most importantly, it's easy for the audience to understand. A presentation isn't the place for a very complex chart with lots of bells and whistles—lines, bars, boxes, arrows, and so forth—because such detail will be lost on anyone sitting at a distance from the screen, and unless everyone in your audience is extremely familiar with the data, they won't necessarily understand it. Stick to simple charts in an onscreen presentation. If you need to give the audience a complex chart, give it to them in a printed handout, along with a text description or explanation.

If you do want to switch to a different chart type, however, it's easy to do. Just click the Chart Type tool and choose the type of chart you want. You can pick from nine different types, plus three different column shapes—cones, cylinders, and pyramids, as shown here.

You can also choose Chart | Chart Type, which opens the Chart Type dialog box. This dialog box will look very familiar to anyone who has created a chart in Excel—it's identical to the first step in the Chart Wizard. You can pick from several chart type categories and subcategories, and you can see your data in the selected type by clicking the Press and Hold to View Sample button. This can be easier than using the Chart Type tool's palette, especially if you're not sure which type of chart you need to use for your data.

Customizing the Chart

The chart you build in PowerPoint will include colors that match the color scheme of your presentation template. This helps make your chart look as if it belongs in your presentation, but it can also be a bit limiting. You might not like one or more of the colors, or two of the colors might be too similar, making it hard to tell different columns, lines, or pie slices apart. You might also want to make changes to the location of your legend or add or edit chart titles. Whatever changes you want to make, PowerPoint makes it very simple to do:

1. Click the chart element you want to format. Handles appear around the element.

2. Click the Format menu. The first menu command will match the element you selected—Selected Legend, Selected Data Series, and so on.

16

3. Choose the first command and work within the resulting dialog box (you'll get a different one depending on which chart element is active). You'll find that the dialog boxes you see at this point are nearly identical to those you saw in Chapter 13, on charting in Excel.

If you'd like to make general changes to several items in your chart from one main dialog box, choose Chart | Chart Options. The Chart Options dialog box opens (see Figure 16-5), through which you can work in any of six tabs—Titles, Axes, Gridlines, Legend, Data Labels, and Data Table. This is the exact same Chart Options dialog box you work with in Excel.

You can also resize your chart by dragging its handles, and you can reformat its text and axis label formatting through the Formatting toolbar. If you want to convert your value axis labels to currency, click the axis, then use the Currency Style button on the toolbar. If you want to make your chart title bigger, click the title and use the Font Size or Increase Font Size tool to apply a larger point size to the text in the title. A quick way to recolor a data series (group of columns or a pie slice)? Use the Fill Color button on the Drawing toolbar.

Building an Organization Chart

An organization chart shows who works for whom and what they do. It also shows how different departments, divisions, or factions of your organization work together, as shown on the opposite page in Figure 16-6. This sort of information can be very useful in certain presentations, and PowerPoint provides a very simple, yet powerful tool for building these charts.

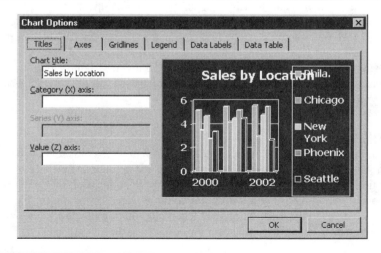

FIGURE 16-5   Tinker with every aspect of your chart—its titles, axes, legend, or anything you want to add or reformat.

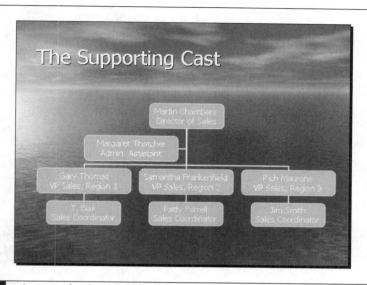

The Supporting Cast

An organization chart is a graphic representation of your organization's staff and departmental structure.

If your company or department has more than 10 or 12 people in it, it's impossible to include them all on a single organization chart and have anyone in the audience be able to read their names and titles on the slide. To solve this problem, break the group into smaller subgroups, and make an organization chart for each of them on separate slides.

To start your organization chart, click the Insert Diagram button on the Drawing toolbar to add a content placeholder to your slide. Once the placeholder appears, click the Diagram icon (the middle icon in the bottom row of icons) to open the Diagram Gallery (see Figure 16-7). If your slide already has a content placeholder, click the Diagram icon, which also opens the Diagram Gallery. Within the Diagram Gallery dialog box, choose the first option in the upper left—the organization chart—and click OK.

Filling in the Chart Boxes

As soon as you select the organization chart, the beginnings of a chart (in the default pyramid style) and a floating Organization Chart toolbar appear onscreen. Notice that handles appear around the top box in the chart—your first step should be to type the text for that top box. Start doing so without clicking your mouse, as the box is already selected. To type the person's name on the first line and his or her title on the second, just press ENTER at the end of the name, and you're automatically on the next line.

You can then continue filling in the rest of the chart's boxes (the default three boxes that you start with—more can be added later) by simply clicking the remaining boxes, one by one, and typing the names and titles of the people whose information needs to appear on the chart.

16

FIGURE 16-7 The Diagram Gallery shows you all your diagramming options.

Boxes can be edited by clicking within the existing text—just use BACKSPACE and DELETE or your mouse to select text that should be deleted or changed, and type your edited content.

Adding New Boxes to the Chart

After filling in the starter boxes (one top box and three boxes on the first tier), you can add boxes for various positions/departments within your organization. To add them, follow these steps:

1. Click an existing box that has a relationship to the box you're about to add.

2. Click the Insert Shape button (on the Organization Chart toolbar) and choose the type of box you want to add—a subordinate, coworker, or assistant—relative to the active box.

3. Continue adding boxes, using the Insert Shape button and choosing new boxes based on their placement in the hierarchy.

4. Once you have one or more new boxes, you can click them, one by one, and add the names and titles for the people or departments represented by these boxes.

TIP *If you make a mistake and place a box in the wrong spot, simply drag it to where it belongs, attaching it to the right superior, subordinate, or coworker.*

Formatting the Organization Chart

Just like the column or pie chart that you built through PowerPoint, the colors in the organization chart are selected for you, based on the template you chose for your presentation. This is normally a good thing, and you should probably leave the chart as is in terms of color unless you find that you don't like the colors or think the font will be hard to read.

Use the following tools to make changes to the appearance of your chart's components:

- The Font button can be used to change the font of any selected text. You can select text within a single box, an entire box, or several boxes, and then choose a new font.

- The font size can be adjusted for legibility's sake by using the Size button on the Formatting toolbar. Use the Increase and Decrease Font Size buttons to make incremental changes, sizing the text "by eye" until it's the size you want.

- Use the Text Color button on the Drawing toolbar to change the color of your box text.

- Use the Fill Color and Line Color tools on the Drawing toolbar to change the color of boxes and the lines surrounding and connecting them, respectively.

Creating a Diagram

The same button that inserts an organization chart can be used to insert a variety of other structural graphics—diagrams that consist of several shapes, linked by lines or other shapes to visually define or depict relationships, procedures, or systems. The Insert Diagram button, found on the Drawing toolbar, inserts a content placeholder on your slide and opens the Diagram Gallery, the same one you use to insert an organization chart, which is essentially just another type of diagram. To view the name and purpose of each of the Gallery's offerings, click once on each of the diagram buttons.

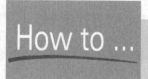 **Make Major Chart Changes**

If you like the idea of making sweeping changes to the entire organization chart, and possibly breaking free of the rather traditional rectangle format of the boxes, you can use the Organization Chart Style Gallery and its collection of preset formats. These formats change the box shape, line styles, and the appearance of text. They also offer different color schemes, so pick one that will work with your current template. To open this gallery, click any box in the chart and then click the AutoFormat button on the Organization Chart toolbar.

You can change the layout of your chart, switching from the traditional pyramid to a "hanging" chart structure that stacks boxes on the same hierarchical level rather than placing them in horizontal rows. Click the Layout button on the Organization Chart toolbar to access this structural option, along with options for automatic scaling and resizing of the chart.

16

Once you've chosen a diagram type, the diagram appears on the active slide. To build the diagram, you need only insert the data—text and/or numbers—to define the areas of the diagram, as shown here. The radial diagram provides instructions on each of the circles.

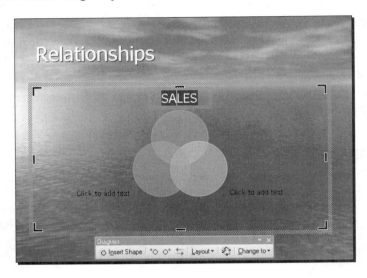

As with an organization chart, you can use the Fill Color, Line Color, Font Color, Font, and Font Size tools to reformat some or all the elements of your diagram. Just select the part or parts and then use the appropriate tool. You can also use the AutoFormat button on the Diagram toolbar to choose from a variety of preset formats for the type of diagram you're building, or you can click the Change To button if you want to switch to a different type of diagram.

Chapter 17

Building an Effective Multimedia Slide Show

How to...

- Preview a slide show
- Give a presentation that grabs and maintains audience attention
- Apply slide transitions
- Animate slide elements
- Create hyperlinks to give your slide show depth and reach
- Publish your presentation to the web

All the great text content, valuable data, and eye-catching graphics don't accomplish anything if they're in a disorganized or lackluster slide show. Too many multimedia bells and whistles can be distracting, and not enough of them can result in a show that leaves the audience napping. The goal of this chapter is to give you tools and ideas for building a slide show that does your presentation proud. All the time and effort you put into designing a great presentation should culminate in a slide show that grabs and keeps the attention of your audience, informing and entertaining them along the way.

Previewing Your Slide Show

One of the best ways to proof your presentation is to run through it once in Slide Show view. This allows you to see how the presentation will look to the audience, and to get a slightly different (bigger) perspective on the presentation without the clutter of the menu and toolbars and other visual distractions. To run the slide show on your screen, choose View | Slide Show or press F5. You can also click the Slide Show button in the lower-left corner of the PowerPoint window.

Rearranging, Duplicating, and Deleting Slides

One of the most common outcomes from a slide show preview is the realization that you need to rearrange your slides, and there are as many reasons for it as there are slides in any presentation. Perhaps slide 4 includes a reference to data that you're not showing until slide 7, so 4 needs to come after 7. Maybe you don't want to bring up the new commission program until you've pumped up the audience about the new sales promotions that are being set up for the next quarter—remember, bad news usually goes down better after good news.

To rearrange slides, you can drag them up and down in the list of slides on the left side of the workspace (the Slide panel), or you can switch to Slide Sorter view and work with a mosaic of your presentation's slides, as shown in Figure 17-1. To work in Slide Sorter view, click the Slide Sorter View button in the lower-left corner of the window or choose View | Slide Sorter.

While you're in either the Slides panel or Slide Sorter view, you can duplicate slides (click a slide and press CTRL-D), delete slides (press DELETE), and cut or copy slides (Edit | Cut or Copy) to use them in another presentation. If what you want to do—duplicating within the same presentation or copying for use in another—involves multiple slides, you can select a series of contiguous slides or a group of random slides. It all depends on your technique:

- To select a series of contiguous slides, click the first slide in the desired series, press and hold SHIFT, and click the last slide in the series.

- In Slide Sorter view, drag your mouse from the starting slide to the last slide you want to select. This works for groups of contiguous slides.

- Press CTRL and keep it pressed as you click all the contiguous and noncontiguous slides you want.

Once your slides are selected, you can hide them, if you don't want them to display during a particular run of the presentation. To hide one or more slides, select the slide or slides and choose Slide Show | Hide Slide. This will prevent the slide(s) from appearing in any slide show, and the slide number will be crossed out in the Slides panel or Slide Sorter view. To bring back a hidden slide, click it and choose Slide Show | Hide Slide again.

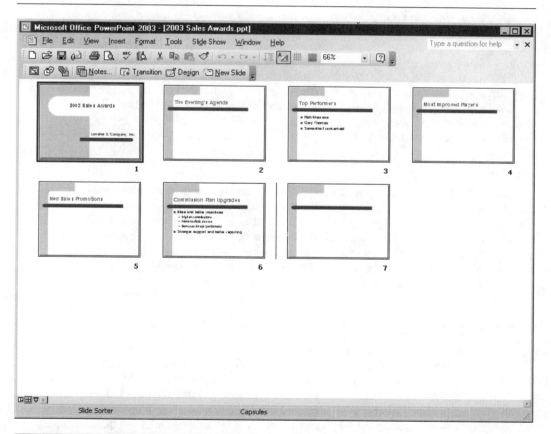

FIGURE 17-1 Drag your slides and watch for the vertical line—where it appears is where your slide will end up when you release the mouse.

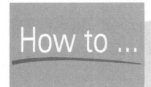

Mistake-Proof Your Presentation

What screams "amateur" or "sloppy" in a presentation? Typos and misspellings. Luckily, the Spelling feature in PowerPoint works just like the one you find in Word. In fact, they share the same dictionaries—both the main one that comes with Office and the custom one you build as you use the Add command to build a list of terms and names that aren't in the main dictionary. You can run the Spelling program (Tools | Spelling) and work through the entire presentation using the Spelling dialog box, or you can right-click words that PowerPoint flags with a red underline and choose a correction from the shortcut menu. Remember that words with more than one capital letter in them will not be compared to the dictionaries' word lists, so you'll have to proof them yourself. Don't skip doing a manual proofread, either—or better yet, get someone else to do it. You may have mistakes in your text that aren't spelling errors, and you won't want your audience to be the first ones to spot them!

To further proof and troubleshoot your presentation, preview your presentation in the setting and on the equipment that will be in use the day of the "real" presentation. This means running it on the screen or with the projection device that will be used, in the room where the presentation will take place. This allows you to determine whether your sound system is adequate and all your slides are legible. It also enables you to establish the overall effectiveness of your presentation as it will be seen by your actual audience. These things usually cannot be determined solely by previewing the presentation at your desk, on your monitor.

Another idea for presentations that are identical except for one or two slides that should be seen in one but not the other—you can use the Slide Show | Hide Slide command to create two versions of the same presentation, each one customized to include only the slides a particular audience should see. After building a presentation with all the slides that any audience would need or want to see, save that presentation with a different name. Then go back to the original version and hide the slides a given group doesn't need to view. When naming the two versions, use names that will help you or another presenter tell them apart.

Applying Slide Transitions

Even if you've proofed, previewed, and made all the changes you think you need in your presentation, it still may not be ready for your audience. If you'll be showing your slides electronically—either on a large monitor or by projecting your monitor's display onto a wall or screen—you should take advantage of PowerPoint's multimedia tools for animating slides and their individual elements. This adds visual interest to your presentation, and the first step in this process is to apply slide *transitions*—animations that occur as one slide leaves the screen and another appears.

Another benefit of using transitions is the potential for sending subtle messages. For example, if a slide in your presentation discusses an old procedure and why it's being phased out, an effective transition from that slide to the next might be Fade or Dissolve. To transition into a slide that discusses a new product or procedure you want to generate enthusiasm about, use an upsweeping transition affect—something that moves up and to the right. Why is "up and to the right" an effect that can generate enthusiasm? Because people subconsciously perceive things that move up and/or to the right as positive, and things that move down and/or to the left as negative.

Transitions can be applied to each slide individually, enabling you to choose a different transition for each slide, or to the entire presentation, so that each slide transitions in the same way. To apply a transition to an individual slide, follow these steps:

1. Switch to Slide Sorter view and click once on the slide for which you want to set a transition.

2. Click the Transition button on the Formatting toolbar. The Slide Transition task pane appears, as shown in Figure 17-2.

FIGURE 17-2   The task pane offers transition options for the selected slide when you click the Transition button.

17

3. From the Apply to Selected Slides list, choose a transition effect.

4. As needed, change the speed of the transition effect. You can choose between Fast, Medium, and Slow.

5. If you want a sound to coincide with the transition, click the Sound drop list and pick one.

6. Set the Advance Slide method. The default is On Mouse Click, which allows a live presenter the sort of pacing control that he or she will need. If your presentation will be self-running, set a time in the Automatically After text box, using the hh:mm format.

7. To see the transition previewed, click the Play button. If you don't like what you see, go back and repeat steps 2 through 6 for a different transition effect.

To set a transition for the next slide or any other, click the desired slide and repeat this procedure. If you want to apply a single transition to all slides, click the Apply to All Slides button. When a transition has been applied to a slide, a small star symbol appears beneath the slide.

Animating Individual Slide Elements

The next step in turning your presentation into a multimedia event is the animation of the individual items on your slides—the text, graphics, and chart objects you've built. Note that adding animation is more than just window dressing. It allows you to present charts and bulleted lists one item at a time, thus enabling you to discuss individual data points at your own pace without your audience rushing ahead.

To access PowerPoint's animation tools, make sure you're in Normal view (so you can select individual slide elements) and choose Slide Show | Custom Animation. The Custom Animation task pane appears, as shown in Figure 17-3.

Animating Text

Using your slide in Normal view and the Custom Animation task pane, click the text object to be animated. Follow these steps to apply an animation to the selected text object:

1. Click the Add Effect button. A list of four effects categories is displayed, enabling you to choose when and how they appear on the slide (Entrance), make them move or change size (Emphasis), determine how they leave the slide, if they're not staying (Exit), or make them move from point A to point B (Motion Paths).

2. Click one of the effects and view its submenu. The submenu lists the specific effects available for the main effects. The Entrance submenu is shown next:

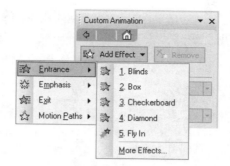

3. Choose when the effect should start. The default is On Click, although you can choose With Previous or After Previous, if another slide item was animated before the one you're working on now.

4. Based on which effect category and specific effect you chose, the second option within the Modify section of the task pane will vary—it may be Direction or Size, and the two

FIGURE 17-3 Animate individual slide elements through the Custom Animation task pane.

drop lists beneath it will vary also, as shown here. Make selections from the two drop lists appearing below the Start option.

5. Set the speed at which the effect should occur.

6. The white box contains a list of all the effects you've applied to the selected element. You can click the items in this list and click the Remove button to get rid of them, or you can click the drop arrow next to the item and choose a specific aspect of the effect to customize.

7. If more than one item appears in the effects list, you can use the Reorder option's up- or down-pointing arrow button to move a selected item up or down in the list, respectively, changing the order in which the animation effects take place. You can also change their order by dragging them up and down within the list.

8. When you've set everything for the selected text object, click another object and repeat steps 1 through 7.

Animating a Bulleted List

To make a bulleted list appear one bullet point at a time, click the text object that contains the list, click the Add Effect button, and choose Entrance. From the Entrance submenu, choose the way you want the selected bullet point to appear onscreen. Fly In is the most commonly used (and quite effective) choice, and you can choose From Left or From Bottom for a rightward or upward movement.

If your bulleted list has only first-level bullets, click the drop arrow for the animation item and choose Effect Options from the shortcut menu. In the resulting dialog box, click the Text Animation tab, and in the Group Text field choose By 1st Level Paragraphs. If any of your bullet points have subpoints associated with them, choose By 2nd Level Paragraphs so that the subpoints are animated individually, rather than appearing with their parent bullet point.

There's one more thing you can do with bulleted lists that applies further control over audience attention—you can dim the points that have already appeared and been discussed, which prevents people in the audience dwelling on something you've already addressed. To dim your previous bullet points, follow these steps:

1. Click the bullet list text object and then click its border so that the entire list is selected.

2. Display the Effect Options dialog box for the bulleted list effect you applied.

3. Click the Effect tab.

4. In the After Animation drop list, choose a color that matches your slide's background, or at least one that's close to it. This will render the text virtually illegible as soon as you go on to the next point.

5. Click OK to apply the effect option and close the dialog box.

Applying Animation to Charts and Diagrams

The Chart Animation or Diagram Animation tab of the Effect Options dialog box allows you to choose how or if the parts of your chart or diagram will be animated individually. For charts, this is especially useful, because it is often necessary to discuss the chart's data in stages. Diagrams are no less served by animation. Imagine a diagram that shows the steps in a procedure appearing one step at a time. This can really help the audience understand the diagram, and it helps the presenter address the diagram at his or her own pace.

To animate a chart or diagram, you first animate the object as a whole and then choose how the chart or diagram's parts will be animated. For example, if you want to have each data point in a chart animated separately, select By Element in Series for the Group Chart field on the Chart Animation tab. If your animated object is a diagram, the Diagram Animation tab in the Effect Options dialog box will offer appropriate choices for animating the type of diagram you've selected.

Making Pictures and AutoShapes Move

Animating graphic elements on a slide is very much like animating text. Once you choose an effect, you have to pick a specific effect (Entrance, Fly In, for example) and then modify the way that effect takes place. If you want to be able to apply animation to parts of a graphic image, you can ungroup a piece of clip art by selecting the clip art image and choosing Draw | Ungroup. You'll be prompted that proceeding will change the nature of the image, and you should agree to continue. After that, the image is broken into as many parts as it required the artist to create when building the image in the first place. Each part can then be animated separately, just as you would animate individual AutoShapes you drew yourself.

Setting Up a Slide Show

Regardless of whether you've applied slide transitions and/or animated your slide elements, you probably need to customize your show, setting it up to run in a way that's compatible with how the show will be presented. If someone will be controlling the speed of the presentation and manually moving from slide to slide (and animating individual slide elements) by mouse click, the default slide show settings we've discussed thus far should suffice.

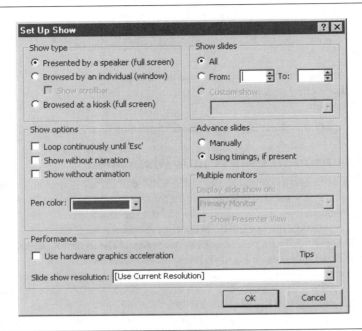

FIGURE 17-4   Set up your slide show so that it runs compatibly with the presentation venue.

If, on the other hand, the show will be run on its own on a continuous loop (on a table at a convention, for example) or if the presentation will be left running on a computer and people can stop and interact with it themselves, you'll want to tweak some of the defaults accordingly. To access these options, choose Slide Show | Set Up Show. The Set Up Show dialog box (see Figure 17-4 above) opens, displaying settings for the type of show, how it will run, and which slides to include.

> **TIP**   *Notice that there's a Pen Color option in the Set Up Show dialog box. You can annotate your slides while the slide show is running by right-clicking anywhere on the slide during the show and choosing Pointer Options | Pen. Your mouse pointer turns into a pen, and you can draw on the slide. To bring your arrow pointer back, right-click the slide again and choose Pointer Options | Automatic.*

Inserting Links to Files, Presentations, and Web Content

Many presentations run from slide 1 through to the last slide without any digression—no cutting to another presentation, no stopping to display a web page or bring up a file that contains related information. Although that's often the norm, PowerPoint makes it easy to set up *hyperlinks*—

interactive text or graphics that when clicked go to another presentation, file, or even website—provided the computer running the presentation is online at the time.

Hyperlinks can be created from elements already on your slides—pictures, text, charts, diagrams, drawn shapes, or clip art. They can also be created through the use of Action buttons—graphic symbols that you add to your chart for the expressed purpose of linking to something else. The following shows a slide with a text hyperlink (underlined) and a chart that serves as a hyperlink to the Excel worksheet file that provided the charted data. It also contains an Action button that, when clicked, takes the viewer to a specific web page. Graphic links and buttons reveal themselves through the pointing mouse hand.

Using Slide Elements as Hyperlinks

To turn something on your slide—text, a graphic, a chart, a diagram, a drawn shape or line—into a hyperlink, you need to select that item and choose Insert | Hyperlink. You can also click the Insert Hyperlink button on the Standard toolbar (it looks like a globe with links of chain under it). Figure 17-5 shows the resulting Insert Hyperlink dialog box.

To choose where the hyperlink will take you when it's clicked, choose an option from the left-hand panel in the dialog box. Here are your choices:

- ■ **Existing File or Web Page**   This option allows you to choose another file—an Excel workbook, Word document, or any other kind of file, even a graphic, displayed in a graphics or illustration application window—or to specify a web page the viewer should be taken to when the hyperlink is clicked. When you're prompted for a web address (known as a *URL*, which stands for *Uniform Resource Locator*), be sure to type the entire address, including the "http://" that precedes the www.domain.com.

- ■ **Place in This Document**   If you choose this option, the dialog box changes to show a list of the slides in the current presentation, and allows you to preview each slide within the dialog box to help you make a choice.

- ■ **Create New Document**   If, for example, you want your hyperlink to open Word with a blank document ready for typing, choose this option. For a presentation run by a live

17

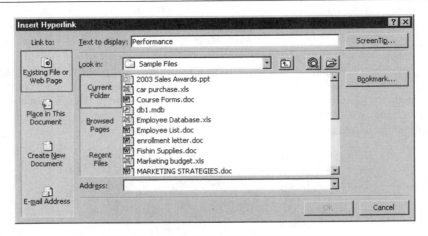

Where will your hyperlink point? To another slide in the same presentation, another presentation, a file, or a web page?

presenter, this is probably not a logical option. Imagine, however, a training presentation that is showing someone how to set up a worksheet in Excel. The link could open a blank worksheet, and the viewer could then test and play with all the things the presentation had taught him or her about using Excel.

■ **Email Address**   This, too, is an option best suited for a presentation viewed by one person sitting at a computer. With an email hyperlink, clicking the link will open a blank message window, already addressed, complete with a subject line.

If you want your hyperlink to have its own identifying or instructional ScreenTip, click the ScreenTip button to type the text that will appear when someone moves the mouse over the link object. "Click here to …" is a good choice, where "…" is replaced by whatever will happen or where the viewer will end up if the link is clicked.

Working with Action Buttons

If you don't want to use one of the elements on your slide as a hyperlink, you can add a small Action button and squirrel it away in a corner, to serve as an unobtrusive link object. To add an Action button to your slide, follow these steps:

1. Display the slide you want to add an Action button to.

2. Choose Slide Show | Action Buttons. The Action Buttons palette appears:

3. Click the Action button you want to add to your slide. Your mouse pointer turns into a crosshair.

4. Move your mouse onto the slide and draw a box the size you want the Action button to be.

5. As soon as you release the mouse after drawing the button, the Action Settings dialog box appears. Through this dialog box you can choose what the button does—link to a file, slide, or web address (among many other choices), run a program, or play a sound.

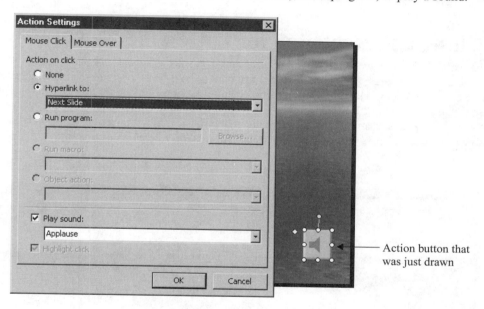

Action button that was just drawn

6. Click the tab that represents how the Action button should be used: either Mouse Click or Mouse Over. The latter option is a bit risky, because a viewer or presenter can accidentally make something happen by simply passing the mouse over a button.

7. The Mouse Click and Mouse Over tabs are identical in terms of how you use them to set up the action associated with the button. Choose an option:

- ■ **None** Choose this if you already have some action associated with the button and want to stop it without removing the button.

- ■ **Hyperlink To** Click the drop list here and choose what the button will link to—a file, a slide, or a web page.

- ■ **Run Program** If you pick this option, you have to provide the path to, and name of, the program file that should be run when the button is clicked or a mouse is moved over it.

- ■ **Play Sound** Want to play a song or other sound clip when the button is clicked? This can be handy if you want to play the sound of someone's voice, perhaps introducing himself or herself, or welcoming the audience to the presentation. When you click this option, you have to choose one of the preset sounds from the drop list, or to

17

choose a sound file of your own, scroll down in the list to Other Sound. This will open the Add Sound dialog box, through which you can pick any WAV format sound file on your computer.

8. Click OK to set up the Action button and close the dialog box.

After your Action button is set up, you can move and resize it as you would any other graphic. If you delete it, all its associated actions are deleted, too.

Publishing a Presentation for Use on the Web

There are really three ways to view a presentation: live, with a presenter speaking and controlling the slide show; on paper; and online. The first two options have been covered in this and the previous chapter, and that leaves us with viewing a presentation online. Why cover this in a chapter on setting up a slide show? Because a presentation published to the web doesn't appear as a series of static web pages. It appears as an interactive slide show, run by the visitor to the website. As shown in Figure 17-6, a presentation that's published to the web consists of multiple frames—

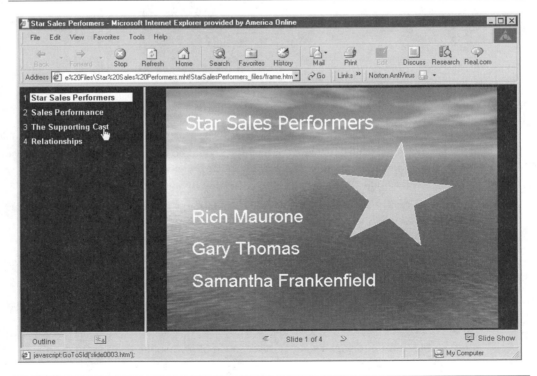

FIGURE 17-6   Your presentation appears in a set of frames, arranged much like the PowerPoint Normal view workspace.

one that lists the slides in the presentation and allows the visitor to click them at his or her own pace and in the order he or she prefers, one that shows the slides (including any transitions and/or animations you set to occur on their own schedule), and one that shows any speaker's notes that the visitor needs to read for supporting information or instructions.

Publishing a presentation to the web is extremely easy—much easier than you'd imagine, seeing all the automation built into the published presentation. To begin, choose File | Save as Web Page. The familiar Save As dialog box appears. After giving the file a name (it will have an HTM extension by default) and choosing a folder to save it in, click the Publish button.

Next, the Publish as Web Page dialog box appears, as shown in Figure 17-7. Through this dialog box, you can choose which slides to include, whether or not to include speaker's notes on the page, and which web browser software you expect most of your site visitors to be using. Based on your choice, certain functionality might be added or omitted.

At the very bottom of the Publish as Web Page dialog box is an important option, and it's on by default—Open Published Web Page in Browser. If you leave this option on, as soon as you click the Publish button, an Internet Explorer window will open, displaying your web page as it will appear online.

Of course, after you publish your presentation as a web page, you have to upload it to a web server in order for it to be accessible online. You can read more about that process in Chapter 27. Although that chapter pertains to posting FrontPage-created web pages to the web, the basic uploading instructions for using an FTP application to connect to and upload files to a web server can be applied to your presentation-turned-web page.

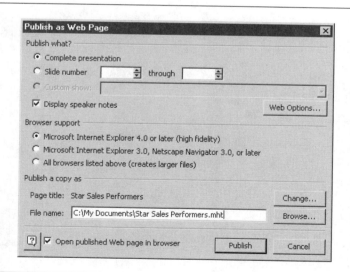

FIGURE 17-7   Customize the way your presentation is converted to a web page.

Part V

Managing Data with Access

Chapter 18

Getting Started with Access Databases

How to…

- Understand database concepts and terminology
- Set up tables to store your data
- Relate tables in your database to expand the ways your data can be used

Ever need a piece of information in a hurry and you find yourself fumbling through the papers on your desk for that information? Databases can help you organize large volumes of related information and place that information at your fingertips. In this chapter, we'll discuss databases and how to use them in some real-world examples. You'll also learn how to create and relate tables, the building blocks of a database. Tables are the most important design element of a database. If you don't set them up right, your database won't work properly.

What Is a Database?

Simply put, a database is a container for organizing and storing information. You have probably been using a database of some kind for years without even knowing it. The classic example is a telephone book. It holds information (names, addresses, and phone numbers) about people in a certain geographical area. It is organized so that you can easily find the information you need.

Electronic data-management systems such as Access allow you to store mass quantities of information without taking up mass quantities of physical space. Imagine a telephone book that encompasses everyone in the United States. That would be a huge book! Further, imagine trying to find your friend John Smith in that book. Talk about a page-turner! That same telephone book stored in an electronic database would take up a fraction of the physical space and offer tools to help you quickly find your friend John Smith among all the other John Smiths based on anything that's unique about him.

Understanding Database Concepts

There are two common types of electronic databases: relational and flat-file. A flat-file database is a single list, such as the type you can create in Excel. A relational database such as Access consists of multiple lists that can be joined together, related by one or more common elements. The main advantage of a relational database is that it requires less repetition of data. For example, suppose you were creating a database for your small business. Your business sells software and you want to track your orders. With a flat-file database, each time an existing customer places an order, you'd have to enter their shipping and payment information on the order. With a relational database, you can maintain two lists: the first with all the customer information, and the second with the order particulars. The relational database allows you to join the two lists together by a common field, such as an assigned customer number, so that you don't have to repeatedly enter customer information for each new order.

Understanding Database Objects

Access is an object-oriented application. It consists of a series of objects that when put together make up a database. Some of the objects are used for advanced features that allow you to automate and customize Access, whereas others are required to build even the simplest of databases. In this section, we will discuss the four basic Access objects. Later in this chapter and book, we will explore these objects in much more detail.

The first and most important database object is called a *table*. A table is a container for data that shares something in common. The first step in building a database is to determine how to organize your data into tables. This is often the hardest step. Tables are to databases what foundations are to houses. If your house has a poorly designed foundation, its walls will eventually come crumbling down. If your tables are poorly designed, your database will not give you the information you need in the way that you need it. The focus of this chapter is to show you how to build the proper foundation, through suitable table design, for your database.

Forms are used to provide a user-friendly interface for data entry and viewing. Forms can contain items such as check boxes and list boxes to make data entry easier. In addition, you can build your forms to improve the accuracy of the data being entered. Chapter 19 will go into more detail on building forms and entering data in them.

Queries are used to extract data from tables. What's the point of having all this information stored in a database if you can't easily get to it? Queries allow you to select the data you need and order it the way you want. You can even perform complex calculations with queries as well as add and remove data from your tables. Chapter 20 takes a closer look at queries.

Reports show you the data from your database in a printable format. Queries allow you to select the data you want, and reports allow you to display that data in a professional manner. Reports are the pot of gold at the end of the database rainbow. Chapter 21 will get you started with Access reporting.

Viewing Objects in Your Database with the Database Window

When you open an Access database, the first thing you usually see is the Database window (see Figure 18-1). The Database window allows you to navigate to the various objects that make up your database. The Objects bar, located down the left side of the Database window, categorizes database objects for easy access. Click a category button, such as Tables, on the Objects bar to see the objects, if any, for that category. The toolbar across the top of the Database window contains tools to manipulate objects. You can easily access the Database window by pressing F11 or by selecting Window | <*database name*>:Database.

Designing Tables to Store Your Data

Before you create your first table, you must decide what information you are to capture. It helps to write down the answers to the following questions:

- What is the overall purpose of the database?

18

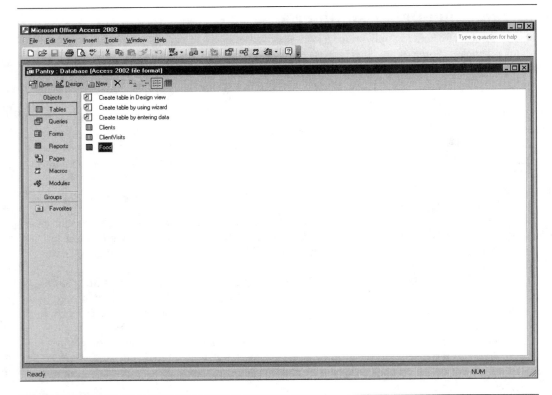

FIGURE 18-1   The Database window for the Pantry database.

- What categories of information do I need to store?
- What subcategories of information do I need to store?

Let's look a little closer with a specific example. Suppose you work for the local food pantry. The pantry distributes food to needy people in your area. You've decided to volunteer your time at the pantry to design its database. Table 18-1 gives you some ideas on what to think about before you start your design.

The food pantry example has been simplified for the purposes of our discussion. Building an actual database for a food pantry would most likely be more complex than the example used here. We want to keep the example simple so that you don't get bogged down in the details but rather learn the concepts.

When answering the questions in Table 18-1, pay close attention to subcategories. If you find yourself repeating subcategories for a group of information, you probably need a new table. In

Question	Answer	
What is the overall purpose of the database?	To track information required to run the pantry	
What categories of information do I need to store?	Food inventory, clients, client visits	
What subcategories of information do I need to store?	**Category**	**Subcategory**
	Food inventory	Item, quantity needed, quantity on hand, food type
	Who is served?	Name, address, phone, date of birth, income
	How often served?	Name, date of visit

TABLE 18-1   Initial Questions for the Food Pantry Database Design

the food pantry example, you might have started with two tables: one for food inventory and one for clients that includes client visits. With that design, however, each time a new client visit is entered, client names, addresses, phone numbers, and so on must be repeated. The client particulars include information that has already been entered. What's new here is the visit information. So, it would make sense to have a table for client particulars to eliminate the data-entry repetition and a third, new table for visit particulars.

What You Need to Know about Tables Before You Begin

Tables are divided into smaller groups of related information called *fields*. A collection of field information about one item (such as a food item in our Pantry database) is called a *record*. Each table should have one or more fields designated as a *primary key*. A primary key is a unique identifier for each record in a table. The primary key helps Access locate records faster when you ask for them. Usually, an ID field is created in each table to uniquely identify each record within that table. Access can generate the ID number for you, or you can use your own manual numbering scheme.

Not only must you think about how to categorize your data into tables and fields, you must also decide what type of data can be entered in a field. Access requires you to assign a data type to each field. For example, the Number data type will accept numbers but not letters or other nonnumeric characters. Assigning data types properly can help prevent erroneous data entry in tables. We'll discuss data types in more detail later in this section.

Finally, you will have to set properties for each table field. A *property* describes something about the field. For example, the Field Size property describes how many characters will be allowed in a field. Set the Field Size property to 2, and only two characters or fewer will be allowed in the field. If the field in question were a state field, this would prevent the user from spelling out the name of the state and force him or her to use a two-character or less abbreviation. You don't want some people entering "California," others entering "CA," and yet others entering "Calif." You want everyone to enter it the same way. Why? Because it's easier to ask for all records containing CA than to ask for assorted variations of the spelling. So, properties help streamline the type of data that is entered in a field.

The secret to good database design is to categorize data properly into tables and fields. That's why it's so important to spend time thinking this through before you begin the actual design. If you don't do the thinking up-front, you will find yourself redesigning tables later on. Because tables are used as the basis for queries, forms, and reports, you will not only end up changing your table design but also the forms, queries, and reports that are based on the tables. That's like trying to change the foundation after the house has been built. It can be done, but it's not easy!

Viewing a Table and Its Data

All Access objects, whether they are tables, forms, queries, or reports, can be viewed in several ways. Every object has a Design view. Design view allows you to create and modify the object components that make up the object. Figure 18-2 shows a table in Design view. Notice that not

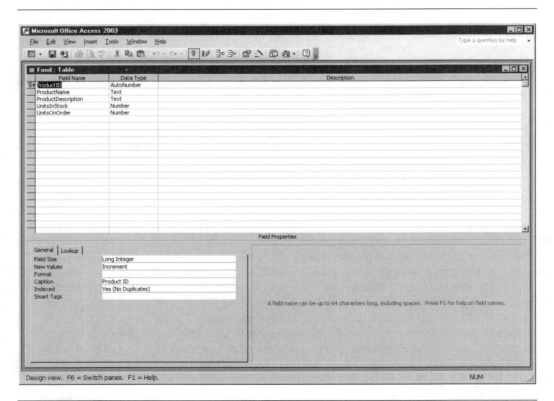

FIGURE 18-2   The Food table in Design view.

only can you input the name of each field within your table but also the type of data the field will hold, a description of the data in the field, and some properties about the field, such as its size and format.

Tables can also be displayed in Datasheet view. Datasheet view displays the data contained in the table in a spreadsheet-like format (see Figure 18-3). You can enter data directly into your tables in Datasheet view very much as you would enter data in a spreadsheet. To do so, use the mouse or ENTER or TAB to navigate to the record and field where you want to enter data. Then, type the data for the field and press ENTER or TAB to move to the next field. When you reach the end of a record, press ENTER or TAB to move to the next record. Although data entry is sometimes done in Datasheet view, it is most often done in a form. Forms provide an easier interface for data entry and are discussed in detail in Chapter 19.

When working with tables, you will constantly be switching back and forth between Design and Datasheet view. Okay. Enough discussion. Now that you have the proper foundation to begin designing your database tables, let's get to work.

Creating a Table

You can create a table in Access in several ways. The two most common are via the Table Wizard and manually. A *wizard* is a tool that helps you complete a task. Each of the four database objects

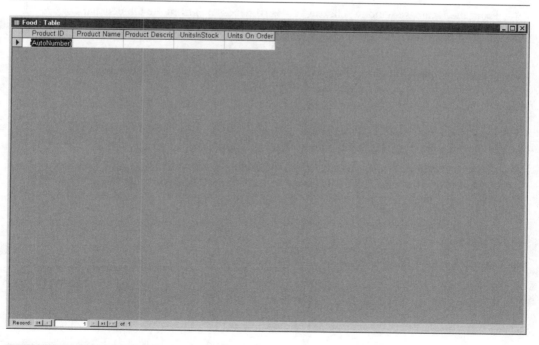

FIGURE 18-3   The Food table in Datasheet view.

18

we discussed earlier in this chapter come with their own creation wizard. Some wizards are more useful than others. I think you will find the Table Wizard extremely useful in that it handles much of the table design for you. It provides a suggested list of fields, chooses the proper data type, and sets some properties for you. If you manually create tables, you must enter all this information yourself. So, why not use the wizard all the time? Because although the wizard contains examples for creating common types of tables, it may not offer examples for the type of table you require, so you'll need to create the table manually.

The Table Wizard

The general rule of thumb in creating tables is to use the wizard if possible. You can take what the wizard gives you and customize the result when the wizard is finished. Let's use the Table Wizard to create the first table—Food—in our Pantry database. Here's how:

1. If Access isn't already running, launch it from the Start | Programs menu.

2. Click Blank Database from the New section of the task pane at the right of the screen. You will be prompted for a file name for the new database.

3. Select a folder to store the database file and type **Pantry** in the File Name box. Click the Create button. A new, blank database will open in the Database window. The task pane will automatically close.

4. From the Database window, choose Tables (if necessary) from the Objects bar.

5. Double-click the Create Table by Using a Wizard icon. The Table Wizard appears (see Figure 18-4).

6. Select Business from the option group on the left side of the wizard screen. A list of business tables appears in the Sample Tables list.

7. Choose Products from the Sample Tables list.

8. Double-click ProductID, ProductName, ProductDescription, UnitsInStock, and UnitsOnOrder from the Sample Fields list.

9. Click the ProductDescription field from the Fields in My New Table list. Click the Rename Field button. Change the word *Description* to **Type** and click OK.

10. Click the UnitsOnOrder field from the Fields in My New Table list. Click the Rename Field button. Change *OnOrder* to **Needed** and click OK.

11. Click the Next button. The second screen of the wizard appears.

12. Enter the name **Food** for your table in the name box at the top of the wizard screen and click Next. The last screen of the Table Wizard appears.

13. Choose Modify the Table Design from the list in the middle of the dialog box.

14. Click the Finish button. The new table will appear in Design view.

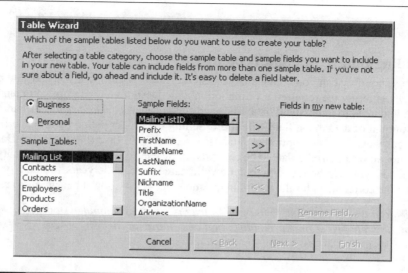

FIGURE 18-4 The Table Wizard

TIP
On subsequent uses of the Table Wizard, a new screen will appear prompting you to select a join relationship between the new table and an existing table in the database. Tables are joined on a common field or fields (usually ID fields) to allow access to data from both tables simultaneously. We will discuss relationships in more detail at the end of this chapter.

Here's your first big test. See if you can create the "who is served?" table using the wizard. Try using the Employees sample table and naming the table "Clients." While using the wizard, you will be prompted to relate your new table to the Food table. Just click Next. The two tables should not be related.

Here are the fields you'll need:

- ClientID (use the Employee ID field and rename)
- First Name
- Last Name
- Address
- City
- State
- Postal Code
- Home Phone

18

- Birth date
- Income (use the Salary field and rename)

Understanding Data Types and Properties

As stated earlier, not only can you create a table with the Table Wizard, but you can also create one manually by entering the required information in table Design view. Before you manually create a table, you need to understand data types and field properties. *Data types* further define the type and amount of data that a field will allow. Setting the proper data type for each field can improve data-entry accuracy and optimize database size. As Table 18-2 illustrates, the Date/Time data type will not allow a nonvalid date to be entered. So, by choosing the Date/Time data type for all your date fields, you will be forced to enter a valid date between the years 100 and 9999. You might not enter the correct date for the record in question, but at least you'll be entering a real date!

NOTE *Some data types refer to sizes in bytes. A byte is a unit of computer storage equivalent to approximately two digits for numbers and one character for text.*

Data Type	Size	Type of Data Allowed
Text	Up to 255 characters.	Text or combinations of text and numbers, as well as numbers that don't require calculations, such as phone numbers.
Memo	Up to 65,535 characters.	Lengthy text or combinations of text and numbers.
Number	Up to 8 bytes.	Numeric data used in mathematical calculations.
Date/Time	8 bytes.	Date and time values for the years 100 through 9999.
Currency	8 bytes.	Currency values and numeric data used in mathematical calculations involving data with one to four decimal places.
AutoNumber	4 bytes (16 bytes if the Field Size property is set to Replication ID).	A unique sequential number or random number (incremented by 1) assigned by Access whenever a new record is added to a table. AutoNumber fields can't be updated.
Yes/No	1 bit.	Yes and No values and fields that contain only one of two values (Yes/No, True/False, or On/Off).
OLE Object	Up to 1 gigabyte (limited by available disk space).	An object (such as an Excel spreadsheet, Word document, a graphic, a sound, or other binary data) linked to or embedded in an Access table.
Hyperlink	Hyperlink addresses can contain up to 6,144 characters.	Text or combinations of text and numbers stored as text and used as a hyperlink address.

TABLE 18-2 Access Field Data Types

Size is a key factor in database design. Always try to keep the size of your database as small as possible. Do this by choosing the proper data type and Field Size property setting for each field you create. Keeping the database small will make your queries and reports run faster.

The Number and Text data types have an adjustable Field Size property that further defines the amount of data stored. The Field Size property is set on the General tab in table Design view. Table 18-3 lists the settings for the Field Size property for the Number data type. The Text data type will allow entry of up to 255 characters in a field.

> **TIP** *Use the Text data type for all numeric fields that do not require a calculation or contain leading zeros. ZIP codes are a perfect example. In many cases, text fields use less space than number fields.*

As you can see, some field sizes reserve more space than others. The Byte field size uses much less space than the Decimal field size. If your field was to store movie ratings, and the rating numbers could be between 1 and 10, you certainly wouldn't want to choose the Decimal field size. That would be like building a garage the size of a 747 for your bicycle. It's unnecessary and wastes space. Instead, you would choose the Byte field size because it is the smallest field size that will allow the entry of the maximum value for your field. So, choose your data types and field sizes carefully. Always choose the size that requires the minimum amount of space yet will allow the maximum value required for the field.

Creating a Table Without the Table Wizard

Now that you know more about data types and field sizes, you are ready to manually create a table. Sometimes it makes more sense to create a table manually. Perhaps the wizard doesn't

Setting	Decimal Precision	Storage Size	Description
Byte	None	1 byte	Stores numbers from 0 to 255 (no fractions).
Decimal	28	12 bytes	Stores numbers from $-10^{28}-1$ through $10^{28}-1$.
Integer	None	2 bytes	Stores numbers from −32,768 to 32,767 (no fractions).
Long Integer	None	4 bytes	(Default) Stores numbers from −2,147,483,648 to 2,147,483,647 (no fractions).
Single	7	4 bytes	Stores numbers from −3.402823E38 to −1.401298E−45 for negative values and from 1.401298E−45 to 3.402823E38 for positive values.
Double	15	8 bytes	Stores numbers from −1.79769313486231E308 to −4.94065645841247E−324 for negative values and from 1.79769313486231E308 to 4.94065645841247E−324 for positive values.

TABLE 18-3   Field Size Property Settings for the Number Data Type

offer an option close enough to the table you need to create, or maybe your table requires only a few fields. Tables are created manually in table Design view.

Here are the steps to manually create the "how often served" table (which we'll call ClientVisits) from our food pantry example:

1. From the Database window, choose Tables (if necessary) from the Objects bar. Three icons appear in the Database window to the right of the Objects bar beginning with the word *Create*.

2. Double-click the Create Table in Design View icon. A new table opens in Design view.

TIP *Access object names such as table and field names can be up to 64 characters long. Try sticking with letters and numbers. Make the name descriptive of the object's contents. Finally, avoid spaces. Any Access object name that contains spaces must be surrounded by brackets ([ ]) when it is referred to in a query, on a form, or in a report. You'll quickly grow tired of typing those extra brackets!*

3. In the first row of the Field Name column, type **VisitID**. In the Data Type column select AutoNumber. The AutoNumber data type will generate a unique sequential ID number for each client visit record. Type a brief description of the field in the Description column.

TIP *The contents of the Description column for a field will display in the status bar when entering data in that field. This can be helpful in prompting for what to enter in the field.*

4. In the second row of the Field Name column, type **ClientID**. In the Data Type column select Number. Confirm that the Field Size property is set to Long Integer. Type a brief description of the field in the Description column.

NOTE *Most ID fields are AutoNumber fields. For example, the ClientID field from the Clients table is an AutoNumber field. When adding it to a secondary table, such as the ClientVisits table, always choose the Number data type and the Long Integer field size. If you don't, you won't be able to join the two tables together so that you can simultaneously retrieve information from them. More on joins later in this chapter.*

5. In the third row of the Field Name column, type **VisitDate**. In the Data Type column select Date/Time. Type a brief description of the field in the Description column, such as "Enter the date of this visit."

6. Choose File | Save As from the menu bar. You will be prompted for a table name. Enter **ClientVisits** and press ENTER.

7. Access will next ask if you want to set a primary key. Choose Yes, and the VisitID field will be set as the primary key because you chose the AutoNumber data type. Note the key icon indicating the primary key next to the VisitID field.

8. Close the table design window for the ClientVisits table.

In Access, saving is a little bit different than it is in other Office products. Access requires that you save only the objects you create. It will prompt you to do so when you close that object after creating or modifying it. Unlike Word, Excel, and PowerPoint, in which you must manually save data entered with the Save command, Access saves data entered for each record after you leave that record. So, Access saves your data for you automatically.

More Table Properties

Most Access objects have myriad properties that could be written about for hours on end. If you decide to become an Access expert, you will have to become familiar with many of these properties. Because you're not yet an expert and might never want to be, we'll discuss only three more field properties. All three—Format, Decimal Places, and Caption—can be set on the General tab in table Design view (see Figure 18-5).

For more in-depth coverage of Access, try a book such as Microsoft Office Access 2003: The Complete Reference *by Virginia Andersen (McGraw-Hill/Osborne, 2003).*

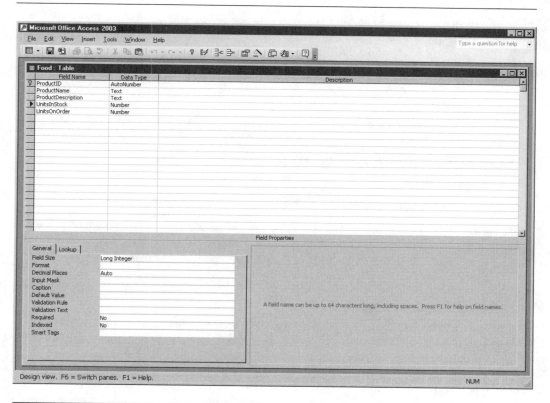

18

FIGURE 18-5   Setting the Format, Decimal Places, and Caption properties

The Caption property allows you to set a description for each field as it will appear on a form, report, or as a column heading in Datasheet view. If you don't set a Caption property, the field name is used. Enter **Last Visit** as the caption for the VisitDate field in the ClientVisits table of the Pantry database and you will see Last Visit as the description for that field wherever it appears throughout the database.

Make sure that the correct field is selected in the Field Name column before you change a property.

The Format and Decimal Places properties go together. The Format property applies to all data types except OLEObject and determines how data in a field will appear. For certain number field Format properties, the Decimal Places property sets the number of decimals that will display. Access Format properties are similar to Excel Format properties. The Percent format adds a percent sign to a number, the Currency format adds a dollar sign, and so on. Choose the format you want for your numbers and that format will apply to the field wherever it appears in your database. The following steps explain how to change the Caption and Format properties for a field in the Pantry database.

If you choose to ignore setting these properties for a field, you will have to set them every time you use that field on a form or report. In this case, a little more work up-front can save hours of work later on.

1. Open the ClientVisits table in Design view.

2. In the Field Name column, select the VisitDate row.

3. On the General tab in the Field Properties section, click in the Format row. Select the Short Date format.

4. Click the Caption row and type **Last Visit**.

5. Close the table.

6. Choose Yes when prompted to save. Figure 18-6 shows the resulting table in Datasheet view.

CAUTION

Formatting a number in a field does not change the actual number itself, only how that number appears throughout the database. So, formatting the number 3.14 to zero decimal places displays the number only as 3. However, any calculations performed on the number will use its actual value of 3.14.

Manually Setting the Primary Key

Sometimes you will need to change or add a primary key after a table has been created. This is done in table Design view. Remember, setting a primary key improves query performance, so most tables should have one, especially those that will be queried often. By setting a field as the primary key, you are telling Access that no two records in the table will contain duplicate information in that field. So, make sure you select a field that will be unique to each record. If you don't, Access will not allow you to enter certain records in the table.

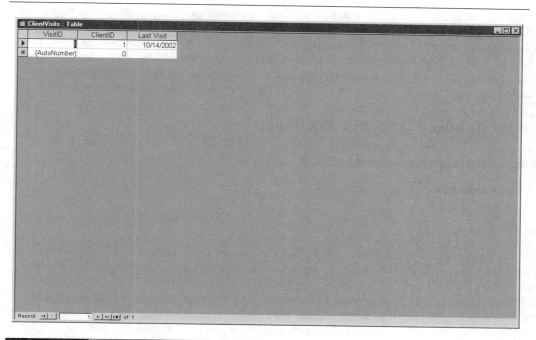

FIGURE 18-6   The ClientVisits table after formatting properties have been set.

For example, suppose you're using Phone Number as the primary key field. Everyone has a unique phone number, right? Well, not always. John and Jane Doe are both clients. They share the same phone number. You could enter Jane without a hitch. However, when it came time to enter John, Access would display a message that essentially tells you that you cannot enter that phone number because another record already contains that value.

Here's how to set the primary key manually:

1.   Open the table in Design view.

2.   In the Field Name column, select the field that you want designated as the primary key.

3.   Click the Primary Key button (You guessed it. It's the one with the key on it!) on the Table Design toolbar.

NOTE   *It is best to set the primary key before entering any data. If duplicate data exists in a field you try to designate as a primary key, Access will not let you set that field as the primary key.*

18

How to Connect Tables with Relationships

When we hear the word *relationship*, most of us think of a bond between two people. In Access, you can play matchmaker. It won't, however, be between human beings but rather between tables.

Doesn't sound like quite as much fun, does it? Table relationships make possible the pulling of information from more than one table at a time. The whole point of a relational database is to economize on data entry by excluding repetitive information. So, you'll need a way to connect tables so that you can access their information at the same time. You relate (more often referred to as *join*) the tables in Access to connect them. As with setting field properties during table design, setting relationships up-front can save you time in the long run by speeding query design.

Understanding Relationship Types

In the human world, we have friendships, marriages, and casual and serious relationships. In the Access world we have the following relationships:

- One to many
- One to one
- Many to many

The most common relationship by far is the one-to-many relationship. So, we will limit our discussion to this type of relationship. In a one-to-many relationship, a record in Table 1 can have many matching records in Table 2, but a record in Table 2 has only one matching record in Table 1. We will use this type of relationship in our Pantry database when relating the Clients table to the ClientVisits table. A client can have many visits, but a visit cannot exist without a client.

Besides relating tables, you will also have to decide if you want Access to enforce referential integrity between the two tables. When referential integrity is turned on, a record in Table 2 cannot exist without a corresponding record in Table 1. In other words, you cannot enter a client visit without first entering the client.

NOTE
To enforce referential integrity in a one-to-many relationship, the related field in Table 1 must be the primary key of that table, whereas the related field in Table 2 cannot.

This sounds perfectly reasonable. Why would you ever want to enter a visit for a client that does not exist? Most of the time you would not. So, most of the time turning on referential integrity makes sense. Just keep in mind that with referential integrity on, you could never record a client visit, then go back later to fill in the client information. Maybe someone else on staff had that information, and the only information currently available was the visit information. Referential integrity improves the quality of your data by eliminating bogus records such as client visits for nonexistent clients.

When choosing to enforce referential integrity, you will have the options Cascade Update Related Fields and Cascade Delete Related Records. The former will update the primary key data in Table 2 if it changes in Table 1. The latter will delete all visit records from the ClientVisits table if the client is deleted from the Clients table. If you do not choose Cascade Delete Related Records, you will not be able to delete a client record from the Clients table without first deleting all that client's visits from the ClientVisits table.

Creating Relationships

Relationships are created in the Relationships window by dragging a shared field from Table 1 on top of its counterpart from Table 2 (see Figure 18-7). A line will connect the two fields. If you

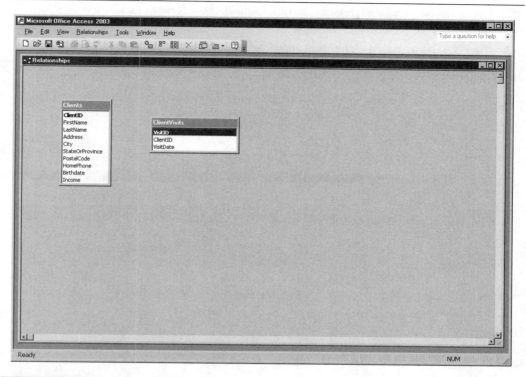

FIGURE 18-7   The Relationships window

make a mistake and join the wrong fields, you can delete the relationship by clicking the join line and pressing DELETE.

Follow these steps to relate the Clients and ClientVisits tables in the Pantry database:

1. Activate the Database window if necessary.

2. Choose Relationships from the Tools menu. The Relationships window will appear, displaying the Show Tables dialog box.

3. Double-click the Clients and ClientVisits tables from the list of tables on the Tables tab.

4. Close the Show Table dialog box.

5. Click and drag the ClientID field from the Clients table on top of the ClientID field from the ClientVisits table and release the mouse. The Edit Relationships dialog box will appear.

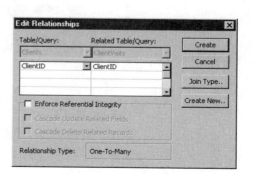

18

6. Check the Enforce Referential Integrity, Cascade Update Related Fields, and Cascade Delete Related Records check boxes.

7. Click the Create button. A line will appear joining the two tables on the ClientID field (see Figure 18-8). The "one" table will have a 1 near it on the join line, whereas the "many" table will have an infinity symbol (<<Unicode: 38>>) near it on the join line.

8. Close the Relationships window. When prompted to save the relationship layout, choose Yes. The relationship is saved automatically when you create it.

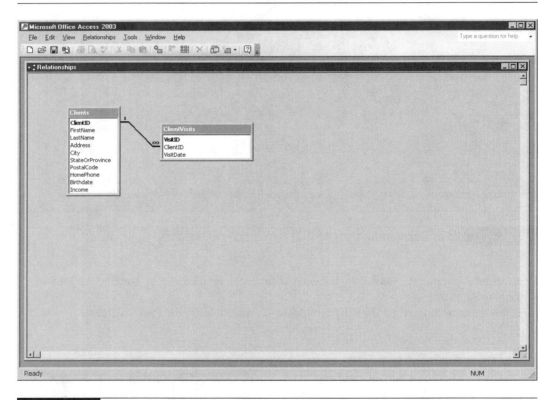

FIGURE 18-8   The Relationships window showing the join line between the Clients and ClientVisits tables.

Chapter 19

Simplifying Data Entry with Forms

How to...

■ Build a form with the Form Wizard

■ View a form's design and data

■ Add and edit text, combo, and check boxes

■ Enter data in a form

Forms are an easy-to-use gateway to your table data. Although data can be entered directly into tables, doing so can be difficult. Access provides the form as a tool to arrange your table data for data entry however you prefer, as shown in this example. Such flexibility is not possible with tables and makes for easier data entry.

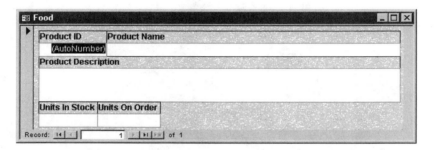

Forms can also be used to create custom dialog boxes, such as the one shown next. Through custom dialog boxes, you can carry out an action based on information the user enters in the dialog box. For example, you can build a dialog box form that lists the reports you have created in your database. With your reports dialog box, the user can select a report and preview or print it.

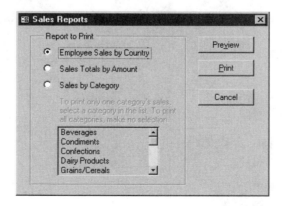

Finally, you can use forms to open other forms. Many professionally developed Access databases contain a switchboard, shown next, with buttons that are used to navigate to the data-entry forms and reports within the database. This is especially important if the users of the database aren't familiar with how to use Access. A switchboard makes the database easier to use.

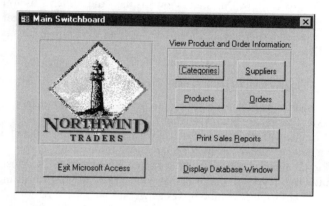

NOTE *Creating switchboards and custom dialog boxes requires some advanced knowledge of Access. These topics are beyond the scope of this book.*

Creating a Form with the Form Wizard

The Form Wizard is a powerful tool that can quickly make a data-entry form for you. I think you will find yourself starting with the Form Wizard for each form you create, with very few exceptions. Once the Form Wizard has finished, all you need to do is fine-tune the form to suit your needs. In many cases, this means moving or sizing objects on the form and adding or editing labels. How much fine-tuning is required often depends on how well you set field properties in your tables. For example, if you don't set a caption for each field, the Form Wizard will use field names as captions. Often, field names do not work well as captions.

How to See the Form Design and Data

Access offers three common ways to view a form. All three are available on the View menu or with the View tool on the Forms toolbar.

The first is Design view. Here you can set properties for the form, such as what data it will display. In addition, it is in Design view that you can alter a form's appearance.

The second is called Form view. Form view lets you see data in the form. So once the form is designed and complete, you will use Form view to view, add, delete, and modify your data.

The final view is Datasheet view. Datasheet view displays the contents of your form in a spreadsheet-like format, just like it appears in the table Datasheet view. Datasheet view is usually used for a type of form called a *subform*. Subforms are beyond the scope of this book and therefore will not be discussed any further.

Understanding Some Basic Form Concepts

Before we create a form with the Form Wizard, let's discuss a few concepts about forms that you'll need to know. Most forms are bound to what Access calls a *record source*. A record source is the name of a table or query that contains the data the form will display. The Form Wizard will prompt you to select a table or query for the form's record source.

The objects used to label and display data on a form are called *controls*. Most Windows dialog boxes contain the same types of controls that you can add to your forms in Access. These controls include check, text, list, and combo boxes as well as labels and buttons. The *Toolbox* is the toolbar used to add these controls to a form. If you do not see the Toolbox when opening a form in Design view, choose View | Toolbox from the menu bar to show it. Forms and controls have *properties*. These properties determine how the form or control will appear and what it will do.

Using the Form Wizard to Create a Form

The Form Wizard will ask you several questions and create a form based on your answers. Here are the questions:

- What table or query contains the data you want the form to display?

- What fields from the table or query will the form display?

- What layout will the form have? *Columnar* will display controls in columns on the form. Use this layout if your table or query contains many fields. *Tabular* will display controls in rows on the form. Use this layout if your table or query has a small number of fields and you want to display more than one record at a time. *Datasheet* will display the form in Datasheet view. This layout is commonly used for subforms. *Justified* will give the controls on the form a uniform size.

- What style will your form have? Access comes with some form templates that will give your form a professionally designed appearance. You can click a style name in the wizard to see how your form will appear.

- What name will your form have?

- How do you first want to see the new form, in Design or Form view?

Let's once again use our Pantry database—this time to create a form for the Clients table. Follow these steps:

1. Press F11 to display the Database window, if necessary.

2. Click the Forms button on the Objects toolbar.

3. Double-click the Create Form by Using Wizard icon. The Form Wizard appears.

4. The first screen of the Form Wizard asks for the table or query that contains the data you want the form to display and the fields to display on the form. Select Table:Clients from the Tables/Queries list.

5. Click the double right chevron (>>) button to choose all fields in the Clients table. When you click it, all the fields from the Available Fields list are moved to the Selected Fields list.

6. Click the Next button. The layout screen of the Form Wizard appears.

7. Click a layout name to see an example of how your form will be laid out. Select the Justified layout.

8. Click the Next button. The Style screen of the Form Wizard appears.

9. Click a style name to see an example of that style. Select the SandStone style.

10. Click the Next button. The last page of the Form Wizard appears.

11. Leave the default name of Clients for the form. Choose the Modify the Form's Design option.

12. Click the Finish button. The new form will appear in Design view (see Figure 19-1).

Modifying Your Form

In many cases, the Form Wizard creates a form that requires no modification. However, it does have limitations that might require some manual intervention on your part. In Design view, you can move, size, add, delete, and format controls.

Managing the Controls on Your Form

Before you can modify a control in any way, you must select it. To select a control, click it with the mouse. To select multiple controls, press and hold SHIFT as you click the controls. You can also draw a box around the controls to select them. If you've worked with graphics before, such as clip art, you should have no trouble working with Access controls.

To size a control, try this:

1. Open the form in Design view.

2. Select the control.

3. Roll the mouse pointer to one corner of the control. A diagonal double arrow will appear. Drag to resize.

19

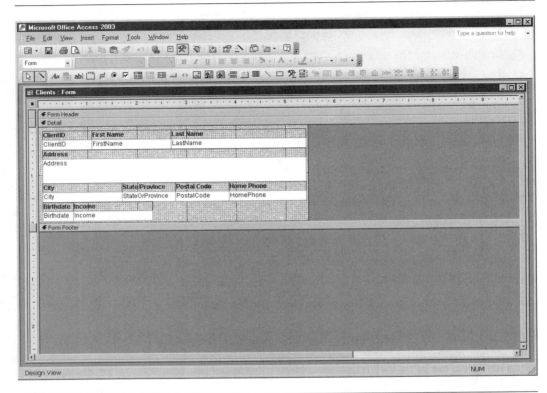

FIGURE 19-1   The Clients form in Design view.

To move a control, follow these steps:

1. Open the form in Design view.

2. Click the control to select it.

3. Roll the mouse pointer over the edge of the control but away from the corners. An open hand will appear. Drag the control to its new location. The control's associated label will also move.

NOTE   *Most data-entry controls are created with an associated label. When you move or delete the control, its label is moved or deleted as well.*

4. To move a control independent of its label, and vice versa, roll the mouse to the upper-left corner of the control or label. A hand with the index finger pointing will appear. Drag the control or label to its new location.

TIP

Controls can be sized and moved with more precision using the keyboard. To size a control, press and hold SHIFT, then press a directional arrow. To move a control, press and hold CTRL, then press a directional arrow.

Here's how to delete a control:

1. Select the control.
2. Press DELETE.

TIP

Remember when working with controls that you can undo up to the last 20 actions. So if you make a mistake, use the Undo tool on the toolbar or press CTRL-Z to reverse your mistake. If you want to undo multiple actions in one step, click the arrow to the right of the Undo tool and select the action you want to undo. When you undo an action, you also undo all actions above it on the list.

Let's try working with some controls on the Clients form. Here's what to do:

1. Open the Clients form in Design view (as shown in Figure 19-1).
2. Click the text box containing the text StateOrProvince. The text box will be white, whereas its associated label containing the text State/Province will be transparent.
3. Press DELETE to delete it. Notice that the text box and label are deleted simultaneously.
4. To reduce the width of the Income control, click the Income text box.
5. Press and hold SHIFT to select the Income label.
6. Roll the mouse pointer to the right side of either the text box or the label and look for a double arrow.
7. Press and drag to the left to make the control about three quarters of its original size.
8. Roll the mouse pointer to the left of the Postal Code label.
9. Press and drag over the Postal Code and Home Phone text boxes and labels to select them.
10. Press and hold CTRL and press LEFT ARROW several times to move the selection.

Making a Pick List with the Combo Box Control

Whenever designing a form, you always want to make the form as easy to use as possible so that data entry is simple and data-entry errors are reduced. The combo box control is effective in both these areas. With it, you can provide the data-entry person with a list of items for the field. In addition, you can limit the user to selecting one of those items so that you can better control the data that is entered into the field (search the Help system for Limit to List for more details). Let's add a combo box to our Clients form that will provide a state pick list:

1. View the Clients form in Design view.

2. Select the Combo Box tool on the Toolbox.

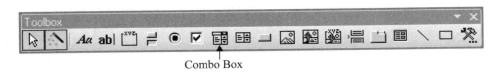

Combo Box

3. Roll the mouse pointer slightly to the right of the upper-right corner of the City text box. Press and drag just to the left of the bottom-left corner of the Postal Code text box. Release the mouse. The Combo Box Wizard will appear.

4. Select "I Will Type the Values That I Want" from the first screen of the wizard.

5. Click Next.

6. The food pantry is located on the border of New Jersey (NJ) and Pennsylvania (PA). It serves people from both states, so we will add those states to the pick list. Click in the first row under the Col1 label and type **NJ**. Do not press ENTER or you will be taken to the next screen of the wizard.

7. Click in the next row and type **PA**.

8. Click the Next button.

9. Select the arrow on the Store That Value in This Field combo box, choose StateOrProvince, and click Next.

10. Type **State** as the label for the pick list.

11. Click the Finish button. The State combo box will appear with its label to the left of the combo box. Its color is not the same as the text boxes. We will address this later on in this chapter.

12. Click the State label to select it.

13. Roll the mouse over the upper-left corner of the control. Look for the hand with the index finger for the mouse pointer shape.

14. Drag the control over the top of the State combo box.

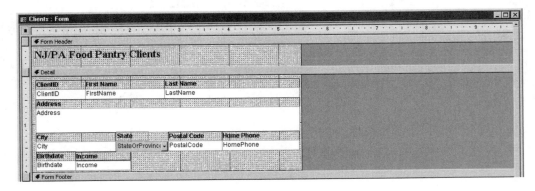

15. Select View | Form View from the menu bar.

16. Click the State combo box arrow and select a state.

17. Close the form and save it.

Adding a Title to Your Form

A form is divided into sections. The following table defines the sections that are displayed by default:

Section Name	Definition
Form Header	Data in this section will display at the top of the form in Form view. This is often used for titles.
Detail	This section displays records from the form's table or query record source.
Form Footer	Data in this section will display at the bottom of the form in Form view. This is sometimes used to display custom command buttons or instructional labels.

Sometimes you will need to add additional text to a form to further define its contents or to title the form. The Label control allows you to do this. Although the Form Wizard does much of the work, it does not provide a title for the forms it creates. The Label control can be used to title a form. To add a title to the Clients form, follow these steps:

1. Open the Clients form in Design view.

2. Place the mouse pointer on the line dividing the Form Header and Detail section buttons. A vertical double-arrow shape will appear.

3. Drag the Form Header section down about one half inch to make room for the title.

4. Select the Label tool from the Toolbox.

5. Draw a rectangle about the size of the Form Header section and release the mouse.

6. Type **NJ/PA Food Pantry Clients**.

7. Click the label again to deselect it.

Changing the Appearance of Controls by Formatting

The easiest way to format a control is with the Formatting toolbar.

This toolbar appears in Design view of a form and contains common buttons from other Microsoft Office applications—some you might know. To format a control, select it, then click the appropriate button from the Formatting toolbar (see Table 19-1 for a description of each tool).

19

Tool Name	Function
Object	Lists all objects on the form and selects the object chosen from the list.
Font	Sets the font of the selected control.
Font Size	Sets the font size of the selected control.
Bold	Bolds the selected control.
Italics	Italicizes the selected control.
Underline	Underlines the selected control.
Align Left	Left aligns text within the selected control.
Center	Centers text within the selected control.
Align Right	Right aligns text within the selected control.
Fill/Back Color	Fills the selected control with a color or removes the color.
Fore/Font Color	Sets the font color of the selected control.
Line/Border Color	Sets the border color of the selected control.
Line/Border Width	Sets the width of the selected control's edge.
Special Effect	Gives the selected control an appearance such as sunken, raised, or etched.

TABLE 19-1   The Formatting Toolbar Icons

Here's how to use the toolbar to format our new controls on the Clients form:

1. Make sure you are still displaying the Clients form in Design view.

2. Click the title label in the Form Header section to select it.

3. Click the Font tool on the Formatting toolbar and select Times New Roman to change the label's font.

4. Click the Font Size tool on the Formatting toolbar and select 16 to change the size of the label.

5. Select the State combo box by clicking it.

6. Click the arrow on the Fill/Back Color tool (looks like a pouring bucket) from the Formatting toolbar and select the color white from the resulting color palette.

7. Choose File | Save from the menu bar to save the latest design changes.

8. Display the form in Form view to see your changes.

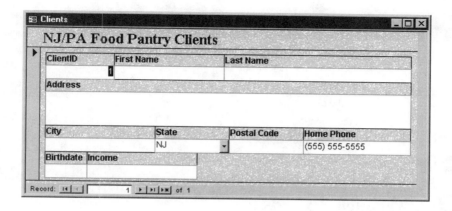

Entering Data in Your Form

Now that you know how to make and modify a form, you'll want to start entering some data in that form. To do so effectively, you'll need to know a little about form navigation. In addition, we'll look at some data-entry shortcuts to improve data-entry time.

Data-Entry Tips

Of course, there is no way around typing much of the data that is to go in your data-entry forms unless of course you hire someone to do it for you! However, there are some keyboard shortcuts that can make that data entry and editing a little bit easier. Table 19-2 lists them and what they do.

Keystroke	Function
END	Move to the end of a single line of data in the current field.
HOME	Move to the beginning of a single line of data in the current field.
CTRL-RIGHT ARROW	Move to the next word.
CTRL-LEFT ARROW	Move to the previous word.
TAB	Move to the next field.
SHIFT-TAB	Move to the previous field.
CTRL-; (semicolon)	Insert the current date.
CTRL-: (colon)	Insert the current time.
CTRL-' (apostrophe)	Insert the value from the same field in the previous record.
CTRL-+ (plus sign)	Add a new record.
CTRL- – (minus sign)	Delete the current record.
SHIFT-ENTER	Save changes to the current record. Remember, moving to a new record also saves changes to the current record.

TABLE 19-2   Data-Entry and Editing Shortcuts

19

Keystroke	Function
SPACEBAR	Switch between the values in a check box or option button.
CTRL-ENTER	Insert a new line in a text field.
CTRL-Z	Undo the last entry.
CTRL-C	Copy the selection.
CTRL-X	Cut the selection.
CTRL-V	Paste the selection.

TABLE 19-2 Data-Entry and Editing Shortcuts *(continued)*

Navigating Through Records

Many forms, such as the Clients form, display your data one record at a time. The record navigation buttons are located in the lower-left corner of a form, as shown in Figure 19-2, and help you move through the form's records.

As the amount of data in your table increases, these buttons will be especially helpful in navigating through the data. Another useful tool to help you navigate to a specific record is the Find command, located on the Edit menu. The Find command lets you type in a search word or phrase and then searches the data in your form to locate that word or phrase. To use the Find command, follow these steps:

1. Click in the field that will contain the data you want to find.

2. Choose Edit | Find from the menu bar. The Find and Replace dialog box appears.

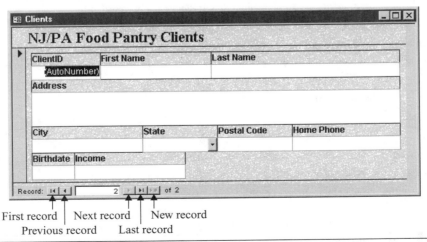

FIGURE 19-2 The record-navigation buttons

3. Type the text you are looking for in the Find What box.

4. The Look In list should already name the field you want to search.

5. From the Match list, choose Any Part of Field. This choice gives you the most flexibility in finding the text you typed in the Find What box because it instructs Access to locate your search text, whether it is part of a word or a whole word.

6. Click Find Next. The first record containing the text you are seeking will be highlighted in the field on the form. Sometimes you have to drag the dialog box aside because the text you seek can be covered up by the Find dialog box.

TIP   *You can also use CTRL-F to open the Find dialog box.*

19

Chapter 20

Extracting Data with Queries

How to...

- Differentiate between query types
- View query designs and data
- Create queries that select specific records from a table
- Write comparison criteria to help you find specific data
- Create queries that select records from multiple tables

Now that you've learned how to create tables and put data into them for safekeeping, we will concentrate on extracting data from tables. After all, what's the point in storing all this data if you can't get to it? In this chapter, we will discuss the Access tool for working with data: the query.

Normally, the next step after table and form design in the development of a database is to enter some sample data, usually about 10 to 15 records per form. If you find yourself typing the same data repeatedly, you might want to reconsider your table design. This usually means that you need at least one or more tables joined back to the original table where the duplication is taking place. You might also find yourself thinking of things you left out, which means adding some fields. Take the time at this stage in the development of your database to fine-tune its design. The worst thing that could happen is that you have thousands of records entered, all your forms, queries, and reports written, and you then discover a major design flaw. A major flaw found toward the end of the design process means a lot of query, form, and report editing.

We will switch gears in our examples, from being the benevolent creator of a food pantry database to a corporate database developer for the Northwind Traders Corporation. We are doing this not because we are suddenly abandoning those in need, but rather because Access comes with a sample database named Northwind.mdb that has a lot of data in it for us to play with.

NOTE   *The Northwind database is located in a subfolder of the Office folder called Office\Samples. If the file is not in this folder on your PC, you must install it from the Office 2003 installation CD. For instructions on installing Northwind, search the Help system for the word Northwind and select the topic Open the Northwind Sample Database.*

Queries and reports go hand in hand. Although it is possible to print the results of a query in Datasheet view, it's unlikely that you would do this, especially if you were printing the results to give to others. Instead, most queries are attached to reports. Reports provide a visually appealing way to display query results, and in Chapter 21, you'll learn how to create and format them.

Understanding Query Types

Although it is true that queries do allow you to extract data from a table or tables, they can do much more. Queries can also perform specific actions on a subset of data that you specify, such as delete a group of records, add records from one table to another, or update a group of records. For example, suppose an area code changed for a group of contacts in a contacts table. An Update query can update the existing area code to the new one in less than a second! Before you can fly though, you need to try a little walking. Therefore, we will concentrate on the extracting type of query in this chapter, which is called the *Select* query. By far, the Select query is the most common Access query type.

Viewing Query Designs and Data

Like tables and forms, the query has a Design and Datasheet view. And like those other objects, the Design view lets you build the object, whereas the Datasheet view lets you see the data. Unlike those objects, however, the query has a view unique to it called the *SQL view.* SQL stands for *Structured Query Language*—a language common in one form or another to all relational database management systems. It is also the language used to manipulate table data in relational databases.

The SQL view displays the SQL statement that will extract your data. Don't worry; you don't have to become an expert in SQL to write an Access query. That's because Access allows you to design a query using something called the *QBE grid.* The QBE grid appears in Design view. The letters QBE stand for *query by example.*

In effect, the QBE grid allows you to graphically design a query. After you enter the necessary information in the QBE grid, Access builds the SQL statement for you in the background. So, use the QBE grid to ask for the data you want to see and use the Datasheet view to see the results. As you fine-tune your query, you will constantly switch back and forth between these two views.

Using the Simple Query Wizard to Make a Select Query

Access comes with several wizards to help you construct queries. We will use the Simple Query Wizard to construct a Select query. To follow the steps in the example, you must have the Northwind database open with its Database window displayed. Let's create a customer phone number listing using the Simple Query Wizard. Here's how:

1. Choose Queries from the Objects bar.

2. Double-click the icon labeled Create Query by Using Wizard. This is the second icon on the list located on the right side of the database window. The first screen of the Simple Query Wizard appears.

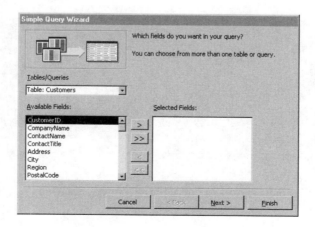

3. From the Table/Queries list, select Table: Customers.

4. Double-click the fields CompanyName, ContactName, City, Phone, and Fax from the Available Fields list. This will add the fields to the Selected Field list.

5. Click the Next button. You will be prompted for a title for your query.

6. Type the title **CustomerPhoneList** in the title box.

7. Click Finish. A list of customers will appear in Datasheet view for the new query.

Designing a Query in the QBE Grid

Although the Simple Query Wizard is helpful in getting you started, it does have its limitations. For example, you can't specify sorting through the wizard. You might find, therefore, that it is best to design your queries directly in the QBE grid.

Figure 20-1 shows the CustomerPhoneList query in Design view. Note that the QBE grid is divided into halves. The top half is where you identify the tables that contain the data you would

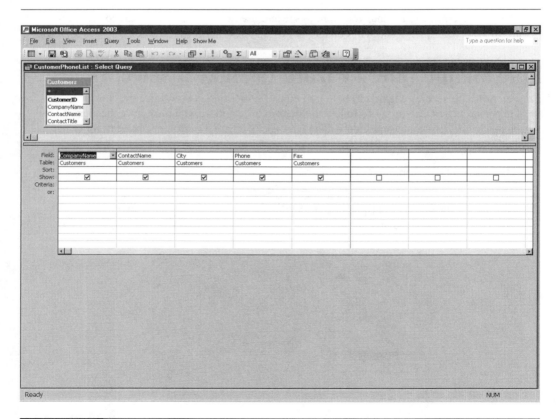

FIGURE 20-1   The CustomerPhoneList query in Design view showing the QBE grid.

like extracted. If you specify more than one table, you also indicate how those tables are related in the top half of the grid.

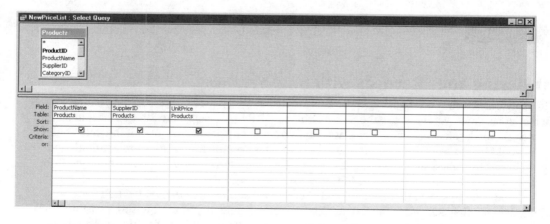

NOTE   *If you relate your tables as described in Chapter 18, they will already be joined when added to the top half of the QBE grid.*

The bottom half is where you specify the fields that you want displayed, the sort order of the data, and *criteria*.

Criteria are a set of restrictions you can apply to the query to limit its results to the records you would like to see. Learning to write effective criteria is the key to seeing the results you want. We will discuss criteria in detail later in this chapter. First, we will create a query in Design view.

Suppose, as a developer for Northwind Traders, it's your job to create a product price list. Here are the steps you would follow:

1.   Select the Queries button on the Objects bar.

2.   Double-click the icon labeled Create Query in Design view. This is the first icon on the list located on the right side of the database window. The QBE grid will appear, as will the Show Table dialog box.

3.   Double-click Products from the Tables tab. This will add the Products table to the top of the QBE grid.

4.   Click the Close button to close the Show Table dialog box. A field list from the Products table will appear in the top half of the QBE grid.

5.   Double-click the fields ProductName, SupplierID, and UnitPrice from the field list at the top of the grid. Each field name will appear in a column on the bottom half of the grid.

6.   Choose File | Save from the menu bar and name the query **NewPriceList**.

7.   Switch to Datasheet view by choosing View | Datasheet from the menu bar to see the query results (see Figure 20-2).

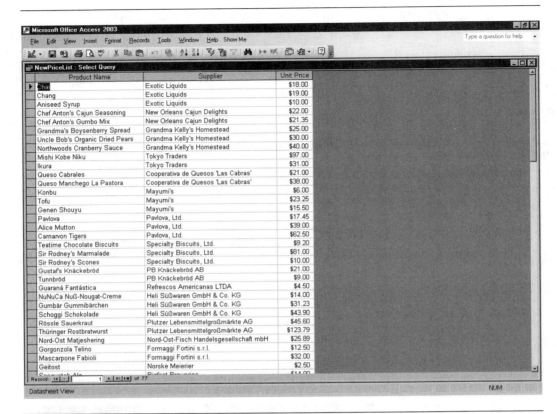

FIGURE 20-2 The completed NewPriceList query in Datasheet view showing the query's results.

Ordering Your Records with the Sort Row

In many cases, you'll want your query results ordered in a very specific way. To put your records in a particular order, you must use the Sort row in the QBE grid (see Figure 20-3). To begin sorting a specific field, select Ascending or Descending from the list in the Sort row of the field column you would like to sort. An *ascending* sort will order the records from *A* to *Z* for text fields and from lowest to highest for number fields. *Descending* is just the opposite. To remove sorting from a field, select (Not Sorted) from the Sort row list.

If you want to sort more than one field, Access will sort records first on the leftmost sort field, then the field second to the left, and so on. For example, if you want to sort a customer list by city, then by company within a city, you must arrange those fields in the grid so that city is before company. Here's how to easily rearrange fields in the grid:

1. Roll the mouse pointer over the column header button above the field name in the QBE grid. The column header button is a thin gray horizontal bar. A downward-pointing arrow will appear.

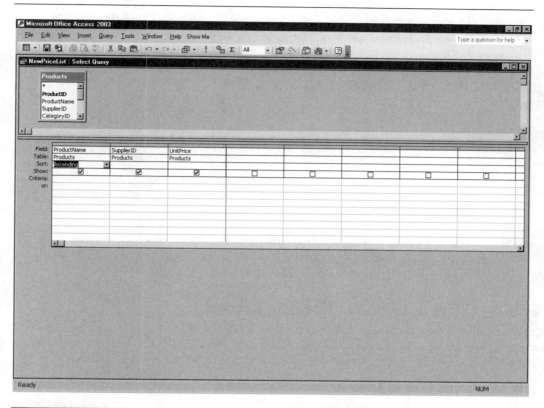

FIGURE 20-3   The NewPriceList query with ProductName as the sort field.

2. Click to select the column.

3. Point to the column header again, and a diagonal left arrow will appear.

4. Press and drag left or right to move the field.

Once you have the fields arranged properly in the grid and you have chosen a sort order in the Sort row, view the query in Datasheet view to see the sorted results.

Here's how to sort records in the CustomerPhoneList query by city, then by company:

1. View the CustomerPhoneList query in Design view.

2. Select the City column.

3. Press and drag the column to the left until it is the first column in the grid.

4. Choose Ascending from the list in the sort row of the City column.

5. Choose Ascending from the list in the sort row of the CompanyName column.

6. Save the query using the File | Save command.

7. View the results in Datasheet view. Notice that the customers are in order by city, then by company name within each city.

You can also sort records directly in Datasheet view. First, click any record in the field you want to sort. Then click either Sort Ascending (the button with a stacked AZ on it) or Sort Descending (the button with a stacked ZA on it) on the Query Datasheet toolbar. Don't worry about Access mixing up your data. It won't happen!

Writing Criteria to Select Specific Records

Criteria allow you to select very specific records from a table or tables. There is a certain way criteria are written, called the criteria's *syntax*. Fortunately, Access will often help you with that syntax as you are writing your criteria. Here are some general rules that you must follow:

■ In text fields, surround your search text with quotation marks ("").

■ In date fields, surround dates with pound signs (#).

You do not have to type the quotation marks or pound signs around the criteria that you type in the Criteria row. Type the text or date that you are looking for and press ENTER. Access will add the quotation marks and pound signs for you.

Here's how to find customer contact Ann Devon using the CustomerPhoneList query:

1. Open the CustomerPhoneList query in Design view.

2. Type **Ann Devon** in the first cell of the Criteria row in the ContactName column.

3. Press ENTER. Note that Access adds quotation marks around your criteria.

4. Show the query in Datasheet view to see the record for Ann Devon:

City	Company Name	Contact Name	Phone	Fax
London	Eastern Connection	Ann Devon	(171) 555-0297	(171) 555-3373

Using Operators to Find Records with Numbers

Much like finding specific text, you can find a specific number by typing it in the Criteria row of the field that contains the number. Suppose, however, that you want to find a group of records that follow a pattern, such as all products priced at $50 or more. Writing this type of criteria requires you to use *operators*. An operator is a symbol that represents a type of numeric comparison. I'm sure you've seen some of the numeric operators listed in the following table.

Operator	Description
>	Greater than the specified number
<	Less than the specified number
=	Equal to the specified number
>=	Greater than or equal to the specified number
<=	Less than or equal to the specified number
<>	Not equal to the specified number

> **TIP** *You don't have to type the equal sign when trying to exactly match a number because "equal to" is implied. Simply type the value.*

Follow these steps to find products priced at or more than $50 using the NewPriceList query:

1. Open the NewPriceList query in Design view.
2. In the first criteria cell in the UnitPrice column, type >=**50**.
3. Switch to Datasheet view to see the results. You should find seven products priced at or more than $50.

Product Name	Supplier	Unit Price
Mishi Kobe Niku	Tokyo Traders	$97.00
Carnarvon Tigers	Pavlova, Ltd.	$62.50
Sir Rodney's Marmalade	Specialty Biscuits, Ltd.	$81.00
Thüringer Rostbratwurst	Plutzer Lebensmittelgroßmärkte AG	$123.79
Côte de Blaye	Aux joyeux ecclésiastiques	$263.50
Manjimup Dried Apples	G'day, Mate	$53.00
Raclette Courdavault	Gai pâturage	$55.00
*		$0.00

Using Wildcards to Find a Group of Related Records

You've seen that operators are used to find groups of records that contain numbers. To find groups of records that contain text, you use *wildcards*. Wildcards are special characters that you type as part of a criteria expression, and they can help you find records that match a specific pattern. The most commonly used wildcard by far is the asterisk (*). The asterisk matches any number of characters in a text field. For example, if you were looking for a customer company named

Berglunds snabbköp and you couldn't remember how to spell it, you would type **Ber*** in the Criteria row of the CompanyName field. In return, Access would show you all customers whose name starts with the letters *Ber*.

The other common wildcard character is the question mark (?). The question mark matches any single character in a text field. For example, typing "bl?ck" in the criteria row would match the words *black* and *block*. Here are some other examples using wildcards:

Criteria	Result
555	Finds 000-555-0000 or 000-000-5550
* Smith	Finds John Smith, Jane Smith, and Joe Smith
m*s	Finds Maria Anders and Mario Pontes
b?g	Finds bag, bug, and big, but not brag

> **NOTE**   *Access will add the Like operator to any wildcard criteria you type. Therefore, "m*s" will be changed to Like "m*s" when you press ENTER after typing the criteria.*

Try these steps to find customers whose company names start with *h* and end with *s* using the CustomerPhoneList query:

1. Open the CustomerPhoneList query in Design view.

2. Remove any existing criteria by rolling the mouse to the left edge of the first cell of the criteria row. A black right arrow will appear. Click when you see the right arrow. The entire criteria row will be selected.

3. Press DELETE. The criteria will be erased.

4. Type **h*s** in the first criteria cell of the CompanyName column.

5. Press ENTER. Access will change h*s to Like "h*s".

6. Switch to Datasheet view. You should find that three companies matching the criteria are found.

City	Company Name	Contact Name	Phone	Fax
Cork	Hungry Owl All-Night Grocers	Patricia McKenna	2967 542	2967 3333
Rio de Janeiro	Hanari Carnes	Mario Pontes	(21) 555-0091	(21) 555-8765
San Cristóbal	HILARIÓN-Abastos	Carlos Hernández	(5) 555-1340	(5) 555-1948

Selecting Data from Multiple Tables

In Chapter 18, we discussed table relationships or *joins*. To extract data from multiple tables in Access, those tables must be joined by a common field. For example, the Northwind database has both a Products and a Suppliers table. To display a list of products and the supplier contact for each product, you would join the two tables on the common field they share, which is SupplierID.

When extracting data from multiple tables, you will sometimes have to add a table to the QBE grid. You can do this by choosing Query | Show Table from the menu bar. The Show Table dialog box will appear. Double-click each table you want added to the query and then close the dialog box.

If you did the work up front in the Relationships window, you shouldn't have to join too many tables in the QBE grid. However, it is sometimes necessary to join tables in the grid. The procedure is exactly the same as it is in the Relationships window. Drag the common field from the field list of one table on top of that same field in the field list of the other table. Once the tables are joined, all you have to do is select the fields you want to see in the results and then specify sorting and criteria.

Now that you know what you'll need to query multiple tables, try these steps to create a list of products and supplier contact information:

1. To take a look at the relationships already created in the Northwind database, make sure the Database window is active and then choose Tools | Relationships from the menu bar. The Relationships window will open. Note that the Suppliers and Products tables are joined in a one-to-many relationship on the SupplierID field.

2. Close the Relationships window by clicking the Close button in the upper-right corner of the window.

3. In the Database window, select the Queries button on the Objects bar.

4. Double-click the icon labeled Create Query in Design View. This is the first icon on the list located on the right side of the database window. The QBE grid appears, as does the Show Table dialog box.

5. Double-click Products and Suppliers from the Tables tab. This will add the Products and Suppliers tables to the top of the QBE grid.

6. Close the Show Table dialog box. Notice that field lists from the Products and Suppliers tables appear in the top half of the QBE grid. The two tables are joined on the SupplierID field.

7. Double-click the ProductID and ProductName fields from the Products table. These fields will be added to the bottom half of the QBE grid.

8. Double-click the CompanyName, ContactName, Phone, and Fax fields from the Suppliers table. These fields will also be added to the bottom half of the QBE grid.

9. Choose Ascending in the Sort row of the ProductName column.

10. Choose File | Save from the menu.

11. Name the query **ProductSupplier**.

12. Switch to Datasheet view to see the query results:

Product ID	Product Name	Company Name	Contact Name	Phone	Fax
17	Alice Mutton	Pavlova, Ltd.	Ian Devling	(03) 444-2343	(03) 444-6588
3	Aniseed Syrup	Exotic Liquids	Charlotte Cooper	(171) 555-2222	
40	Boston Crab Meat	New England Seafood Cannery	Robb Merchant	(617) 555-3267	(617) 555-3389
60	Camembert Pierrot	Gai pâturage	Eliane Noz	38.76.98.06	38.76.98.58
18	Carnarvon Tigers	Pavlova, Ltd.	Ian Devling	(03) 444-2343	(03) 444-6588
1	Chai	Exotic Liquids	Charlotte Cooper	(171) 555-2222	
2	Chang	Exotic Liquids	Charlotte Cooper	(171) 555-2222	
39	Chartreuse verte	Aux joyeux ecclésiastiques	Guylène Nodier	(1) 03.83.00.68	(1) 03.83.00.62
4	Chef Anton's Cajun Seasoning	New Orleans Cajun Delights	Shelley Burke	(100) 555-4822	
5	Chef Anton's Gumbo Mix	New Orleans Cajun Delights	Shelley Burke	(100) 555-4822	
48	Chocolade	Zaanse Snoepfabriek	Dirk Luchte	(12345) 1212	(12345) 1210
38	Côte de Blaye	Aux joyeux ecclésiastiques	Guylène Nodier	(1) 03.83.00.68	(1) 03.83.00.62
58	Escargots de Bourgogne	Escargots Nouveaux	Marie Delamare	85.57.00.07	
52	Filo Mix	G'day, Mate	Wendy Mackenzie	(02) 555-5914	(02) 555-4873

The Northwind database is a great tool for you to use in learning Access—beyond its use for demonstrative purposes in this chapter, you can use it yourself to see how various database features are utilized and how a well-built database management system is crafted. The fact that it comes with lots of records already entered also makes it a great resource, because you can play with a lot of different query, form, and report variations and have plenty of data to work with. If you didn't install the Northwind database when you installed Office, you can use the Office CD to install it now.

Chapter 21

Documenting Your Data with Access Reports

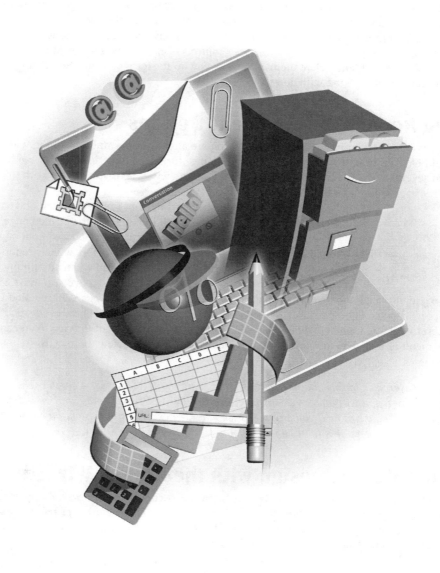

How to...

- Work in the report Design and Print Preview views
- Simplify report design with the Report Wizard
- Change margins and paper orientation

Reports are the payoff for your hard database development work. You can use a report to quickly view data from a table or query. You can preview a report or print it out. So, the report allows you to see what you want to see in a polished format that is easy on the eye.

Report and form design are very similar. Just as forms have controls such as text, check, and combo boxes, so do reports. Working with these controls is exactly the same as it is for forms. You move, size, format, and delete them exactly as you do for form controls. See Chapter 19 for more information on working with controls.

Exploring Report-Development Options

Report design is very similar to form design. If you are already comfortable working with forms, you should have no trouble with reports. As with tables, forms, and queries, reports can be viewed in several ways. Of course, reports have a Design view, where you do the work to create and modify your report (see Figure 21-1).

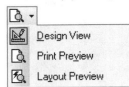

You can also view your report in Print Preview, where you can see onscreen what the entire report will look like on the printed page. From Print Preview, you can move between pages, zoom in and out on a page, and adjust page layout settings. Finally, you can view your report with Layout Preview. This view is especially helpful when attempting to preview a large report. When viewing the full report, you must wait for Access to gather the data to display the pages. The Layout Preview shows an abbreviated version of the report with just enough data in all parts of the report so you can see how every section will look. Therefore, large reports display onscreen much faster using Layout Preview. You can use the View menu or the View tool on the Report Design and Print Preview toolbars to switch between views.

NOTE *The exercises in this chapter were written using the HP LaserJet 4 printer. The printer you are using will affect the way a report displays in Print Preview and on the printed page. Because of this, you might not see what the exercises in this chapter say you will see. Please keep this in mind when doing the exercises that follow.*

Simplifying Report Design with the Report Wizard

The Report Wizard is the most commonly used wizard that comes with Access. Every report that I've ever made in Access I've started from the Report Wizard. The wizard does the vast majority of the work, leaving you to fine-tune its results. The Report Wizard will ask you a few questions that you must answer. Here are the questions and what they mean:

■ *Where is the data that you want to see on the report?* Usually, the data is in a query that you select from the list of data sources. You can, however, attach a report to a table as well. Remember that a table will show all records, whereas a query allows you to select the records you want to see as well as records from multiple tables.

■ *What fields from the data source do you want to see?* Here you select the fields—in order from left to right or top to bottom—as you would like to see them on the report. On average, you cannot fit more than ten columns on a page turned sideways, so you should keep that in mind when selecting fields. This number might vary depending on how much data there is to display in each column. Sometimes six will fit. Sometimes 16 will fit. It all depends on the data.

■ *What grouping would you like? Grouping* is the process of lumping like records together on the page. Suppose you are printing a customer list from the Northwind database. You can group customers by country so that a country heading appears when the list of customers who live in that country is below the heading.

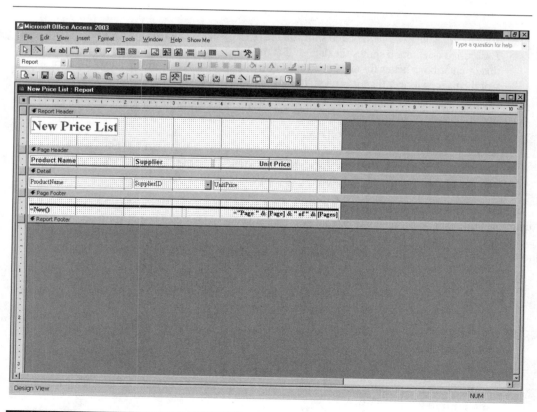

FIGURE 21-1   A report in Design view

■ *What sorting would you like?* Here you can select how you want Access to order the records on the page. You can select up to four fields and ascending or descending order for each field.

NOTE *When you add grouping to a report that contains numeric data, the Report Wizard adds a Summary Options button to the sort screen. Click the Summary Options button to add totals such as sums and averages to the end of the group. If you're grouping orders by date, for example, the Summary Options button allows you to add a total to the bottom of each day's group of records.*

■ *What layout would you like? Columnar* will display controls in columns on the report. Use this layout if your table or query contains many fields. *Tabular* will display controls in rows on the report. This is the most common report layout because it lets you show multiple records on a page. *Justified* will give the controls on the form a uniform appearance.

NOTE *When grouping is added to a report, the Report Wizard provides other layout options, such as stepped and blocked. These are variations of the Tabular layout. Choose a layout and look at the preview pane, located to the left of the layout list, to see an example of that layout.*

■ *Which way would you like data to show on the page?* Access calls this *orientation. Landscape* orientation shows the data so that the page is wider than it is long. In most cases, this orientation is better for tabular layouts. *Portrait* is just the opposite. It shows the data so that the page is longer than it is wide. In most cases, Portrait is better for columnar layouts.

■ *Do you want Access to adjust the field width so that the data fits on the page?* Normally what Access does is see what field size you have chosen for a field in table design and make the column for that field on the report equal to its field size. So, if the field size of one of your selected fields is 25 characters, the Report Wizard will make that field 25 characters wide on the report. When you tell Access to adjust field widths to fit the page, it will ignore field size and adjust each field's column width so that all columns fit on the page.

If you select this option with too many fields to display, some of your data will be cut off in the column. If you don't select this option, some of the fields you've selected might spill onto the next page. When this happens, you'll wind up with something like five columns of a record on page 1 and five more on page 2. This is where you have to experiment to see which option works best.

■ *What style do you want for your report?* Access comes with some report templates that will give your report a professionally designed appearance. You can click a style name in the wizard to see how your report will appear.

■ *What title do you want for your report?* The title you enter will display on the top of the first page of the report.

TIP *Because the Report Wizard is quick and easy, try experimenting with its options. This might mean creating the same report three or four times until you end up with one that is closest to what you want.*

Creating a Report with the Report Wizard

Now that you understand what options the Report Wizard offers, let's create two reports. The first will be a simple report without grouping, whereas the second will use grouping.

We will start with a report using our NewPriceList query from Chapter 20. Here are the steps to follow:

1. Open the Northwind database, if necessary.

2. Select Queries from the Objects bar.

3. Design the NewPriceList query. If you did not do the exercise to create this query, turn to the section "Designing a Query in the QBE Grid" in Chapter 20.

4. Delete any criteria from the query.

5. Save and close the query.

6. Select Reports from the Objects bar.

7. Double-click the Create Report by Using Wizard icon. This is the second icon on the list on the right side of the Database window. The first screen of the wizard appears.

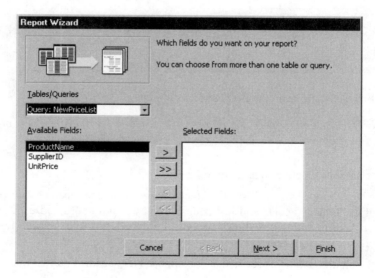

8. Select Query: NewPriceList from the Tables/Queries list.

9. Click the double-chevron (>>) button to bring over all fields from the query.

10. Click the Next button. The grouping screen will appear.

11. If SupplierID is specified as the group field on the grouping screen, double-click directly on it to remove any grouping. You can tell whether SupplierID is selected for grouping by the color and position of its text in the preview pane located on the right side of the grouping screen. If it is in a rectangle by itself and colored blue, it is selected for grouping.

12. Click the Next button again. You will see the sorting screen.

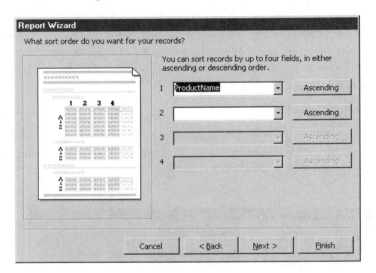

13. Choose ProductName from the first list of sort fields.

NOTE *If a report is based on a query and records are sorted in the query, the sort order is inherited by the report.*

14. Leave the default direction of ascending.

15. Click the Next button. You will see the layout screen, where you can choose layout options of Columnar, Tabular, and Justified, as well as a Portrait or Landscape orientation. My Report Wizard dialog box shows options of Stepped, Blocked, Outline 1, Outline 2, Align Left 1, and Align Left 2.

16. Leave the defaults on the layout screen and choose Next again. You will then see the style screen.

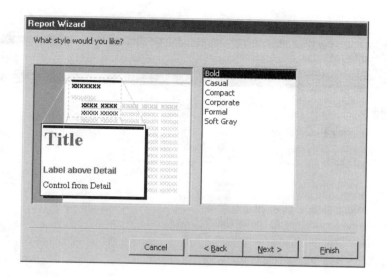

17. Select the Bold style from the list, if necessary.

18. Click Next to see the name screen.

19. Enter the name **New Price List**. Notice that the wizard is set to display the report in Print Preview.

20. Click Finish. The new report displays onscreen in Print Preview.

21. Use the Page arrow buttons on the lower-left corner of the Print Preview screen to move between pages.

22. Figure 21-2 shows a report with Product Name, Supplier, and Unit Price. The finished result from the last 16 steps produces a different report, with SupplierID, Product Name, and Unit Price.

23. Close the report window.

Here's how to make a customer report with grouping:

1. Press F11 to activate the Database window, if necessary.

2. Select Reports from the Objects bar.

3. Double-click the Create Report by Using Wizard icon. This is the second icon on the list on the right side of the Database window. The first screen of the wizard will appear.

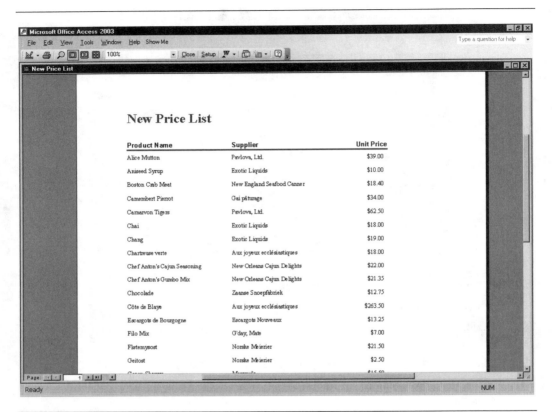

New Price List

Product Name	Supplier	Unit Price
Alice Mutton	Pavlova, Ltd.	$39.00
Aniseed Syrup	Exotic Liquids	$10.00
Boston Crab Meat	New England Seafood Canner	$18.40
Camembert Pierrot	Gai pâturage	$34.00
Carnarvon Tigers	Pavlova, Ltd.	$62.50
Chai	Exotic Liquids	$18.00
Chang	Exotic Liquids	$19.00
Chartreuse verte	Aux joyeux ecclésiastiques	$18.00
Chef Anton's Cajun Seasoning	New Orleans Cajun Delights	$22.00
Chef Anton's Gumbo Mix	New Orleans Cajun Delights	$21.35
Chocolade	Zaanse Snoepfabriek	$12.75
Côte de Blaye	Aux joyeux ecclésiastiques	$263.50
Escargots de Bourgogne	Escargots Nouveaux	$13.25
Filo Mix	G'day, Mate	$7.00
Fløtemysost	Norske Meierier	$21.50
Geitost	Norske Meierier	$2.50

FIGURE 21-2 The completed New Price List report in Print Preview.

4. Select Table: Customers from the Tables/Queries list.

5. Click the double-chevron (>>) button to bring all fields from the Available Fields list to the Selected Fields list.

6. Double-click CustomerID from the Selected Fields list to remove it. It will return to the Available Fields list.

7. Click the Next button. The grouping screen will appear.

8. Double-click Country from the list of fields on the left side of the wizard screen. The preview pane to the right of the field list shows you how the grouping will effect the report's layout.

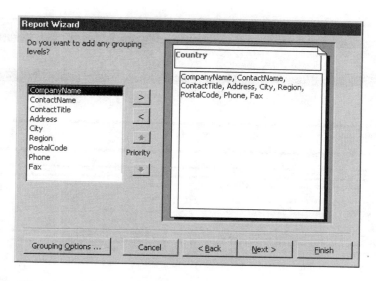

9. Click the Next button. You will see the sorting screen.

10. Choose CompanyName from the first list of sort fields.

11. Choose ContactName from the second list of sort fields. The report will be sorted by company name, then by contact name within each company.

12. Leave the default direction of ascending for each field.

13. Click the Next button. You will see the layout/orientation screen.

14. Select the Align Left 1 layout. Select Landscape orientation. Note that Adjust the Field Width So All Fields Fit on the Page is checked. Access will adjust the fields so that they all fit on the page.

15. Choose Next again. You will see the style screen.

16. Select the Bold style from the list. It is good design practice to use the same style for each report in your database.

17. Click Next to see the name screen.

18. Enter the name **Customer List**.

19. Click Finish. The new report displays in Print Preview (see Figure 21-3).

20. Use the Page arrow buttons at the lower-left corner of the Print Preview screen to move between pages. Notice that some data does not fit in its column, and the title shows only on page 1. We will fix these problems later in this chapter.

21. Close the report window.

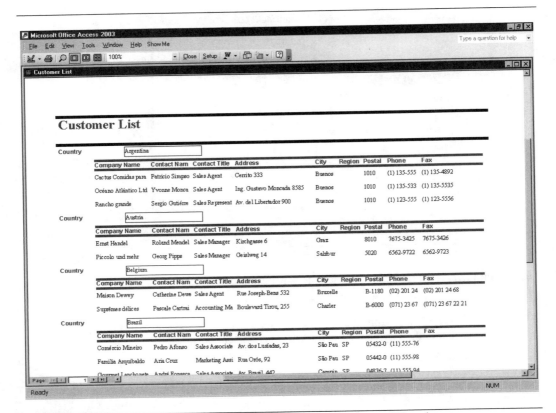

FIGURE 21-3   The Customer List report as created by the Report Wizard.

Changing the Margins to Fit More Data per Page

Sometimes you have to change margins to fit more data on a page either horizontally or vertically. You can change margins with the Page Setup command directly in Print Preview. This is one of the few design elements that Access does not require you to change in Design view.

Let's complete the Customer List report by changing its margin settings to fit more records on a page. Here's how:

1. Select the Customer List report from the Reports list in the Database window.

2. Click the Print Preview button on the toolbar to see the report with its data. Only one record for Brazil appears at the end of page 1.

3. Click the Setup button on the Print Preview toolbar. The Page Setup dialog box displays.

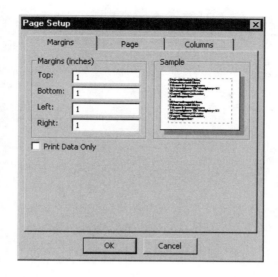

4. Select the text in the Top text box and type **.5** to replace it.

5. Select the text in the Bottom text box and type **.5** to replace it.

TIP   *Some printers can print closer to the edge of the paper than others. You can type **0** in a margin box if you like. Access will adjust this to the lowest possible value your printer will accept.*

6. Click the Page tab. Here is where you can change orientation.

7. Choose OK to lock in your new settings.

8. Close the Customer List report.

Printing Your Reports

After all that hard work, it is time to enjoy the fruits of your labor by printing a completed report. Access gives you several printing options. All are available in the Print dialog box. Here are the most common:

■ Select a printer

■ Print multiple copies

■ Print a page range

You must use the File menu or press CTRL-P to display the Print dialog box. If you click the Print button on the Print Preview toolbar, you will send one copy of the entire report to the currently selected printer.

Part VI

Keeping in Touch and on Schedule with Outlook

Chapter 22

Communicating with Email

How to...

- Set up your email accounts
- Address, compose, and send a message
- Reply to incoming mail
- Forward messages to others
- Set up an email signature
- Organize stored messages in folders

Outlook is an application that does many things—it allows you to send and receive email messages, track your schedule through a calendar, maintain to-do lists, store names and addresses, and even keep a journal. In this chapter, you'll learn all about email, from setting it up to making use of both its everyday features and its most powerful ones.

About Email Accounts

Unlike the rest of the applications in the Office suite, which function "as is" and don't require any setup from you, Outlook needs to know some basic information about your email accounts before it can go to work for you. Specifically, Outlook requires your account name, password, and the name of the email server(s) that receives and stores your incoming and outgoing mail. You can get this information from your network administrator or Internet service provider (ISP), who will typically supply you with the following:

- The type of account (Exchange Server, POP3, IMAP, HTTP, or other)
- Name of your incoming server and outgoing server
- Your email address, username, and password

To add an email account to Outlook, do the following:

1. Open Outlook.
2. From the menu bar, select Tools | Email Accounts to open the Email Accounts Wizard.
3. In the first dialog box, click the Add a New Email Account radio button and then click Next.

22

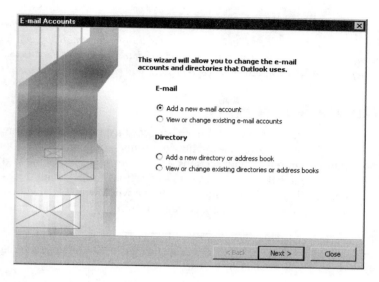

4. Select your account's email server type from the choices provided—Microsoft Exchange Server, POP3, IMAP, HTTP, or Additional Server Types. The server type for your account is identical to the type of account you have. If you have a POP3 account, you're using a POP3 server. Click Next.

5. Enter the account information provided by your ISP or system administrator, as shown next. Unless otherwise instructed by your ISP or system administrator, all server and address information should be entered in lowercase. Some ISPs may use a combination of uppercase and lowercase letters in passwords to add additional security. Click Next to continue to the last panel. Then click Finish.

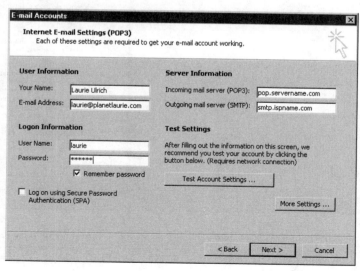

To make sure your settings and entries are all correct, click the Test Account Settings button. Outlook will (assuming you're online) connect to the designated email servers, sending and receiving messages with the information you provided. If any portion of the process fails (you'll see each step tried, and it will either succeed or fail), you can make changes and retest.

Touring the Outlook Interface

Like the rest of the Office suite, Outlook relies on a basic set of simple tools to accomplish its tasks so you don't need to learn an entire new application from the ground up. The Outlook application window is divided into five main sections—three message panes, one set of toolbars and menus, and a Navigation pane that contains a series of buttons for switching between Outlook's major components. Figure 22-1 shows the Outlook window in its default condition, with Mail selected, the Inbox active, and a message being viewed in the Reading pane.

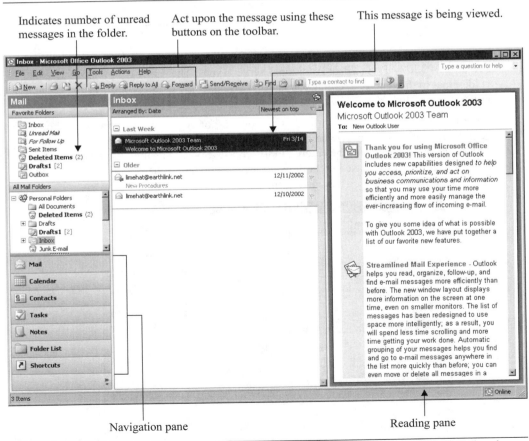

FIGURE 22-1   Outlook's tools and onscreen features are unique, but logically placed and easily identified.

You can customize the appearance and placement of the panes within the Outlook window by resizing them (point to their borders and drag your two-headed mouse pointer, shown in Figure 22-2) or by choosing where and how the Reading pane will appear. The View | Reading Pane menu offers options for Right, Bottom, and Off.

Working with Messages

Given that sending and receiving email is Outlook's primary function, let's get started with the process of creating an outgoing message. After all, other than the "spam" (junk email) that everyone gets whether they want it or not, you have to send a message in order to get a reply.

Composing an email message is very simple. With the Mail view displayed (click the Mail button in the Outlook Navigation pane), click the New button on the toolbar. Because you're in Mail, the New button automatically gives you a new message window—if you were in Calendar, the New button would be used to create a new appointment, as you'll discover in Chapter 23. In

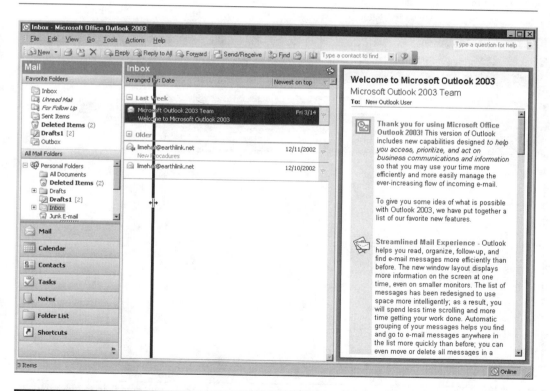

FIGURE 22-2   Want to see more of this and less of that? Resize the panes to suit your needs.

the new Untitled Message window shown in Figure 22-3, you can see that the basic tools for addressing and composing your message are right there, all within a very familiar-looking window. You'll recognize several of the formatting tools from Word on the Formatting toolbar, and on the Outlook toolbar, you'll find a small group of easily learned and remembered buttons for utilizing various email-handling tools.

Because your cursor is already in the To box, either type the recipients' addresses (if you know them) or click the To button (the word "To…" is a button) to access your Address Book. You'll only have Address Book entries if you imported them from whatever email program you were using previously, or if you've added entries to it manually. If you have no entries, you can learn to build them in Chapter 24. For now, just type the address of each recipient of the new message. If you will be sending to more than one person, use a semicolon to separate the addresses.

If you want to send a copy of your message to one or more people, use the Cc… box. You can click the Cc… button to access the Address Book (with the aforementioned considerations),

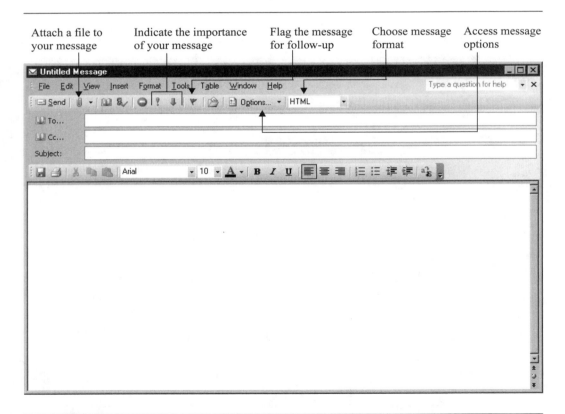

Everything you need to address, compose, and format a message is in the Untitled Message window, and you'll use familiar Word tools for much of your work.

or you can type email addresses directly into the box. If you want to send "blind carbon copies" (Bcc... copies), click the Options drop list and choose Bcc from the submenu. When you do, a Bcc address line will appear in the Message window.

> **CAUTION** *Blind carbons are sent to the people whose email addresses are listed in the Bcc field, but none of the other To or Cc recipients will know that anyone has been blind carboned. Be careful when using the Bcc feature, and consider letting the Bcc recipients know, through another message, that they've been blind carboned—otherwise, they might not notice that their address doesn't appear in the To or Cc box and might reply to the message, thus revealing their having been included in your mailing.*

After addressing your message, give it a subject, which will tell the recipient what your message is about. If you leave the Subject field blank, your recipients will see a blank in their list of incoming messages, which some people find annoying. It's a good idea to always include a subject, even if it's just "Hello from Bob" (if your name is Bob, of course). Once you've done that, press TAB to be taken automatically to the message box, where you'll simply start typing your message. After there is text in the box, the formatting tools will become available, and assuming your message format is set to HTML or Rich Text, you'll be able to choose fonts, sizes, colors, and apply alignment, bullets, and numbering formats to your text.

Attaching Files to Messages

Sending file attachments is the most common way of getting documents from one person to another. You have a Word document or Excel spreadsheet that you need to pass off to a coworker? Just attach it to an email message and—voilà—there it is on the other side of the office. If you're sending an attached file to people outside of your office, you'll need to be aware of any file size limitations their email provider may have. In general, you don't want to send an attachment that is larger than 5MB in size. In some cases the limitation might be even smaller. For example, AOL won't accept any attachment over 2MB.

> **TIP** *If you have a large file or group thereof to attach to a message, you can try zipping (compressing) the file(s) with a program such as WinZip. This can take several megabytes of attached files and reduce them to a single, manageable-sized file. Of course, the amount of size reduction you'll achieve varies by file type—but you'll get some reduction in all cases. If you don't have WinZip, you can download a trial version and then later purchase the software from www.winzip.com.*

You can attach a file to an email message in a number of ways. You can select Insert | File from the Message window's menu bar or click the Insert File button (which looks like a paperclip) on the toolbar. Each of these methods opens the Insert File dialog box (see Figure 22-4), from which you can select any file on your PC to attach to your message. If you want to attach multiple files, just press the CTRL key as you click the individual files (assuming they're all in the same folder). Then, when all the files you want to attach are selected, press ENTER. If the files are not all in the same folder, simply attach one file and then repeat the Insert File process to attach the others from other folders.

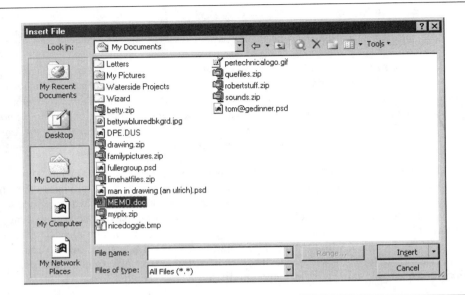

FIGURE 22-4 Navigate to the folder containing the file you wish to attach and then double-click the file to attach it to your message.

You can also attach a file by simply dragging the icon of the file you want to attach from anywhere in Windows (the Desktop, Windows Explorer, My Computer) and then dropping it into the body of the Message window.

Working with Message Flags, Levels, and Receipts

Before you send your message, think about any last-minute things you'd like to do. Would you like to be told when the message is received and read? Would you like to mark the message important so that the recipient doesn't delay reading it? Would you like to insert a flag that tells the recipient what you'd like him or her to do upon reading your message? All these extras are easily applied to your new message, simply by clicking buttons on the main toolbar or using the Options button and its submenu.

Setting Message Importance

The importance of a message can be set to High, Normal, or Low. The default is Normal, and you'll see High and Low buttons on the toolbar (red exclamation point for High, blue down-pointing arrow for Low). Depending on which importance you choose, an icon will appear next to the message in the recipient's Inbox, letting him or her know that your message is either very important and should be opened immediately or not terribly important, and he or she can open other more pressing messages first.

Flagging a Message

You can add a flag icon to a received message to act as a reminder for yourself, or you can add flags to outgoing messages to indicate a course of action for the recipient. To apply a flag, click the Flag button on the toolbar and use the resulting Flag for Follow Up dialog box to choose from a series of actions for the recipient to take based on your message (such as Follow Up, Forward, Read, Reply, and so on). You can also pick a due-by date if the action is time-sensitive. Note that a calendar will display when you click the Due By drop list, and you can click the month and day you'd like associated with your flagged action.

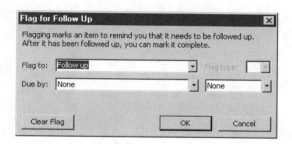

TIP   *To get rid of a flag, click the Flag button and then use the Clear Flag button in the Flag for Follow Up dialog box.*

Asking for a Receipt

Don't you hate it when people claim to have not received your email and you just know they got it? Well, you can foil their attempts to evade your email by asking for a receipt—either when the message is received, read, or both. Of course, your recipients can foil you by setting their Outlook to refuse requests for receipts, but many people don't bother to do this, so you can still "catch" them having received and/or read your message.

Receipts can be requested on a per-message basis (using message options within a given message window) or globally, by establishing an automatic request for receipts on all sent messages. I prefer to ask for them on a per-message basis, because given the volume of mail I send, I could be inundated with receipts. If, however, you absolutely must have receipts for all your sent messages, you can set Outlook up to ask for receipts on all outgoing mail. Just follow these steps:

1. In the main Outlook window (with Mail selected in the Navigation pane), choose Tools | Options.

2. Click the Preferences tab.

3. Click the Email Options button. The Email Options dialog box opens.

4. Click the Tracking Options button, which opens the Tracking Options dialog box.

5. Under the For All Messages I Send heading, choose Read Receipt or Delivery Receipt (or both).

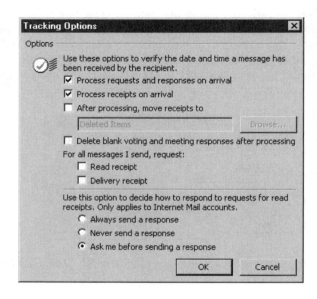

To request a receipt for just one message (assuming you have *not* turned on the aforementioned automatic request for all outgoing messages), follow these steps:

1. In the new Message window, click the Options drop list and choose Options from the resulting submenu.

2. In the Message Options dialog box (see Figure 22-5), click the Request a Delivery Receipt for This Message box and/or the Request a Read Receipt for This Message box.

3. Click OK to apply your settings and return to the message in progress.

Sending Your Message

Once your message is addressed, composed, flagged, and formatted (find out more about that process later in this chapter) and you've set an importance level and attached any files that need to go with the message, you can send it. The process of sending a message is unbelievably easy—

An alternate method of marking the message's importance

You can choose another address to which replies to this message can be sent.

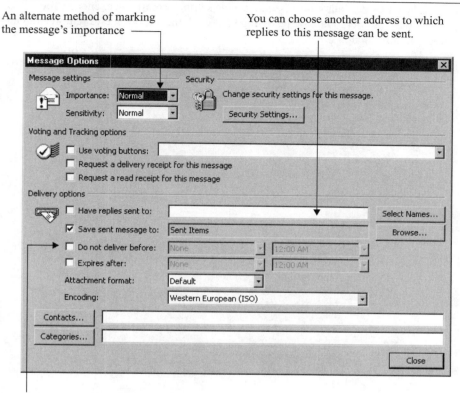

Put your delivery of the message on hold here.

FIGURE 22-5   Control the settings for your individual message, asking for receipts or setting up alternate delivery options.

just click the Send button in the message window. The message will go to your Outbox, where it will languish until either you click the Send/Receive button or a default automatic Send/Receive session is initiated by Outlook.

To determine what kind of automatic Send/Receive settings are in place, choose Tools | Options and click the Mail Setup tab. In the dialog box, click the Send/Receive button and view the Send/Receive Groups dialog box:

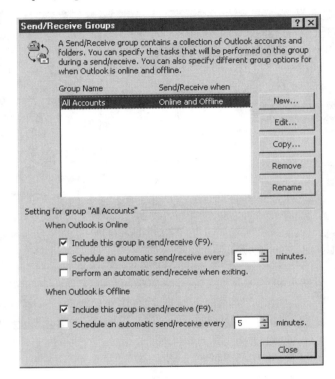

If you have more than one email account, the top area of the dialog box allows you to choose which one to set up. If you want to schedule Outlook to send all the messages in your Outbox automatically, enter a number of minutes and click the check box under When Outlook Is Online. There you also have the option to have Outlook perform an automatic send/receive upon exiting the program, but note that this is a bit risky—you may forget you have something in the Outbox that you chose not to send yet.

CAUTION *I prefer to turn off all automatic Send/Receive sessions, including the one that happens when you start Outlook (it's on by default) and the one that you can set to send all outgoing mail whenever you exit Outlook. I like to let messages build up in my Outbox and then review the list before sending—that way I don't risk firing off a message I wrote in haste or anger without a chance to review it or to change my mind about sending it at all.*

Replying to Messages

Replying to messages you've received is yet another straightforward operation. You have the option of replying to either the sender or to all recipients of the message, including the sender. Simply select the message to which you want to reply and click either the Reply button or the Reply To All button on the toolbar. You can also right-click any of the messages displayed in the View pane and select the same commands from the shortcut menu that appears.

When you choose Reply or Reply to All, a RE: message window opens, as shown in Figure 22-6. This window looks almost exactly like an Untitled Message window (for a new outgoing message), but there are three main differences:

- The title bar has "RE" on it, meaning that the message is REgarding an existing received message.

- The Subject field is already filled in, with RE: followed by the subject text from the message to which you're responding.

- The body of the message to which you're responding appears in the message area, below the cursor. The cursor is awaiting your response, and the message you're responding to appears below it so that the recipient of your response knows what you're responding to.

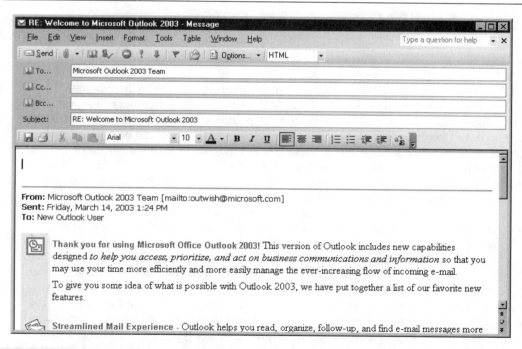

FIGURE 22-6   Reply to the sender or to everyone the sender included in the To and Cc boxes when he or she composed the message.

It's wise to use the Reply to All feature with discretion. Sometimes, even if other people were included in a message you received, your response may really only be appropriate for the sender, and he or she might not want all the other recipients to see your response. In these cases, use Reply instead so that only the sender gets your response, or use Reply to All, but be prepared to edit the list of recipients to remove anyone who might not like what you have to say. If, on the other hand, your response is for everyone's eyes—every single recipient included in the original mailing—go ahead and use Reply to All and keep the conversation going and everyone "in the loop."

Forwarding Messages

Forwarding a message is much like replying to one, except that instead of automatically entering the To and Cc data, Outlook leaves that blank—obviously, it can't know to whom you intend to forward this message. After selecting the message you wish to forward, simply click the Forward button on the toolbar or right-click the message to be forwarded and select the Forward command from the shortcut menu. Then enter the email address of your intended recipient(s) in the To and Cc fields and compose a note to go with the forwarded message—normally some sort of explanation as to why you're forwarding it. When you've composed your note, go ahead and click Send.

Formatting Email Messages

Outlook can send and receive your messages in three different formats: HTML (default), Rich Text, and Plain Text. To switch between these formats, use the Message Format drop list, found on the Outlook toolbar.

When choosing a format, bear in mind that only two of them allow any formatting—HTML and Rich Text. Plain Text allows no formatting of any kind, and your message will appear in a simple 10-point Courier font. HTML supports much of the same formatting of text you find in Word, including numbered lists, bulleted lists, text alignment, pictures, and background images. Many email applications support HTML messages; however, there are some that don't. In those cases, your message will appear as plain text with all the HTML code visible. You will want to know the capabilities of your recipients' email applications, particularly if you intend to send complex marketing material via email or if the contents of your message rely intricately on the specific formatting you've added. If you're using Outlook on a local area network, you won't have to worry about these things because everyone on the network will presumably be using Outlook.

If you find out that your recipients can't accept HTML mail (some email servers strip out the formatting, as stated earlier, and others simply reject HTML-based mail because it could be "spam" or junk email), you can still format the appearance of your message text if you choose Rich Text format. With Rich Text, you can apply text colors, fonts, sizes, and bullets and numbering. You can also select a URL within your message and click the Insert Hyperlink button to turn the text of the URL into a clickable hyperlink for the recipient. The Insert Hyperlink button is dimmed if you choose Plain Text.

Setting a New Default Font

By default, Outlook is set to use 10-point Arial when you're composing messages. This is a clean, neat, and professional-looking font, but what if it just doesn't suit your taste? Change it! Like most of the configuration settings in Outlook, this will take you back to the Options dialog box, reached by selecting Tools | Options from the menu bar.

Just as you did when setting the default email format, click the Mail Format tab and look at the middle section of the dialog box, titled Stationery and Fonts. Click the Fonts button, and in the resulting Fonts dialog box, shown next, use the Choose Font buttons to select the fonts you want used for composing messages, replying and forwarding messages, and reading and composing plain text.

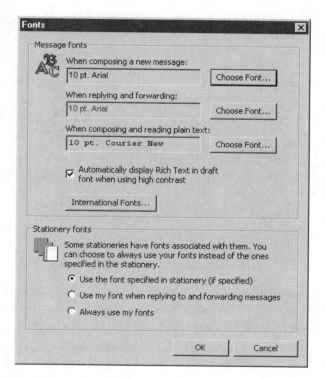

TIP

Although you'll want to pick a font that's "you," you'll also want to choose one that is legible and reasonably popular, so that your recipients can display it on their computers.

Choosing Stationery

Outlook comes with some very nice stationery options that allow you to personalize the messages you send with a graphical background, preset fonts, colors, and text layout. Selecting a stationery package of your choice is just like setting your default font—and it will apply to all outgoing messages, so make your selection with that fact in mind. To apply a default stationery to your messages, follow these steps:

1. Choose Tools | Options, and in the resulting Options dialog box select the Mail Format tab.

2. Click the Stationery Picker button. This opens the Stationery Picker dialog box. To preview the listed stationery choices, just click each item in the Stationery list. A preview of the stationery appears in the big box in the lower half of the dialog box.

If you don't see any stationery that suits your fancy, try clicking the Get More Stationery button. This will connect you to the Microsoft Office Download website (assuming you're online at the time), where you can look for more stationery to install on your machine.

TIP   *If you want to apply the look of stationery to a single outgoing message, use that message window's Format | Background command to choose from solid colors and Fill Effects to place behind your text. You can also use the Format | Theme command to choose from a variety of presets—fonts, sizes, and bulleting and numbering styles that have names such as Arctic, Canyon, and Travel. Make your choice from the list of themes, preview it, and click OK if you like it and want to apply it to your message. Be aware, however, that the size of your message (and therefore the time it will take dial-up users to receive it) will be increased by using Themes.*

Formatting Message Text

The actual formatting of text when in HTML format is similar to formatting text in Word, and exactly like formatting text in FrontPage, because they are both HTML-editing tools. The Formatting toolbar, found in any message window, is nearly identical to Word's Formatting toolbar, and it allows you to format headings and paragraph styles; select fonts, font sizes, and colors; set physical styles (bold, italic, underline); set alignment; create lists; and insert horizontal rules. If you change the format of the message to Plain Text, the Formatting toolbar will be dimmed, and text will appear in the default font you set for plain text in the Fonts dialog box.

Working with Signatures

A signature is a closing—typically your name, title, phone number, and/or web address—that appears at the foot of all outgoing messages, replies, and forwards. As shown in Figure 22-7, using a preset signature saves you typing the same information at the end of all your messages, and it prevents any messages going out without any "sign-off" or indication of your identity as the author of the message, which can be considered rude.

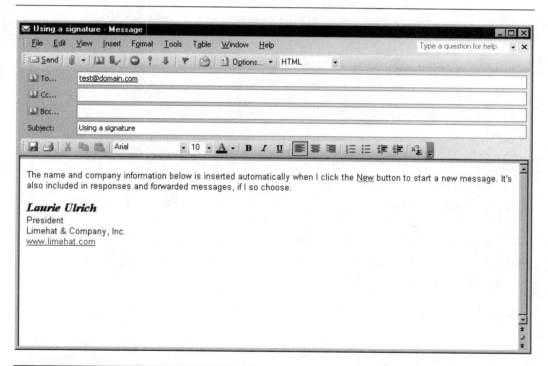

FIGURE 22-7   Create an automatic closing for your messages.

Creating a Signature

To create a signature, choose Tools | Options and click the Mail Format tab. In the resulting dialog box, click the Signatures button, found in the Signatures section of the dialog box. The Create Signature dialog box opens, through which you can create a new signature, edit it, and apply formatting to some or all of the signature content.

To continue creating a new signature, follow these steps, starting inside the Create Signature dialog box:

1. Click the New button.

2. Type a name for your signature (preferably your name or the name of the email account with which you plan to associate the signature).

3. Leave Start with Blank Signature selected and then click Next.

4. In the resulting Edit Signature dialog box, type your signature into the white box where you see your cursor blinking.

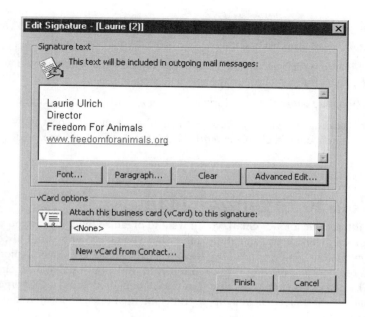

5. Use the Font button if you want to apply a different font, size, or color to some or all of your signature text. Always select the text to be formatted (using your mouse) before clicking the button.

6. If you want to change your signature's alignment, click the Paragraph button and choose Left, Center, or Right. You can also apply bullets.

7. When you've typed and formatted your signature as desired, click Finish. This places you back in the Create Signature dialog box, where you can create another signature (starting with New again) or click OK to go back to the Options dialog box.

Establishing Signatures for Different Email Accounts

New to Outlook 2003, you can set up signatures for individual email accounts. In the past, you could have multiple signatures on file, but whichever one you had selected as the default would apply to all outgoing messages, replies, and forwards. You could switch between the defaults, but it was a tedious process, and people often forgot to switch signatures when using one email account or another.

To apply a signature to a specific email account (assuming you have more than one established through Outlook), follow these steps:

1. Choose Tools | Options, and in the Options dialog box click the Mail Format tab.

2. In the Signature section of the dialog box, click the Select the Signature to Use with the Following Account drop list and choose one of your email accounts.

3. Click the Signature for New Messages drop list and pick the signature you want to use for the email account you chose in the previous step.

4. Choose a signature for replies and forwards for the selected email account.

5. Go back to the drop list where you chose an email account and repeat steps 2 through 4 for each of your accounts, choosing a different signature for each one, as desired.

6. Click OK.

Creating Folders to Organize Email

Assuming that you'll receive a lot of email, you'll want to organize them just as you would your Word documents, Excel worksheets, and all the other files you create with your Office and other manufacturers' applications. To organize those files, you can use the Windows Explorer or My Computer, creating folders and moving files from folder to folder until you have them just where you want them. The process is simple because it mimics the method you'd use to organize paper files in a file cabinet—you'd place them in appropriately named folders and store them alphabetically in a drawer.

This same concept and a very similar process is used in Outlook to organize your email, both incoming and outgoing, as you create folders within your Inbox and Sent Items folders to store email messages by nearly any organizational criteria you can imagine—topic, sender, recipient, or date, just to name the more common choices.

Setting Up Inbox and Sent Items Folders

Setting up folders inside your Inbox (for incoming mail) or the Sent Items folder (for mail you've sent) is no different from creating folders anywhere in Windows. First, you'll want to make sure you've selected Mail from the Navigation pane so that your Inbox and folders lists (Favorite Folders and All Mail Folders) are displayed. After that, it's just a matter of right-clicking the Inbox or the Sent Items folder in the Folder list and selecting New Folder from the shortcut menu.

After making this selection from the shortcut menu, you're prompted by the Create New Folder dialog box, shown next, to enter the name for the folder and choose the type of information the folder will contain. The dialog box also displays the folder hierarchy with the folder you right-clicked highlighted. If you change your mind about where you want to create the new folder, you can select the proper folder here.

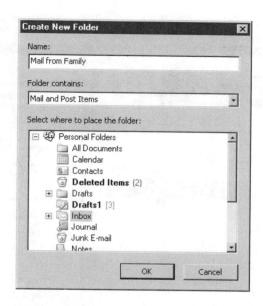

After you've named your folder (you can ignore the Folder Contains option because the default, Mail and Post Items, is fine), click OK to create the folder. You can repeat the process for as many folders as you need, and you can put folders within folders—for example, if you create a folder in the Inbox called "Mail from Family," you can create subfolders within that folder for each branch of your family, for particular family members, or for family events, such as "Reunion Mail."

Moving Messages Between Folders

Once your folders are created, you can move messages into them very simply—just drag the envelope icon for the message you want to move over to the Folder list and drop it on the folder of your choice. When the target folder is highlighted, release the mouse to drop the message into that folder, as shown in Figure 22-8.

If you want to move multiple messages from one folder to another, you can select them by holding down the SHIFT key to choose a continuous range of messages or by holding down the CTRL key to pick a number of noncontiguous messages in the list. After making the group selection, drag them en masse to the folder of your choice. If you prefer keyboard shortcuts, you can use CTRL-C to copy or CTRL-X to cut your messages and then open the folder of your choice and use CTRL-V to paste the message files in place.

NOTE   *The Favorite Folders portion of the Folders pane contains a folder for mail that requires follow-up and a folder for unread mail. These are considered virtual folders in that they don't physically exist the way that the Inbox and Sent Items folders (and subfolders within them that you create) do. They're conceptual folders that help categorize mail that requires some action over and above its categorization by topic, sender, recipient, or whatever criteria you'd use to place a message in a real folder.*

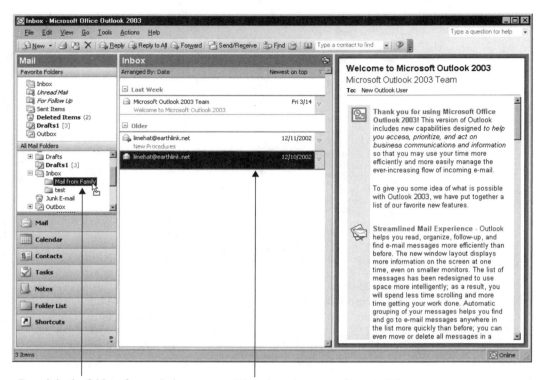

Drop it in the folder of your choice.   The selected message from the Inbox

FIGURE 22-8   Drag and drop your messages from one folder to another.

Deleting Messages

Deleting messages is equally simple and no different from what you're already used to. Select the message you want to delete and press DELETE to move the message to the Deleted Items folder within Outlook. You can also drag messages to the Deleted Items folder just as you might drag a file from your desktop onto the Recycle Bin. Just like the Recycle Bin, the Deleted Items folder will hold on to the messages placed inside it until you empty the folder manually. Then, and only then, are files truly "gone." To empty the Deleted Items folder, right-click it and choose Empty "Deleted Items" Folder from the shortcut menu. You'll be prompted to confirm your intention to delete all the messages in that folder, and assuming you want to do so, click Yes in response to the prompt.

Filtering Junk Email

Many senders of junk email (also known as *spam*) use HTML content in the message itself to verify that you are an actual email user, with a valid email address. They do this to eliminate dead email addresses from their mass-mailings so that their future emails don't go to people who don't really exist. This "web beacon" technique is blocked by Outlook 2003, through its tools that block any external content included in an HTML-based email. You can customize how your email is protected from spammers through the Junk Email Options dialog box, shown in Figure 22-9.

To access this dialog box, choose Actions | Junk Email, and from the submenu choose Junk Email Options. The submenu also includes Add commands for building a list of senders you trust (so all their email will be accepted) and a list of those you know to be junk email senders.

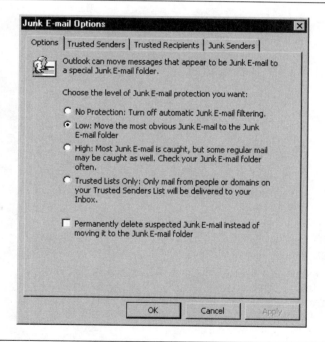

FIGURE 22-9   Set the level of spam-interception you want through the Options tab and choose whether or not to permanently delete mail deemed to be "junk."

Chapter 23

Scheduling Tasks and Appointments

How to...

- View the Outlook calendar from daily, weekly, and monthly perspectives
- Add one-time and recurring appointments and events to the calendar
- Schedule meetings with your coworkers
- Customize the calendar to meet your needs
- Build and maintain a list of to-do items
- Print your schedule

Outlook has a tightly integrated calendar and scheduling module that is tied into your email, contacts list, and a host of other Outlook features. Simply titled the Outlook Calendar, it is essentially an electronic version of any organizer you might purchase at an office supplies store. What's nice about this one is that you aren't limited to one type of layout. You can view a single day by hour, the whole work week by day and hour, the week as just blocks of days, or the entire month like a giant desk pad. You can schedule appointments and events, even setting audio reminders to get your attention and color-coded entries to quickly pick out important appointments at a glance.

> **TIP** *Can't be tied to your desktop? Not a problem! Outlook can be synchronized to a number of handheld devices so you can carry your calendar, task list, and contacts wherever you go. Check the documentation that comes with your handheld device for more information.*

A Tour of the Outlook Calendar

Accessing the calendar requires only a click of the Calendar button on the Navigation pane. You can also choose Go | Calendar. The view you see (Day, Week, or Month) is dictated by which view you had open last. Day and Week (or Work Week) views allow you to see the entire calendar workspace, including the TaskPad, as shown in Figure 23-1, whereas Month view's full calendar dominates the Outlook window, as shown in Figure 23-2.

The calendar is divided into three primary areas:

- **Appointments list** This area displays the hours of the day while in Day, Week, and Work Week views. Notice that the hours before 8:30 A.M. and after 5:00 P.M., and all hours on weekends, are shaded, indicating they are not traditional work hours. You can click any time increment and begin typing to enter information.
- **Date Navigator** This is how you get around in the calendar. While in Day view, click any date to see the schedule for that day. In Work Week view, click any day to have the entire five days displayed. You can also use LEFT ARROW and RIGHT ARROW keys to move forward and back. In the regular Week view, the arrow keys will move you forward

Banner indicates day-long event   Choose your view from these buttons on the toolbar.   Date Navigator   TaskPad

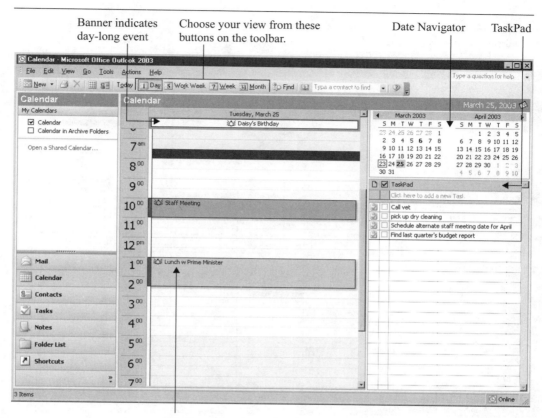

An appointment appears in a color chosen by the user.

FIGURE 23-1   The Outlook Calendar in Day view allows you to focus on a single day's activities.

and backward, whereas clicking an individual date will pop you into Day view. Use the two arrow buttons on either side of the Date Navigator (see Figure 23-1) to scroll through the months of the year. You can also click each month's heading to see a drop list from which you can select from a seven-month range—three months before and three months after.

■ **TaskPad** This tool is for (you guessed it!) entering tasks. Some people like to see it onscreen while in any view of the calendar, and others prefer to see their tasks only when Tasks is chosen from the Navigation pane. If you want to see your to-do list while viewing your calendar, choose View | TaskPad.

The displayed month is
mirrored in the Date Navigator.

A vacation event
spans several days.

Scroll through the years
with the vertical scroll bar.

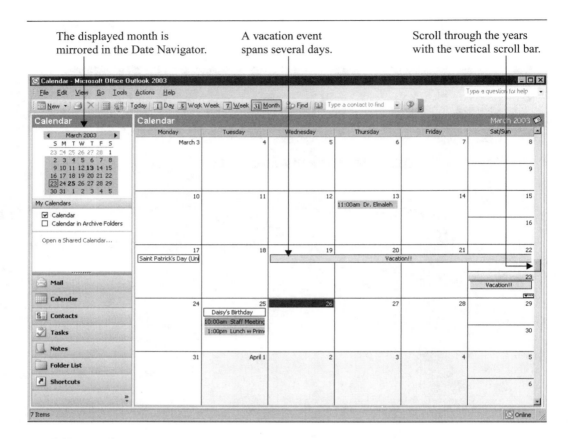

FIGURE 23-2 If you need to see your schedule from a greater distance (and with less
extraneous information included), choose Month view.

Understanding Calendar Entries

The Outlook Calendar recognizes three kinds of entries, and their terminology and parameters
operate under the assumption you are using Outlook in a cooperative office environment. This
certainly doesn't mean you can't take full advantage of the calendar in a standalone capacity,
as many people do.

■ **Appointments** These are individual activities that don't require you inviting other
people in your workgroup. When you create an appointment, you can choose how you
want your calendar to appear to the other members of your group, displaying that time

as Out of Office, Busy, Tentative, or Free. Alternatively, you can make appointments private, so others can't see them at all. You not only have the ability to schedule appointments in your own calendar, but permissions can also be granted allowing others to schedule and edit appointments in a coworker's calendar. This is useful, for example, when an administrative assistant is responsible for maintaining an executive's appointment book.

■ **Meetings**   Unlike appointments, which involve only your time, meetings involve inviting other coworkers and reserving office resources such as conference room space or setting up video or phone conferences and the equipment required. When you schedule a meeting in Outlook, you select the people to invite and whatever resources are required. The request for a meeting goes out to your coworkers in the form of an email, and you receive their responses (indicating their ability to attend) in your Inbox.

■ **Events**   Unlike meetings and appointments, events are at least day-long occurrences— for example, your vacation, a business trip, or someone's birthday. An event doesn't appear as a consumed block of time in Day or Work Week view, but rather as an event name banner running across the top of the dates specified for the event.

Creating Appointments, Events, and Meetings

The nice thing about the Outlook Calendar is that the same basic dialog box is used for each type of calendar entry, so once you know how to create one type you know how to create the others.

Setting Up an Appointment

Select the day for which you want to schedule the appointment, either using the Date Navigator or clicking the date in Month view. Then do one of the following:

■ Click the New button on the toolbar.

■ Double-click an hour in Day or Week (or Work Week) view.

■ Right-click any day or hour block in the Month, Day, Week, or Work Week view and choose New Appointment from the shortcut menu.

Any of these methods opens the Appointment dialog box, shown in Figure 23-3.

From here, enter the subject and location for the appointment in the fields provided. Each time you enter a new location, Outlook remembers it so you can quickly select it again using the location drop arrow. Next, select start and end times and enter a reminder interval if you choose. The Show Time As field will automatically be set to Busy. You can, of course, set it to any option you prefer, such as Free, Tentative (so others know you'd be willing to reschedule in favor of something else), or Out of Office. In the Appointment dialog box, if your start and end values are greater than 23 hours, the entry will be displayed as an event.

If the appointment is going to be repeated at regular intervals, click the Recurrence button on the toolbar to display the Appointment Recurrence dialog box. There you can define parameters

Select a color that establishes a category and/or
level of importance for the appointment.

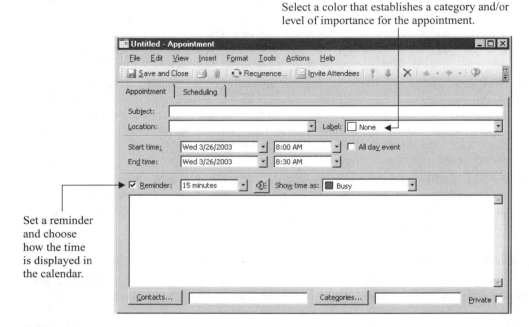

Set a reminder
and choose
how the time
is displayed in
the calendar.

FIGURE 23-3 Enter the dates, times, and a description of your appointment.

such as the recurrence pattern (how often the appointment occurs) and the date range across
which the appointment repeats. Click OK to return to the Appointment dialog box.

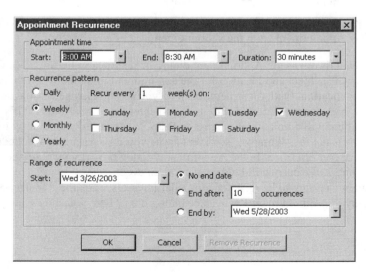

> **TIP** *You can edit recurring appointments or events so that just one occurrence or all the appointments/events are affected. This makes it possible to change or delete just one instance of a recurring staff meeting, doctor's appointment, or event and leave the rest of the series of recurrences intact.*

Once you've entered all the necessary information for your appointment (don't forget to apply a color label—it really helps you when you view your entire schedule later), click the toolbar's Save and Close button to see your appointment displayed in whichever calendar view was last active. Depending on the length of the description (some of the text will be truncated in Month view), it should look pretty much the same in each view, within the confines of the view itself.

If you need to edit the appointment, simply double-click it wherever it appears in the calendar to open it in the Appointment dialog box. If you want to quickly modify the duration of an appointment in Day or Work Week view, simply drag its borders: top (to adjust the start time) or bottom (to adjust end time). To move an appointment to another day, just point to it and immediately drag it to the desired date. Don't click and pause because Outlook will think you want to edit the appointment description, in place. You can also duplicate an appointment by dragging it to another date while holding CTRL down—be sure to release the mouse before releasing CTRL when the appointment duplicate is positioned on the date you want.

> **TIP** *You can enter appointments directly into the Day or Work Week view by simply clicking in a time slot on the Appointments list and entering your information directly into the view.*

Entering an Event

Entering event information is no different from creating an appointment, except that you check the All Day Event check box. This removes the Start and End time interval drop lists from the dialog box, leaving you with only the date ranges. If you want to include the times, as mentioned earlier, as long as the duration spans a full day, it will be displayed as an event. Anything less will just be seen as an extremely long appointment.

How to ... Use the Reminder Option for Appointments, Events, and Meetings

Use the Reminder check box (above the large text box in the Appointment dialog box) and set a time prior to the appointment, event, or meeting for which you should be given an alert or reminder. If you want a sound to play (in addition to the prompt dialog box that appears when the designated time prior to the appointment is reached), click the button with a speaker on it and choose the sound file that you'd like to play. The default is reminder.wav, part of the Office suite's group of preset sounds. Something to remember: When choosing how far in advance of the appointment to set the reminder, make sure you're allowing enough time to get to the appointment—if it takes an hour to drive to the appointment location, a reminder that appears just 15 minutes in advance won't be very helpful!

Scheduling a Meeting

Meetings obviously require people to meet with, a place to meet, and occasionally, other resources. Outlook's meeting scheduler has the ability to scan the availability of individuals you work with, as well as to reserve things such as conference rooms and equipment needed for the meeting.

To schedule a meeting, simply create an appointment as described previously and then click the Invite Attendees button on the toolbar. The Appointment dialog box displays a To field above the subject and location fields, and it changes the Save and Close button to Send, just like an email. You can now click the To button and select coworkers from your address book, or you can type their addresses manually, if you know them.

Next, click the Scheduling tab to see the availability schedule of the people you've invited, as shown in Figure 23-4. Beside each invitee's name is a bar, running across the time graph, displaying their availability. Use the legend at the bottom of the dialog box to determine if they're free to meet, busy, tentatively scheduled elsewhere, or out of the office. If your original meeting time is no good, you can easily click a time that shows better availability for the people you need to meet with. Once you're satisfied with your choices, simply click the Send button to deliver your meeting request to your desired attendees.

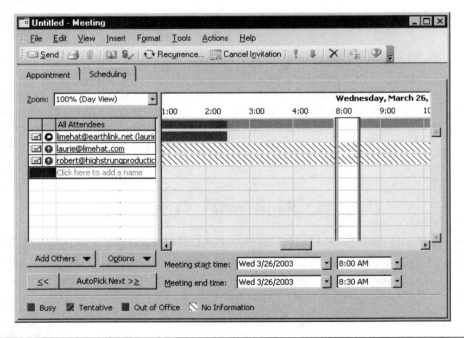

FIGURE 23-4   Use the Scheduling tab to see who's available and when to attend your meeting.

NOTE *Reserving resources requires you to use Microsoft Exchange. You'll know if you're on a Microsoft Exchange server when you create your email account as described in Chapter 22. If your account has been set up by your system administrator at work, simply ask him or her if you're using Microsoft Exchange and have the ability to schedule resources for meetings—if you are, you can add the meeting room or piece of equipment just as you would invite a person to the meeting. The individual resources will appear as entries in your address book.*

Customizing the Calendar

Even though Outlook's Calendar feature offers four different views of your calendar, which would seem to accommodate just about any need you'd have to see or not see some aspect of your schedule, you may want to customize the way one or more of your Calendar views looks.

If you want to tinker with the way the calendar looks and works, choose Tools | Options and click the Calendar Options button on the Preferences tab. In the resulting dialog box (see Figure 23-5), you can change the days of the week that you consider a "work week," change your

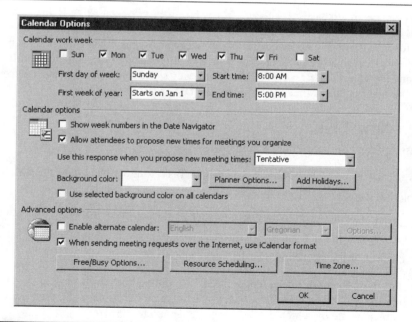

FIGURE 23-5 Choose how your calendar looks and functions and make it a friendlier tool for the way you work.

background color for Day and Week views, and even add holidays from one or more countries—your own country, and then perhaps the holidays of a country where you have clients or coworkers, and want a heads-up as to days they may be off work. You can also choose a different time zone if you'll be working in a far-off place for a while.

> **TIP** *Use the Options dialog box and the Preference tab buttons to customize virtually every aspect of Outlook—Mail, Calendar, Tasks, Journal, and Notes. The latter two are not covered in this book because (a) they're not as widely used and (b) they're easy enough for you to figure out on your own.*

Working with Tasks

The Outlook TaskPad is your electronic to-do list. You can enter tasks for yourself for a personal to-do list, or you can delegate work and assign task requests to people in your work group. The ability to delegate tasks works if you're on a network and Outlook is set up to allow you to do so, or if you delegate to another Outlook user—all you have to do is follow through on the assignment process (described later in this section) and send them the task. For many users, the TaskPad is simply a to-do list for oneself, where you keep track of what you have to do and when, in a clear, simple list that can be edited easily.

When you build tasks, you can type anything you want for the task description, and you can pick any date for the task to be completed. Tasks can be recurring, just like appointments, meetings, and events. What's more, you can track a task from inception through to completion, following its progress—and if you put a task on the list after it's already started, you can estimate a percentage of completion so that you know that only some of the task is left to be done.

Creating a New Task

To create a task, use any of the following methods:

- Click in the text box Click Here to Add a New Task, found at the top of the task list.
- Double-click anywhere on the TaskPad.
- Click New | Task on the toolbar (assuming you've chosen Tasks from the Navigation pane).
- Select File | New | Task from the menu bar.
- Press CTRL-SHIFT-K on the keyboard.

All but the first of these methods opens the Untitled Task dialog box, shown in Figure 23-6. If you use the Click Here to Add a New Task box, you can type a description and then use the Due Date drop list to pick a date by which the task must be complete.

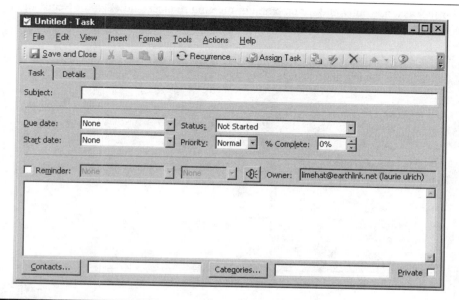

FIGURE 23-6   Set up all the particulars for your new task.

In the Untitled Task dialog box, enter a short description for your task in the Subject box, as well as the date by which the task is due and the date the task will be started, using the fields provided. If you want the task to be recurring, click the Recurrence button on the toolbar and use the Task Recurrence dialog box to set up the frequency of the recurrences and the length of time over which the task will recur. The dialog box is virtually identical to the one you see when you set up a recurring appointment. Use the Regenerate New Task radio button if you want the task to recur at a specific time *after* it is initially completed. You can use the Details tab to keep track of total hours worked, actual hours worked, mileage, billing information, and so on. When you're finished, click the Save and Close button on the toolbar.

Assigning Tasks

This procedure is very similar to scheduling a meeting, in that you're using a To field (like a message sent to invite people to a meeting) and choosing the person or persons you'd like to perform the task. To start the process, simply click the Assign Task button on the toolbar, which displays the To field and changes the Save and Close button to Send, as shown next. Enter a recipient for the task, as you would for an email or meeting request, and click the Send button when you're ready.

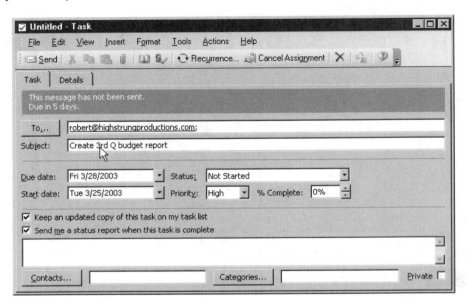

When assigning tasks, if you want to track their progress, select the Keep an Updated Copy of This Task on My Task List check box and the Send Me a Status Report when This Task Is Complete check box. To make sure these check boxes are selected automatically, on the Outlook menu bar, choose Tools | Options to open the Options dialog box. From here, click the Task Options button and select the appropriate check boxes from the Task Options dialog box.

Printing Your Schedule

Outlook accepts the fact that sometimes nothing beats a hard copy. Therefore, it's no problem at all to print out a copy of all your appointments for a given period. While in Calendar view, simply select Print from the File menu, or press CTRL-P on your keyboard. This opens the Print dialog box, where you can select the print style you prefer. Your choices are intuitively named—Daily Style, Weekly Style, Monthly Style, Trifold Style, and, for those who want the details of their appointments, Calendar Details Style. Use the Start and End fields to select the date range you want printed and then click the Page Setup button if you want to change your page orientation or margins or to add a header or footer (recurring titles on the top and/or bottom of the page).

If you want to print a blank calendar to write on manually, create a new folder by selecting File | New | Folder from the menu bar. This opens the Create New Folder dialog box:

In this dialog box, enter a name for the folder. In the Folder Contains field, select Calendar Items. In the Select Where to Place the Folder field, select Calendar and click OK. Now view the Folder list and select the new folder you just created. You can now print this blank calendar as described previously.

Chapter 24

Building a Contacts List

How to...

- Create a list of names, addresses, phone numbers, and Internet contact information
- Edit Contacts list entries
- Import an address book from Outlook Express
- Print your Contacts list

The Outlook Contacts folder is where you store the names, addresses, phone numbers, email addresses, and other pertinent information about the people with whom you do business. It can also contain the names, addresses, and email/web information for friends, family, and personal associations, including pictures of the individuals whose information you choose to store. Using the information you keep in your Contacts list, Outlook can add addresses to your email messages, flesh out your meeting requests, and provide a list of potential performers for tasks you assign. In addition to supporting vCards (the Internet standard for sharing virtual business cards), you can also use the Outlook Address Book as the source of data for a mail merge in Word—its uses are virtually unlimited.

> **TIP**   *If your recipient's email server is set up to filter out spam (junk) email, or if there's a firewall in place, your vCard may be stripped out of your message before it's delivered.*

Working with Contacts

By clicking the Contacts icon on the Navigation pane, you can display your address book in the main Outlook window, as shown in Figure 24-1. You start out in Address Cards view, but you may prefer views that place your contacts in a particular order, such as by company name, rather than contact name. You can switch between views of your address book by choosing View | Current View, or by using the buttons in the task pane on the left side of the screen.

You can view your contacts in any way that facilitates your working style: by last name, first name, nickname, company, or any other classification that works for you.

The amount of possible information you can enter for a single account is enormous, including multiple addresses and phone numbers, detailed information such as birthdays and anniversaries, the name of the person's secretary, and as many personal notes and comments as you desire.

> **NOTE**   *New to Outlook 2003 is the ability to share your contacts. While you're in Contacts, click the Open Shared Contacts link in the Navigation pane and click the Name button in the resulting small dialog box. A list of your contacts appears, from which you can select those contacts you wish to share. Select them (with the CTRL key to make multiple selections) and then click OK. Once shared, the contacts can be viewed by those people to whom you've given access to your Outlook data, through your network. If you're unable to perform these steps, check with your network administrator to see about possible problems with your setup.*

Choose a view
from this pane.

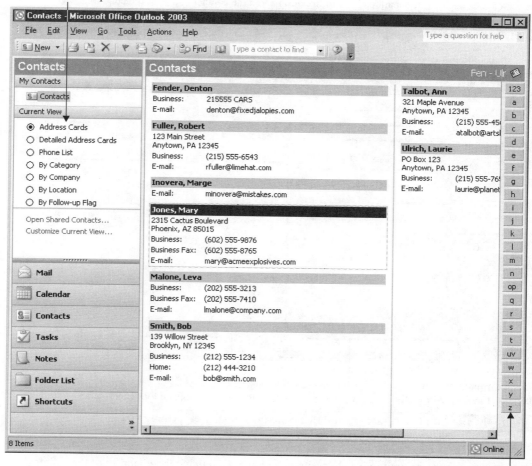

Click a letter of the alphabet to move to
the first record starting with that letter.

FIGURE 24-1   The Address Cards view shows you all the information you've entered into
each contact's fields.

Entering a New Contact

The Contact dialog box, shown in Figure 24-2, is potentially more useful than any pocket
knife the Swiss Army ever came up with, providing more than 120 possible fields to record
information about your contact. With three possible addresses, 20 telephone numbers, three
email addresses, web page and Instant Messenger fields, and plenty of space to enter general

Click Full Name if you want to keep the person's name and title separate.

Use these tabs to store more information about the contact.

Selects a picture of the contact

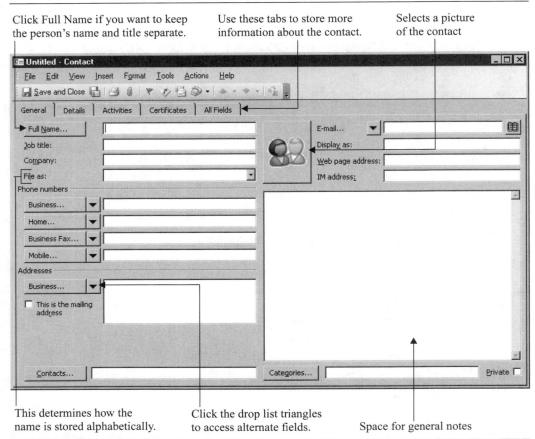

This determines how the name is stored alphabetically.

Click the drop list triangles to access alternate fields.

Space for general notes

FIGURE 24-2   Build a contact record that contains virtually everything you know about a person or an organization.

notes, you can create an entire virtual dossier on anyone. Granted, only a handful of these fields are viewable from the General tab at any one time. You can, however, click the All Fields tab and then use the Select From drop list to browse through them all, divided by category.

To open a blank Contact dialog box and begin entering a new contact, use any of the following methods:

- Double-click in an open area of the Address Cards view.
- Right-click in the Address Cards view and select New Contact from the context menu.
- While in Address Cards view, click the New button on the toolbar.
- Choose File | New | Contact from the menu bar.

24

Once you're faced with an Untitled Contact dialog box, you can begin entering the record—enter a name (it doesn't matter if you enter first name or last name first, you'll have a choice later to file the entry by first or last name) and then press TAB to move to the next field. Before doing so, however, you can click the Full Name button to open a separate dialog box, which allows you to enter precise name information one field at a time. You'll also see Business, Home, Business Fax, and Mobile buttons next to the fields where you can enter those pieces of information—again, the buttons open dialog boxes for detailed entry. For most records, however, you'll just move through the fields with TAB, entering information into the fields that you care about or for which you have information—you may not, for example, know someone's mailing address if you've only ever spoken to him or her on the phone or exchanged email. You might not have multiple phone numbers for some people, or you might not know where a distant cousin or acquaintance works, so the Company field will remain blank.

TIP   *If you only want to store someone's name and email address, just right-click his or her email address in a recent message from that person and choose Add to Contacts from the shortcut menu. A contact record will be created, with the information that's part of his or her email address—potentially, the person's name and email address, as in "Mary Smith <msmith@company.com>."*

Editing Contact Information

Outlook allows you to edit your contact information from any of the views available while within Contacts, whether you're in the default Address Cards view or any of the other possible views accessible from the View menu. Select the contact by clicking it once and then clicking the field you want to change, as shown in Figure 24-3. Once your cursor is blinking within the data, you can use BACKSPACE and DELETE to remove unwanted content and then type whatever you do want to appear in the field.

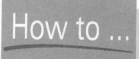

Import Your Address Book from Outlook Express

If you've been using Outlook Express for email prior to installing Office 2003, you can take your address book with you. In Outlook 2003, choose File | Import and Export, which opens the Import and Export Wizard. Choose Import Internet Mail and Addresses and then click Next. Choose your current version of Outlook in the next step of the wizard and then choose whether or not to import both your mail and your address book—you can choose one or both. Click Next, and the import begins. In the end, you'll see your Outlook Express address book entries appear in the current Outlook 2003 Contacts view, and you can use and edit the addresses as you would those you enter manually.

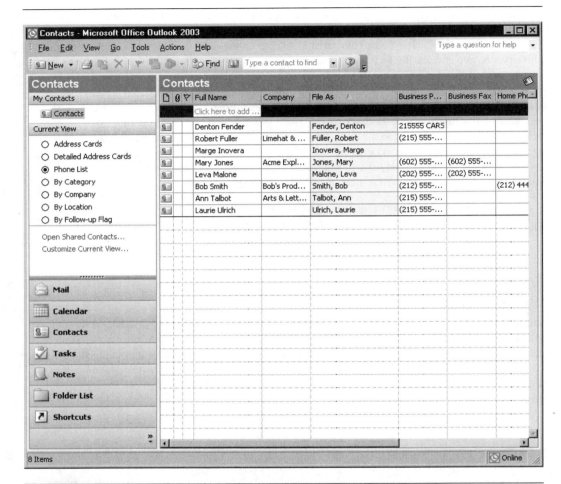

FIGURE 24-3 The Phone List view, as selected from the View menu. Simply click one of the fields and update the information to edit the contact.

Of course, you can also open the contact in the Contact window and make any changes there as well. To reopen the Contact window for any contact in the address book, just double-click the record name in the current view, and the window opens. You can also right-click the record (on any of the displayed data) and choose Open from the shortcut menu.

TIP *Deleting records is almost too easy. Simply select the contact in any of Outlook's possible views and either press DELETE to send it to the Deleted items folder or right-click the contact and choose Delete from the context menu. You can also click the X (Delete) button on the toolbar while the record is selected.*

Contact Tracking

The Activities tab of the Contact dialog box allows you to see all email messages, appointments, tasks, notes, and documents related to that contact. You tie these items to a contact via links. Outlook will automatically create links when you send or receive email messages, schedule meetings, or assign tasks involving someone on your Contacts list. You can manually link contacts to Outlook items and other Office documents using any of the following methods.

Linking a Contact to a Preexisting Outlook Item

Open the contact to which you want to link an item, and select Actions | Link | Items from the menu bar. This displays the Link Items to Contact dialog box, shown next.

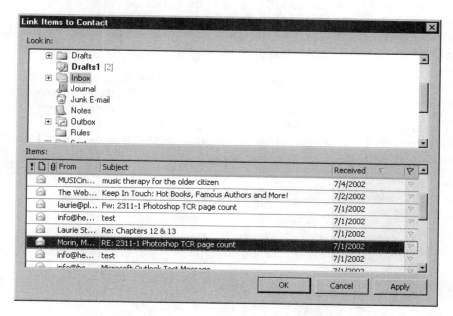

Use the Look In field to select the folder you want to look in, and use the Items field to choose the specific Outlook items you want linked to this contact.

Linking a Contact to New Items

When composing a new message, click the Options button on the message window's toolbar and then click the Contacts button at the bottom of the Message Options dialog box. When creating appointments, meetings, and event items, simply use the Contacts button located at the bottom of their input windows.

Linking a Document to a Contact

Just like linking a contact to a preexisting Outlook item, open the contact to which you want to link a document, select Actions | Link, but then choose File from the menu bar. This opens a standard Choose a File dialog box from which to locate a file on your hard drive.

Printing Your Contacts List

You can print out your contacts in much the same way you print out a calendar. You can print your entire Contacts list or print only a subsection—for example, if you're going out of town and only need the contacts for a specific city.

To print your entire Contacts list, switch to Address Cards view, as this provides the most print style options, and then choose File | Print from the menu bar. You can also press CTRL-P on your keyboard. In the Print dialog box, select the style you prefer in the Print Style area (see Figure 24-4) and then click OK. You may want to use the Preview button first to get an idea how your printout will look.

If you only want to print a selection of contacts, go to the View menu and choose Current View | Customize Current View. In the View Summary dialog box, click the Filters button. In the resulting dialog box, shown next, use the available fields to narrow your contacts down to the ones you want. You could use the Search for the Word(s) field and enter the name of a city, or you could use the Email button to pick out individuals from your Contacts list. Use in In field

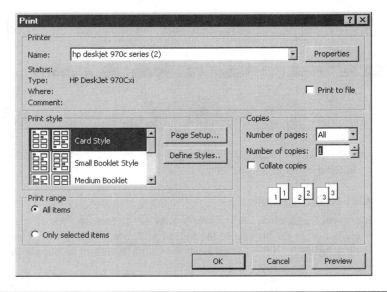

FIGURE 24-4   Choose the desired style for your printout of the Contacts list.

to choose which fields to search for that criteria. Once you've customized the view to only include the contacts you want to print, follow the preceding steps to print them out. You'll probably want to reset the current view back to how it was originally when you are done. You can do this by going through the same procedure and using the Clear All button at the bottom of the Filter dialog box.

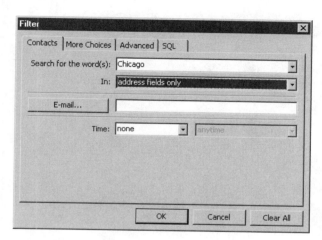

24

Part VII

Designing Web Pages with FrontPage

Chapter 25 Planning a Website

How to...

- ■ Choose the type of website you need
- ■ Gather content for your site
- ■ Storyboard your site

What does a website do? Essentially, it's a little piece of real estate on the web that a person, organization, or business uses to say, "Here I am, and this is what I'm doing/thinking/selling." Sites are used to share points of common interest, disseminate information, and provide services for visitors. Websites can live on the Internet, being available to millions of potential visitors around the world, or can reside on an organization's intranet, closed but to the select people who work for, or are in some way associated with, that organization. Regardless of the site's physical location, before actually building the website, you'll need to establish what you want your site to do. Once the site's mission is clear, thought needs to be given to its design and content, and where that content will come from. If you're simply making your own personal home page and using it as a hobby to teach yourself about web technology, the topics discussed here aren't going to be as pressing on you as they might be if you're trying to establish an ecommerce presence or build a website to distribute information about an important cause. Whatever your long-term web goals are, it always helps to have a strategy laid out so you aren't caught flat-footed with an unexpected obstacle right in the middle of developing your site.

What Are Your Online Goals?

What do you want to accomplish with your site? Will this website be a resource for information? Is it an entertainment site? Will you use it to sell a product? Once you establish your site's purpose—what it's going to be and do—every decision you make afterward will be simple. Some examples of questions to ask yourself include:

- ■ *Who will the site's visitors be?* Think of a typical visitor, and then imagine other types of people who'd be likely to visit the site. Will they be mostly men? Mostly women? Would people of a particular age or with a particular interest or political affiliation be drawn to your site?

- ■ *How do you want your visitors to move from one area of your site to the next?* Imagine the navigational strategy for your site—from where your navigational tools (buttons, text links) will be located to the way people will move from top-level pages (such as the home page) to lower-level pages.

- ■ *What hardware and software will your visitors be using to view your site?* Internet Explorer or Netscape Navigator? PC or Mac? Both? Clues to the answer to this question lie in the first question about the audience for your site.

■ *What sort of design do you want for the site?* The tone, color scheme, the overall "look"—imagine it and think about whether it will appeal to the typical visitor and whether it matches your site's subject matter.

What follows isn't intended to be an exhaustive list of every type of site on the Internet—after all, there are nearly as many flavors of sites out there as there are people who've decided to carve out their niche in cyberspace. Instead, this is an overview of the more common methods for employing websites. One of these might be right up your alley, or you could very well blaze an entirely new trail.

Personal and Family Websites

We've all seen these types of sites in our travels, and with the number of free hosting options available through Internet service providers and sites such as Yahoo!, Lycos, and Angelfire, to name only a few, it's not surprising that these "freebie" sites make up a good percentage of the sites on the web. Individuals who are more serious about their web presence may go to the effort to purchase their own domain names (http://www.*your_name_here*.com) and develop a more unique presence on the web rather than just being a small section within a larger domain.

Personal sites are great for the beginning web developer. You don't have to worry about "staying on message," marketing data, sales and site statistics, or any of the other concerns a corporate web presence demands. Have some snaps from the family picnic you want the rest of the extended clan to see? Put together a little page and load them all up to the web server, then send your cousins an email. Have a pet subject you want to share with the world? Create your own cyber-shrine and put it on the web for all the other enthusiasts to see.

Sites that Advertise

Sites that advertise basically say, "Hi! Here we are, and this is what we do. Please contact us for all your *(place a subject here)* needs!" As you can see, the personal category could easily merge in here if it were an online résumé. I differentiate the advertisement site from a site that sells a product only by the fact that it is not a true ecommerce site allowing customers to make purchases directly from within the site itself. This doesn't mean that a site that advertises can't be selling a product, but only that you can't buy its products using the site. A site that advertises doesn't even need to be pushing a product. There are plenty of nonprofit organizations whose sites simply function to let the public know about the work they do.

Sites that Sell

When I refer to sites that sell, I mean *ecommerce*. Ecommerce is hard-core online selling. "Hi! Welcome to our site. This is what we sell, and if you provide us with the necessary information, we'll have your order off to you in no time flat (hopefully)!" You can set up your own secure server to process the credit card transactions with the bank, installing and running a relational database and writing a custom program to process orders from an inventory and shipping perspective. Alternatively, you can subcontract the "shopping cart," the software and services that allow people to click a product, enter a quantity, type in their credit card, billing, and shipping address, and have the sale processed online.

As you might expect, the first option can prove to be expensive to implement and maintain, whereas the other costs more per transaction but doesn't require you to be hardware and ecommerce software savvy. The choice is yours. What both solutions demand is that your site be pleasant on the eye and easy to use so that people enjoy their shopping experience.

> NOTE *An intranet is a private network contained within an organization. It may consist of many interconnected local area networks (LANs) and may also be part of a larger wide area network (WAN). Typically, an intranet includes connections through one or more gateway computers to the outside Internet. The main purpose of an intranet is to share company information and computing resources among employees. An intranet can also be used for teleconferences to facilitate working in groups.*

Planning Your Site's Content

Before you actually sit down and start constructing the site you decide to make, it's a good idea to have as much of the site's contents at your fingertips as possible. By having all your individual site assets ready to go at the beginning, you make the construction phase of the site move much more quickly and easily. You'll want to gather any images you plan on using or create them if needed. You'll also want to have located/created the text components—any articles or other longer text elements that you wouldn't want to type from scratch when you sit down to create your pages. Have all these items in one folder, preferably called "site content" or something like that. The more centralized the storage of your site content is, the more quickly you'll be able to find it later, and the simpler your filing procedures will be as you find new graphics, articles, and so forth for your site over time.

Understanding Graphic Requirements

It would be wonderful if you could grab any old image file you had and drop it into your website. Just like with most things in life, however, it's rarely that simple. First off, there are only a limited number of file types that web browsers are capable of displaying, and secondly, regardless of file type, file size is another important issue. The smaller a file is, the quicker your visitors can access it over their Internet connection. If the images you use in your site are of astronomical size, your visitors will be left waiting interminably for your site to load.

Choosing the Right Web-Friendly Graphic Format

To date, the two most widely supported graphic file formats by web browsers are GIF (Graphic Interchange Format), shown with a .gif file extension, and JPEG (Joint Photographic Experts Group), which uses the .jpg file extension. When it comes to creating images in either of these formats, this general rule applies: Use JPEGs for photographs and photo-realistic images, and use GIFs for simpler images such as clip art, line art, and grayscale graphics (including black and white photos).

GIFs only support up to 256 individual colors. Consequently, they are great for images that don't have a lot of detail or don't contain a great deal of color variation. JPEGs, on the other hand, support millions of colors, so they can handle more of the subtle shades of color that exist in a photograph, or the kinds of photo-realistic images you can create with image editors such as Adobe's Photoshop. If you have an image that isn't in either of these formats, you can open it in the image editor of your choice and either save or export the file as one of these formats.

Reducing File Size for Quick Page Loading

Now on to the second part of the equation: file size. The smaller an image file is, the quicker a visitor's browser can display it. So how do you ensure a minimum file size for the graphic you want to use? Image optimization. Any program used to edit graphics for the web, such as Adobe's Photoshop/Photoshop Elements and Macromedia's Fireworks, offers tools that allow you to optimize web graphics (see Figure 25-1). There are some programs, such as Equilibrium's

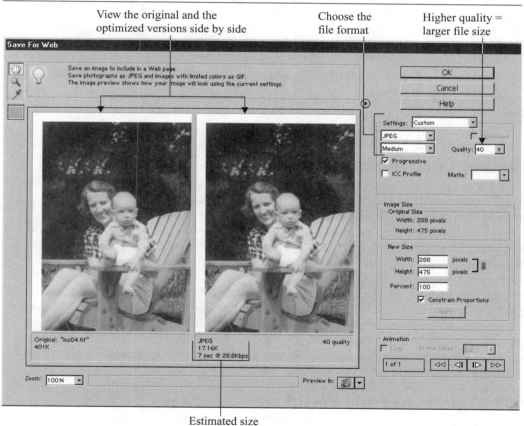

FIGURE 25-1 The Photoshop Elements Save for Web dialog box provides all the tools you need to take any kind of image and make it web-ready.

DeBabelizer, that instead of being an image editor, do nothing but optimize and convert graphics for the web and other media.

Working Within Color Limitations on the Web

Unlike designing for print, where you have ultimate control over the finished product the viewer will see, web-based content has as many variables governing how visitors experience a site as there are potential visitors. Each copy of this book is virtually identical, and each person who reads it will experience it in nearly identical fashion, but each person who views your web page has control over his or her own computer—its graphic card, monitor, operating system, and web browser. Designing for this extremely unlevel playing field is a challenge for the conscientious web designer. In addition to using commonly supported graphic file formats, another strategy designers employ to ensure a consistent experience for their visitors—regardless of what hardware and software configuration they may have—is to use the web-safe color palette.

The term *web-safe* refers to the 216 colors that will be displayed consistently in both Netscape Navigator and Internet Explorer (both Mac and PC) when that computer is running in 256-color mode. Any color that falls outside the 256 range would be pushed to its closest web-safe neighbor on any machine not capable of displaying more than 256 colors. The reason designers try to conform to the web-safe palette, even though many newer computers are capable of displaying millions of colors, is to make sure their sites look the same across the greatest number of computers.

> **TIP** *An advantage to using FrontPage is its preexisting collection of themes, which contain graphic elements and web-safe color schemes. For the first-time webmaster, these are a useful starting point.*

Gathering Your Graphic Images

So you know what graphic file formats to use, and which format is best for each type of graphic (photos vs. line art). Does your site really need graphics? Without hesitation, yes. The saying "a picture's worth a thousand words" hasn't hung around for centuries because it's not true! Your website needs graphics—whether it's your company logo or a photo of your product, you can say a lot about yourself, your organization, your cause, or your product if you use pictures. The pictures can be photographs, drawings, clip art, or simple line art images—anything that does the job.

But where are all these images coming from? You have three basic options: create them yourself, scan printed artwork, or gain access to preexisting digital graphics from either free or commercial sources. If you're an aficionado of Photoshop, Fireworks, or some other graphics application, creating web graphics shouldn't be much of a problem for you, and these tools are perfectly suited to the task. On the other hand, you may have no prior experience with these tools and thus be resigned to the other two options.

Scanning Photographs and Line Art

Provided you have a scanner, FrontPage makes this option extremely easy using the Insert | Picture | From Scanner or Camera command. This launches your scanning software, from which you'll make choices about how you want the image scanned.

Remember it's rare that the image you scan is perfect "as is" for the web. Because of this, think of scanning as simply the process by which you bring the image into your computer. From here, you'll refine the image to your specific needs. A general rule of thumb for scanning images for the web is to bring in more than you're going to use. By this I mean scan at a high dpi (dots per inch) setting to gain the biggest, clearest manageable image you can get to work with. From here you'll use your image-editing software to pare it down to something usable on the web. A computer monitor is only 72 dpi, and chances are the printed image or photograph you're scanning is much higher than that to begin with. If you scan at 72 dpi, you'll be losing valuable image data. Scan at 300 to 600 dpi, then work your image down using your image editor—*after* doing any restoration or retouching, which will benefit from the higher dpi. A discussion of this process is a book unto itself, and it's easy to locate a book devoted specifically to using the image editor of your choice for creating web graphics.

25

TIP   *If you want to find out more about the "gold standard" for image editing and photo retouching, consider* Photoshop 7: The Complete Reference, *published by McGraw-Hill/Osborne (2002) and written by the author of the book you're reading now.*

Utilizing Commercial Resources for Graphics

Commercial graphics vendors have been the friends of the graphic designer for ages. Volumes of images sorted into thousands of categories are available on CD-ROM and for download from many different vendors. Corbis and Photodisc are two of the better-known commercial retailers of images.

The advantage of using these resources is simple: The images are of extremely high quality. The downside, of course, is that they cost money and you may still need to further edit an image once you've paid for it to make it fit in exactly with your design.

Finding Free Images Online

If you do a web search for "royalty free graphics" or "free web graphics" in your favorite search engine, you are sure to find hundreds of thousands of sites dedicated to the subject. These sites have the commercial sites' pros and cons reversed. The graphics don't cost anything, but they may not be the highest quality. Hey, beggars can't be choosers. If you poke around, you're sure to find something that suits your needs. It just requires a little more work on your end.

Once you get to the site and view the images it has to offer, the site will usually offer a Download button next to each image or provide instructions for copying the file to your local drive (typically, this involves right-clicking the image and choosing Save Picture As from the resulting shortcut menu, which opens the Save Picture dialog box). The other downside of mining the web for images is that everyone else in need of graphic images is mining the same supply, and people start to recognize images that get used a lot.

Collecting Text Content

All the graphics in the world won't mean a thing if your site has nothing to say, and to say something you'll need text. If you're creating a personal or family site, the text you use is most likely going to be something you come up with yourself. If you're building an advertising or ecommerce site, you may have the advantage of using preexisting marketing materials from which to gather your text. It's nice if such sources are still in their electronic form, such as some type of word processing or print layout file. Then you can simply cut and paste into FrontPage and format as needed. Otherwise, it's time to start typing. You can also scan text materials using a method called *OCR* (which stands for *optical character recognition*). OCR "reads" the words in the image and generates a text file that you are then free to use any way you like. Depending on the quality of the original document you're scanning—photocopies, documents containing ornate fonts, and folded or stained paper—you may not get the most accurate scan. It's always advisable to go back over the scanned text with the original in hand to fix what the software failed to interpret accurately. If all this extra proofing sounds too arduous for you, consider having to retype a two-page article yourself. Some proofing and editing of the scanned text is a small price to pay.

Of course, you won't be inserting the scanned and saved text files (or the other electronic files that you accumulate for your website) into your web pages. You'll be opening them in their native applications (Word or Notepad, for example) and copying the text to the Clipboard (CTRL-C or Edit | Copy). Next, you'll position your cursor on the web page at the spot where the text should appear and then paste it (CTRL-V or Edit | Paste). The text will appear in your web page in a normal paragraph style. You can then do any necessary reformatting using the techniques discussed in Chapter 26.

NOTE | *It pays to watch the competition, even if you aren't competing. If your site isn't geared toward some business venture, it can still be useful to take a look at what other folks have done in sites similar to the one you want to build. You may be creating a site about a particular topic, in which case using the web as a research tool to find information is perfect. If the site you intend to build is marketing a product or service, you certainly want to see what other sites are out there. Perform your search using multiple search engines to get a solid overview of what your potential audience will find. Remember, search engines are simply individual databases of links, so the top 50 returns at Google will differ from those at Yahoo! or AltaVista.*

Building Your Website Blueprint

You've decided what kind of website you want to build, you've gathered your graphics and textual content, and you've researched your competition. Now give a little thought to your site's layout and structure, creating, in essence, a blueprint for your site. It makes no difference whether you sit down with pencil and paper or a graphics program to do this. You want to have a simple site map or flow chart depicting the individual pages of your site and their navigational relationship to one another, as well as a visual mockup of what the pages should look like.

Creating a Site Map

A *site map* is a flow chart that shows how your pages are connected—which page leads to which page. The site map's primary function at this stage is to help you organize your navigational structure so you know how your visitors will go from one page to the next. In large ecommerce sites, these things can become fairly complex, particularly in a site where an action taken by the visitor on one page determines the page he or she will see next. For example, a page may ask if the visitor is a new customer or a returning one who has already provided information necessary to making a purchase. Again, this is something you can determine on paper or on your PC. This map will represent the physical hyperlinks between the documents of your sites.

Site maps can be drawings or sketches of the navigation process, as shown in Figure 25-2. You can draw simple boxes that represent your site's pages and start jotting down the headings

25

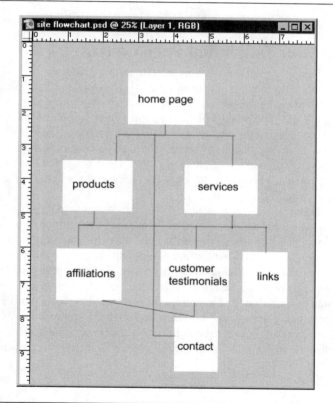

| FIGURE 25-2 | An electronically produced site map is easier to update as you add, move, or delete pages. |

and making quick representations of the graphics you intend to use inside them. Simplicity is the key word here. Next, draw lines connecting the pages, showing which ones will be connected by hyperlinks. By drawing lines that point away from your collection of pages, you can indicate links to the outside world. Jot down the URLs of the sites that these external links will point to.

It's a simple process, no more complex and no less essential than creating an outline before writing a report or a story. To create these sketches, you can stick with the paper and pencil, or you can create computerized images using any of a variety of simple programs. PowerPoint's organization chart tools lend themselves nicely to this task, and you can read all about using PowerPoint to create your sketches in Chapter 16.

When you're planning out your site, imagine you're the visitor. Think about what information you'll be providing through your pages, what decisions you'll be asking your visitors to make, what tools you'll use to compel them to read, buy, act—whatever you want them to do. It's important to maintain the visitor's perspective in all your design decisions, and the site map process is a great place to start.

Storyboarding Your Individual Page Content

With your overall site blueprint in place, it's time to start planning how the individual pages will look. Again, you can sketch these out on paper or create them electronically. This is essentially mocking up a rough draft of each page so you have something to work from while you're actually in FrontPage building the site. The process of creating this rough draft is called *storyboarding*.

Although you may be alone in the web design process, the value of the storyboarding process is not diminished. If anything, the objective "voice" of your visions onscreen or on paper is even more important when there's no one else there to say, "No, I don't like that, but how about this?" Your site map and page mockups become your sounding board, and it's a step in the design process that I don't recommend skipping.

If drawing isn't your cup of tea, you may want to use the computer to create your storyboards. You can use something as simple and accessible as Paint, one of the Windows accessories (Start | Programs | Accessories | Paint), or a more powerful illustration program such as Photoshop or Fireworks, as shown in Figure 25-3. Literally, any graphic illustration application will do. You can also use PowerPoint or Word, utilizing the freeform and shape drawing tools available in the AutoShapes menu on the Drawing toolbar. If you have the budget for extra software, you can also look into programs that are designed expressly for creating flowcharts—programs such as Microsoft's Visio, which has a website diagram included among its templates. Again, though, if you start with a program you've never used before, you'll have to think about the program's tools, and that may slow down your drawing/charting process unless you're very proficient with the software.

It's helpful to insert indications of where text links and other navigational tools will be placed.

Shapes are used to represent the places where graphics will be used.

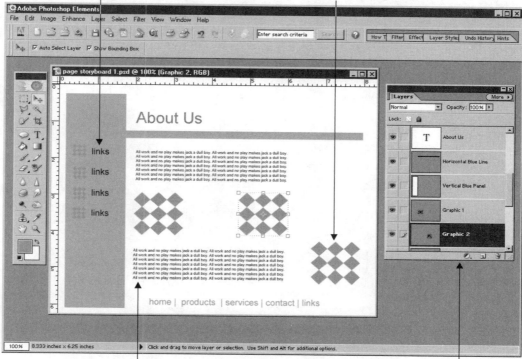

Filler text represents where real text will be pasted or typed.

Each component of the "page" is stored on a separate layer, allowing each one to be moved, resized, hidden, or displayed separately.

FIGURE 25-3 Use a product you know well enough to use the basic tools with ease. This allows you to concentrate on your design, and not on the software you're using to plan it.

If you want quick and easy, stick with paper and pencil. You can use graph paper if you want to keep your lines straight and to have 90-degree angles on your boxes' corners (though that's not important to the process). Paper's a nice choice because you can store it anywhere—in your briefcase or handbag—and take it with you with a minimum of fuss. Also, other than encountering a strong wind or fire, there's not much chance of the paper malfunctioning.

Chapter 26

Building a Website

How to...

- Set up a new site using FrontPage templates
- Build a website from scratch
- Add pages to the site
- Designate a home page
- Link pages within your site
- Add text and graphics to your pages
- Structure page content with tables
- Set up navigation bars and buttons

FrontPage is what is known as a WYSIWYG (What You See Is What You Get, or *wizzy-wig*) editor. Instead of having to be proficient with HTML (Hypertext Markup Language), you simply use the same type of menus and commands you're already familiar with from Office's other applications. With FrontPage, you can see your site project through from inception to conclusion—laying out your site's basic structure, developing the site's individual pages, and then uploading the completed site to your web server.

Getting Started with FrontPage

FrontPage provides you with multiple views to see the individual files in your site, as well as the relationships between them. You will create and edit your website documents in Page view, examine the contents of your website in Folders view, and design your site navigational structure in Navigation view.

FrontPage's site development and management tools provide everything you need to create, manage, and maintain any website you design. The advantage to you, being a user of Microsoft Office, is that FrontPage will be easier to learn because you really already know how to use it—it works just like the rest of the Office suite.

Starting a New Website

The first thing you'll want to do is view the task pane, which allows you to open pages within a website, add new pages, and create new websites, either from scratch or using any of FrontPage's templates. To open the task pane, either select File | New | Page or Web Site or select View | Task Pane from the menu bar; the task pane, shown next, will then appear on the right side of the application window.

On the task pane, click More Web Site Templates. This opens the Web Site Templates dialog box (see Figure 26-1), from which you select what type of site you plan to make. Click any of the templates, and a description appears on the lower-right side of the dialog box. If you want a simple blank website to build up from scratch, select the Empty Web Site template.

Next, you'll want to specify where on your hard drive you want this site created. By default, FrontPage will place it in the C:\My Documents\My Webs directory created on your C drive and will give it a name such as *myweb1*. For convenience sake, keep the new site in the My Webs directory but simply change the last directory name in the file path to something appropriate for your site—for example, C:\My Documents\My Webs*your_website_name,* where *your_website_name* is the domain name of the site.

Once you've done this, click OK. Depending on the site template you've selected, either a blank page will then open, awaiting your creative touch, or a full, multipage site with predefined FrontPage themes will appear, in some cases launching wizards to help you make choices about structure and content.

TIP   *FrontPage offers website templates, many of which require that FrontPage Extensions be installed on the computer being used to develop the site. If you do a complete install of FrontPage, the extensions should be there for you already. If you didn't do a complete install, you can go back and install them later. These extensions allow the FrontPage-specific code to be properly interpreted as you develop and test your pages. As you'll also find in Chapter 27, the web server storing your FrontPage websites must have FrontPage extensions on it as well.*

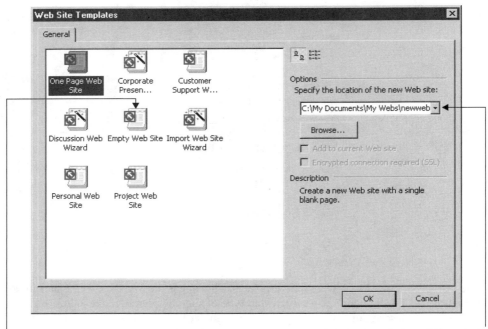

The Empty Web Site template offers the most flexibility to build whatever kind of site you want.

By default, the website will be stored in My Webs, a subfolder of My Documents.

FIGURE 26-1   The Web Site Templates dialog box offers several options for starting a new website.

Adding Pages to Your Site

Adding pages to a site is pretty straightforward stuff with FrontPage. The easiest way of doing this, whether you're adding pages to a new empty site, an existing site, or one of the template-based sites, is to switch to Navigation view by clicking its icon in the View pane (shown in Figure 26-2).

As you can see in Figure 26-2, the home page is the first added. Each subsequent page you add (by clicking the New Page button) will have the default title of Top Page, and then if you click one of the Top Page icons and click the New Page button, you'll get a new page. Don't worry

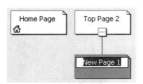

about these generic page names—you can easily re-title each document by pressing TAB or by clicking once on the page icon and then once again to highlight the page title. From here you can simply enter the title you prefer. By clicking TAB once you're finished, the next document title in the sequence is selected and you can move through the entire site structure, re-titling your pages one by one.

By default, the first page added is the home page, indicated by this icon.

Click the New Page button to add pages.

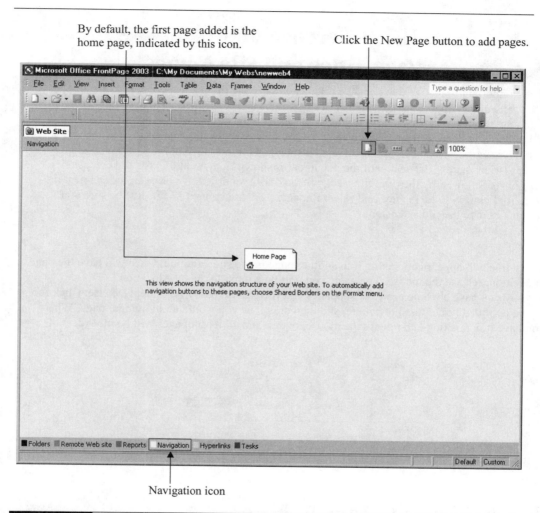

Navigation icon

FIGURE 26-2 Click the Navigation icon to switch to Navigation view.

Rearranging the Site Structure

One of the nice things about using FrontPage is being able to quickly and easily restructure your website without losing the link relationships between pages. Just like adding pages, restructuring is done in Navigation view. This functionality gives you a lot of freedom when first setting up your site. Don't think that page should be attached there? No problem, just click the page you want to relocate. It will change from yellow to blue. As you begin dragging the page, FrontPage will display an outline of the page icon. When you drag the outline into new potential locations,

 **Did you know?**

The Difference Between Page Titles and File Names

It's important to realize that a page's title is not the same thing as its file name. The title of a document appears in the title bar of the web browser when the page is displayed, and it's the value found between the <title> and </title> tags in the head section of the HTML file's source code. To see the difference between the two, re-title your pages and then click Folders view. You'll see your documents displayed similarly to Windows Explorer when set to view details. The name of the document is shown first, including the file extension (*.htm), followed by the title, file size, type, and date modified. If you want to rename a file, right-click it in Folders view and select Rename from the context menu. Just be sure you don't change the file extension.

a gray line will appear connecting it to another page in the site structure. Once you have the page in position, release the mouse. The page icon will then jump to the new location.

Say you have a whole group of subpages you feel should really be someplace else. Click the top page of that "tree," as shown here, and then drag it as you would an individual page. When you have it in position and release the mouse, both it and all its subpages will be moved.

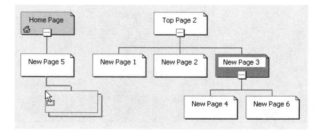

Applying a Theme to Your Website

Once you've created your pages—at least those you know you need right now, as more can be added later—it's time to apply a theme. You can leave your website without a theme and build graphic content such as a background image, fonts, colors, and so forth from scratch, but it's faster and easier to choose one of FrontPage's themes. To choose and apply a theme to your entire site, follow these steps:

1. Select all the pages in your site by switching to Navigation view in the Folders pane and clicking the Home Page icon. Press and hold SHIFT as you click the last page listed—this will select the home page and all pages between and including the last page.

2. Choose Format | Theme. The Theme task pane (shown in Figure 26-3) appears, giving you an extensive selection of themes.

3. Scroll through the themes and find one you like. You can always change your mind later.

4. Click once on the theme you'd like to use, and when the drop list arrow appears on the theme's thumbnail, click it and choose Apply to Selected Pages.

At this point, the selected theme is applied to all the pages you selected in step 1, and if you go to Page view of the pages individually, you'll see the background graphic and/or colors of the selected theme in place.

Leave these options on in order to include the main elements of the selected theme in your pages.

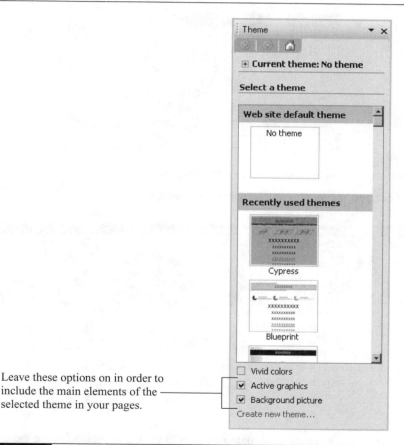

FIGURE 26-3   Select a theme from this vertical list of thumbnail images.

Adding Page Banners

Each page in your site needs some sort of identification. You can achieve this through graphic images you create in an application such as Photoshop, or you can take the quick-and-easy way out and let FrontPage insert a page banner for you. Your banner can be a graphic or simple text. To insert a graphic banner (with the name of your page incorporated into it), follow these steps:

1. Double-click a page from within the Navigation view so that the page is displayed onscreen.

2. Click at the top of the page and choose Insert | Page Banner. The Page Banner Properties dialog box opens.

3. Type the text you want to appear in the banner (leave the Picture option selected).

4. Click OK. The page banner appears, its nature dictated by the theme you've chosen.

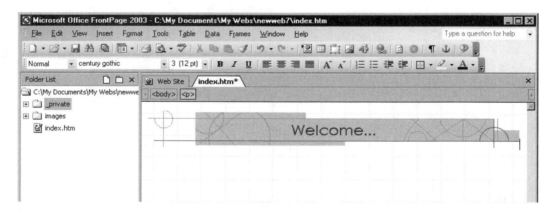

5. Repeat steps 1 through 4 for all the remaining pages in your site—at least those that should have some sort of identifying image on them to let visitors know which page they've come to.

Inserting Navigation Bars

Now that you have your pages set up and some identifying element on each of them, you're ready to create the buttons that will help visitors move around within your site—from the Home page to a subpage, between subpages, back to Home, and so on. You'll also be able to add links to external web pages—pages on other websites of your, or someone else's, creation, but that comes later. For now, we're going to create consistently located, and consistently designed navigation bars and place them on each page within your site.

Adding Navigation Buttons to the Home Page

The navigation bar for your home page will be different from the ones you place on your subpages. Why? Because the home page has no hierarchical equal—it's at the top of the website food chain. For this reason, you'll employ a slightly different set of instructions for inserting the home page navigation bar, as follows:

1. Double-click the Home Page icon in Navigation view to open that page onscreen.

2. Click below the page banner.

3. Choose Insert | Navigation. The Insert Web Component dialog box opens (see Figure 26-4), and the Link Bars component is automatically selected on the left side of the dialog box.

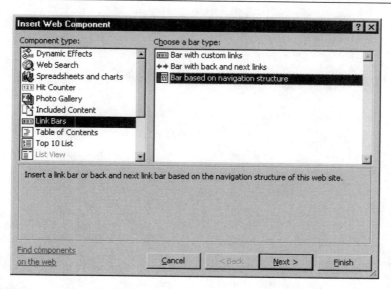

| FIGURE 26-4 | View the list of potential web components that can be added to your active page. |

4. On the right side of the dialog box, choose Bar Based on Navigation Structure (from the Choose a Bar Type list). This means that the bar you create will be based on your existing website's page hierarchy.

5. Click Next to move to the next step in the process.

6. Click Next again to accept the fact that whatever bar is created will be based on the existing theme. What you see in the Choose a Bar Style preview box will not necessarily match your theme, so don't worry.

7. Choose the orientation of your bar—vertical or horizontal. Your choice will be dictated by aesthetics and your planned layout for the page (based on your storyboards, as created in Chapter 25).

8. Click Finish. This takes you to the Link Bar Properties dialog box (see Figure 26-5), where you indicate the navigational structure of your bar. For the home page, choose Child Pages Under Home.

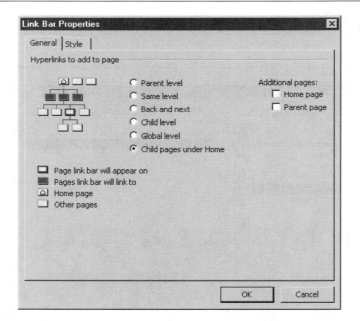

FIGURE 26-5 The home page is the "parent" to all the subpages you've created, and it's a grandparent to those subpages' subpages, if any.

9. Click OK. The navigation bar appears, with buttons for each of your subpages, as shown here.

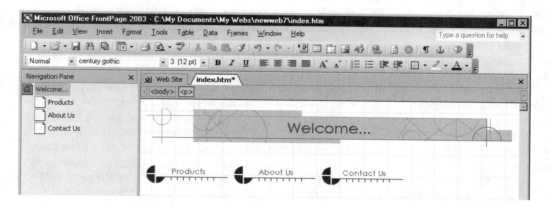

Adding Navigation Buttons to Subpages

The process of creating navigation buttons for your subpages is virtually identical to that which you employ for a home page—except for the choice you make in the Link Bar Properties dialog box. To create a navigation bar in your first subpage, double-click it in Navigation view so that the page is displayed onscreen and then click below the page banner (if you have one on the page). From there, follow the steps you used for inserting a navigation bar on the home page, but when you click Finish and see the Link Bar Properties dialog box, make the following choices:

- ■ Same Level
- ■ Home Page (from the list of two options under Additional Pages)

These options will build buttons for each of the subpages that are on the same hierarchical level as the active page, as well as a button to return to the home page. If you have subpages of subpages, you can repeat the process and add buttons for those pages by choosing Child Level while on the page that is the parent to those sub-subpages.

Building Web Page Content

What we've covered up to now is the stuff involved in getting the backbone of your site in place so you have something on which to hang your content. We've discussed the basics involved in setting up a site, applying a theme, and taking advantage of FrontPage's navigational features to make structuring your pages easier. But what about formatting and inserting the content that's specific to the home page and subpages? You've already got the consistent stuff done—the banners, the buttons, the consistent look and feel applied by the theme you chose. Now it's time to fill each of your pages with the graphics and text that pertain to the topic of your individual pages.

Inserting Text Content

You use FrontPage to speed the development of your sites, letting the application deal with the actual coding of HTML, scripting, and style sheets so you can focus on larger issues such as design and content. Therefore, if you're entering and formatting text, the best way to do that is with tools similar to the ones you're already used to in your word processor. Because it's a forgone conclusion you'd be using Word for that task, the FrontPage text-formatting tools are nearly identical.

The simplest way to get going is to click inside an open document and just begin typing. When you reach the right margin, your text will automatically wrap. You can select text just as you would in your word processor, using the cursor or holding down SHIFT while using the arrow keys. You can copy and paste text in all the ways you're familiar with as well, either inside the document or from one document to another, whether they're inside FrontPage or not. If you can copy it to the operating system's Clipboard, you can paste it into your web page.

As for formatting, you'll notice that the FrontPage Formatting toolbar is virtually identical to those in the rest of the Office suite. There are a few differences to conform to the limitations of HTML, such as a point size equivalent paired with an HTML-based font size number on the Size button. Other than that, however, the tools work the same way—simply select the text you want to format and then click the button that applies the format you want. The HTML code is generated in the background, as shown in Figure 26-6.

Making Text Links to External Web Pages and Sites

The buttons in your navigation bar are not the only links you'll have in your website. Some pages will need to connect to websites other than your own, and you'll want to make text links to do the job. To turn text into a hyperlink, just select the text you want to turn into a link and either select Insert | Hyperlink from the menu bar or press CTRL-K to view the Insert Hyperlink dialog box.

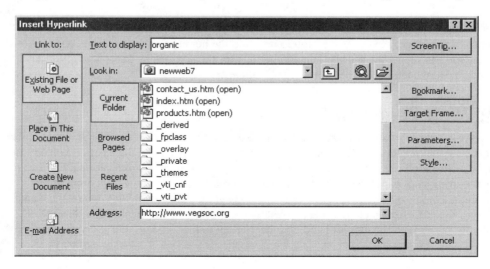

The <p> tag indicates a blank line has been inserted.

Each HTML tag and its attributes tell a web browser what to display.

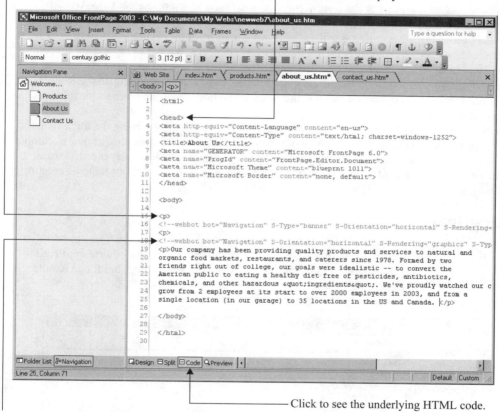

Click to see the underlying HTML code.

The <!—webbot...> tags are FrontPage-specific code for your theme-based banner and navigation bar.

FIGURE 26-6   Every word you type and each format you apply contributes to the HTML code that makes your document a web page.

Your options within the dialog box include:

- Entering the full URL (web address) for the website you want to link to, such as http://www.domain.com

- Creating a text link to a page within your own site

- Creating an email link—one that, when clicked, will open a blank message window, with the message already addressed to a particular person

Adding Images to Your Web Pages

Placing images in your web pages is another relatively simple procedure. Open the document you want to add an image to in Page view, then choose Insert | Picture. Select Clip Art if the image you want to insert is a piece of Microsoft clip art, or From File if your image is a GIF or JPEG that you've already created, scanned, or downloaded from the web and saved to your local hard drive. If you select From File, the Picture dialog box opens, shown in Figure 26-7. From here you can browse your hard drive to find the GIF or JPEG you want to insert.

Selecting Clip Art launches the Insert Clip Art task pane. Here you can use the search interface to locate clip art, or you can use the links at the bottom of the pane to locate clips online at Microsoft Office Online.

Once inserted, images can be centered, left-aligned, or right-aligned using the alignment tools on the Formatting toolbar. You can gain greater control over their placement by positioning them within table cells, which enables you to place images next to blocks of text or to create an array of pictures in a grid, such as shown in Figure 26-8. You'll learn about tables—creating, formatting, and otherwise manipulating them—later in this chapter.

Editing Images

A feature that separates FrontPage from other web design tools is that it allows you to edit images right within the interface, without having to go to an outside image-editing application. Granted, it doesn't have the power of tools such as Fireworks or Photoshop, but it can handle

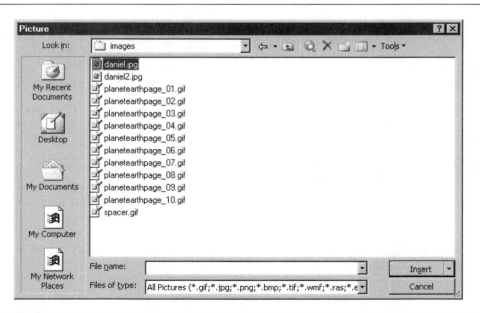

FIGURE 26-7 Use the Picture dialog box to locate the image you want to insert.

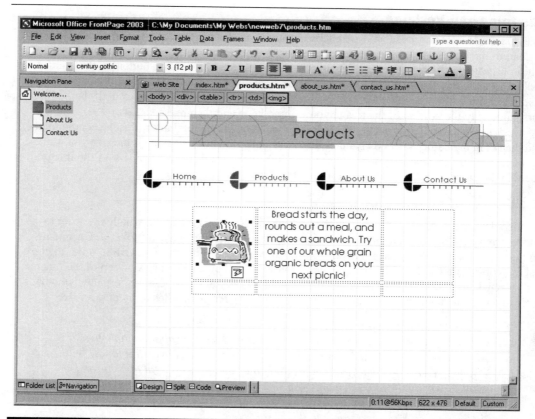

FIGURE 26-8   Images can appear "loose" on the page and be aligned like text, or through the use of a table they can be positioned among text and/or other graphics.

simple resizing and the addition of text to an image. The first step in making these types of changes is to have the Pictures toolbar visible by right-clicking any visible toolbar and selecting Pictures from the shortcut menu. The toolbar appears in Figure 26-9.

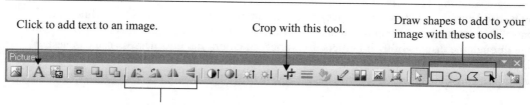

FIGURE 26-9   Some familiar button faces appear on the Pictures toolbar, providing an extensive set of tools for simple manipulation of your image within FrontPage.

Cropping and Resizing

Imagine you've got an image whose dimensions are just a tad too big for what you have in mind. Instead of having to use another application to make your edits, you can crop or resize the image within FrontPage. To crop your image, simply select it and click the Crop button on the Picture toolbar (it's the one that looks like two interlaced right angles). This will place a border with resize handles within the dimensions of the image. From here, drag the handles until the outline surrounds only the portion of the image you want to keep and then press ENTER.

Resizing is basically the same procedure without using the Crop button. Just select the image and then drag the corner selection handles inward or outward until the image is the size you want. By using the corner handles, you can control both the horizontal and vertical size of the image, keeping the current width-height proportions if desired.

Working with Images and Text

It's also possible to add text to certain types of images. Select the image to which you want to add text and click the Text button on the Pictures toolbar, which looks like a capital *A*. Depending on the type of image, FrontPage may alert you that it must be converted to a GIF in order to carry out the command. Click OK to proceed, and FrontPage will place a text box on top of the image you selected. From here you can enter and format your text as you see fit (use the Formatting toolbar's tools to adjust the appearance of the text) and use text-box resize handles to modify its size.

TIP   *If the image in question is a photograph or very detailed image with lots of colors, shading, and intricacies, you may want to edit it in another application where it can have text added to it but remain a JPEG image. The conversion to GIF will seriously reduce the quality of photos and other images with a lot of color and detail. If you don't want to change your image to a GIF just so you can add text to it, Photoshop, Photoshop Elements (with a more pleasing price tag than Photoshop), or Fireworks can handle the job.*

Structuring Pages with Tables

Just as the table is a powerful tool for structuring documents in Word, it's also a powerful tool for structuring web pages in FrontPage. Used to control the placement of text and graphics, the HTML table is the single most common web page element used to lay out documents, and FrontPage makes constructing and formatting tables a fairly straightforward process. Your FrontPage tables can be used purely as a structural device, providing an invisible set of blocks to confine and control the placement of text and graphics. They can also become a graphical component of your page through the display of their borders in a variety of colors and thicknesses. You can nest tables within other tables, and you have a full set of table-formatting tools at your disposal for customizing the dimensions and other visual aspects of the table.

Inserting a Table

The easiest method for inserting a table is to simply select Table | Insert | Table from the menu bar, thus opening the Insert Table dialog box (see Figure 26-10). From here, you specify the number of columns and rows in the table, where the table should be aligned, the table's width, its cellpadding and cellspacing, and its border width. Most often, when you're using a table

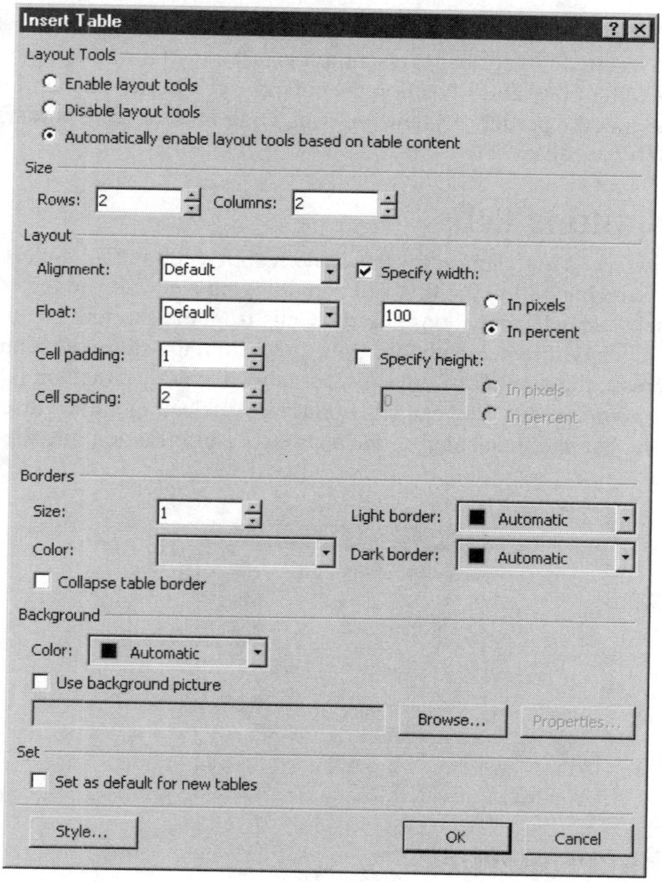

FIGURE 26-10   The Insert Table dialog box is used to define a table's properties.

as a page-layout device, the borders of the table are set to zero, making them invisible to the person visiting the site. Borders are unnecessary because the table is simply acting as a container for individual page elements.

In HTML, cellpadding is the amount of whitespace between a table cell's contents and its perimeter. Cellspacing, by contrast, is the amount of whitespace between individual table cells. Both these table attributes are measured in pixels.

Resizing Tables

Once you have a table inserted in your page, resizing it is just a matter of dragging its borders. Want to increase the width of the table? Position the cursor over a borderline until it becomes a two-headed arrow and drag the border to a new position. Drag interior table borders to increase or decrease the size of inner cells.

Merging and Splitting Cells

Say you need to join two cells together or, for that matter, split a cell in two. Select the two cells you want to merge by clicking within the first cell and dragging across it and the adjacent cell. Then right-click the selected cells and choose Merge Cells from the shortcut menu. To split a cell, you simply right-click within it and choose Split Cells from the shortcut menu.

If you need to increase the number of rows in your table, the easiest method is to place the cursor in the last cell and press TAB. You can add columns by selecting Table | Insert | Rows and Columns from the menu bar and then entering the appropriate information into the Insert Rows or Columns dialog box.

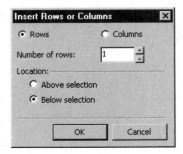

Modifying Table Properties

The shortcut menu is a handy way to access other dialog boxes that help you format your tables and cells. For example, right-click anywhere on a table and select Table Properties from the shortcut menu to view the Table Properties dialog box, shown in Figure 26-11. In the Layout section of the dialog box, you can change the table's alignment, set the cellpadding and cellspacing values, and modify the table's dimensions.

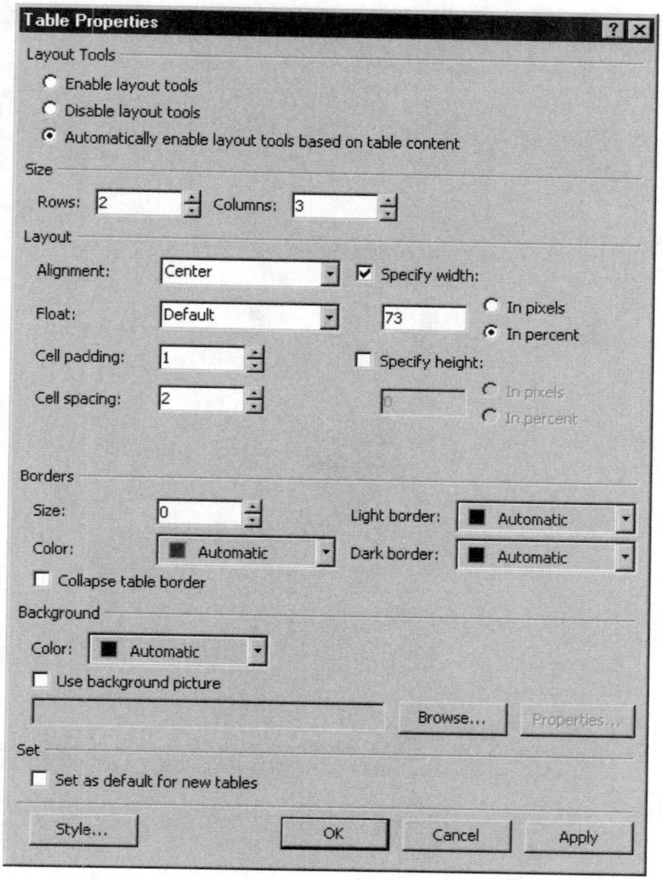

FIGURE 26-11 Use the Table Properties dialog box to modify the various attributes of your table.

You can use the fields in the Border section to change the border thickness, as well as modify the border color. Below this is the Background section, where you can specify a background color for your table. You can also add a background image using the Browse button to locate an image on your hard drive.

Once your table is created, you can begin inserting its content. Of course, not every cell needs to have something in it—sometimes leaving one or two cells empty or just inserting a little bit of text can have a dramatic structural effect, as shown in Figure 26-12. To insert text into a table cell, simply click in the cell and begin typing. The text will wrap to the cell's current

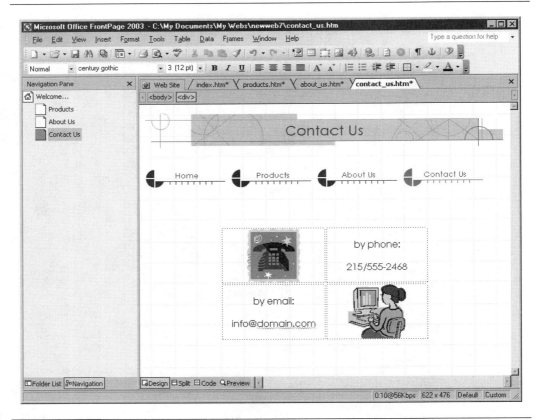

FIGURE 26-12 Create a checkerboard with images in every other cell in a table.

dimensions. If you want more text to fit inside the cell or for the wrap to have a different effect, simply resize the cell.

To add graphics to a cell, click inside the cell and use the Insert | Picture command (and submenu, as described earlier). The image can be aligned within the cell using the alignment buttons on the toolbar. You can place more than one image in a cell, but it's usually best to have one image per cell—it gives you that much more control over the alignment and position of the image relative to the table, the text within the table, and the page overall.

Chapter 27

Posting Pages to the Web

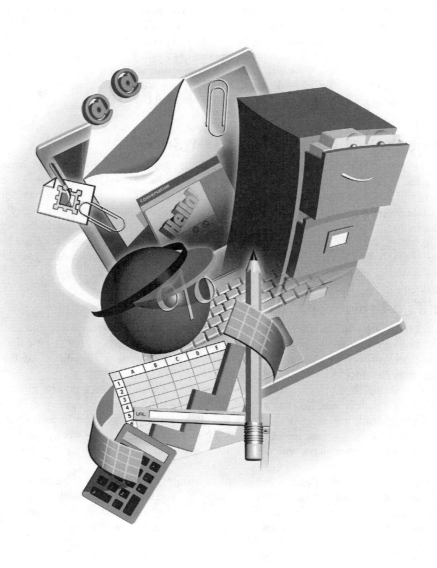

How to...

- Test and troubleshoot a website
- Set up folders on the web server
- Upload your pages to the web
- Keep your site up-to-date

You've worked hard and built a great website, and now you want to put it up on the World Wide Web for everyone to see. Hang on a minute, though. Have you tested your site? Are all the links functioning properly? Do all the images appear where you expect them to? Does the site function adequately in (at least) the most popular web browsers? Is anything taking too long to load? You don't want to put anything up on the web for a public showing until you've got any and all bugs worked out. Oh—and don't forget to do a spell check before you put a site online. You don't want everyone in the world to know you never won a spelling bee, do you?

Previewing Pages Through a Browser

Although it is possible to get a general idea of what your page will look like in a web browser by clicking the Preview tab at the bottom of the Page view window, you really want to open your creation in an actual browser to truly see what you've got. Fortunately, FrontPage makes this another painless operation and provides a toolbar button for precisely this purpose. The Preview in Browser button, shown in Figure 27-1, is located on the Standard toolbar, just to the right of the Print button, and by clicking it you can open your page in the browser you define for FrontPage. If you haven't saved your page at all or since changes have been made, you'll be asked if you want to save—click Yes to save and proceed with the preview.

Selecting a Preview Browser

By default, FrontPage will launch your page in Microsoft Internet Explorer when you click the Preview in Browser button. Viewing your page through different browsers isn't particularly difficult, and it's something you'll need to do to be sure your site looks as good as possible in as many browsers as possible.

To view your page in a browser other than Microsoft Internet Explorer, choose File | Preview in Browser from the menu bar. You can also click the drop list next to the Preview in Browser button. Either technique will display the Preview in Browser list of browsers in which you can preview your page. Here you can select not only which browser to preview your page in, but also the browser's window dimensions, which will mimic how much of your web page will be displayed at different screen resolutions.

The nice thing about FrontPage is that when it's installed, any browsers you currently have on your PC are automatically added to the list of browsers you can use to preview a page. However, if you install another browser after you already have FrontPage on your machine, you'll need to add that browser to the list yourself. This is an easy operation. Simply choose Edit Browser List

The web page, previewed in Internet Explorer

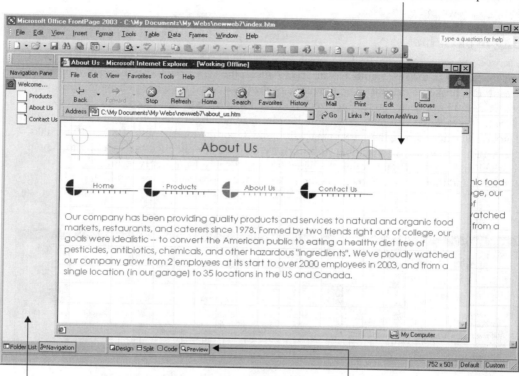

The FrontPage window is behind the browser window.   Preview in Browser

FIGURE 27-1   Just click the Preview in Browser button to view your page in Microsoft Internet Explorer.

in the Browser drop list/submenu, and in the dialog box that results, enter the name of the browser you want to add in the Name field. Then click the Browse button to locate the appropriate browser's executable file (.exe).

Checking Your Site for Errors

FrontPage allows you to check your site using its powerful set of reporting tools so you aren't limited to doing a page-by-page site check in your browser to find any possible errors. After all, you're only human. Why not put your PC to work to do the mundane stuff such as link checking? Call up the Reporting toolbar by selecting View | Reports from the menu bar. This makes accessing the reporting functions of FrontPage a whole lot easier. When you're ready to run a site report, select Site Summary from the submenu to display the site summary in the main FrontPage window, as shown in Figure 27-2.

Fixing Broken Links

The most common error to occur in a website is a link that leads nowhere. When this happens it means that the page the link points to can't be found on the server. Any of a number of problems can result in a broken hyperlink. The file name of the page could have been changed, the link reference could have been entered incorrectly, or the file may have been moved or deleted.

Not to worry, to err is human, and though FrontPage is certainly not divine, it can solve your link problems. After running the site summary from the Reporting toolbar, if the Broken Hyperlinks category indicates you have a number of broken hyperlinks, simply click that heading to view a list of the broken links. Double-click the listed links to display the Edit Hyperlink dialog box, shown next, and then use the Browse button to locate the appropriate page to which the link

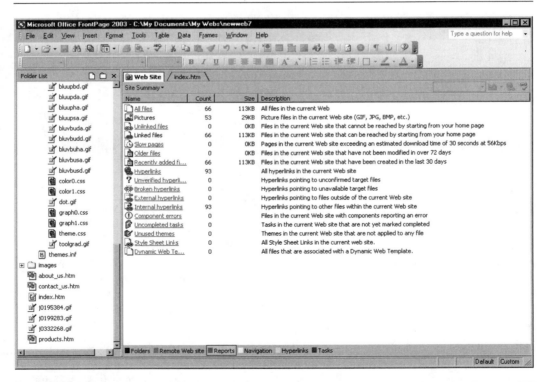

FIGURE 27-2   The site summary provides you with a breakdown of your site's components and possible errors.

should point. The radio buttons beneath the Replace Hyperlink With field allow you to select whether all links to this page should be fixed site-wide or only in the specific document to which this error refers. Once you've made your changes, click Replace.

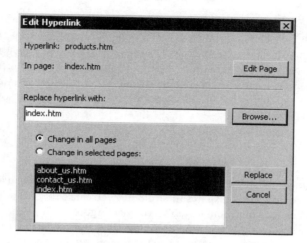

Virtually every troubleshooting process is identical to this. Simply check the site summary for the list of errors, click the link for a specific category to view the errors individually, and then double-click the individual error to launch a dialog box that addresses it.

Publishing Your Website

After you've fixed any errors in your pages, you're ready to upload your site to a web server. Before you can do this, however, you'll need to know the server address and have a username and password in order to log in to the server. Check with your web server administrator, Internet service provider (ISP), or hosting service if you need help.

If your ISP has FrontPage server extensions installed (and they must be if you're going to publish a FrontPage-created site to the server), you can publish to the web server via Hypertext Transfer Protocol (HTTP), in which case you can enter an address such as http://www.*your_web_server*.com. Otherwise, you can publish via an FTP server, and your address would read ftp://ftp.*your_web_server*.com. Again, check with your server administrator, ISP, or hosting service to find out the appropriate method. If your server requires a username and password, you will then be prompted to enter them.

FrontPage extensions enable your FrontPage web pages to work properly—providing the necessary support for the proprietary code that's inserted when you build your web page using FrontPage. Interactivity within your site, access to data, and overall functionality—these things all depend on FrontPage extensions being on your web server. If you don't know whether your host has placed these extensions on the server where your pages will be stored, take the time to check, and if they're not already added, get them added. There shouldn't be a charge (or a significant one) to include the extensions, because FrontPage is a popular web design tool.

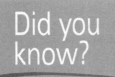

SharePoint Services

When reading about what's new in FrontPage 2003 (online or through various Office mailing lists and forums), you may hear about SharePoint Services and wonder what they are. SharePoint Services allow you to package a portion of your website and turn it into a functional module that other people can use in their sites. By enabling you to convert a custom web package into a single file format, SharePoint Services allow your FrontPage-created web solutions to be easily shared and transported.

Once you have all the necessary information in hand, open the website you want to publish in FrontPage and click the Publish Site button on the Standard toolbar. You can also select File | Publish Site from the menu bar. This displays the Remote Web Site Properties dialog box, into which you enter the address of your remote web server (see Figure 27-3a). Also found in the Remote Web Site Properties dialog box is the Publishing tab—from this tab (see Figure 27-3b) you can tell FrontPage which pages to publish once the remote server is contacted. For example, if you've already uploaded pages, you can choose to publish only the pages that have changed since that last upload.

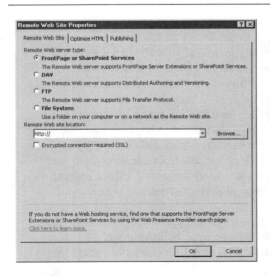
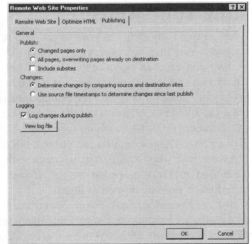

FIGURE 27-3   a). Use the Remote Web Site tab to provide your remote server's address and choose the remote server type. b). The Publishing tab controls the upload of pages.

After you provide FrontPage with all the information it requires to connect to your remote web server, the Publish Web view appears in the Web Site tab, as shown in Figure 27-4. This two-sided window allows you to pick which local files will be uploaded to the remote location, and through the View Your Remote Web Site link (on the left and below the two-sided local/remote windows), you can create folders on your remote server so that you have the same folder structure there that you have locally.

To perform the upload, click the Publish Web Site button in the lower right. The files are uploaded to the remote server, and a status bar and file list in the Status area of the window show

The local window shows the files you're about to upload.

The remote window shows what's on the server now.

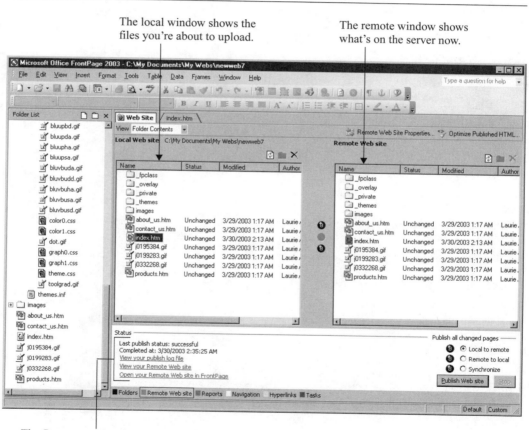

The Status area shows you the date and time of the last upload.

FIGURE 27-4 The Publish Web dialog box is the interface through which you will pass files from your local machine to the web server.

you how the upload is progressing. For smaller sites or for pages that don't have a lot of graphic content, the upload may go so quickly that you don't even get a chance to read what appears in the Status area as the files are uploaded. When the upload is complete, the Status area displays the time and date of this successful upload, and you see your files in the Remote side of the window.

TIP   *You can also drag and drop files from one side of the Publish Web dialog box to the other to quickly transfer files from server to PC, or vice versa.*

Index

References to figures and illustrations are in italics.

3-D formula references, 205–206

A

Access

adding titles to your forms, 325
AutoCorrect, 13
backing up, 13
changing report margins, 352–353
connecting tables with relationships, 313–316
controls, 320
creating relationships, 314–316
creating reports, 347–352
creating tables, 305–313
data entry tips, 327–328
data types, 308–309
database concepts, 300–301
database objects, 301
Database window, 301, *302*
defining databases, 300
designing a query in the QBE grid, 334–340
designing tables to store data, 301–313
error-checking, 13
fields, 303
Form Wizard, 319–321
formatting controls, 325–327
Formatting toolbar, 325–326
forms, 301, 318–329
joins, 314

making a pick list with the Combo Box control, 323–325
managing controls on forms, 321–323
manually creating tables, 309–311
manually setting the primary key, 312–313
modifying forms, 321–327
navigating through records, 328–329
new features, 13
new look, *5*
ordering records with the sort row, 336–338
primary keys, 303, 312–313
printing reports, 353
properties, 303–304, 308–309, 311–312, 320
QBE grid, 333, 334–340
queries, 301
query types, 332–333
record sources, 320
relationship types, 314
relationships, 313–316
Report Wizard, 344–353
reports, 301
selecting data from multiple tables, 340–342
Simple Query Wizard, 333–334

SQL view, 333
subforms, 320
Table Wizard, 306–308
tables, 301
Toolbox, 320
using operators to find records with
  numbers, 339
using wildcards to find a groups of
  related records, 339–340
viewing forms, 319–320
viewing query designs and data, 333
viewing reports, 344
viewing tables and data, 304–305
workspace, 18, *20*
writing criteria to select specific
  records, 338–340
alerts, 8
aspect ratio, 48
AutoCorrect, 13, 85–87
  creating entries, 87–88
  editing and removing entries, 88
AutoFilter, 217–218
AutoSum
  in Excel, 199–202
  in Word, 161

C

charts
  building, 228–230
  chart axes, 227
  customizing, 275–276
  data points, 226
  data series, 226
  deleting, 233
  editing chart text, 233
  elements, 226–227
  formatting, 232
  gridlines, 227
  legends, 227
  making major changes, 279
  organization charts, 276–279
  plot area, 227
  PowerPoint, 273–276

  repositioning slice values and names
    on a pie chart, 233
  resizing and moving charts, 233, *234*
  selecting data for charting, 228
  setting up a new chart, 228–230
  titles, 227
  types, 224–226, 232, 275
  updating and changing, 230–234
  using to enhance Excel worksheets,
    224–227
  See also Excel; PowerPoint
Clipboard, 28–34
  customizing the Clipboard task pane,
    33–34
  deleting content, 32–33
  displaying the task pane, 32
  moving content with the
    Cut command, 29
  pasting selections, 30–32
  sharing content with the Copy
    command, 29–30
  storing multiple selections, 32
  using the Paste Special command to
    insert content, 34–39
columns, 137
  applying to existing text, 139–140
  customizing, 141–142
  newsletter documents, 138–139
  setting up before typing, 140
  setting up multiple configurations
    in one document, 142
compatibility with previous Office versions, 15
Copy command, 29–30
Cut command, 29

D

databases
  concepts, 300–301
  defining, 300
  objects, 301
  See also Access
Drag and Drop, 78–79

E

ecommerce, 409–410
email
    adding accounts in Outlook, 358–360
    asking for receipts, 365–366, *367*
    attaching files to messages, 363–364
    composing messages, 361–363
    creating signatures, 374–375
    default fonts, 371
    deleting messages, 378
    establishing signatures for different
      email accounts, 375–376
    filtering junk email, 379
    flagging messages, 365
    folders, 376–378
    formatting messages, 370–373
    formatting message text, 371–372
    forwarding messages, 370
    Inbox folder, 376–377
    moving messages between folders,
      377–378
    replying to messages, 369–370
    sending messages, 366–368
    Sent Items folder, 376–377
    setting message importance, 364
    sharing images via, 57–59
    signatures, 13, 373–376
    stationery, 371–372
    See also Outlook
embedding selections, 37–39
error messages, 8
Excel
    3-D formula references, 205–206
    absolute addressing, 203–204
    adding and deleting worksheets, 178
    advanced filters, 218–219
    aligning worksheet content, 191–192
    applying color to text and numbers, 191
    applying numeric formats, 189
    AutoFilter, 217–218
    AutoSum, 199–202
    borders, 194–195

    building a list, 212–213
    building charts, 228–230
    built-in functions, 206–207
    changing fonts and sizes, 190–191
    changing the angle of text, 191–192
    chart elements, 226–227
    chart types, 224–226, 232
    combining workbooks in a formula,
      205–206
    combining worksheets in a formula, 205
    conditional formatting, 193
    controlling page breaks and page count,
      238–241
    controlling your print area, 237
    copying cell formats, 195
    creating simple formulas from scratch,
      202–204
    custom lists, 201
    database requirements, 212
    editing cell content, 183
    editing formulas, 203
    entering worksheet content, 181–185
    fields, 210
    filtering, 211, 217–219
    Formatting toolbar, *188*
    formatting worksheet content, 188–195
    Formula Bar, 183
    freezing database field names, 213
    grouping and ungrouping worksheets,
      179–180
    header rows, 214
    headers and footers, 242–243
    inserting rows and columns, 185
    interface, 176
    margins, 238–239
    Merge and Center button, 192
    naming worksheets, 179
    navigating worksheets, 180–181
    new features, 12
    new look, *6*
    order of operations, 204–206
    Page Break Preview, 240–241
    paper orientation and size, 240

password-protecting worksheets, 186
PivotTables, 219–222
Print dialog box, 236–237
printing an entire workbook, 237–238
printing a range of cells, 238
printing individual worksheets, 238
publishing content to the Web, 243–245
records, 210
relational vs. flat file databases, 212
relative addressing, 201–202, 203–204
resetting default font and size, 191
saving a new workbook, 186
saving a workbook as a template,
   186–188
saving a worksheet as a web page,
   243–245
saving workbook files, 185–188
scaling printouts, 240
searching for specific records, 217–219
selecting a block of cells, 184
selecting entire columns and rows, 185
selecting multiple cell ranges, 184–185
shading worksheet cells, 193
smart tags, 12
sorting, 210–211, 213–214
spreadsheet calculations, 198–199
starting a new workbook, 176–181
subtotal reports, 214–216
switching between worksheets, 178
terminology, 210–211
updating and changing charts, 230–234
working with print options, 241–242
worksheets, 177–180
workspace, 18, *19*
wrapping and shrinking text to fit, 192
exporting, pictures, 59
Extensible Markup Language. *See* XML

F

faxing, via the Internet, 8
File menu, most recently used files, 24

FrontPage
adding images, 432
adding navigation buttons to
   subpages, 429
adding navigation buttons to the home
   page, 427–429
adding pages to your site, 422–423
checking your site for errors, 441–443
collecting text content, 413–414
commercial graphics vendors, 413
cropping and resizing images, 434
editing images, 432–434
extensions, 421
file formats, 410–411
file size, 411–412
finding free images online, 413
fixing broken links, 442–443
graphic requirements, 410–412
inserting tables, 435–436
inserting text content, 430, *431*
making text links to external web pages
   and sites, 430–431
merging and splitting cells, 436
modifying table properties, 436–438
page banners, 426
page titles vs. file names, 424
personal and family websites, 409
planning your site's content, 410–414
previewing pages, 440–443
publishing your website, 443–446
rearranging site structure, 423–424
resizing tables, 436
scanning photographs and line art,
   412–413
selecting a preview browser, 440–441
SharePoint services, 444
site maps, 415–416
sites that advertise, 409
sites that sell, 409–410
starting new websites, 420–424
storyboarding individual page content,
   416–417

structuring pages with tables, 434–438
templates, 421, *422*
themes, 424–425
web-safe colors, 412
website goals, 408–410
working with images and text, 434

G

graphics
    adding images to websites, 432
    adding images to Word documents,
        46–51
    capturing images digitally, 54
    changing text flow in Word documents,
        49–50
    creating shortcuts to your images, 56
    cropping and resizing images for
        websites, 434
    editing images for websites, 432–434
    editing your digitally captured images,
        60–62
    exporting pictures, 59
    moving images in Word documents, 51
    opening an image, 56
    Picture Library, 9, 55–59
    renaming images, 56–57
    resizing images in Word documents,
        47–49
    sharing images via email, 57–59
    using clip art and photos in PowerPoint,
        53–54
    using images in Excel worksheets, 53
    using the Picture toolbar in Word, 51–52
    working with images and text for web
        sites, 434

H

handles, 47, *62*
help, 42–43. *See also* Office Watson

I

images. *See* graphics
instant messaging, 14

K

kerning, 73, 105
keyboard
    setting indents from, 108
    shortcuts, 24

L

labels, 167
    choosing the right label, 168–169
    merging data with, 169–172
    printing, 172
    selecting your data source, 169, *170*
linking
    creating paste links, 35–37
    severing links between source and
        target, 36–37
    updating linked content, 36

M

mail merge, 164
    creating a form letter, 164–167
    creating mailing labels, 167–172
    troubleshooting, 172
Media Player, 12
menu bar, new look, *4*
menus, 23
    common menu enhancements, 23–24
    customizing display of, 8
    ellipses, 24
    making selections, 23
    submenus, 24

O

Office 2003
    new look, 4–8
    upgrading to, 14–15

Office Watson, 8
optical character recognition (OCR), 414
Options dialog box, accessing, 24
orphans, 110
Outlook
    adding email accounts, 358–360
    Address Cards view, 396, *397*
    appointments, 384–387
    Appointments list, 382
    asking for receipts, 365–366, *367*
    assigning tasks, 391–392
    attaching files to messages, 363–364
    Calendar, 14, 382–390
    composing messages, 361–363
    Contacts, 396–403
    creating new tasks, 390–391
    creating signatures, 374–375
    customizing the calendar, 389–390
    Date Navigator, 382–383
    default fonts, 371
    deleting contacts, 400
    deleting messages, 378
    editing contact information, 399–400
    email folders, 376–378
    email signatures, 13
    entering new contacts, 397–399
    establishing signatures for different
        email accounts, 375–376
    events, 385, 387
    filtering junk email, 379
    flagging messages, 365
    formatting email messages, 370–373
    formatting message text, 371–372
    forwarding messages, 370
    importing address books from Outlook
        Express, 399
    Inbox folder, 376–377
    interface, 360–361
    linking contacts to new items, 401
    linking contacts to preexisting
        Outlook items, 401
    linking documents to a contact, 402
    meetings, 385, 388–389
    moving messages between folders,
        377–378
    new features, 13–14
    new look, *6*
    printing Contacts list, 402–403
    printing schedules, 392–393
    Quick Flagging, 13
    Reading pane, 13
    Reminder option, 387
    replying to messages, 369–370
    Search folders, 13
    sending messages, 366–368
    Sent Items folder, 376–377
    setting message importance, 364
    setting up appointments, 385–387
    sharing contacts, 396
    signatures, 373–376
    stationery, 371–372
    TaskPad, 383
    Tasks, 390–392
    thread management, 14
    web beacon, 13
    workspace, 18, *21*

P

pagination, 110–112
Paste Special command, 39
    inserting Clipboard content with, 34–37
Picture Library, 9, 55–59
PivotTables, 219–222
PowerPoint
    action buttons, 292–294
    adding clip art and photographs,
        268–269
    adding new boxes to charts, 278
    aligning graphic objects, 273
    aligning text objects, 261
    animating bulleted lists, 288–289
    animating text, 286–288

applying animation to charts and diagrams, 289
applying fills and outlines, 271–272
bulleted text, 256–258
changing the stacking order of graphics and drawn objects, 273
chart types, 275
charts, 273–276
choosing slide layouts, 254–256
creating notes and audience handouts, 265
customizing charts, 275–276
deleting slides, 255–256
diagrams, 279–280
Draw menu button, 269
drawing lines and arrows, 270
drawing shapes, 270
Drawing toolbar, 269, *270*
environment, 251–252
filling in chart boxes, 277–278
formatting bullet characters, 257–258
formatting graphic elements, 271–273
formatting organization charts, 278–279
formatting slide text, 263
grouping and ungrouping objects, 273
hyperlinks, 291–292
inserting extra text boxes, 259
inserting links to files, presentations, and web content, 290–294
inserting new slides, 254–255
inserting slide text, 256–259
making major chart changes, 279
making pictures and AutoShapes move, 289
marking up with pen/tablet device, 12
multiple bullet levels, 257
new features, 12
new look, *5*
organization charts, 276–279
organizing presentation content, 251
Package to CD, 12
planning presentations, 250–251
previewing slide shows, 282–284
printing color options, 264–265
printing slides, 263–265
proofing and troubleshooting presentations, 284
publishing presentations on the web, 294–295
rearranging, duplicating and deleting slides, 282–284
repositioning text objects, 260–261
resizing text objects, 261–263
rotating shapes and lines, 272
saving presentations, 263
setting up a slide show, 289–290
spell checking, 284
templates, 252–254
Thesaurus, 12
transitions, 284–286
typing paragraphs, 258–259
typing shapes, 272
Viewer, 12
Windows Media Player, 12
workspace, 18, *20*
printing
    Access reports, 353
    Excel workbooks and worksheets, 236–243
    labels, 172
    Outlook Contacts list, 402–403
    Outlook schedules, 392–393
    PowerPoint slides, 263–265
    Word documents, 92–93

R

readability statistics, 91–92
Red Eye link, 61, *62*
Research button, 8
Research task pane, 8
ruler
    indenting text from, 108–109
    setting tabs from, 123–124

S

SharePoint services, 444
smart tags, 27–28
    in Excel, 12
    expanded use of, 8
    in Word, 70
source files, 29
speech recognition, 39
    dictating documents, spreadsheets
      and presentations, 41
    giving commands verbally, 41–42
    training the speech tools for your
      voice, 40–41
    turning speech on, 39–40
styles, 114–115
    building new styles, 116–117
    creating styles by example, 116
    editing and deleting, 117–118
    locking, 118–119

T

tables
    adding and deleting columns and rows,
      151–152
    AutoSum, 161
    borders, 153–154, 157
    building a uniform grid, 144–147
    changing table size, dimension and
      alignment, 157–158
    drawing table cells, 155–156
    entering content, 147–148
    erasing table cell walls, 156–157
    fields, 159
    formatting, 149–155
    freeform, 155–160
    header rows, 159
    Insert Table dialog box, 146–147
    inserting from the toolbar, 144–146
    merging cells to consolidate table
      structure, 153
    navigating, 148
    nesting, 160
    resizing columns and rows, 149–151
    restoring table defaults and
      uniformity, 150
    selecting columns, rows, and cells,
      148–149
    setting cell margins and spacing,
      150–151
    shading tables cells, 155
    sorting table content, 158–160
    splitting cells to increase table
      dimensions, 152–153
    structuring web pages with, 434–438
    summing rows or columns of
      numbers, 161
    Tables and Borders toolbar, 157–160
    See also FrontPage; Word
tabs
    adjusting tab positions, 126–127
    alignment, 123–124
    changing tab stop alignment, 127
    creating a tabbed list, 122
    creating bar tabs, 124
    default, 122–123
    editing tab settings, 126
    positioning tab stops, 124
    setting from the ruler, 123–124
    setting up multiple tabbed lists in
      a single document, 126
    Tabs dialog box, 125–126
target files, 29
task panes
    Clipboard, 32, 33–34
    displaying different, 26
    Home, 7–8, 24–26
    Styles and Formatting, 115
    turning off, 26
templates
    building content, 97–98
    creating new documents from, 99
    PowerPoint, 252–254
    saving workbooks as, 186–188
    tips and techniques, 99

toolbars
    button equivalents, 24
    buttons, 21–22
    customizing display of, 8
    displaying different, 22
    Drawing, 269, *270*
    Formatting, 21, 102, *188*, 325–326
    moving, 22–23
    new look, *4*
    Picture, 51–52
    Standard, 21
tracking, 105
troubleshooting, mail merge, 172

U

upgrading to Office 2003, 14–15

W

websites
    adding images, 432
    adding navigation buttons to subpages, 429
    adding navigation buttons to the home page, 427–429
    adding pages, 422–423
    checking for errors, 441–443
    collecting text content, 413–414
    commercial graphics vendors, 413
    cropping and resizing images, 434
    editing images, 432–434
    file formats, 410–411
    file size, 411–412
    finding free images online, 413
    fixing broken links, 442–443
    goals, 408–410
    graphic requirements, 410–412
    inserting tables, 435–436
    inserting text content, 430, *431*
    making text links to external web pages and sites, 430–431
    merging and splitting cells, 436
    modifying table properties, 436–438
    page banners, 426
    page titles vs. file names, 424
    personal and family, 408–410
    planning content, 410–414
    previewing pages, 440–443
    publishing, 443–446
    rearranging site structure, 423–424
    resizing tables, 436
    scanning photographs and line art, 412–413
    selecting a preview browser, 440–441
    SharePoint services, 444
    site maps, 415–416
    starting, 420–424
    storyboarding individual page content, 416–417
    structuring pages with tables, 434–438
    templates, 421, *422*
    that advertise, 409
    that sell, 409–410
    themes, 424–425
    web-safe colors, 412
    working with images and text, 434
    See also FrontPage
widows, 110
Windows Media Player, 12
Word
    accepting Word's suggested completions, 71
    AutoCorrect, 85–88
    AutoSum, 161
    blank documents, 66–68
    bulleted lists, 113–114
    changing paragraph alignment, 106–107
    columns, 137–142
    Comments feature, 10, *11*
    creating a form letter, 164–167
    creating consistent indents, 73
    creating mailing labels, 167–172
    customizing page layout, 119–122
    customizing proofing tools, 89–91
    editing text, 78

Find and Replace dialog box, 135–137
first-time saves, 94–96
Font Format dialog box, 104
fonts and font size, 103–104
formatting tables, 149–155
formatting text, 102–106
Formatting toolbar, 102
freeform tables, 155–160
getting started, 66–70
grammar check, 84–85, 90
handling errors as you type, 83–84, 91
headers and footers, 131–133
indenting text, 107–109
Insert Table dialog box, 146–147
keyboard navigation techniques, 74–75
Layout tab, 121–122
line spacing, 109–110
locking styles and formatting, 118–119
mail merge, 164–172
margins, 119–120
moving around with the mouse, 74
navigating documents, 73–75
new features, 10–12
newsletter documents, 138–139
Normal template, 66–68
numbered lists, 112–113
page numbers, 130–131
page orientation, 120
Page Setup dialog box, 119–122
paper size, 121–122
paragraph and line breaks, 71–73
printing, 92–93
proofing documents, 82–85
readability statistics, 91–92
Reading Layout view, 10, *11*
rearranging text, 78–79

replacing special codes, 136–137
replacing text, 136
saving documents, 94–97
saving documents with a new name,
    96–97
section breaks, 133
selecting text via the keyboard, 76
spelling check, 84–85, 89
starting with a template, 68–70
structuring documents and text with
    tables, 144–149
Style Locking, 12
styles, 114–119
tables, 144–161
tables of contents, 134–135
tabs, 122–127
Tabs dialog box, 125–126
templates, 97–99
text color, 104–105
text special effects, 105–106
text-flow controls, 110–112
Track Changes, 10
typing document content, 70–73
updating saved files, 96
using Find to move through a document,
    135–136
using your mouse to select text, 76–77
word wrap, 71, *72*
workspace, 18, *19*
Zoom percentage, 68
workspace, common elements, 18–21

X

XML, 10

INTERNATIONAL CONTACT INFORMATION

AUSTRALIA
McGraw-Hill Book Company
Australia Pty. Ltd.
TEL +61-2-9900-1800
FAX +61-2-9878-8881
http://www.mcgraw-hill.com.au
books-it_sydney@mcgraw-hill.com

CANADA
McGraw-Hill Ryerson Ltd.
TEL +905-430-5000
FAX +905-430-5020
http://www.mcgraw-hill.ca

GREECE, MIDDLE EAST, & AFRICA
(Excluding South Africa)
McGraw-Hill Hellas
TEL +30-210-6560-990
TEL +30-210-6560-993
TEL +30-210-6560-994
FAX +30-210-6545-525

MEXICO (Also serving Latin America)
McGraw-Hill Interamericana Editores
S.A. de C.V.
TEL +525-1500-5108
FAX +525-117-1589
http://www.mcgraw-hill.com.mx
carlos_ruiz@mcgraw-hill.com

SINGAPORE (Serving Asia)
McGraw-Hill Book Company
TEL +65-6863-1580
FAX +65-6862-3354
http://www.mcgraw-hill.com.sg
mghasia@mcgraw-hill.com

SOUTH AFRICA
McGraw-Hill South Africa
TEL +27-11-622-7512
FAX +27-11-622-9045
robyn_swanepoel@mcgraw-hill.com

SPAIN
McGraw-Hill/
Interamericana de España, S.A.U.
TEL +34-91-180-3000
FAX +34-91-372-8513
http://www.mcgraw-hill.es
professional@mcgraw-hill.es

UNITED KINGDOM, NORTHERN,
EASTERN, & CENTRAL EUROPE
McGraw-Hill Education Europe
TEL +44-1-628-502500
FAX +44-1-628-770224
http://www.mcgraw-hill.co.uk
emea_queries@mcgraw-hill.com

ALL OTHER INQUIRIES Contact:
McGraw-Hill/Osborne
TEL +1-510-420-7700
FAX +1-510-420-7703
http://www.osborne.com
omg_international@mcgraw-hill.com

Know How

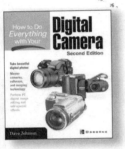

**How to Do Everything
with Your Digital Camera**
Second Edition
ISBN: 0-07-222555-6

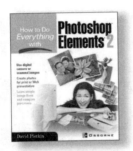

**How to Do Everything
with Photoshop Elements 2**
ISBN: 0-07-222638-2

**How to Do Everything
with Photoshop 7**
ISBN: 0-07-219554-1

**How to Do Everything
with Your Sony CLIÉ**
ISBN: 0-07-222659-5

**How to Do Everything
with Macromedia
Contribute**
0-07-222892-X

**How to Do Everything
with Your eBay Business**
0-07-222948-9

**How to Do Everything
with Your Tablet PC**
ISBN: 0-07-222771-0

**How to Do Everything
with Your iPod**
ISBN: 0-07-222700-1

**How to Do Everything
with Your iMac,**
Third Edition
ISBN: 0-07-213172-1

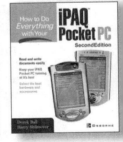

**How to Do Everything
with Your iPAQ Pocket P**
Second Edition
ISBN: 0-07-222950-0

Mc